SOUTH KOREA AT THE CROSSROADS

A COUNCIL ON FOREIGN RELATIONS BOOK

YDER

SOUTH KOREA
AT THE CROSSROADS

Autonomy and Alliance in
an Era of Rival Powers

Columbia University Press / New York

Columbia University Press
Publishers Since 1893
New York   Chichester, West Sussex
cup.columbia.edu
Copyright © 2018 Columbia University Press
All rights reserved

Library of Congress Cataloging-in-Publication Data
Names: Snyder, Scott, 1964– author.
Title: South Korea at the crossroads : autonomy and alliance in an era of rival
powers / Scott A. Snyder.
Description: New York : Columbia University Press, 2017. | "A Council on
Foreign Relations book." | Includes bibliographical references and index.
Identifiers: LCCN 2017024120 (print) | LCCN 2017045106 (ebook) |
ISBN 9780231546188 (e-book) | ISBN 9780231185486 (cloth : alk. paper)
Subjects: LCSH: Korea (South)—Foreign relations—1960–1988. |
Korea (South)—Foreign relations—1988-2002. | Korea (South)—Foreign
relations—2002– | Korea (South)—Foreign relations—Korea (North) | Korea
(North)—Foreign relations—Korea (South). | Korea (South)—Foreign
relations—United States. | United States—Foreign relations—Korea (South) |
Korea (South)—Foreign relations—China. | China—Foreign
relations—Korea (South)
Classification: LCC JZ1747 (ebook) | LCC JZ1747 .S69 2017 (print) |
DDC 327.5195—dc23
LC record available at https://lccn.loc.gov/2017024120

∞

In memory of Lee Sang-Seol,

Richard H. Solomon,

and Barnett Baron

CONTENTS

CONTENTS

FIGURES AND TABLES

FIGURES

TABLES

PREFACE

THE STORY OF Korea has historically been one of survival and resiliency in the face of external threats from great-power neighbors. It is a story that combines the extraordinary stubbornness necessary to hold one's ground with exhibitions of remarkable adaptability necessary to survive in the face of geopolitical reality. It is the story of life on a geopolitical fault line in which external events can put everything at risk yet strategic choices also contribute to national prospects for survival and prosperity.

Having observed the story of Korea from many different angles over the past three decades, I have accumulated many debts to a long list of teachers who have contributed to my understanding of how Koreans think and act when making strategic choices. This project benefited from the perspectives I have gained by watching the evolution of South Korean foreign policy as a manifestation of South Korea's democratization and modernization. I am thankful for the opportunity to hold countless conversations with South Korean diplomats, academics, and Korea watchers, each of which helped me to deepen my understanding of the determinants of South Korea's strategic choices.

The immediate catalyst for this research project was the opportunity to hold a workshop on South Korea's strategic choices in the summer of 2015 involving American and South Korean specialists, cosponsored by the Seoul

Forum for International Affairs, co-organized with Chung Min Lee of Yonsei University, and supported financially by the Smith Richardson Foundation and the Korea Foundation. The conversations held during the workshop jumpstarted my thinking and contributed to the overall structure and content of the book. I am grateful to Al Song at the Smith Richardson Foundation and Yu Hyun-seok, Lee Shi-yong, and Seayoun Lee at the Korea Foundation for their support, encouragement, and patience throughout the project.

I was aided in research and drafting of the manuscript by two able research associates, Sungtae (Jacky) Park and Darcie Draudt, with additional research support from Andrew Park, Daniel Jung, Cris Lee, Lynn Lee, and Myeong Park. I benefited from constructive comments by two blind reviewers and the editorial support of Anne Routon and Stephen Wesley at Columbia University Press. I am thankful to Trish Dorff, James Lindsay, and Richard Haass at the Council on Foreign Relations for providing the institutional support for this project and for reading and making invaluable suggestions for improving the draft manuscript.

Finally, I thank SoRhym, Elliana, and Elyssa Snyder for their patience with my travel absences and for their encouragement and understanding.

SOUTH KOREA AT THE CROSSROADS

1

SOUTH KOREA'S
STRATEGIC CHOICES

T HE KOREAN PENINSULA has historically been a victim of the tragedy
of great-power politics, given its geographic location at the vortex of
great-power rivalry in Northeast Asia. Yet South Korean leaders
have historically had little ability to determine their country's fate. Having
had no viable choice but to rely on the United States as an effective protector
in the decades since the Korean War, South Korea faces a strategic choice
that will determine its future and influence the direction of the regional order in Northeast Asia. In this context, it must reevaluate its strategies in the
face of an uncertain strategic environment generated by China's rise and
by questions regarding the durability of its own security alliance with the
United States. Should the country continue to rely for its security and prosperity on that alliance or side with a rising China as a new security guarantor, or does the country have sufficient capabilities to protect itself without
external help? To avoid renewed victimization as a result of intensifying regional rivalries, South Korea must use its diplomatic capabilities to make
smart strategic choices and avoid entrapment in those rivalries, all the while
working with great powers to deal with the growing threat from North Korea. Yet South Koreans also face the possibility of American withdrawal or
underappreciation of South Korea's strategic importance to regional stability in Northeast Asia, which could lead to drastic limitations on South
Korea's security options and to increased dependency on China.

During the late nineteenth and early twentieth centuries, Korea was the chief victim of conflict among imperial powers, as a result of which it even lost its sovereignty. With the decline of China's Qing dynasty at the hands of Western imperial powers, a weakened China became vulnerable to challenges from imperialist Japan. Korea, a country that was in China's sphere of cultural and political influence but was strategically important to Japan, became an object of contestation, resulting in the Sino-Japanese War of 1894–1895. Japan then defeated Russia in a war over Korea in 1904–1905. The Taft–Katsura Memorandum (1905) and the Treaty of Portsmouth (1905) soon paved the way for Japan's formal annexation of Korea in 1910.

Korea's liberation from Japanese colonial rule in August and September 1945 at the end of World War II proved illusory for independence-minded Koreans as the Korean Peninsula again became the focal point for competition, this time between the occupying forces of the Soviet Union and the United States. At the start of the Cold War, rival Korean clients of the United States and the Soviet Union sought supremacy over the entire peninsula, resulting in the hardening of borders, the establishment of the two Koreas, and the tragedy of the Korean War (1950–1953). Following three years of fighting and millions of casualties, the Korean Armistice Agreement of 1953 hardened political divisions without resulting in a peace treaty. The competition between South Korea and North Korea to claim the entire Korean Peninsula has endured for more than seven decades.

As part of arrangements that brought about the end of the Korean War, a mutual defense treaty was established between the United States and the Republic of Korea (ROK) to guarantee security and stability in the latter. For decades, the alliance has deterred conflict and protected South Korea from renewed military aggression by the North and provided it with investment and a ready market that enabled the country's export-led liberalization and opening to the outside world. A poverty-stricken economy with few natural resources following the Korean War, South Korea was among the world's poorest countries in the 1950s, but its successful economic modernization allowed it to become one of the top-fifteen economies in the world by the year 2000. South Korea's economic growth also enabled its transition in the late 1980s from authoritarianism to democracy. These accomplishments are remarkable for a country that was invaded and almost wiped out by its neighbor to the north less than two years following its establishment in 1948 and that many had diagnosed as an economic "basket case," trapped in poverty with little hope of improvement. South Korea has moved from net consumer to net provider of international security goods through contributions to international peacekeeping, international financial architecture in the G20, global health, and international development. Unlike its successful southern counterpart, North Korea, which has sought self-reliance since its founding, has lost allies and has survived by perpetuating a personality cult around its leader, exerting draconian control over its population, and closing itself off from the rest of the world.

The prospect of renewed inter-Korean conflict continues to hold South Korean security and prosperity at risk. Moreover, South Korea's foreign policy is a product of factors that shaped the strategic environment and Koreans' choices before the country's establishment. First, the establishment and survival of South Korea as an independent state following the end of World War II depended on security guarantees provided by a distant great power, the United States. Second, the evolution of South Korean foreign policy has been accompanied by an ongoing struggle between the impulse toward inward-centered parochial nationalism and the demands of internationalism that have accompanied the country's economic growth. This struggle has played out against the backdrop of political divisions between conservative and progressive factions that were magnified through South Korea's transition from authoritarianism to democracy. Third, South Korean leaders have continuously pursued unification as a national objective.

For the first time in decades, South Korea faces an active debate over alternative strategies to safeguard its security and prosperity. China's rise has uncovered latent tensions and rivalries that are gradually reshaping the regional context and reopening domestic debates over South Korea's strategic choices, including the question of the durability of its alliance with the United States. If China successfully challenges U.S. global leadership, or if South Korea comes to regard U.S. security guarantees as unreliable, South Korea will have to pursue alternative strategic pathways to preserve its security and prosperity. It has long feared the possibility of abandonment by the United States, but preparation for possible alternatives to alliance with the United States will generate friction and stress in U.S.–South Korean relations.

This book sets out to examine the major factors that influence South Korean strategic choices. Every South Korean leader has struggled to balance the need to maintain a strong alliance with the United States, on the one hand, with the aspiration for greater national autonomy, on the other. The book shows how a once weak South Korea, focused primarily on the North Korean threat, began to pursue a more internationalist foreign policy as its economy grew. However, the nature of South Korea's strategic environment has often constrained its room to maneuver and has resulted in heavy dependence on the alliance with the United States, even during the period following South Korea's democratization. The interplay between South Korea's domestic politics and its strategic environment highlights the fact that external factors have been the most important influences on its foreign policy, whereas its domestic political divide between conservatives and progressives influences the direction of its foreign policy primarily when the country's strategic environment is comparatively benign. South Korean foreign-policy makers will face a more challenging environment in which they must navigate between domestic politics and international rivalries, but possibly without assurances that have heretofore been provided by the alliance with the United States.

As South Korea's domestic debates over its future direction and the competition among great powers grow more intense, South Korea will face greater pressures even as it questions the durability of the U.S. commitment to it and weighs the alternatives of aligning with a rising China or pursuing autonomy rather than relying on an external protector. A review of the evolution of South Korea's foreign policy and a careful evaluation of its relative power and strategic options indicate that the only viable way forward for the foreseeable future is for South Korea to continue to rely on the United States to meet its security needs and to take further measures to strengthen alliance cooperation with the United States. Despite South Korea's improved capabilities, the country is unlikely to be able to assure its security absent the credible assurances and commitments of a dependable alliance partner. China's rise has enabled it to assert growing economic and political influence on Seoul, but China does not yet have sufficient power, influence, or commitment to become an alternative security guarantor for South Korea.

Despite the possibility of American retrenchment, it is unlikely that the United States will abandon its commitment to defend South Korea, and the United States remains the most capable, committed, and strategically aligned alliance partner available to Seoul. To forestall concerns about U.S. commitment and to secure the necessary assurances of the U.S. will to meet those commitments, South Korea will need to continue to invest in the U.S.-ROK alliance. However, to the extent that a rising China emerges as a potential alternative provider of security to South Korea or as a viable security partner for a unified Korea, South Korea may be tempted to hedge and accommodate China. Under these circumstances, Sino-U.S. major-power competition for South Korea's allegiances is likely to heat up, South Korean domestic debates over the country's strategic choice are likely to intensify, and South Korea will continue for as long as possible to avoid hard choices and to hedge against both the negative effects of China's rise and the persisting uncertainties regarding U.S. commitment. However, despite sharper debates and increasing friction over South Korea's future direction, the U.S.–South Korea alliance will remain an essential instrument for assuring South Korea's security given its relative weakness compared to its neighbors.

SOUTH KOREA'S FOREIGN-POLICY ASPIRATIONS VERSUS GEOPOLITICAL CONSTRAINTS

Like any other state, South Korea has sought to achieve the central strategic objectives of securing and promoting its own economic well-being. As one part of a divided state, it has also consistently pursued the strategic objective of national unification. In its pursuit of national security and prosperity, it desires to achieve greater autonomy for itself not only in relation to the United States but also vis-à-vis other major powers. At the same time, as its capabilities have grown, South Korea has sought to define its place in the global community by contributing to global welfare in specific areas such as global development and health.

DESIRE FOR AUTONOMY VERSUS NEED FOR ALLIANCE

The primary and enduring tension in South Korean foreign policy and the pursuit of its primary strategic goals of security, prosperity, and national unification is the classic dilemma facing small states surrounded by major powers: the desire for autonomy versus the necessity of alliance with a more powerful security guarantor. South Korea's desire for autonomy versus the necessity of the alliance with the United States has been a source of tension underlying almost every foreign-policy decision made since the country's establishment following World War II. This tension is a natural by-product of South Korea's uniquely situated geography, in which it exists both as a pivotal partner and as a vulnerable neighbor located on the periphery and yet central to larger neighbors' security interests.

PAROCHIALISM VERSUS INTERNATIONALISM

South Korea's foreign policy has also been shaped by a contest between inward-focused parochialism, at one extreme, and economic-interdependence-driven internationalism, at the other. South Korea's initial parochial outlook was driven both by its weakness and by the existential threat posed by a stronger North Korea. The gap between South Korea's peninsular focus and U.S. global interests has been a perennial source of tension in managing differing perspectives in the context of the security alliance. However, the two Koreas' unification policies inevitably have an international dimension to the extent that the international and regional context influences the feasibility and likelihood of unification. Following the Korean Armistice of 1953 that marked the end of military conflict, the competition for legitimacy between the two Koreas went international as both sides mobilized global support for their positions.

As the country's economy grew and became integrated with the rest of the world, South Korea emerged as a more consistently globally involved actor and as a constructive contributor to global governance. This evolution reflects South Korea's development of an extensive international network based on trade and development and its attractiveness as a model for developing countries that seek to replicate its economic modernization path. South Korea's gradual shift toward internationalism over the past two decades has changed the nature of its international outreach from one focused on trying to win the legitimacy competition with North Korea to one focused on making contributions to global leadership in international security and development.

CHARTING THE DEVELOPMENT OF
SOUTH KOREA'S FOREIGN POLICY

Since the founding of South Korea in 1948, schools of foreign policy have reflected tensions arising from the debates over parochialism versus internationalism and alliance dependence versus greater autonomy. As shown in figure 1.1, these tensions have meant that there are four possible distinct options that South Korean leaders might consider as part of the nation's foreign-policy debates: (1) parochial alliance dependency, (2) alliance-enabled internationalism, (3) internationalization plus autonomy, (4) independence through neutralization.

PAROCHIAL ALLIANCE DEPENDENCY: COLLABORATING
WITH A STRONG ALLY TO ACHIEVE SECURITY

An approach to foreign policy reflected in the initial development of South Korea's foreign policy is the mix of alliance and parochialism. This approach is expressed most clearly in the patron–client relationship that characterized South Korea's interaction with the United States during the Cold War. In this period, South Korea was weak, was singularly focused on the North Korean threat, and had no alternative but to depend on the United States as the primary guarantor of its security. During the Cold War, most of South Korea's major foreign-policy decisions—including normalization of relations with Japan, dispatch of Korean troops to Vietnam, outreach to North Korea in the early 1970s, and even President Park Chung-hee's decision to pursue a covert nuclear weapons program in the mid-1970s—were framed by perceptions of the level of U.S. commitment

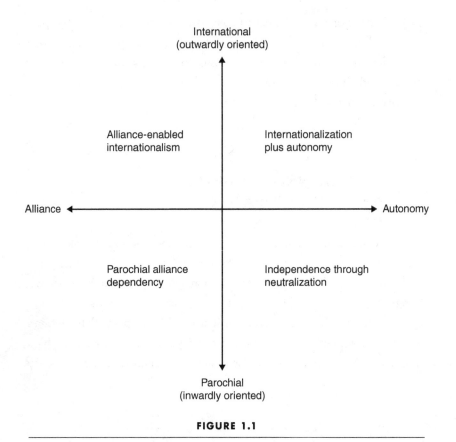

FIGURE 1.1

A Framework for Understanding South Korea's Foreign Policy

to South Korea and, most importantly, concerns about abandonment by the United States.

ALLIANCE-ENABLED INTERNATIONALISM: LEVERAGING INTERNATIONAL PRESSURE TO ACHIEVE SOUTH KOREA'S GOALS

The second approach is South Korea's search for an expanded international role and set of relationships while maintaining a strong alliance with the United States as the foundation for its foreign policy. This school is reflected in South Korea's cautious but eager efforts at the end of the Cold

War to take advantage of new opportunities to expand the scope of its diplomacy. Under Roh Tae-woo (1988–1993), South Korea moved to develop new relationships with the Soviet Union, China, and other Communist countries, but always in close coordination with the United States. President Kim Dae-jung (1998–2003) sought to pursue a more internationalist and "sunshine" policy of improved relations with North Korea but under strong U.S. backing. Under Presidents Lee Myung-bak (2008–2013) and Park Geun-hye (2013– 2017), South Korea has become a net contributor to global goods while working in lockstep with the United States to mobilize international support against North Korea. In this respect, although the expansion of South Korea's international role and reach enabled it to pursue a more autonomous foreign policy, South Korea was always solicitous of U.S. support to bolster its diplomatic leverage on the international stage and to ensure that the United States did not perceive it as abandoning the centrality of the U.S.-ROK alliance as a main pillar underlying its diplomatic orientation.

INTERNATIONALIZATION PLUS AUTONOMY: THE SEARCH FOR COOPERATIVE SECURITY

A third possible approach combines greater autonomy from the alliance with pursuit of foreign-policy multilateralism and a broader scope of interests to include issues that go beyond the Korean Peninsula. South Korea's pursuit of cooperative security frameworks in Northeast Asia goes back to the end of the Cold War and has relied on its greater capabilities to participate effectively in global affairs. Its efforts to use multilateralism and to participate in and lead multilateral gatherings on a range of subjects from nuclear security to the G20 to global health are a reflection of the maturation of its foreign policy. In terms of overall foreign policy, however, the only time Seoul came close to truly pursuing autonomy was during the early years of the Roh Moo-hyun administration (2003–2008), which considered but ultimately abandoned a foreign-policy model based on South Korea's acting as an influential "balancer" to bring about cooperative security in Northeast Asia and to become a more influential global nation. The Roh administration and to a lesser extent the Kim Young-sam administration (1993–1998) wanted to pursue this approach but never actually implemented the idea, in large part because South Korea's relative weakness vis-à-vis its neighbors made such an approach impractical.

INDEPENDENCE THROUGH NEUTRALIZATION

The fourth approach involves the pursuit of independence through neutralization of the Korean Peninsula. Through this idealistic pathway, South Korea seeks to assert its autonomous role in foreign policy either by declaring itself neutral and thereby isolating itself from the contending negative influences of major-power rivalry or by seeking independence within or from the necessity of alliance. Although the idea of a neutral and independent Korea has been explored from time to time within academic circles and in South Korean debates over strategy, no South Korean government has ever seriously considered this option.[1]

* * *

These four approaches are not mutually exclusive. Certain South Korean administrations clearly fall in one school or another. Some are on the lines that divide the different schools, and some have elements of more than one of these foreign-policy types. Given the vibrancy of South Korean domestic politics, these types have become an enduring part of the domestic debate and have become contending influences in South Korea's ongoing debate over its foreign-policy choices.

FACTORS INFLUENCING AND CONSTRAINING SOUTH KOREAN FOREIGN POLICY

In addition to the tension within South Korean foreign-policy debates between the aspiration for autonomy and the necessity of alliance as well as between parochialism and internationalism, South Korea's geopolitical situation, growing capacity, and domestic politics have influenced the course of its foreign policy. Among these factors, the nature of Northeast Asia's strategic environment, notably the balance of power and level of competition, and South Korea's own indigenous capacity have been the most important, while domestic politics has played a lesser role, although it becomes more influential when the regional environment is relatively benign.

GEOPOLITICAL ENVIRONMENT

The geopolitical context of the Korean Peninsula has been the most important factor influencing South Korean foreign policy. The balance of power and the degree of competition in Northeast Asia inevitably limits South Korea's choices given that the country has to live in an environment that has been shaped largely by the capacities and preferences of larger major-power actors. South Korea's alliance with the United States has been the most important feature of this dynamic, although the end of the Cold War and South Korea's economic growth have somewhat lessened the degree to which dependency on the alliance with the United States and the preferences of South Korea's neighbors have constrained its foreign policy.

In addition, the high degree of South Korea's economic interdependency and reliance on the effective functioning of international markets have also become important facets of the international context to which South Korea is particularly sensitive. Slowdowns in global economic growth, risks of financial contagion, and the major powers' economic policies may influence prospects for Korean exports, and South Korean leaders have little to no ability to control such events or trends.

SOUTH KOREA'S CAPACITY

The second factor influencing South Korea's foreign policy is its economic, military, and developmental capacity, which must be considered in relation to the capacities of its immediate neighbors, the United States, and the rest of the world. The country's economic growth has enabled the strengthening of its national capabilities, which has translated into various ways to influence—but not necessarily to control—its strategic environment. Economic growth has also changed the nature and mode of expression of tensions between South Korea's desire for autonomy and its need for alliance. When South Korea was a developing country facing considerable internal challenges in adequately providing a living for its own population and a relatively narrow set of political relationships with its neighbors, Seoul had little to no capability to influence those neighbors or the United States. This lack of influence naturally meant that the primary focus of South Korean foreign policy was on maintaining good relations with its alliance protector, the United States. Despite (or perhaps because of) South Korea's relative powerlessness in those circumstances, its leaders have continuously challenged the United States in various forms as a relatively safe way of asserting symbolic agency despite South Korea's weakness.

In the post–Cold War period, the scope, reach, and aims of South Korean foreign policy have expanded, with economic modernization serving as the primary driving factor. For one thing, growing exports and overseas business opportunities provided reasons for South Korea's diplomatic relationships with the rest of the world to expand. This shift in its capacity has increased its ability to influence its own environment, to enhance its autonomy, and to allow it to be a better alliance partner. South Korea's economic modernization expanded the scope of its foreign policy beyond its original almost exclusive focus on the alliance with the United States. The country's growing economic capabilities provided opportunities to develop diplomatic relations with many new countries based on preexisting trade and investment relations. In some cases, South Korea's economic modernization facilitated the transformation of relations with former enemies, enabling it to build new relationships with countries such as China and the Soviet Union. In addition, its economic modernization changed the dynamic of the inter-Korean relationship as its economic capabilities surpassed and eventually dwarfed those of the North. Within the U.S.-ROK security alliance, South Korea's rising capabilities generated a different dynamic as it was more able to contribute to its own self-defense and eventually to make international contributions both independent of and complementary to the alliance. As a result, the nature and scope of the

U.S.-ROK alliance has transformed from a patron–client relationship to a comprehensive security alliance.

DEMOCRATIZATION AND THE RISE OF DOMESTIC POLITICS

The third factor that has shaped formation of South Korean strategic choices is the transformation of domestic politics, especially following the country's democratic transition and consolidation of democratic governance. South Korea's democratization has expanded the number of interest groups that have the capacity to influence foreign policy. These groups range from specific business constituencies—including the powerful *chaebol*s, conglomerates, that have taken the lead in expanding the range of South Korea's economic relationships globally, often forging the way for new political and diplomatic opportunities—to local public-interest groups. South Korea's legislature has also taken the lead in expanding civilian exchanges through outreach to fellow parliamentary bodies.

The resulting structure of South Korea's domestic politics reflects deep and long-standing ideological polarization between progressive and conservative camps with distinctly different orientations, priorities, and preferences. The domestic divide pits conservatives, who have traditionally been aligned with upper-class elite interests, support for the U.S.-ROK security alliance, and a hard-line position toward North Korea, against progressives, many of whom have fought Korean authoritarianism, objected to perceived U.S. support for authoritarian leaders, and sought reconciliation and unification with the North by prioritizing ethnic unity over ideological division. Although not as powerful as the external factors, ideological polarization has influenced South Korean foreign policy, depending on the ideological orientation of the administration in power.

South Korea's democratization has enabled public preferences to influence the parameters and direction of foreign policy, most often serving as a constraint on the country's political leadership but also ensuring that South Korea's foreign-policy formation is both aligned with the public will and conducted in an open and transparent manner. Under authoritarian rule, the president's decision was often decisive regardless of the public will. Under democracy, the president must work to gain public support in a transparent fashion or risk having foreign-policy initiatives blocked or overturned.

HOW THESE FACTORS HELP DETERMINE SOUTH KOREA'S FOREIGN-POLICY ORIENTATION

As table 1.1 shows, South Korea's foreign policy has moved over time from a parochial outlook to an international one as the country's capacity has grown. Regardless of its geopolitical environment and capacity, the country has pursued a foreign policy based on the alliance with the United States. Nevertheless, the degree to which it has depended on the alliance has differed depending on the nature of the strategic environment in Asia. During the Cold War, South Korea depended heavily on the United States. In the 1990s and through the Roh Moo-hyun administration, however, it depended less because the regional environment was relatively benign. But then as the North Korean threat and regional rivalries began to increase, South Korea returned to a foreign policy based on heavy dependence on the alliance with the United States, albeit with an increasingly internationalist outlook as South Korea's capacity grew.

South Korean domestic politics has been a secondary factor in shaping foreign-policy choices compared to the geopolitical environment and South Korea's own capacity. When South Korea's strategic environment was comparatively benign in the 1990s and early 2000s, conservative and progressive leaders alike sought to pursue a more autonomous foreign policy. During this period, the progressive Roh Moo-hyun administration came closest to pursuing autonomy over alliance. But even Roh ultimately could not abandon the alliance with the United States because of both international and domestic political factors. Thus, as figure 1.2 shows, every administration has continued to hold fast to the alliance with the United States despite pressure to expand the country's autonomy, while South Korea has adopted an increasingly internationalist foreign-policy orientation in line with its expanding capabilities. However, China's rise and America's perceived retrenchment have stimulated debates that could lead future leaders to a fundamental reevaluation of South Korea's strategic choice.

STRUCTURE OF THE BOOK

Whenever South Korea faced critical strategic decision points, the issues of capacity, domestic politics, and the international political context have played a role in influencing the direction of its foreign policy. I argue in this book that following seven decades of reliance on the alliance with the United States as the foundation for its security, debates over the country's strategic options are intensifying as it faces the geopolitical impact of China's rise and uncertainties accompanying U.S. retrenchment. As a result, South Korea will actively consider alternative strategic choices to alliance with the United States, including the possibility of a closer security relationship with China. I contend that despite growing international pressure and intensifying domestic debates, South Korea's only viable strategic option for the foreseeable future is continued cultivation and strengthening of the alliance with the United States. Based on the framework laid out earlier, I present broad patterns and influences on South Korea's past foreign-policy choices as well as factors likely to influence its future strategic decisions.

The book is structured roughly in two parts. First, I describe the evolution of South Korea's foreign policy and then apply the primary determinants underlying Korean thinking to three main issues the country faces today. From chapter 2 to chapter 7, I analyze the evolution of South Korea's foreign policy using the framework laid out in this chapter. Chapter 2 examines efforts by South Korea's authoritarian leaders to counter the risk of abandonment by the United States. Park Chung-hee offered a solution to President Lyndon B. Johnson's political needs during the Vietnam War by negotiating dispatches of South Korean troops to Vietnam, but those efforts failed as the Vietnam War wound down, heightening Park's fear of abandonment. The U.S. retrenchment during the 1970s precipitated South Korean self-help efforts to build nuclear weapons. The alliance relationship also deteriorated because of Park's poor human rights record and his nuclear-development efforts after the election of Jimmy Carter, but Ronald Reagan's renewed assurances to Chun Doo-hwan (1980–1988) diminished South Korean fears of abandonment by the United States.

TABLE 1.1 FACTORS INFLUENCING SOUTH KOREA'S FOREIGN-POLICY ORIENTATION BY ADMINISTRATION

PRESIDENT	RELATIVE CAPACITY	GEOPOLITICAL ENVIRONMENT	IDEOLOGICAL ORIENTATION	RESULTING FOREIGN-POLICY ORIENTATION	DEGREE OF PAROCHIAL VERSUS INTERNATIONAL ORIENTATION	LEVEL OF DEPENDENCE ON THE ALLIANCE
Syngman Rhee (1948–1960)	Low	Hostile, Cold War confrontation	Authoritarian conservative	Parochial alliance dependency	Very parochial	Very heavy
Park Chung-hee (1961–1979)	Low, growing	Hostile, Cold War confrontation	Authoritarian conservative	Parochial alliance dependency	Very parochial	Very heavy
Chun Doo-hwan (1980–1988)	Low, growing	Less hostile, easing Cold War confrontation	Authoritarian conservative	Parochial alliance dependency	Less parochial	Heavy
Roh Tae-woo (1988–1993)	Low, growing	Benign, post–Cold War era	Conservative	Alliance-enabled internationalism	Parochial but increasingly internationalist	Moderate

Kim Young-sam (1993–1998)	Low/Middle	Benign, post–Cold War era, but with security tensions with North Korea	Conservative	Alliance-enabled internationalism	Parochial but increasingly internationalist	Moderate
Kim Dae-jung (1998–2003)	Middle	Benign, with inter-Korean cooperation	Progressive	Alliance-enabled internationalism	Internationalist	Moderate
Roh Moo-hyun (2003–2008)	Middle	Benign, with inter-Korean cooperation and growing U.S.–North Korea tensions	Progressive	Alliance-enabled internationalism	Parochialism despite internationalist tendencies	Autonomy within alliance
Lee Myung-bak (2008–2013)	Middle	Increasing regional tensions, inter-Korean conflict, and growing U.S.–North Korea tensions	Conservative	Alliance-enabled internationalism	Internationalist	Alliance partnership
Park Geun-hye (2013–2017)	Middle	Increasing regional tensions, inter-Korean conflict, and growing U.S.–North Korea tensions	Conservative	Alliance-enabled internationalism	Internationalist	Alliance partnership

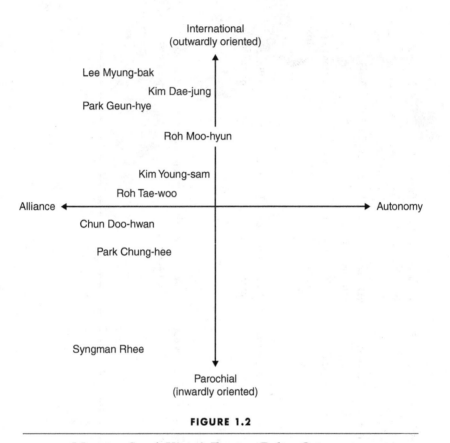

FIGURE 1.2

Mapping South Korea's Foreign-Policy Orientation

Chapter 3 examines the strategic opportunities South Korea faced with the end of the Cold War and the advent of democratization as well as Roh Tae-woo's efforts to capitalize on those challenges through Nordpolitik, a policy of outreach to the Soviet Union, the People's Republic of China, and North Korea. Roh's policy led to the normalization of diplomatic relations with the Soviet Union and the People's Republic of China, a breakthrough in inter-Korean dialogue and a landmark agreement on exchanges and cooperation, and Kim Young-sam's efforts to pursue "globalization" while also deepening domestic reform in South Korea's transition to democracy.

Chapter 4 examines South Korea's first democratic power transition and Kim Dae-jung's effort to lead the international community in a switch from containment of to engagement with North Korea. Chapter 5 examines the ways in which South Korea under Roh Moo-hyun pursued autonomy through parallel efforts to seek autonomy from the alliance and to seek autonomy within the alliance. This approach was most clearly expressed in Roh's balancing policy, designed to enable South Korea to bridge relations between China and Japan as well as between China and the United States.

Chapter 6 examines Lee Myung-bak's effort to restore the U.S.-ROK alliance as a platform that has enabled unprecedented international visibility and influence for South Korea on international issues such as financial stability, climate change, and international development. Chapter 7 evaluates Park Geun-hye's efforts to grapple with an increasingly dire nuclear challenge from North Korea, to address "Asia's paradox" by using the U.S.-ROK alliance as a platform upon which she might lead and invite the United States to join as a "co-architect" in the development of multilateral security cooperation in the region, and to confront the challenge posed by extended paralysis of South Korean political leadership resulting from the corruption scandal that engulfed Park's presidency.

The second part of the book analyzes three main issues that preoccupy South Korea's strategists now that its strategic pathways are in greater flux. Chapter 8 considers the implications of South Korea's thinking about its role and prospects as a middle power in its future diplomacy. Chapter 9 considers South Korea's strategic thinking regarding its relative position between the United States and China. Chapter 10 examines South Korean strategies with regard to how to manage peaceful unification of the Korean Peninsula. Finally, the epilogue discusses the implications of South Korea's strategic choices and the implications of possible American retrenchment for the U.S.-ROK alliance.

2

STRATEGIC CHOICES UNDER
AUTHORITARIAN RULE

T HE CONFLICT BETWEEN South Korea's aspirations for autonomy and its
need for alliance has been the main source of tension besetting its
foreign-policy decisions since the signing of the U.S.-ROK alliance
on October 1, 1953. South Korea's first president, Syngman Rhee, struggled
with this contradiction as he tried to reconcile his country's absolute dependency on the United States for its security with his unquenchable desire to restore a free, independent, and unified Korean state. This tension
naturally became a continuous source of contention in Rhee's relationship
with U.S. officials. Despite his need for U.S. support, Rhee clashed with
American authorities and agitated for a "march north for unification"
(*puk-chin t'ong-il*), a unified Korea restored to Korean rule. The mutual
security treaty of 1953 was the price President Dwight D. Eisenhower ultimately paid to secure Rhee's acquiescence to the Korean Armistice Agreement that brought about a truce and ended the military conflict between
the North Korean military/Chinese People's Volunteers and the U.S.-led
United Nations (UN) Command, which included the South Korean
army. The U.S. security commitment to South Korea was intended in part
to prevent the possibility that an independent-minded Rhee would reiniti-
ate military conflict with the North and its patrons.[1]

In contrast to Syngman Rhee's direct challenge to the United States
and the U.S. need to restrain Rhee so as to avoid the risks of renewed

military conflict, Park Chung-hee, an authoritarian leader who prioritized South Korea's modernization, took a less confrontational tact than Rhee. In the 1960s and 1970s, instead of antagonizing his American patrons at a time when they were focused on other priorities, Park tried to make Korea useful and even essential to the achievement of U.S. political priorities and military objectives in Vietnam—even sending a combined total of more than 300,000 troops between 1964 and 1973 to serve there alongside U.S. forces[2]—as a means to gain leverage to negotiate the desired levels of assistance from the United States and to assuage his fears of abandonment by the Americans.

As successful as Park Chung-hee's strategy was in generating American military and economic support for Korea's defense as a collateral benefit of dispatching Korean military forces to Vietnam, it began to lose its effect as the United States wound down its engagement in Vietnam and announced pullbacks from Asia under the Nixon Doctrine of 1969. As a result, Park embarked on two new initiatives. First, he began to explore ways to reach out to the Communist bloc, in particular China and the Soviet Union. Second, he began an indigenous arms buildup, which included pursuit of a covert nuclear weapons program. When the United States discovered Park's efforts, the program nearly pushed the U.S.-ROK alliance to a breaking point. Moreover, Park's efforts to squelch domestic opposition and assert authoritarian political control became a source of friction in the alliance and led to aborted efforts by U.S. president Jimmy Carter to withdraw U.S. ground forces from South Korea.

In the aftermath of Park Chung-hee's assassination in 1979 and despite successor Chun Doo-hwan's bloody crackdown on pro-democracy activists in Gwangju, a provincial capital in southwestern Korea, the following year as part of his own coup d'état and consolidation of power, the United States sought to balance peninsular stability in the context of continued Cold War confrontation with North Korea with efforts to save the life of pro-democracy activist Kim Dae-jung. The Reagan administration reaffirmed U.S. alliance commitments to South Korea, but at a cost to U.S. reputation from perceptions within South Korea that the United States had backed authoritarian rule over democracy in South Korea.

During decades of South Korean authoritarian rule, the geopolitical context of the Cold War and South Korea's dependency on the United States to meet the challenge from a more powerful and aggressive North Korea were the defining factors that shaped South Korea's foreign policy. Given its weakness and the enduring inter-Korean confrontation during the Cold War, the country had little choice but to rely on U.S. pledges to ensure its security.

SYNGMAN RHEE AND THE ORIGINS OF THE ALLIANCE

South Korea's first president, Syngman Rhee, had spent most of his life in exile as a leader of the Korean independence movement during Japanese colonization. At seventy years old by the end of World War II, Rhee was a relatively senior figure but had little practical experience with management or administration. Educated at George Washington University (BA), Harvard University (MA), and Princeton University (Ph.D.), Rhee had spent decades trying unsuccessfully to draw U.S. attention to and support for the seemingly lost cause of Korean independence from Japanese colonial rule. He was articulate and committed to his conviction and vision of a free and united Korea, but his stubbornness and inflexibility tended to feed rivalry and enmity among his cohorts rather than to win cooperation, even from those who shared his vision. When given power, Rhee used it to crush opposition rather than to build support for his views. He was authoritarian in practice despite his rhetorical commitment to freedom and democracy. His obstinacy would come to vex his American patrons.[3]

The clash between Rhee's dependency on the United States and his desire to pursue his own goals independent of U.S. interference became a constant centerpiece of tension between him and the United States. His obstinacy tested the limits of both sides and ultimately gave birth to the U.S. security commitment to South Korea.[4] Rhee was such a big headache to his American patrons that debates arose periodically before, during, and after the Korean War among senior U.S. policy makers about removing him from South Korea's leadership. Following two years of intermittent and fruitless armistice negotiations at the village of Panmunjom near what was eventually to become the Korean Demilitarized Zone (DMZ), U.S. domestic support for continued fighting had declined, Stalin died, and Chinese supporters of North Korean leader Kim Il-sung saw little strategic advantage in continuing the fight. Chinese premier Zhou Enlai made a speech containing concessions on the issue of prisoner-of-war exchanges in March 1953 that signaled a likely breakthrough in concluding an armistice agreement, despite Rhee's staunch opposition. Rhee threatened to withdraw ROK forces from the UN Command and to continue the fight alone but at the same time requested a security treaty with the United States.

On the eve of the conclusion of armistice negotiations, in which South Korea refused to participate, Rhee unilaterally released twenty-five thousand anti-Communist North Korean prisoners of war who had not agreed to be repatriated, causing a setback to armistice negotiations and raising questions about whether the UN Command could secure compliance with the agreement from the South Korean side. Rhee's unilateral action generated both exasperation and serious U.S. consideration of Rhee's removal, but it also catalyzed negotiation of a defense treaty, which was Rhee's price for not obstructing the armistice. Thus, the establishment of the U.S.-ROK security alliance was a direct product of the clash between South Korea's need for security supplied by the United States to ensure South Korea's future and Rhee's ongoing desire to pursue actions against his patron's wishes.

The conclusion of the Korean Armistice Agreement and the subsequent failure of an envisioned political conference in Geneva in 1954 to determine the political future of the Korean Peninsula marked a shift in international and U.S. political attention away from the peninsula. Rhee's preoccupation with extracting concessions and commitments from the United States revealed the absence of a South Korean option beyond dependency on the alliance for the near future. For Rhee, extraction of U.S. security and economic support for South Korea became the main objectives of South Korea's foreign policy. The alliance arrangements became an instrument through which the United States provided economic assistance to South

Korea. According to one source, "Foreign aid constituted a third of the total [South Korean] budget in 1954, rose to 58.4 percent in 1956, and was approximately 38 percent of the budget in 1960." U.S. assistance accounted for up to 40 percent of South Korea's national budget in the 1950s and provided more than half of the defense budget.[5] The United States eventually tired of the ROK's economic strategies focused on maximizing U.S. development assistance rather than on building a self-sustaining economy of its own. Rhee's unilateral bluff to "march north" continued to be a useful tool for preserving domestic South Korean support for him and a means by which to antagonize his American patrons. Otherwise, his pledges rang hollow given the likely consequences of a renewed conflict with a North Korean adversary that had experienced a rapid economic recovery and was relatively stronger than the South.[6]

During and immediately following the negotiation of the Korean Armistice Agreement, Rhee's defiance of his patron's wishes seemed to put at risk support that was in fact essential to South Korea's survival. However, Rhee also recognized that America needed to preserve South Korea as an alternative to unification of the Korean Peninsula under Communist rule. This reality empowered him to bluff and to take American support for granted. An important consequence of his unilateral defiance, bluff, and bluster was that he gained a security commitment from the United States that proved to be vital to South Korea's survival and eventual prosperity. The U.S.-ROK security alliance originated both as a product of American mistrust and as an instrument by which the United States imposed restraint on Rhee. It also happened to serve shared security interests in the preservation of South Korea against the expansion of Communist rule in Asia and became the dominant framework that has defined South Korea's foreign policy ever since.

PARK CHUNG-HEE'S VISION FOR SOUTH KOREA

Unlike Syngman Rhee, who had lived in the United States for decades, Park Chung-hee's formative experiences were shaped by his time as a student in a Japanese military academy and as a soldier in the Japanese Imperial Army in Manchuria. Although Park paid lip service to liberal values to maintain good relations with the United States, he was neither liberal nor democratic in practice. He compared the democratic system in Korea under Syngman Rhee to the corrupt, incompetent, and faction-ridden political system of the old Joseon dynasty monarchy that had ruled Korea until the dawn of the twentieth century but that was unable to effectively deal with external challenges and pressure and was eventually annexed by Japan in 1910.[7]

In contrast, Park Chung-hee sought to build a Korea that was self-reliant and not dependent on great powers for its security. Much like Kim Il-sung in North Korea, Park believed that a nation must rely on its own strength to survive in a hostile environment and that "virtues [such] as loyalty, legalism, or even human compassion are but *weaknesses* before the interlocking interests of the Big Powers." For Park, international politics was a "question of who is winning rather than who is right." He believed that South Korea had to do away with its shrimp-among-whales mindset, believe in its own abilities, and become self-reliant because "help is offered only when one helps oneself."[8] Whereas Kim Il-sung was talking about *juche*, Park was writing about *jaju*. Both were aiming for self-reliance.[9] Park wrote ardently about "the soldiers of the Koguryo Kingdom, [who,] far outnumbered by enemies from Shui and Tang China, successfully fought off and repelled the aggressors; after over ten years of tenacious struggles, the small Kingdom of Silla finally succeeded in unifying all of Korea by defeating the Tang Chinese troops."[10] In the international arena, Park wanted Korea to be a more assertive and confident nation. In his memoir *The Country, the Revolution, and I*, he laments: "Despite all these accumulated sufferings [administered by foreign powers], we have never once undertaken a foreign excursion by turning the tide."[11]

To strengthen South Korea, Park Chung-hee wanted his fellow citizens to look to the military as a model organization to be emulated. He wanted to copy Japan's war economy during the 1930s and 1940s.[12] As a general-president, he sought to run South Korea with military precision and efficiency.

CONSTRAINTS ON SOUTH KOREAN FOREIGN
POLICY UNDER PARK CHUNG-HEE

Despite the fact that Park Chung-hee envisioned a self-reliant Korea, he faced massive constraints that inevitably led to his heavy dependence on the United States. It is easy to forget just how dependent South Korea was on the United States in the late 1950s and early 1960s. Not only was it re-covering from the ravages of the Korean War, but it was also doing so more slowly than its North Korean foes. South Korea's fragility left the country utterly dependent on the United States both for economic suste-nance and for security. Its per capita gross domestic product (GDP) in 1961 was about $100 per year. Outside assessments of the country's economy were grim. Donald Macdonald, a top U.S. State Department official on Korea, recalled about a White House meeting in 1960, "The majority posi-tion was that Korea was an economic basket case that would always de-pend on American handouts for its existence."[13] United States Agency for International Development officials during the early 1960s privately echoed that assessment and believed that aid was going down a "rat hole."[14] In fact, the Philippines and Burma, following Japan, were supposed to be the economies in East Asia with the greatest potential to industrialize, according to a World Bank report published in 1961.[15]

Following the Korean War, the United States maintained a significant operational capability in South Korea up through 1960. U.S. economic as-sistance to South Korea in the late 1950s accounted for more than half of the South Korean government's national budget and 72 percent of the de-fense budget.[16] The U.S. support infrastructure in country included five hundred economic advisers at the U.S. Operations Mission, responsible for overseeing aid money, budgetary allocations, and in large part control-ling South Korean economic policy.[17] Figures 2.1 and 2.2 show the level of U.S. economic and military assistance to South Korea during this period.

South Korea's dependency on the United States was virtually complete. Abandonment by the United States would surely have meant communiza-tion under Kim Il-sung's rule. Put in contemporary terms, U.S. influence over South Korea's financial and economic policies in the 1950s was far

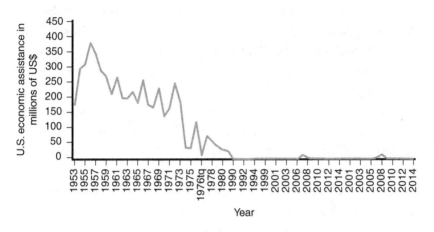

Year

FIGURE 2.1

U.S. Economic Assistance to South Korea, 1953–2014

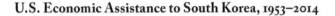

Note: "1976tq" refers to transitive quarter 1976.
Source: United States Agency for International Development, *Country Summary*, n.d.,
http://explorer.usaid.gov/data-download.html

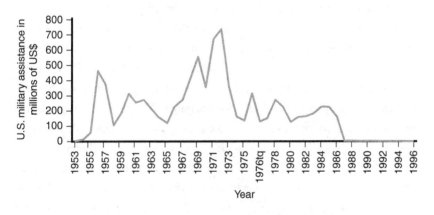

Year

FIGURE 2.2

U.S. Military Assistance to South Korea, 1953–1996

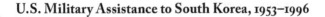

Note: 1976tq refers to transitive quarter 1976.
Source: United States Agency for International Development, *Country Summary*, n.d.,
http://explorer.usaid.gov/data-download.html.

greater than China's influence over the budget of North Korea today. Yet U.S. ability to dictate political outcomes or to control South Korea's direction and policies remained limited, just as China has found that its influence on the North is limited despite Pyongyang's economic dependency on Beijing.

The United States dealt with competing priorities in its Korea policy. On the one hand, its most important goal was to defend South Korea against North Korea. On the other hand, the United States wanted to encourage South Korea's democratization and development. But it failed to integrate security and economic interests into a comprehensive strategy following the Korean War, with the result that American economic and security bureaucracies that had entrenched themselves in South Korea found themselves in competition with each other for control over limited assistance to South Korea. Second, South Korea's leaders in the aftermath of the war focused more on dependency-perpetuating aid extraction from the United States than on building capabilities that would enhance autonomy and prospects for indigenous growth. The United States had potentially enormous leverage as a result of South Korea's near-total dependency on U.S. economic assistance, but the need for cooperation with South Korean leaders also tempered U.S. political pressure.[18]

South Korea also faced dilemmas resulting from its parallel dependencies on the United States for economic and security assistance. It needed U.S. support in order to survive and deter the threat from a North Korea that was experiencing greater postwar economic growth than the South, and thus it had no choice but to accommodate U.S. intrusion and guidance on a wide range of domestic economic issues. The structure and composition of U.S. financial support focused primarily on the military need to deter a more rapidly recovering North Korea in the 1950s, but American security investments would not be sustainable in the absence of a South Korean economic recovery. Nevertheless, the United States and South Korea had divergent priorities regarding the direction of South Korean structural and economic reforms.

As a former Japanese military officer who came to power through a coup, Park Chung-hee needed the support of ambivalent U.S. officials who on the one hand hoped for enlightened economic mobilization but on the other hand opposed Park's inclination to set aside democratic practice. Park's ascension to power tested the relative priority of U.S. support for democracy, commitment to South Korea's security, and need to stabilize the country's economy. Park's ambitious vision of rapid industrialization and economic growth clashed with a more incrementalist U.S. policy that sought economic stabilization and more realistic economic planning.

Park Chung-hee, however, was far more pragmatic than Syngman Rhee. Rhee was too obstinate to back down from an open confrontation with the Americans and was wily enough to resort to sabotaging U.S. initiatives to get his way. In contrast, Park, even as he longed for Korean autonomy, recognized that he needed the alliance with the United States and so sought to make himself and his contributions to the U.S. struggle against communism indispensable, shifting from a posture of confrontation to one of bargaining within the patron–client relationship as the best hedge against the risk of abandonment.

Throughout the 1960s and 1970s, Park Chung-hee constantly worried about abandonment by the United States and took extraordinary measures to obtain reassurances of U.S. commitment both to his political leadership and to South Korea's national security. The most important of Park's efforts in aligning South Korea with the United States was his decision to dispatch some of South Korea's most capable forces in support of U.S. efforts in Vietnam in the mid-1960s. The move had both a security purpose and an economic purpose. On the security front, Park feared the potential reallocation of U.S. troops on the Korean Peninsula to Vietnam and believed that the withdrawal would invite a North Korean invasion. Sending Korean troops to Vietnam also provided much needed combat experience and U.S. modernization assistance for the South Korean military. On the economic front, the war in Vietnam created growth opportunities for nascent South Korean firms that produced goods to support the war effort. In an indirect sense, U.S. financial burdens resulting from the war also provided the United States with a strong incentive to normalize relations between Japan and South Korea. The net effect of the Park government's participation in the Vietnam War was that South Korea became more capable militarily and economically.

PARK CHUNG-HEE'S FOREIGN POLICY DURING THE 1960S: CLOSE ALIGNMENT WITH THE UNITED STATES

Despite his aspirations to build a self-reliant Korea, Park Chung-hee could not ignore the fact that when he came to power in 1961, South Korea remained extraordinarily vulnerable and that Kim Il-sung had already made great strides in revitalizing the North Korean economy, had consolidated his domestic political standing, and had secured security treaties with his major patrons, China and the Soviet Union. Kim was also taking advantage of the political turmoil in the South: North Korean incursions along the DMZ increased from around 200 per year to 736 incidents in 1961 alone.[19] Given the circumstances, Park clearly recognized his dependence on the United States and feared abandonment by an ally that was increasingly preoccupied by the war in Vietnam. His concerns were likely heightened by reductions in the annual U.S. economic assistance to South Korea from $230 million in 1959–1963 to $110 million in 1964–1968.[20] Park needed to find a way to shore up the U.S. commitment both to South Korea and to his personal leadership.

Thus, Park simultaneously sought U.S. support for his leadership and deflected U.S. pressure to democratize in the form of either a U.S. decision to back an alternative leader or a U.S. withdrawal of economic or political support deemed vital to South Korea's stability. Park's main strategy in achieving these objectives involved classic issue-linkage bargaining. In return for normalization of South Korea's relations with Japan and contributions to U.S. war efforts in Vietnam, he sought U.S. political backing, support for his economic agenda, and continued tangible expressions of commitment to South Korea's security. Meanwhile, the top U.S. priorities, according to a National Security Council task force on South Korea, were Korea's national development, civilian rule, and recognition of the United States Forces Korea (USFK)–UN Command authority to exercise operational control over Korean forces.[21] The United States was initially reluctant to support Park in the absence of a stronger commitment to return to civilian rule.[22] At the same time, the Americans were mindful of the need for South Korea to achieve political stability and were moderately hopeful regarding Park's commitment to economic development. After Park's visit to Washington in November 1961, U.S. ambassador to South Korea Samuel Berger determined that U.S. backing for Park would contribute to Korean stability while indirectly enhancing his legitimacy within South Korea.[23] However, the United States continued to worry about Park's resistance to a return to civilian rule. It was particularly concerned about the power, influence, and methods of the notorious Korean Central Intelligence Agency run by Park's brother-in-law, Kim Jong-pil, whom Americans viewed as nationalistic, anti-American, and possibly influenced by leftists.[24]

SOUTH KOREA'S PARTICIPATION IN THE VIETNAM WAR

Park Chung-hee sought to earn U.S. trust and commitment by volunteering his support for the U.S. war effort in Vietnam. As a major contributor to the war, South Korea under Park preserved limited autonomy and gained U.S. acquiescence to Park's pursuit of his own domestic political and economic agenda.

Park first volunteered to send Korean troops to Vietnam "if requested" during his state visit to Washington in 1961. Two years later, in August 1963, he told close associates that in the event of an American request that South Korea dispatch troops to Vietnam, South Korea would be "obliged out of both economic and security considerations."[25] When the U.S. request for support did come, Park responded quickly by providing noncombat personnel in May and December 1964 and subsequently by providing combat troops in July 1965 and June 1966. Although there were concerns in South Korea's National Assembly over the wisdom of the troop dispatch on grounds that it might weaken South Korean security or unnecessarily entrap South Korea in a faraway conflict, Park easily managed to overcome domestic opposition to his decision.[26] With these moves, the Park administration solidified U.S. commitment to economic and military benefits as well as security assurances, which included the maintenance of U.S. troops on the Korean Peninsula at a steady level, assistance in military modernization, and promises of combat-duty pay and death-disability compensation for South Korean troops at the same level received by U.S. forces. Of these three benefits, the first was the most important for Park because he feared that the withdrawal of U.S. troops would prompt a North Korean invasion. He remarked in 1967, "I will give you a more frank reason for the troop deployment. . . . We could have chosen not to deploy our troops when asked. Then the two U.S. divisions deployed in South Korea would have been transferred to Vietnam. How could we have been able to stop them while not sending our own forces? We could not have."[27]

At the height of the war in Vietnam, South Korea deployed 50,000 troops, the largest international contingent of foreign forces next to the 550,000 troops deployed by the United States. The troops that Park sent to Vietnam were some of South Korea's best fighting units, the vaunted Tiger and White Horse Divisions. Dispatched in 1965 and 1966, respectively, these Korean divisions were responsible primarily for the restoration of order and rehabilitation of damaged areas behind the front lines. Korean Forces in Vietnam conducted 1,171 large-scale military operations and 576,000 company-based actions, primarily providing defense for U.S. supply lines in coastal areas of South Vietnam.[28] South Korean contributions to the U.S. war effort in Vietnam came at a relatively low cost. For example, the cost of placing one South Korean soldier on the field in Vietnam for one year was $5,000, less than half the approximately $13,000 spent to support one U.S. soldier on the field for one year, making the Korean contribution a relative bargain for the United States.[29]

In return, Park Chung-hee won U.S. gratitude, gained assurances that the United States would not abandon South Korea, and earned political support and acquiescence to both his authoritarian rule and his efforts to promote Korean economic growth. Conditions for the first deployment of Korean Forces in Vietnam included pledges that there would be no reduction in the number of U.S. troops on the Korean Peninsula without first consulting the South Korean government, that the level of U.S. military assistance be maintained at current levels, and that the United States would provide financial support for transport of South Korean troops to South Vietnam.[30]

Park used his efforts during the Vietnam War to obtain assistance from the United States for military modernization, including modernizing defense equipment, upgrading the peninsula-based defense capabilities, giving preferential terms to South Korean suppliers for U.S. government contracts for equipment and services, and providing technical assistance for South Korea in export promotion.[31] Park was particularly shrewd in using the cover of his political and military support to ensure that the United States retained its capabilities in South Korea, or, alternatively, that South Korean capabilities were upgraded in the context of acquiescing to increasingly urgent requests from the United States for the war effort in Vietnam. Kim Jong-pil relates an instance in late 1972 in which U.S. ambassador Philip Habib made an urgent request for South Korea to provide two battalions of F-5A fighter planes to Vietnam. Although the planes were U.S. property, the U.S. government needed Korean acquiescence to divert the planes for use by the South Vietnamese government. In return for his approval, Kim requested a battalion of Phantom F-4D planes that had superior range and capabilities as replacements for the F-5As. So within two years, when the South Vietnamese government collapsed, the F-5As returned to South Korea and remained there at no additional cost to Seoul, as did the Phantom F-4D planes. South Korea proved particularly adept at taking advantage of U.S. needs for both foreign-exchange-earning opportunities and arbitrage arrangements, which provided both a profit for South Korea and a net improvement of its capabilities.[32]

NORMALIZATION OF RELATIONS WITH JAPAN

Park Chung-hee's decision to dispatch forces to Vietnam also knit together South Korean military and Japanese economic contributions as critical supporting elements in the U.S. strategy toward Asia during the Vietnam War. As U.S. concerns in Asia increased with Chinese Communist aggression following nuclear tests in October 1964 and May 1965 and pressure that came with the escalation of the Vietnam War, the United States had strong incentives to promote reconciliation between Japan and South Korea.

With U.S. support, Park Chung-hee took the domestically controversial step of reopening diplomatic normalization talks with Japan. In contrast to Syngman Rhee, who had stood up for Korean independence against the Japanese for decades, Park, with his background as a Japanese officer, was predisposed to developing relations with Japan as a pragmatic measure that would serve South Korea's economic and political interests. In Japan, former prime minister Kishi Nobusuke also saw a clear opportunity to improve relations with South Korea under Park's leadership, recognizing that Park, as an authoritarian leader, would be able to handle domestic politics. Kishi argued, "If we do not do anything and allow Park to fail, most grave consequences will follow. Now is not the time to sit idly by."[33] Yet many in Japan did not feel a strong need to pursue normalization with South Korea. As a confidential background paper by the U.S. government noted in January 1965, "Most Japanese [feel] little urgency about normalization, since a prosperous Japan can do without the Korean market and Japan's security position is protected by the U.S. commitment to the R.O.K."[34]

Therefore, U.S. support and direct involvement were crucial in bringing about the normalization treaty between the two Northeast Asian allies of the United States, particularly as Park Chung-hee was facing the possibility of severe instability in his country due to South Korean protests against the Japan-ROK negotiations. Although Washington had been involved in improving Japan-ROK relations since the 1950s in a more restrained, cheerleading role, it had refused to become directly involved in lobbying for normalization until 1964.[35] With the escalating war in Vietnam and the specter of a more aggressive, nuclear-armed China, the United States finally decided to become directly involved both privately and publicly between 1964 and 1965. The United States assured South Korea of continued U.S. support, supported the Park government publicly and privately, and made backroom maneuvers to persuade the different parties and interest groups in both Japan and South Korea on the need to normalize their relations.

Nevertheless, Park Chung-hee's decision during these negotiations to compromise on whether Japan's colonial rule over Korea should be deemed "legal" or "illegal" and thus to forgo reparations in favor of a package of economic grants and loans was greeted with widespread public dissatisfaction and student protests in Korea. Other issues drawing the South Korean public's ire were the fact that the scope of the treaty covered only South Korea, not extending to the North, and the abandonment of expansive fishery protections that had been enforced under Syngman Rhee. When the near-complete draft of the treaty was revealed in April 1965, massive protests erupted in South Korea and even led to the formation of an opposition group, the Committee for the Struggle Against Humiliating Diplomacy with Japan, which sought to prevent the South Korean National Assembly from ratifying the normalization treaty.[36] Public unrest against the normalization was so intense that Ambassador Samuel D. Berger and USFK commander Hamilton H. Howze recommended that Park declare martial law.[37] By the end of 1965, the two countries' legislatures ratified the treaty on normalization.

The normalization between Japan and South Korea ultimately benefited Park by reaffirming South Korea's importance as a U.S. ally and by bolstering his popularity when economic growth came with Japanese economic assistance.[38] South Korea received $45 million in property claims and a total of $800 million in grants and loans. Within a mere two years of the controversial treaty, Park won his second presidential term in 1967 by a wide margin, ten percentage points over the opposition candidate and former president Yun Posun.

During the first half of his presidency in the 1960s, Park Chung-hee proved to be a shrewd strategist and an effective negotiator in the context of the asymmetrical U.S.-ROK alliance. Rather than pursuing autonomy by challenging the fundamental U.S. aims of stability in favor of Korean unification, as Syngman Rhee had done, Park sought a quid pro quo deal in which he provided political and military support for the highest U.S. security priority in Asia in return for political, economic, and security benefits. He tied the United States more closely to South Korea rather than resisting the United States. With his strategy, Park also gained a degree of autonomy to govern in a fashion that fundamentally challenged U.S. values by prioritizing national security over democracy, centrally directed planning over laissez-faire economic principles, and state repression over civil society.[39] The result was that South Korea was able to launch an extraordinary economic takeoff, which in the long-term was vital in providing it with the enhanced capacity to have a greater voice within the U.S.-ROK alliance. The second half of Park's presidency, however, would prove to be far more challenging than the first.

CHALLENGES TO SOUTH KOREAN FOREIGN POLICY DURING THE 1970S AND PARK CHUNG-HEE'S RESPONSE

The international circumstances that initially enabled Park Chung-hee to make himself essential to U.S. strategy in Asia and in Vietnam eventually shifted. With U.S. withdrawal from Vietnam, Sino-U.S. rapprochement, and retrenchment from the region marked by the Nixon Doctrine of 1969, Park faced the dual threats of abandonment and rising American opposition to his increasing authoritarianism at home.

The shifting international environment resulting from U.S. retreat from Vietnam and the announcement of the Nixon Doctrine led to the draw-down of the 20,000 troops composing the Seventh Infantry Division from South Korea in 1971. These developments and Park's inability to reverse them fanned his fears of abandonment. In 1971, his anxiety was exacerbated by Nixon's opening to China, which was one of North Korea's two main patrons. In response to the announcement of Henry Kissinger's secret visit to Beijing, Park ruminated in front of Western reporters, "How long can we trust the United States?"[40] In the run-up to Nixon's visit to Beijing, Park sought reassurances that the U.S. opening to China would not compromise or affect the inter-Korean situation. Nixon's National Security Council took more than three months to reply to Park, indicating the low level of importance that the United States attached to his concerns. He later described his feelings toward the situation by writing that "this series of developments contained an unprecedented peril to [Korean] people's survival. . . . [The situation] almost reminded one of the last days of the Korean Empire a century earlier, when European Powers were similarly agitating in rivalry over Korea."[41] Figure 2.2 shows that U.S. military assistance dropped steeply during the early 1970s.

The sudden perception of a realignment of power in Asia precipitated a historic set of interactions between Park Chung-hee and Kim Il-sung and led to the first dialogue and joint declaration between the two Koreas since the end of the Korean War. Although both sides had different motives for moving toward a short-lived détente, they agreed to a mutual declaration that the two Koreas would pursue national unification independently, peacefully, and on a basis of great national unity that would transcend differences in "ideology, ideal, and system."[42] A significant aspect of the agreement is that it established the inter-Korean relationship as a sphere in which South Korea was willing to take initiatives in response to perceived geopolitical changes independent of the United States.

Park Chung-hee also challenged the United States on two fronts: he flouted U.S. desires for South Korea's eventual democratization through his increased centralization of power under the Yushin (Revitalization) Constitution (1972) and his efforts to obtain nuclear weapons. The latter seriously jeopardized South Korea's security relationship with the United States. Park never achieved his desire for security and autonomy. The alliance with the United States proved to be a constraint to the self-help approach, even as it provided security benefits to South Korea. In the end, Park chose the alliance over a nuclear weapons program.

Last but not least, Park Chung-hee began to diversify South Korea's foreign policy during the early 1970s from an approach that depended on the United States exclusively to one that reached out to China and the Soviet Union, partially with the goal of better managing North Korea. In this respect, his efforts laid the foundations for subsequent efforts under Roh Tae-woo's Nordpolitik (Northern Policy) that unfolded at the end of the Cold War and normalized Seoul's relations with Beijing and Moscow.

INTER-KOREAN DÉTENTE

Both Park Chung-hee and Kim Il-sung shared surprise at Sino-U.S. entente, but from different perspectives. Park genuinely feared that the United States might abandon South Korea; Kim Il-sung, although taken aback by China's opening to the United States, saw it as a potential opportunity to achieve unification given that North Korea remained stronger than South Korea. With these thoughts in mind, both leaders initiated an extraordinary restoration of direct communication between the two Koreas that had not existed for more than two decades since the Korean War. A series of secret exchanges led to the announcement of an inter-Korean declaration on July 4, 1972, in which the first and foremost point was that "unification shall be achieved through independent efforts without being subject to external imposition and interference." The other two points stipulated that unification was to happen peacefully and that it was to be based on ethnic unity, transcending ideological and institutional difference.[43]

Both leaders saw the inter-Korean declaration as a tactical maneuver and so had rather differing objectives. Through détente with his archenemy, Park sought to reduce tensions on the Korean Peninsula and to buy time needed to achieve self-reliant defense for South Korea by accelerating the development of indigenous arms industries and nuclear weapons.[44] Kim, for his part, believed that he might be able to take advantage of South Koreans' public discontent with Park's rule to weaken and subvert his regime and to use the Nixon administration's retrenchment and rapprochement with China to secure the departure of U.S. troops from the Korean Peninsula.[45] The North Korean position was partially motivated by Chinese premier Zhou Enlai's conversation in July 1971 with Henry Kissinger, who said that it is "quite conceivable that before the end of the next term of President Nixon, most, if not all, American troops will be withdrawn from Korea."[46] In another meeting with Zhou, Kissinger noted that "if the tensions in the Far East continue to diminish, the number of forces in Korea can be expected to be very small."[47] To achieve this, Kim sought to use improved inter-Korean relations to induce a false sense of calm in the South as part of his plan to take over the entire Korea with anti-Park "democratic" forces to achieve subsequent unification.

Naturally, "progress" on inter-Korean relations proved to be rather short-lived because neither side truly came to terms with the other. Kim Il-sung's unrealistic hopes for democratic uprisings against Park Chung-hee faded as Park imposed his dictatorship in the South and clamped down on all opposition movements in late 1972. By the summer of 1973, inter-Korean relations were back to where they were before the joint statement, with both sides accusing each other of abandoning the agreed principles and North Korea seeking to bypass the South to establish a direct dialogue with the United States.[48] The transformation of the international political environment brought about by Sino-U.S. entente instead generated a more complex and subtle form of inter-Korean competition. Each Korea competed globally with the other for diplomatic support while attempting to outmaneuver the other in seeking to reinforce its own legitimacy and moral superiority.

YUSHIN CONSTITUTION: STRENGTHENING CONTROL AT HOME AGAINST U.S. PRESSURE

A major consequence of the changing international environment was Park Chung-hee's decision essentially to do away with checks and balances that could fetter his power by declaring the Yushin (Revitalization) Constitution, whose name was inspired in part by Japan's Meiji Ishin (Meiji Restoration or, more correctly, Revitalization). The new constitution granted Park six-year terms with no term limit, gave him the right to appoint one-third of the National Assembly members, and allowed the president to rule by decrees with little constraints, if any, and backed by control of repressive security institutions, such as the Korean Central Intelligence Agency and the Presidential Security Service.[49]

The promulgation of the new constitution revealed Park Chung-hee's increasing intolerance of internal challenge and dissent. Park also pursued Yushin as a means to continue his economic modernization drive and as a necessary response to a deteriorating external security environment and North Korea's active military provocations. Based on his diary entries and accounts by his close associates, Park might not have intended to remain president forever and might have seen the measures as temporary, although many outside observers saw him as seeking to remain in power indefinitely. As he initially told Kim Jong-pil, "We'll face strong opposition, but later people will say we got through the decade well. It will be temporary until we get over this national emergency."[50] According to other accounts, Park wanted to build a self-reliant defense economy and nuclear weapons program by the early to mid-1980s and then resign.[51]

By the time Park introduced the Yushin Constitution, he had already used the intelligence service, control over the media, and his own penchant for dividing and inducing loyalty among potential challengers at the elite level to strengthen his own authoritarian control. The combination of these methods made his subordinates dependent on his good favor and ensured that Korean politics remained under his control. Nevertheless, there remained wide opposition to his actions among activists and dissidents, notably in academia, religious institutions, and the working class. Although remaining outside of political institutions, aside from some ties with the opposition party in the National Assembly, this network had a broad base of support and resisted Park's excesses.[52]

At the international level, Park Chung-hee's move toward a more powerful dictatorship further strained relations with the United States. Yet the threat of the diminution and even the withdrawal of U.S. support had the ironic effect of reducing Park's deference toward the United States, removing any external inhibitions on his desires to consolidate his rule. His efforts ironically mirrored and were fed by North Korea's own political centralization under Kim Il-sung as inter-Korean competition intensified and as Park tried to close the gap between the South and the North in national capacity and to lessen the South's dependency on the United States. As the United States retrenched in the context of its withdrawal from Vietnam, the political basis and value of South Korean support for U.S. aims simultaneously also diminished.

The factor that allowed Park Chung-hee to strengthen his centralized control despite U.S. opposition was that his dependency on the United States for both economic and military support had declined in a relative sense thanks in part to his economic modernization drive and in part to the economic and security benefits derived from South Korea's involvement in the Vietnam War. The United States remained South Korea's biggest customer and an essential bulwark against the North, but U.S. assistance bought much less leverage for the United States in South Korea as the latter's capabilities increased, and so South Korea's dependency on the United States was no longer near total. U.S. ambassador to South Korea Richard L. Sneider noted in 1975, "The country is becoming a middle size power, though we do not realize it. It is too large an economy to be a client state."[53]

However, because of U.S. opposition, Park Chung-hee could not centralize the South Korean political system, as Kim Il-sung was able to do in North Korea. Americans publicly and privately criticized and pushed back against Park, who ultimately had no alternative security option aside from the United States. In contrast, Kim Il-sung could exploit the Sino-Soviet split to pit his Chinese and Soviet patrons against each other in a competition to win the North's allegiance and favor, effectively discouraging both Beijing and Moscow from interfering in the domestic dynamics in Pyongyang.

Even as Park further centralized the South Korean political system, he took increasingly desperate measures to maintain political support within the United States for keeping U.S. troops in South Korea. Notably, his efforts included direct, illegal congressional lobbying, an incident known as "Koreagate," in which a high-ranking South Korean official attempted to obtain stronger U.S. commitment to South Korea by bribing more than a hundred members of Congress with hundreds of thousands of dollars. The scandal led to further estrangement with Washington in the 1970s. Nevertheless, President Carter agreed in 1978 to establish the Combined Forces Command, which would integrate control of the two allies' military forces on the Korean Peninsula. In addition, Carter offered to restore U.S. economic and military assistance, including increased sales of U.S. jet fighters.[54] In 1979, the U.S.-ROK relationship reached a particularly low point when Carter pushed for the withdrawal of all ground troops from the Korean Peninsula, although he never carried through with the plan due to opposition from Park as well as from Carter's own subordinates within the U.S. government. During a meeting in the summer of 1979, Park promised to spend more than 6 percent of the South Korean GDP in defense spending and committed to take steps toward liberalization in return for Carter's reconsideration of his plan to pull out ground troops from the Korean Peninsula.[55]

DIVERSIFICATION IN FOREIGN RELATIONS: BEGINNING OF NORDPOLITIK

Although Roh Tae-woo, in power from 1988 to 1993, receives much credit for the success of Nordpolitik—a policy of pursuing diplomatic normalizations with China and the Soviet Union in order to pressure North Korea—the policy was initially introduced under Park Chung-hee. As U.S. policy shifted in the context of Vietnam War drawdowns, South Korea's perception of the balance of power in East Asia also shifted. In 1972, Special

Assistant for Foreign and Security Affairs Hahm Pyong-choon wrote in *Foreign Affairs* that "the cold war [*sic*], which had been characterized by bipolar power alignments with strong intra-bloc cohesion, was definitely coming to an end by the time the U.S. involvement in the Vietnam war [*sic*] was reaching its climax."[56] In response, the Park government shifted its foreign policy from one based exclusively on a close alliance with the United States and unequivocal opposition to communism to a more flexible approach with the goal of establishing relations with China and the Soviet Union for the ultimate purpose of isolating North Korea.[57]

The Park Chung-hee administration first reviewed its relations with China, the Soviet Union, and other Communist countries after Richard Nixon's announcement of the Nixon Doctrine in 1969 and began allowing South Korean officials to engage Communist officials abroad while discouraging further expansion of contact with Taiwanese diplomats.[58] In 1971, South Korean foreign minister Kim Yong-sik said that the ROK would deal with the issue of normalization of relations with China and the Soviet Union with "flexibility and sincerity."[59] On June 23, 1973, Park Chung-hee noted in a special address on foreign policy: "The Republic of Korea will open its door to all the nations of the world on the basis of the principles of reciprocity and equality. At the same time, we urge those countries whose ideologies and social institutions are different from ours to open their doors likewise to us."[60] Park's shift in foreign policy was driven by the perception that U.S. commitment had become unreliable and that relations with North Korea's patrons needed to be established in order to better restrain and pressure Pyongyang. This approach was essentially a precursor to Nordpolitik and provided the basis for South Korea to explore relations with long-standing enemies on the other side of the Cold War divide, most notably China and the Soviet Union.

Park Chung-hee's overtures did not lead to a sudden improvement in relations with the two countries, but the early stages of contact with both major powers began to develop during his presidency. In 1973, Moscow began to allow South Korean artists and academics to attend conferences in the Soviet Union and permitted South Korean athletes to participate in competitions there.[61] In 1974, Beijing began allowing Korean Chinese to exchange letters with their relatives in South Korea and began to refer to

South Korea as the Republic of Korea at the United Nations.[62] Beijing also began to allow Korean Chinese to visit or return to South Korea.[63] By the end of the Park presidency, South Korea had established minor but still notable educational, athletic, and cultural exchanges with the Soviet Union and had established indirect trade relations with China. Park's outreach, however, was limited by the intensity of the Sino-Soviet split at the time; both Beijing and Moscow were wary of establishing closer ties with Seoul due to their need to court Pyongyang. The concern was that if either China or the Soviet Union sought to improve its relations with South Korea, North Korea would move away from the offending party and toward the other Communist great power. As long as the Sino-Soviet split existed, the North Koreans could pit the great powers against each other.

PURSUIT OF SELF-RELIANT SECURITY AND DRIVE TO ACQUIRE NUCLEAR WEAPONS

The most drastic decision Park Chung-hee took in response to the Nixon Doctrine was his clandestine pursuit of nuclear weapons. The South Korean cabinet discussed the development of nuclear weapons as early as 1969.[64] By 1970, Park told Kim Jong-pil, "Since we don't know when the U.S. forces will leave, we need to research atom bombs. If the United States stops us, at least we will have the technology to make nuclear weapons."[65] Park believed the United States would be forced to accept South Korea as a nuclear weapons state once the country became one, as the United States had done tacitly with Israel.[66] Park was also motivated by the example of France's Charles de Gaulle, whom he greatly admired as someone who seemed to have restored French security, foreign-policy independence, and prestige through strongman rule and nuclear weapons development.[67]

Park, however, did not make his decision to pursue a nuclear weapons program lightly and did so only after making vigorous efforts to reverse the reductions in U.S. forces on the Korean Peninsula. His suspicions regarding the credibility of U.S. commitment to South Korea's defense occurred against the backdrop of increasing frequency and intensity of North Korean military provocations. North Korea had completed a military buildup under the "four-line military policy" in the 1960s and pursued a series of military provocations in the late 1960s, including an assassination attempt on Park in January 1968, the capture of the USS *Pueblo*, armed guerrilla infiltrations, the shooting down of a U.S. EC-121 reconnaissance plane in 1969, and the abduction of a South Korean patrol boat near Yeonpyeong Island near the inter-Korean maritime border in the Yellow Sea in June 1970.[68] In addition, Park's doubts were fed by the shift in U.S. nuclear strategy in the 1960s from "massive retaliation" to "flexible response" in which the United States reduced dependence on deployment of atomic weapons as the primary component of deterrence.[69] The announcement of Kissinger's secret visit to Beijing in 1971 further fueled Park's sense of abandonment.

In response, Park Chung-hee not only established the Agency for Defense Development to modernize and develop an indigenous arms industry but also created the more covert Weapons Exploitation Committee, which was tasked with developing advanced weapons, reported directly to the president, and eventually recommended nuclear weapons development.[70] In September 1972, Park received the Atomic Fuel Development Plan, which included a plan for developing nuclear weapons. Between late 1972 and 1975, the Park government worked to recruit ethnic Korean nuclear scientists from abroad and to sign deals on obtaining reprocessing technology and facilities from France and heavy-water reactors and technology from Canada. The Park government hoped to have working nuclear weapons by the late 1970s or mid-1980s.[71]

For the first few years, Park's efforts proceeded smoothly, but India's nuclear test in May 1974 sent a sudden wake-up call to the U.S. government, which revamped its efforts to identify potential nuclear weapons states around the world and soon zeroed in on the South Korean program. By late 1974, the U.S. embassy in Seoul determined that Park was pursuing nuclear weapons, and a U.S. government interagency study came to the same conclusion in early March 1975.[72] South Korean efforts to acquire technology for nuclear weapons proved impossible to conceal. External observers easily put the pieces together as ethnic Korean nuclear scientists, including from the United States and Canada, suddenly began traveling to Korea and as the Park government negotiated deals to obtain reprocessing and heavy-water technology and equipment from France and Canada. Moreover, according to Kim Jong-pil, many of the people involved in the program voluntarily revealed their activities.[73]

Although Park's efforts greatly alarmed the United States, Washington was slow to respond at first, spending much of the spring of 1975 internally debating the issue. The U.S. embassy in Seoul pushed early on for the U.S. government to take "a more explicit course" and argued that there was "no need to pussy-foot," and the United States made efforts to have France cancel its deal with South Korea in April 1975.[74] The Americans were in the end able to get the Park government to ratify the Treaty on the Non-Proliferation of Nuclear Weapons (NPT). South Korea's ratification was a positive step, but the main concern in the United States was that Park was intent on obtaining nuclear weapons under the guise of a civilian program. The most contentious issue had to do with South Korea's insistence on acquiring reprocessing technology and facilities from France for "civilian" purposes because reprocessing technology would provide a pathway for the development of plutonium-based nuclear bombs.

Beginning in the summer of 1975, the United States intensified its efforts to persuade Park Chung-hee to cancel South Korea's nuclear deal with France. Washington initially began with an incentive-based approach, promising expanded access to nuclear technology and aid, hundreds of millions of dollars in Export-Import Bank financing for South Korea's nuclear program, and the possibility for South Korea to be part of a "multinational regional reprocessing plant."[75] During a visit to South Korea in August, U.S. secretary of defense James Schlesinger even warned quietly that "the only thing that could undermine the political relationship between the U.S. and the ROK would be the Korean effort to acquire its own nuclear weapons," although Schlesinger did not directly accuse Park of pursuing nuclear weapons (both Washington and Seoul knew what each other knew).[76] Yet the South Koreans continued to rebuff the U.S. request that it cancel the deal with the French, insisting that the deal was essentially done and that the program was peaceful in nature.

By December 1975, the United States had changed its approach to one based on pressure, repeatedly warning the South Koreans of "very adverse implications" and a complete reevaluation of the U.S.-ROK relationship if the Park government did not cancel the deal with France.[77] According to Kim Jong-pil, the United States also threatened South Korea with "critical sanctions."[78] By early 1976, Park Chung-hee caved and scrapped the deal on reprocessing facilities in January and downsized or shut down significant portions of the nuclear weapons program in December of the same year. South Korea continued its research on nuclear weapons development, albeit at a much smaller scale and scope until Park's death in 1979.

In addition to his efforts to acquire nuclear weapons, Park Chung-hee also increased the proportion South Korea spent on defense from 5 percent of gross national product (GNP) to 7.5 percent.[79] In 1976, South Korean defense spending doubled reportedly to about $1 billion in 1977, surpassing that of the North, but South Korea's capabilities still lagged behind the North's both qualitatively and quantitatively.[80] The military balance favored South Korea only if U.S. troops were taken into account, and it was only the U.S. military presence that deterred North Korea from waging war.[81]

CHUN DOO-HWAN: ABANDONMENT OF THE NUCLEAR PROGRAM, REAFFIRMATION OF THE ALLIANCE, AND ADVANCEMENT OF NORDPOLITIK

Park Chung-hee's attempt to develop nuclear weapons shook the alliance to its core, but his assassination in 1979 and the subsequent close cooperation between the Chun and Reagan administrations in South Korea and the United States revitalized the alliance. Just as his predecessor had done, Chun Doo-hwan, a military commander, came to power through force and suppression of dissent in 1979 and became president in 1980. Unsurprisingly, he lacked legitimacy and needed U.S. support to shore up his regime. In return for his pledge to spare the life of South Korea's leading opposition figure, democracy activist Kim Dae-jung, the United States under Reagan promised enhanced security assurances and welcomed Chun as one of the first foreign leaders to visit the White House in

February 1981, greatly bolstering Chun's legitimacy. Reagan's embrace of Chun, however, resulted in public criticisms from Koreans, who saw that the United States backed an authoritarian leader over democracy activists and in May 1980 blatantly tolerated the special forces' massacre of dissidents in Gwangju who were calling for the restoration of democracy. Reagan downplayed his predecessor's human rights concerns and provided credible U.S. security guarantees to South Korea. He promised that there would be no further withdrawals of U.S. forces, nullified Carter's decision to withdraw tactical nuclear weapons in Korea by 1982, and provided South Korea with a large number of advanced weapon systems.[82] With the alliance fully revitalized, Chun completely dismantled Park Chung-hee's nuclear weapons program.[83] Chun also returned to the policy of importing arms from the United States instead of focusing on indigenous development.[84]

The restoration of the U.S.-ROK relationship marked a significant turning point for South Korea's thinking about its pursuit of nuclear weapons. The Reagan–Chun communiqué signed during the summit in 1981 stressed that South Korea would be a "full participant" in any U.S. discussions with North Korea on reunification.[85] Joint security cooperation also increased.[86] At the same time, the Reagan administration made it clear that the improved security relationship was conditional on South Korea fully ending its pursuit of nuclear weapons. A joint communiqué from a meeting of defense ministers in 1982 also explicitly "confirmed . . . the United States' nuclear umbrella."[87] The joint communiqué issued at the end of Reagan's visit to South Korea in 1983 described for the first time the security of South Korea as "pivotal" to the stability of Northeast Asia and as "vital" to the security of the United States.[88]

While revitalizing the U.S.-ROK alliance, Chun Doo-hwan, following Park Chung-hee's lead, also continued to seek better relations with China and the Soviet Union. In 1981, Chun said, "Even with a country with a different ideology, if that country does not take a hostile attitude, [Korea] is willing to conduct people and material exchanges."[89] In March 1982, Foreign Minister Noh Sin-yeong noted that "taking advantage of the Seoul Olympics, [Korea] will move to open diplomatic relations with ten communist countries, including China, the Soviet Union, and Cuba."[90] In fact, Noh's successor, Lee Bum-suk, coined the term *Nordpolitik* in 1983.[91] For the Chun government, establishing relations with the two Communist giants, the Soviet Union and China, was the "primary diplomatic task."[92]

As a gesture of good will to advance Nordpolitik, Seoul unilaterally accorded most-favored-nation status to China, the Soviet Union, and other Communist states in 1982.[93] In 1983, Seoul took advantage of an airplane-hijacking incident involving Chinese civilians seeking asylum in Taiwan in order to make further contact with high-ranking Chinese officials. Instead of reaching Taiwan, the plane had landed on a U.S. military base near Seoul. To deal with the issue, Seoul invited a high-level Chinese Communist Party delegation to visit South Korea, marking the two countries' first official face-to-face contact. The two sides resolved the issue by deciding that Seoul would try the hijackers on Korean soil and would not repatriate them to China, but the plane and its passengers would be returned.[94] During the same year, China began to allow South Korean officials to attend events in China (such as conferences) sponsored by international organizations.[95] In March 1984, Seoul and Beijing conducted what might be called "tennis diplomacy" when a South Korean tennis team traveled to Kunming to play against the Chinese.[96] By 1985, South Korean businesses began to invest directly in China, and the indirect bilateral trade volume between China and South Korea surpassed the volume of trade between China and North Korea.[97]

With the Soviet Union, progress was more uneven. The ROK-Soviet relationship in fact hit a low point when the Soviets shot down Korean Airline Flight 007, a civilian airliner, in 1983, killing all passengers on board. Seoul, however, resumed its cautious outreach to better relations with Moscow by allowing South Korean officials to engage in interactions with Soviet officials in 1984, sending representatives to Soviet conferences, and inviting Soviet officials to visit South Korea.[98] As with China, ROK-Soviet rapprochement proceeded slowly, cautiously, and quietly. Nevertheless, Chun was able to build on the progress made by his predecessor and laid the ground for his successor, Roh Tae-woo, to take advantage of the changing global strategic landscape in the late 1980s and normalize South Korea's relations with both the Soviet Union and China.

Last but not least, the Chun government, unlike the Park government, understood the need to have a far more positive approach toward North Korea as part of the broader policy of Nordpolitik. After becoming president, Chun brought together a group of experts to study Nordpolitik and engagement strategies toward the Communist world. The group concluded in 1985 that outreach to Communist states had to be synchronized with improved relations with North Korea for Nordpolitik to succeed.[99] Even before the study was completed, however, Chun announced in 1982 his plan for unification and cooperation, similar to the calls he had made in 1981. The proposal included the creation of a unification conference with high-level representatives from the two sides; provided the basis for a unification constitution to restore the nation, democracy, and ideals of freedom; and proposed the holding of a free and democratic national referendum in both the North and the South to confirm the constitutional plans and finally to achieve unification by conducting nation-wide elections to form a government. Chun also called for a renunciation of the use of military force, for noninterference in domestic affairs, and for economic and personal exchanges.[100]

The North Koreans never reciprocated Chun's outreach, however. They instead tried to assassinate him and his cabinet members during their visit to the Martyrs' Mausoleum in Rangoon, Myanmar, in October 1983. Chun survived because he happened to be running late on that occasion, but many of his senior cabinet members died when the North Korean bombs exploded. But Chun never tried to come up with a tough response as Park Chung-hee had sought to do after Kim Il-sung's commandos infiltrated Seoul to kill Park. Chun instead continued to pursue outreach to the North. Indeed, he accepted North Korean offers of aid during the flood in the South in 1984, realized the very first inter-Korean family reunions in 1985, and suggested a summit with Kim Il-sung during the same year.[101] Throughout the rest of Chun's presidency and his successor's tenure, the two Koreas would maintain quiet channels of communication.[102] Any progress in inter-Korean relations, however, was thwarted by North Korean provocations. In 1987, two North Korean operatives planted bombs that blew up Korean Airline Flight 858, killing all aboard. Further progress would not materialize until Roh Tae-woo's presidency beginning in

1988, during which South Korea was able to use improved relations with China and the Soviet Union as leverage against the North.

CHANGING KOREAN CAPACITIES AND INFLUENCE ON THE AUTONOMY–ALLIANCE DYNAMICS

South Korea's vulnerability required protection from a more powerful patron, even while its founding leader, Syngman Rhee, continued to voice his unyielding desire to march North for Korean unification. Whether Rhee's obstinate insistence on achieving unification was a realistic possibility, his defiance of Korean Armistice Agreement arrangements and his apparent willingness to continue fighting ultimately proved sufficient to draw in significant economic and military resources and political commitments from the United States to assure South Korea's security. Ironically, U.S. commitments to that security were motivated as much by the Americans' distrust of Rhee's judgment and reliability as by their commitment to preserve South Korea as a bulwark against Communist aggression.

In contrast to Syngman Rhee, Park Chung-hee managed South Korea's alliance with the United States by asserting his autonomy and by protecting his domestic standing within the context of the alliance, although the specific expressions, weights, and tensions between alliance and autonomy gradually shifted in ways that created growing tensions with the United States. Park's cooperation with the United States to provide troops to Vietnam and his decision to normalize relations with Japan paid off handsomely and contributed to his economic-development plans while providing him with leverage to secure continued U.S. commitment to the defense of South Korea.

However, the Nixon doctrine and Sino-U.S. rapprochement created a different context for Park Chung-hee's decisions in the 1970s. The inter-Korean declaration in 1972, Park's pursuit of nuclear weapons, and gradual outreach to China and the Soviet Union were responses to a changed strategic context in which Park increasingly doubted U.S. security assurances and faced growing threats of U.S. abandonment. Under Park, the relative salience of domestic politics was low compared to its status after democratization, but domestic politics still affected critical decision points. This was particularly the case in Park's management of relations with Japan because Park had to contend with public dissatisfaction at the terms of his decision to normalize relations. Meanwhile, the U.S.-led alliance framework enabled South Korea's economic development because export-led industrialization depended on Japanese capital and technology and U.S. markets.

By the late 1970s, the prospect of autonomy from alliance, in the form of self-reliant defense backed by acquisition of a nuclear deterrent as a hedge against U.S. abandonment, pushed the U.S.-ROK patron–client relationship almost to the breaking point. The international context was the dominant factor that influenced South Korean foreign policy during this period, with Park able to manipulate domestic politics to his own advantage from a position of relative strength. Moreover, South Korea's increasing relative capacity enabled by a rapid economic take-off, albeit from a low base, reduced its dependence on the United States and weakened the U.S. capacity to influence South Korea's domestic politics.

By the end of the Park Chung-hee administration, as Hong Kyudok observes, "the United States could still make itself felt in the South Korean political process, but not necessarily in ways that enabled it to achieve specific goals, and certainly not in a matter of regime legitimacy to which the South Korean authorities attached vital political importance."[103] By the time of Park's assassination in October 1979 and the subsequent takeover by Chun Doo-hwan in May 1980, the U.S.-ROK alliance was restored, but at a cost to the credibility of U.S. support for Korean democracy. By the late 1980s, South Korea's democratic activism would enable South Korea's democratic transition and become a more powerful influence on South Korean foreign policy.

Thus, throughout the period of South Korea's authoritarian rule, the international political context of the Cold War provided real constraints on the scope of its foreign policy given its extraordinary dependence on the United States for its security and prosperity. However, South Korea's efforts to expand its economic and military capabilities within the alliance context helped to its assuage fears of abandonment and to generate some room for maneuver, especially as Park's fears of abandonment following the U.S. announcement of the Nixon doctrine led him to pursue greater self-help measures as an alternative to relying on U.S. alliance commitments. These efforts drew the attention and concern of the United States and ultimately led the United States to restore the credibility of alliance commitments sufficiently to assuage South Korean leadership fears, even despite rising opposition within South Korea to authoritarian rule.

3

ROH TAE-WOO AND
KIM YOUNG-SAM

Nordpolitik and Democratization

HERE IS NO starker turning point in the development of South Korea's foreign policy to date than the combination of international
and domestic developments that occurred under the administration
of Roh Tae-woo in the late 1980s and early 1990s and in the efforts to consolidate South Korea's democratic transition under Roh's successor, Kim
Young-sam. It was a moment when the fruits of South Korea's economic
development as one of four rapidly developing "Asian dragons" were recognized internationally and South Korea successfully navigated a difficult
political transition from authoritarianism to democracy.

In 1988, South Korea took a major step onto the world stage with its
hosting of the summer Olympic Games, providing Seoul with an opportunity to host the world for a major international event that featured South
Korean political and economic accomplishments and provided a stepping
stone for further internationalization. By that time, South Korea had already become one of the top-twenty countries in the world in GNP on the
strength of its growing exports, according to the International Monetary
Fund (IMF) and the World Bank.[1] South Korea's conglomerates—such as
Hyundai, LG, and Samsung—paved the way for a broader South Korean
foreign policy by developing global business and political interests on the
expansion of global exports. The Olympics created greater awareness of
the price competitiveness and growing quality of South Korean products.

As South Korean exports impressed people around the world, especially representatives of the Eastern bloc countries, the door to diplomatic normalization with the latter countries became easier to open as they sought out economic ties and investment with a successfully modernizing South Korea. By hosting the Olympics, a South Korea that had faced numerous domestic political and international constraints under authoritarianism during the Cold War was also forced to step out from its own parochialism and think of Korea's goals and purpose in a broader international context.

South Korea's opportunity to expand its international horizons occurred at an opportune moment. While South Korea rapidly rose to eclipse its northern counterpart economically and military, a more relaxed international environment resulted from the end of the Cold War as U.S.-Soviet and Sino-Soviet relations improved and as North Korea came to face increasing isolation from its great-power patrons. These circumstances opened up new diplomatic opportunities for South Korea to normalize relations with China and the Soviet Union under Roh Tae-woo's Nordpolitik, or Northern Policy. The diversification of South Korea's diplomatic relations was a step toward a more independent foreign policy in which South Korea would have the capacity in principle to act autonomously from the United States without antagonizing or working at cross-purposes to its main security guarantor. The outstanding question was whether South Korea's leaders would have the ability to manage these new opportunities effectively. Doing so still required the endorsement of and cooperation with the United States while reflecting significant advances in the scope of South Korean interests and expanded capabilities.[2]

South Korea's domestic political transformation from authoritarian rule to democracy removed a long-term obstacle in the U.S.-ROK alliance and enabled South Korea to claim success internationally both as a modernizing economy and as a fledgling member of Samuel Huntington's "third wave" of democratic transformation.[3] Known as the "June democracy movement," mass protests erupted nationwide during June 1987 to force Chun Doo-hwan to abandon plans to install Roh Tae-woo as his designated successor in favor of allowing direct elections for president under a new South Korean constitution. Roh ultimately won the election by winning a plurality over a divided opposition.

At the same time, South Korea's democratization marked the gradual emergence of the conservative-progressive divide in domestic politics on inter-Korean relations while creating new constraints on the South Korean government's ability to formulate and implement foreign policy as the need to maintain public support became a significant factor.[4] With democratization, South Korean progressives, who had been suppressed under authoritarian rule, were able to express their own views and aspirations for Korea's future in an unconstrained and often contentious fashion to influence the direction of their country's foreign policy. The Roh Tae-woo administration, unlike its predecessors, had to pay attention to domestic politics for the first time, and Roh's successor, former opposition leader Kim Young-sam, prioritized domestic political reform and broadened the scope of South Korea's post–Cold War foreign-policy framework.

Kim Young-sam's signature policy was *segyehwa*, "globalization," which came to be symbolized by South Korea's membership in the Organization for Economic Cooperation and Development (OECD) in 1996. As a former opposition leader who joined the ruling party in a three-party merger in 1990, Kim furthered domestic economic and political reform by instituting the real-name system in domestic financial transactions and ending the South Korean military's involvement in domestic politics, but without disrupting or challenging conservative elites who had supported democratization and national development.

An important area of difference between the Roh Tae-woo and Kim Young-sam administrations involved the implementation of a policy toward North Korea under Kim that resulted in tensions in U.S.-ROK alliance relations. These tensions developed as a result of differences over how to deal with North Korea's nuclear program as well as how to respond to North Korea's first generational leadership succession from Kim Il-sung to Kim Jong-il. The Clinton administration in the United States established direct talks with the Democratic People's Republic of Korea (DPRK), thus bypassing South Korea for the first time in an effort to prevent the North from following through on its announcement in February 1993 that it would leave the NPT. But the opening of direct talks risked sidelining Seoul on matters crucial to South Korean security interests and generated new tensions between the United States and South Korea.[5] Management of differing approaches toward North Korea proved to be one of the most serious sources of strain in the U.S.-ROK alliance during this period, leading some analysts to anticipate the demise of the security relationship as a result of a benign international security environment following the end of the Cold War.[6]

NORDPOLITIK: CONTEXT, OBJECTIVES, AND MAIN THEMES

The end of the Cold War was a moment of diplomatic opportunity for South Korea. Constraints that had long limited the scope of its foreign policy eased with U.S.-Soviet and Sino-Soviet rapprochement during the late 1980s. Pyongyang could no longer manipulate and play its great-power allies against each other and prevent Seoul from achieving rapprochement with Beijing and Moscow. Moreover, South Korea was pulling away from the North economically by the 1980s, with the Olympics in 1988 symbolizing its emergence on the world stage, giving Beijing and Moscow economic incentives to engage Seoul that gradually overwhelmed North Korea's political objections to Chinese and Soviet interaction with South Korea.[7] These developments created an unprecedented opportunity for South Korea to diversify its international relationships and reach out beyond its traditional focus on maintenance of relationships with the United States and the West.

OBJECTIVES OF NORDPOLITIK

Taking advantage of these factors, Roh Tae-woo laid out his administration's strategy, Nordpolitik, five months after his inauguration as South Korea's first democratically elected president. The strategy built on Park Chung-hee and Chun Doo-hwan's diplomatic initiatives toward the Communist bloc, most importantly China and Russia; was influenced by Ostpolitik, proposed in the early 1970s by the West German leader Willie Brandt; and was designed to ease inter-Korean tensions by establishing relations with China and the Soviet Union. Nordpolitik has been assessed as a policy originating from an "elite democracy" that was led primarily by the government, with limited input from the public or civil society.[8] The government in this period still had relative autonomy to lead foreign-policy formation with relatively little consideration for public opinion. At the same time, the administration succeeded in gaining elite consensus for Nordpolitik as well as for the development of a unification plan that advocated gradual, negotiated steps under the Korean National Community Unification Formula, which has remained South Korea's official policy through 2017.[9]

Roh Tae-woo laid out the parameters of Nordpolitik on July 7, 1988, in his Special Declaration for National Self-Esteem, Unification, and Prosperity, which addressed six issues: inter-Korean exchanges, divided families, inter-Korean trade, nonopposition to North Korea's development of economic relations with South Korea's allies, an end to inter-Korean diplomatic confrontation, and the process of implementation of the Nordpolitik policy.[10] The intended purpose of Nordpolitik was essentially to overcome hostile relations with the North, seek ways to promote coprosperity based on nationalism, help improve North Korea's relations with other countries (mainly the United States and Japan), and normalize diplomatic relations with the Communist bloc.[11]

Roh Tae-woo wanted South Korea to lead Nordpolitik but also sought collaboration with all major powers involved on the Korean Peninsula. As expressed by Secretary for Political Affairs Kim Chong-hwi, "Nordpolitik was autonomous in nature. The ROK took the lead on formulating policies for North-South relations despite U.S. concerns; however, the government limited the roles of the United States to cooperating with Korea in maintaining ROK-led diplomatic efforts."[12] South Korean ambassador to the United States Hyun Hong-choo described Nordpolitik as a diplomatic diversification strategy that required U.S. support but "was clearly a Korean initiative and certainly not a subordinate variable of any grand strategy of the superpower." He also wrote that the strategy was "undeniably a pressure tactic against North Korea" in which the North would be weaned of the support of its two closest allies, thereby enhancing the chances of "sincere dialogue and North-South cooperation."[13] Yet, Roh recalls in his memoir, "the intended audience of the declaration was not only the Koreans but also leaders in the U.S., Soviet Union, China, and Japan. I wanted to make it clear to our neighboring countries that Korea has the autonomy and leadership to address its own issues on the peninsula."[14] Along with improving relations with China and the Soviet Union, Nordpolitik eventually opened the door to a series of high-level inter-Korean dialogues at the prime ministerial level, effectively constituting a de facto recognition of the legitimacy of the government on each side of the DMZ.

To a great extent, Nordpolitik as an autonomous initiative was possible because of the changing international circumstances at the time. The policy had its origins in the late 1960s and early 1970s, when Park Chung-hee began to express interest in developing relations with China and the Soviet Union, but it was not fully implemented until the Roh administration, which finally succeeded in achieving the normalization of those relations.

NORDPOLITIK IN PRACTICE

NORMALIZATION OF SOUTH KOREA'S RELATIONS WITH THE SOVIET UNION

The first achievement of Nordpolitik came as Roh took advantage of circumstances created by a relaxed international political environment and the reputational effects of South Korea's increasing economic capacity to expand South Korean diplomacy, with full support from the United States. The main forces behind ROK-Soviet rapprochement were sports diplomacy and economic incentives.[15] These efforts had begun under Roh's two predecessors, Park Chung-hee and in particular Chun Doo-hwan, with South Korea's successful bid to host the summer Olympic Games in 1988. Chun and later Roh wanted to highlight South Korea's increasing status on the world stage by hosting an inclusive and successful event free of the sort of political boycotts that had marred the Moscow and Los Angeles Olympic Games in 1980 and 1984.[16] According to Cho Gab-je, a prominent conservative journalist, holding the event was an immense challenge:

There were numerous complications in the process of pushing ahead with the Seoul Olympics, and there were times the whole plan could have foundered. At the time, the world considered Korea "the most dangerous country" with a prospect of war and called it "Asia's flashpoint." Many criticized that the Olympics should not be held at such a dangerous place. However, we argued that Korea being the "flashpoint" is the very reason that the Olympics should be held so that we can plant the seeds of peace and prevent war. We also argued that the Olympics should no longer be held exclusively in developed countries. . . . These two sets of logic appealed to many non-aligned nations with ROK.[17]

Because there were concerns that Pyongyang might campaign to have its closest allies boycott the games, Seoul reached out earnestly to win the participation of the Soviet Union and the Eastern bloc countries.

The Olympics were the first step toward greater ROK-Soviet engagement in that the event presented a good first impression of South Korea to the Soviets. During the games, Soviet TV viewers saw for the first time that South Korea's level of economic development exceeded their expectations. Moreover, the South Korean public gave a warm reception to Soviet athletes, cheering their participation even more loudly than that of the Americans. All these factors aligned with Roh Tae-woo's interest in cross-recognition as part of South Korea's campaign for UN membership, where avoiding a Soviet veto would be critical.

In addition, South Korea's business conglomerates increasingly showed interest in dealing with the Soviet Union both to expand markets for quality consumer goods and to develop natural resources in the Russian Far East. The Soviets welcomed the Korean interest in investment, especially given that Soviet relations with Japan remained stalled over the territorial disputes and a failure to reach a final postwar settlement. As Don Oberdorfer and Robert Carlin describe in their detailed account of Moscow's opening to Seoul, the prospect of strengthening trade and investment ties was a powerful motive and underlying interest in better relations with South Korea, outweighing North Korea's objections.[18] As early as the summer of 1988, Roh Tae-woo sent a special envoy, Park Chul-un, to Moscow with a letter to the Soviet leader, Mikhail Gorbachev, proposing diplomatic normalization. Park was also told to pay close attention to a speech by Gorbachev in Krasnoyarsk on the eve of the Seoul Olympics in which Gorbachev stated that "within the context of a general improvement in the situation on the Korean peninsula, opportunities can open up for forging economic ties with South Korea" and proposed a multilateral arms-control initiative in Northeast Asia.[19] Gorbachev's proposal was a welcome initiative in South Korea, given that one of Roh's reasons for improving ROK-Soviet ties was "deterring Soviet arms assistance to North Korea for national security."[20] During a Politburo meeting on November 10, 1988, Gorbachev and the top Soviet leadership decided to improve economic relations with Seoul and to dispatch Foreign Minister Eduard Shevardnadze later that month to inform Pyongyang of the decision. Gorbachev also believed that improved Soviet-ROK relations would lead to "maturing of South-North relations."[21] Not surprisingly, the North Koreans did not receive the Soviet foreign minister well, especially given that Pyongyang was already wary of perestroika, the political and economic restructuring within the Soviet Union, and was concerned about the increasing trade between South Korea and the Soviet Union. The North Koreans fought unsuccessfully over the next year to draw Gorbachev's attention and to prevent the Soviets from improving their ties with Seoul.

The Soviets benefited greatly from improving ties with South Korea, mostly in the economic sphere. Gorbachev later stated in his memoirs, "Our interest in South Korea, one of the East Asian dragons which had succeeded in creating an economic miracle, grew in relation to the worsening of the economic situation of the USSR."[22] South Korea took advantage of the opportunities afforded by Soviet economic weakness and offered a $300 million commercial loan and a $40 million project to build a trade center in the Soviet Far East in December 1988. By the spring of 1990, the Soviet Union was nearly bankrupt, and financial markets refused to authorize further credit. A cash-starved Gorbachev secretly sought financing from the West German government and authorized a special envoy, Anatoly Dobrynin, to go to South Korea to propose a summit meeting with Roh Tae-woo in exchange for a $3 billion financing package, $1.47 billion of which was paid out and inherited by Russia as the successor state following the collapse of the Soviet Union.[23]

The two sides even bypassed their respective foreign ministries and agreed that Roh would meet Gorbachev in San Francisco on June 5, 1990, and then with President George H. W. Bush in Washington the next day. The location and U.S. support for the opening served to give the South Korean president cover against domestic critics who might argue that stronger ROK-Soviet ties would come at the expense of the U.S.-ROK alliance. Roh portrayed the meeting as a major step forward for Nordpolitik: "The road between Seoul and Pyongyang is now totally blocked. Accordingly, we have to choose an alternative route to the North Korean capital by way of Moscow and Beijing. This may not be the most direct route but we certainly hope it will be an effective one."[24]

North Korea's response to these developments was outrage. In an attempt to smooth matters over, Shevardnadze visited Pyongyang in September 1990 to deliver the news that the Soviet Union would establish relations with South Korea. When he privately informed Foreign Minister Kim Yong-nam, Kim fought back by arguing that Moscow's decision would give legitimacy to the permanent division of Korea, embolden South Korea to destroy socialism in North Korea, free North Korea to recognize secessionist elements of the Soviet Union, destroy the basis of the security treaty of 1961, and free North Korea to pursue all self-defense measures, including development of nuclear weapons. The meeting went so badly that when Shevardnadze met with his South Korean counterpart on the sidelines of the UN General Assembly later that month, he agreed on the spot to advance the date for ROK-Soviet normalization from January 1, 1991, to September 30, 1990.[25]

With the Soviet Union, Roh Tae-woo's decision to pursue Nordpolitik paid early dividends, driven in large part by the Soviets' economic desperation. South Korea arguably paid too high a price for the relationship, especially when one considers that the issue of unpaid debts was an impediment to a better relationship between Seoul and Moscow for more than a decade. Nevertheless, Roh later recalled that, despite the unpaid debt, improvement in relations with the Soviet Union was "more than the money's worth." The Soviet Union not only minimized its trade of essential natural resources such as petroleum and coal with North Korea but also halted its supply of arms, ultimately contributing to the security and stability of South Korea by reducing the North Korean threat.[26] Furthermore, the

ROK-Soviet rapprochement helped to open South Korea's path to UN membership by removing the prospect of a Soviet veto in the UN Security Council, increased pressure on China to acquiesce to South Korea's membership, and induced North Korea to change its position and join the UN together with South Korea.

NORMALIZATION OF SINO-ROK RELATIONS

Compared to the early returns from ROK-Soviet diplomatic normalization, progress in normalization of relations between Seoul and Beijing lagged. In both cases, South Korea's emergence as an attractive economic partner played a decisive factor, but in the Chinese case the driver was the flourishing of trade relations in the context of China's successful economic reform and growth rather than the demand for economic assistance resulting from economic failure. Growing economic relations between Seoul and Beijing provided a pretext for South Korea to meet China's political need by enabling Seoul to reach out and ease Beijing's political isolation at a relatively early stage following the Tiananmen Square incident in June 1989, eventually leading to the diplomatic normalization in 1992.

The initial opportunity to push toward normalization with China also came with South Korea's hosting of the Seoul Olympics in 1988, in which four hundred Chinese athletes participated against the backdrop of the rapid growth in trade relations. Yet China was still more cautious in approaching South Korea than the Soviet Union was, most probably in deference to continuous expression of concerns from North Korea. As early as 1981, Pyongyang had criticized developing Sino–South Korean economic relations, causing Beijing to artificially suppress trade with South Korea in 1982 and 1983.[27] The Korean Peninsula had always been more important to China than to the Soviet Union. Whereas the peninsula was thousands of miles away from Russia's heartland around the Moscow area, it was right at the footsteps of China's heartland on the Northern China Plain. Therefore, North Korean opposition to growing China–South Korea ties was a major obstacle in normalization.

The eruption of the Tiananmen student demonstrations in Beijing and across China in 1989 temporarily slowed the progress in Sino-ROK relations. As the world focused on the brutal crackdowns on protesters within the country, China came under massive diplomatic pressure. Beijing therefore needed a way to ease the political isolation, improve its public image, and form an environment friendly to economic development by improving relations with neighboring countries in Asia and the West.[28] Taking advantage of the situation, Seoul, unlike most other countries, continued to promote tourism in China.[29] Moreover, South Korea, with China's full knowledge, lobbied to restrain the United States, Great Britain, and other countries from taking much tougher measures against Beijing during the Tiananmen crisis, when China was facing international ostracism.[30] By continuing to engage Beijing at a time of crisis, Seoul was able to lay the foundations for an improved relationship with China.

To deal with China's concerns regarding North Korea, Roh Tae-woo did not oppose the potential establishment of Japan-DPRK and U.S.-DPRK relations, giving Beijing political space to justify normalizing China's relations with South Korea against North Korean objections.[31] Roh's assurance to the Chinese that he was "not thinking, not even in dreams, of a German-style reunification" with North Korea and was simply seeking to "establish a cooperative relationship" also helped to alleviate concerns within the Chinese leadership.[32]

Increasing trade between China and South Korea was another factor facilitating the improvement in the ties between the two countries. By the mid-1980s, South Korea's economic relations with China had outstripped China's economic relations with North Korea. Even with objections from Pyongyang and concerns within Beijing, China and South Korea could still grow their trade indirectly through Hong Kong. Moreover, the development of informal economic ties at the local level across the Bohai/Yellow Sea area continuously challenged central-government efforts to suppress such trade. Even after the Tiananmen incident, the China-ROK trade volume doubled from $3.087 billion in 1988 to $6.3 billion in 1992.[33] The Roh administration even ran temporary trade deficits with China between 1987 and 1992 to accommodate China during a time of internal political and economic uncertainty.[34]

Building on the foundations laid by his predecessors, Roh Tae-woo made the final push to take advantage of the propitious conditions that emerged in the late 1980s to achieve China–South Korea diplomatic normalization. As he had done in reaching out to the Soviet Union, he used Park Chul-un as a special envoy to Beijing to propose normalization, reportedly in exchange for an economic aid package worth $2.5 billion. By May 1991, the two countries had agreed to an exchange of trade offices led by the China Council for Promotion of International Trade and the Korea Trade-Investment Promotion Agency. Later that year China demonstrated interest in the opening of normalization negotiations, but only under conditions of strict secrecy. The two countries formally established diplomatic ties on August 24, 1992, in the waning months of Roh's term in office.

In his authoritative review of Sino-ROK normalization, *Between Ally and Partner: Korea-China Relations and the United States,* Chung Jae Ho identifies several shortcomings in Roh Tae-woo's outreach to China. Chung argues that Roh's overeagerness to complete normalization with China before the end of his presidential term cost South Korea leverage to negotiate better terms and enabled Beijing to dictate the terms of normalization to a great extent. The South Korean side failed to hold the Chinese to a verbal commitment that China would treat the two Koreas equally and would pay more attention to the North Korean nuclear weapons program, a failure owing to the Chinese reluctance to violate their principle of nonintervention in other countries' domestic affairs. The South Koreans also failed to obtain any expression of regret or apology from the Chinese for the Chinese role in the Korean War, similar to those the South Koreans had been able to achieve with the normalization agreement with Japan in 1965. The South Korean side also initially failed to get the Chinese to agree to establish a consulate general in the Shenyang region.[35]

Furthermore, the hurried and secretive nature of the negotiations led South Korea to manage the ending of official relations with the Republic of China (Taiwan) in an unprofessional and undiplomatic manner, giving the Taiwanese only two days over a weekend to vacate their embassy building, which was to be handed over to the Chinese.[36] With the announcement of the severing of relations with South Korea, Taiwan nullified all preferential trade agreements and ended visa services to any Koreans entering Taiwan.[37] Chung perceives South Korea as having sacrificed relations with Taiwan too readily and failing to achieve more progress in isolating Pyongyang in its pursuit of normalization with Beijing. One can argue that South Korea still has not achieved its political objectives of winning full Chinese support in dealing with North Korea, and it took more than a decade to reestablish direct flights between Korean and Taiwanese flag carriers. Roh later defended his decision by arguing that "sometimes we have to sacrifice small things for greater things. We thought the severance of relations with Taiwan was very unfortunate, but inevitable. First, we had an obligation to realistically seek our country's interests; secondly, although Taiwan is our ally, China has had a much longer history of friendship with the ROK."[38]

Chung observes that South Korea's rapprochement with China was conducted "fairly independently of American direction." In this respect, he notes a comment by Kim Young-sam's newly appointed ambassador to Beijing, Hwang Byung-tai, in 1993 that "South Korea–China cooperation over the issue of North Korea's nuclear program should go beyond the current level of simply notifying Beijing what has already been decided between Seoul and Washington. . . . South Korea's diplomacy should break out of its heavy reliance exclusively on the United States." This remark was clarified as the ambassador's personal view, but it stirred a controversy that Chung highlights as a "harbinger" of the idea that South Korea in the future should seek balance in its relations with the United States and China.[39]

DEVELOPMENTS IN ROK-JAPAN RELATIONS

Roh Tae-woo claimed that in order to successfully achieve Nordpolitik, South Korea should engage in a "proactive and balanced diplomacy" that would persuade other nations that a unified Korea would also benefit them.[40] As part of this strategy, Roh considered ROK-Japan relations particularly important in building a stable and prosperous Asia-Pacific region and emphasized that South Korea should deepen its relations with Japan at both governmental and nongovernmental levels.[41] Yet the Roh administration nevertheless held an ambiguous stance toward Japan.

The main factor behind the Roh administration's view of Japan was the concern during the late 1980s and early 1990s that the United States would greatly reduce its security commitment or even leave East Asia with the end of the Cold War, a fear bolstered by the U.S. troop drawdown on the Korean Peninsula during this period. Furthermore, Japan—at the time considered an economy eventually set to overtake that of the United States—was seen as potentially "normalizing" and becoming the new "leader" of the region. To put this concern into the context of the time, according to the IMF Japan's GDP in 1991 was $3.5 trillion, a little more than half the size of the U.S. GDP at the time, while China's GDP was more than eight times smaller than that of Japan at about $411 billion; South Korea's GDP stood at approximately $325 billion at the time.[42] According to the Stockholm International Peace Research Institute, Japan was spending approximately $28 billion on defense in 1991, less than 1 percent of the country's overall GDP, whereas China and South Korea were spending $20 billion and $11 billion, respectively.[43]

The Roh Tae-woo administration showed concern about the prospect of Japan's remilitarization. In defense white papers in 1990 and 1991, the Roh administration expressed its concern about the potential negative effects of Japan becoming more of a normal nation, specifying in the second paper that the Japanese Self-Defense Force was being "transformed into offensive forces for the purpose of forward defense."[44] In October 1990, South Korean foreign minister Choi Ho-joong characterized Japan's deployment of forces abroad as "the starting point of the remilitarization of Japan."[45] Japan and South Korea took a number of steps during the early 1990s to improve their security relations. In 1990, when the chief of Japan's self-defense agency (predecessor to the Ministry of Defense) visited South Korea for the first time since 1979, Seoul and Tokyo decided to increase their consultations over their Air Defense Intercept Zones and established trilateral policy-planning talks with the United States.[46] These developments were essentially responses to the general sense of uncertainty that emerged with the end of the Cold War, the prospect of reduced U.S. commitment in the region, and coordination in response to North Korea's developing nuclear weapons program.

INTER-KOREAN RAPPROCHEMENT

Although engagement with China and the Soviet Union were major components of Roh Tae-woo's Nordpolitik, its ultimate objective was establishment of dialogue with North Korea. Looking back on his presidency, Roh described the strategy in the following manner: "I decided to implement the policy of befriending distant states and antagonizing neighbors, as the first principle of Nordpolitik was to indirectly pressure DPRK by establishing diplomatic relations with the East-European bloc, Soviet Union, and China. It was my goal to 'peel' North Korea like you would peel an onion, starting from the perimeter. This was the best and most proper way to achieve unification without war." Roh believed that previous approaches that focused on inter-Korean relations first were not effective: "I thought that what the July 4 Joint Statement [1972] and June 23 Declaration [1973] could do to improve the North-South relations had serious limitations. We could not overcome our obstacles no matter how hard we tried. . . . Therefore, pressuring DPRK by changing dynamics in the international environment was necessary."[47] His strategy of reaching out to North Korea's great-power allies turned out to be successful to the extent that it led to inter-Korean dialogue.

North Korea's Committee for the Peaceful Reunification of the Fatherland initially rejected Roh Tae-woo's overtures out of hand, preferring dialogue with South Korea's nongovernmental opposition forces as a way of taking advantage of dissent toward a South Korean government that was facing tremendous flux and opposition. However, democratization had tamed the most vicious waves of opposition as the South Korean political system evolved to enable channels for making one's voice heard without going to the streets. While blocking North Korea's calls for nongovernmental gatherings, Seoul eased restrictions on trade with North Korea and supported the efforts by Hyundai Group chairman Chung Ju-young, who had been born in North Korea, to discuss various economic activities with North Korean counterparts.

Eventually, in January 1989, North Korea's prime minister, Yon Hyung-muk, responded positively to a letter from his South Korean counterpart, Kang Young-hoon, calling for prime ministerial inter-Korean talks. North Korea's precise motivations for coming to talks remained unclear. Kim Il-sung was no doubt concerned that improvements in Soviet and Chinese relations with South Korea represented a betrayal and setback for North Korea. In addition, the collapse of the Soviet Union resulted in the end of economic support from one of North Korea's long-standing patrons. These adverse trends may have led Kim to feel that he needed to move toward dialogue and the easing of tensions with the South to forestall the impact of loss of support from the North's primary patrons. Kim may have also accepted talks as a way of exploring the potential for exploiting South Korean domestic political divisions in the context of South Korea's democratic transition, discussed later.

Following over eighteen months of preliminary working-level talks, the prime ministerial inter-Korean talks were established in 1990 and were held eight times to December 1992. These talks took place against the backdrop of a reduction in regional tensions, including a decision by the United States under George H. W. Bush in September 1991 to remove forward-deployed sea- and air-based U.S. nuclear weapons from foreign soil, including the Korean Peninsula. The main achievements of the talks were the landmark Agreement on Reconciliation, Nonaggression, and Exchanges and Cooperation, announced during the fifth round on December 13, 1991, and the Inter-Korean Joint Declaration on the Denuclearization of the Korean Peninsula, announced in January 1992, which pledged denuclearization of the two Koreas and peaceful use of nuclear energy. With regard to the former, Roh stated that "this agreement showed the world that Korea has the willingness and capacity to autonomously achieve peace and reunification on the Korean peninsula [sic]" and considered it the most significant official document after the declaration of July 4, 1972.[48] Indeed, the agreement provided a roadmap for inter-Korean cooperation- and confidence-building measures in security, economics, and sociocultural areas.

Implementation of these agreements, however, was ultimately cut short by the emergence of the first North Korean nuclear crisis. The crisis was precipitated by a standoff between North Korea and the International Atomic Energy Agency (IAEA) that resulted from questions raised by the IAEA over "significant inconsistencies" between North Korea's declaration of its nuclear activities and evidence gathered in June 1991 during IAEA inspections.[49] The nuclear issue eventually ended up preventing South Korea from moving forward toward further cooperation with the North. Some Koreans have regarded this moment as a lost opportunity for inter-Korean reconciliation that might have been able to forestall renewed crisis. The disagreement between the IAEA and North Korea instead led to a decision to resume U.S.-ROK Team Spirit exercises in the spring of 1993, although they had not been held in 1992, causing further tensions between the two Koreas.

IMPACT ON U.S.-ROK RELATIONS

South Korea's democratization and Nordpolitik had mixed effects on the U.S.-ROK alliance. On the one hand, democratization in 1988 removed a major structural limitation—authoritarian rule—on the development of relations between the United States and South Korea. Former South Korean ambassador to the United States Hyun Hong-choo relates his surprise at a meeting with U.S. national security adviser Brent Scowcroft in 1991 when he learned that the United States, in recognition of South Korea's political transformation, would welcome Roh for a state visit that the Roh administration had not even requested, in contrast to the usual scramble for face time and attention that South Koreans had traditionally experienced in negotiating visits to Washington.[50]

Nevertheless, the legacy of South Korean authoritarianism remained an issue requiring management by the two governments. The issue resulted primarily from widespread public perceptions in South Korea that the United States had sacrificed its democratic ideals in support of Chun Doo-hwan and had allowed Chun to crack down on protesters during the Gwangju incident while he mounted a coup d'état. The blowback from this incident shaped the anti-American views of a generation of South Korean youth. These sentiments were manifested in a firebombing of the American cultural center and even in the trespassing on the grounds of the residence of the U.S. ambassador to the Republic of Korea, Donald Gregg.[51] Even today, Korean polls show that the generation that were university students during the 1980s are more negative in their assessments of the United States than their older or younger cohorts.

Moreover, the liberalization of South Korean society that began with its democratic transition enabled fuller expression of anti-American views toward the United States as well as the public airing of many long-standing grievances within South Korean society regarding the U.S. presence. For more than a decade following South Korea's democratic transition, expressions of anti-Americanism on issues related to USFK, American complicity in the Gwangju incident, and even mistaken mass killings of Korean civilians at places such as Nogunri under confusing and stressful conditions during the Korean War added to friction in the relationship between the two countries.[52]

Another notable incident that reportedly occurred under Roh Tae-woo was the resumption of South Korea's nuclear weapons program. According to National Assembly member Suh Su-jong, who was chief policy analyst for the conservative Democratic Liberal Party, Roh created a plan to develop nuclear weapons after receiving reports that suspected that North Korea was developing its own nuclear weapons.[53] Suh also said that another important reason for Roh's decision was that he wanted to reduce South Korea's heavy military dependence on the United States.[54] After all, the United States was in the process of drawing down its troops on the Korean Peninsula. The South Koreans probably felt that they had to build nuclear weapons to prepare for a scenario in which all U.S. troops left. Much of the work took place in the nuclear facilities at Daeduk. During the same year, however, Roh was forced to scrap the program due to U.S. pressure. For this reason, his decision to include abandonment of enrichment and reprocessing as elements of the inter-Korean Joint Declaration on Denuclearization of the Korean Peninsula in February 1992 has been treated—in particular by American specialists—as an important commitment by South Korea to remain a nonnuclear state, regardless of North Korea's subsequent flouting of the agreement.

DEVELOPMENTS IN SOUTH KOREA'S DOMESTIC POLITICS: DEMOCRATIC TRANSITION AND ITS IMPACT ON FOREIGN POLICY

Roh Tae-woo came to office in 1988 as South Korea's first democratically elected president following the country's transition from authoritarianism to democratic rule. However, Roh won the election with only a plurality of the vote against three rivals for power. This meant that he had a weak political mandate, particularly in the domestic realm.[55] Roh had played an instrumental role in defusing mass democratization protests in 1987 by agreeing that his selection as Chun Doo-hwan's successor be subject to a popular election. Yet he could never escape the fact that he was Chun's handpicked successor and close associate. In the end, Roh's election win, with 36.9 percent of the vote, was owing to the opposition's failure to unite behind a single candidate rather than to his own popularity; the two opposition heavyweights, Kim Young-sam and Kim Dae-jung, won 28 percent and 26.9 percent of the votes, respectively.[56] Roh had the double-edged benefit of a strong institutional political base and establishment support from within South Korea's bureaucracy, including a powerful political patronage system that he inherited from Chun and an intelligence apparatus that remained involved in South Korea's domestic politics. These assets allowed him to mobilize resources more effectively than the opposition, but they also damaged perceptions of his legitimacy. Furthermore, public expectations for domestic social change were high, and they generated previously nonexistent domestic economic and social pressures as a result of the empowerment of labor in the democratization process. As a result, economic and social issues arose between South Korea's management and labor, with a rapid expansion in the number of labor strikes and an erosion of the state's coercive capacity. Roh's party also had only minority support within the National Assembly during his first two years as president, limiting his ability to push through legislation. His weak hand in domestic politics and his desire to distinguish himself from his predecessor were important factors that drove him to focus on foreign policy. South Korea's democratization unleashed vibrant forces for social change within South Korea, many of which challenged the government, given that Roh Tae-woo's election as president did not fully satisfy those who wanted a cleaner break from and a more thorough social reckoning with the authoritarian forces that in many aspects were still powerful players in South Korean society.

KIM YOUNG-SAM AND SOUTH KOREA'S
DEMOCRATIC CONSOLIDATION

In January 1990, faced with a confluence of difficult domestic circumstances, Roh Tae-woo moved to negotiate with Kim Young-sam, one of the opposition party leaders, to pursue a grand merger with the ruling party that would also position Kim as Roh's most plausible successor. Kim had been a long-time democracy activist and protester against Park Chung-hee and Chun Doo-hwan, so the alliance with Roh risked painting Kim as unprincipled, but the merger turned out to be effective. The move helped Roh's government function better while helping Kim become the next president. Roh and Kim's ability to compromise and work together was striking because the two main opposition leaders, Kim Young-sam and Kim Dae-jung, had failed to establish a similar cooperative mechanism during the election in 1988, thus enabling the election of Roh Tae-woo as president.

The merger between Roh's ruling party and Kim Young-sam's opposition support base eased South Korea's transition to democracy by maintaining conservative influence within government while incorporating a leadership that had the credentials necessary to push through important domestic institutional reforms that would advance the country's democratization. The melding of conservative leadership with democratic activism provided South Korea with a more gradual transition in the orientation of South Korean politics than would have been possible with a full-scale transition to a new, untested, and inexperienced power base.

As Roh's successor, Kim Young-sam, who came to power in 1993, made important contributions to democratic consolidation in South Korea, including the banning of military associations that served powerful bases from which to intervene in domestic politics and the institutionalization of the real-name system in the financial arena, which imposed transparency in personal finances by making it easier to track hidden wealth, bribes, laundered money, and other illicit financial transactions. These institutional reforms provided an important step forward in combating the role of money in politics. Related to these reforms, South Korean prosecutors were able to pursue high-profile cases of political corruption and extortion by South Korea's largest private-sector firms to generate personal and political slush funds under former presidents Chun Doo-hwan and Roh Tae-woo.

South Korea's democratic transition also had implications for the country's foreign policy as public opinion and public approval of presidential leadership became a more important influence on the president's calculations and actions. Kim Young-sam was known to be sensitive to his popularity ratings, and his leadership and management of foreign-policy issues came to be influenced to a greater degree than before by both public opinion and activism from nongovernmental organizations. As a result, two areas where presidential prerogatives received the greatest public scrutiny and therefore were influenced most strongly by public opinion were policy toward North Korea and relations with the United States. These two areas converged as points of tension during the Kim Young-Sam administration as a result of the emergence of the first North Korean nuclear crisis and the establishment of direct nuclear negotiations between the United States and North Korea for the first time.

TENSIONS IN THE U.S.-ROK ALLIANCE RELATIONS OVER NORTH KOREA: KIM YOUNG-SAM AND THE AGREED FRAMEWORK

Following Roh Tae-woo's lead in pursuit of Nordpolitik, Kim Young-sam initially set out to make his own conciliatory gesture to North Korea in hopes of renewing dialogue by releasing unconverted North Korean prisoners Yi In-mo and others, who had been held in South Korean jails for decades.[57] North Koreans, however, ignored the gesture as part of the brewing nuclear spat with the IAEA, which Pyongyang saw as a proxy for the United States due to perceptions that the IAEA had received U.S. help in the form of satellite information on North Korea's nuclear development. Instead of reciprocating the release of Yi and other prisoners, North Korea upended the card table completely by declaring in 1993 that it would invoke a clause allowing it to withdraw from the NPT within ninety days. This announcement further escalated the nuclear crisis at the UN Security Council, which in a meeting in early April called for member states to take action to try to resolve the crisis.

In response to this call, the United States opened unprecedented direct negotiations with North Korea only a week prior to Pyongyang's withdrawal from the NPT. With the exception of a single meeting the previous year between U.S. undersecretary of state Arnold Kanter and Korean Worker's Party International Division chairman Kim Young-sun, there had been no direct U.S.-DPRK negotiations outside of the UN Command Military Armistice Commission since the end of the Korean War. After several days of negotiations, the United States finally succeeded in crafting a statement based on the UN Charter that North Korea would suspend its withdrawal from the NPT pending further negotiations with the United States.

However, the inauguration of an open-ended bilateral negotiation between the United States and North Korea for the first time since the end of the Korean War created heartburn in Seoul, especially for Kim Young-sam.[58] Despite South Korea's diplomatic and developmental progress, Seoul was exposed as being completely reliant on the United States to address an issue crucial to South Korea's security. In addition, Kim believed that the United States was naive in negotiating with North Korea and was either falling for North Korea's negotiating tactics by giving more than necessary or helping to prop up a regime that was on the verge of collapse as a result of a drastic reduction in subsidies from Soviet and Chinese patrons following the collapse of the Soviet Union.

Another factor that bolstered Kim Young-sam's opposition to the negotiations was concern regarding how a bilateral deal between the United States and North Korea might affect the U.S.-ROK alliance. With the end of the Cold War, the United States seemed to be reducing its commitment to South Korea, as seen in its plans to draw down the number of troops from the Korean Peninsula. Hence, Seoul viewed U.S. bilateral engagement of North Korea as a loss for South Korea in a zero-sum framework.[59] South Korea was naturally sensitive to the likelihood that North Korea would use direct negotiations with the United States to marginalize South Korea or to make the South more vulnerable by trying to split the alliance between Washington and Seoul. South Korea urged the United States to discuss only North Korea's nuclear program and not to talk about a comprehensive political settlement during the negotiations, although the Agreed Framework of 1994 between Washington and Pyongyang ended up including the promise of better political relations between North Korea and the United States anyway.[60] At the same time, Kim did not push the United States to sanction or attack North Korea. However, U.S. officials came to resent the distrust that was evident in South Korea's efforts to influence the content and substance of the U.S. approach to negotiations with North Korea and in its constant need for up-to-the-minute reporting on the content of every bilateral negotiating session. American officials described dealing with their South Korean allies as a "headache" and saw Kim Young-sam as "very emotional and unreasonable."[61]

Kim Young-sam understandably had a need to show that he had not been marginalized on issues that threatened the very security of South Korea. Both North Korea's nuclear development and the possibility that the United States might be unfaithful to South Korean interests were perceived in South Korea as consequential developments that would influence its security and necessitated efforts by Kim to show that he was an influential force in dealing with North Korea.

The overall situation reignited South Korea's discomfort with dependency and desires for autonomy while underscoring the necessity of the alliance framework to deal with the emerging nuclear dimension of the North Korea challenge. The tensions and mistrust that the U.S.-DPRK nuclear negotiations generated were considerable for the U.S.-ROK alliance. Kim Young-sam openly criticized the negotiations in interviews with major news outlets, arguing, for example, in a BBC interview that the United States "must not concede to any additional demands by DPRK" and in a *New York Times* interview that the United States "should withhold DPRK from taking the lead in negotiations on the nuclear issue."[62] At a summit meeting at the White House in November 1993, Kim and President Bill Clinton barely concealed their friction. Kim, frustrated by media reports that the United States had adopted a "comprehensive" strategy toward North Korea that he had not been fully briefed on, sought changes to the approach outlined in working-level consultations in preparation for the summit.[63] In the end, the two sides agreed on a "broad and thorough" approach rather than a "comprehensive" approach to the North Korean nuclear issue to make it seem that Kim was relevant and influential as a partner in shaping U.S. policy toward the North.[64] The two sides, however, failed to bridge their differences in any meaningful way. U.S. negotiators found their South Korean colleagues overbearing because they desired to influence U.S. negotiations and needed to be the first to hear about outcomes as soon as negotiations ended. (It was even more awkward that at the conclusion of the U.S.-DPRK agreement, U.S. negotiators had to shuttle to Tokyo and Seoul with a tin cup looking for funding to implement the agreement, which caused South Korean diplomats who had waited outside the negotiating rooms to wryly complain about "taxation without representation.")

Kim Young-sam's frustrations with the U.S.-DPRK negotiations held in Geneva over the summer and fall of 1994 following the Carter intervention did not mean that he opposed the U.S. talking to North Korea but simply that he believed South Korea should be in the lead in such talks and not marginalized. His desire to be a central actor in dealings with the North was more fully exposed at the time of Jimmy Carter's visit to Pyongyang at the peak of the nuclear crisis in June 1994. The Kim administration gave Carter a somewhat cold shoulder in advance of his trip to Pyongyang and was distrustful of his involvement in the negotiations. However, in meetings prior to Carter's visit to Pyongyang South Korean senior officials did suggest to him the possibility of an inter-Korean summit meeting between Kim Il-sung and Kim Young-sam. Although South Korea was uncomfortable with Carter's role in jump-starting diplomatic negotiations, Kim Young-sam was very pleased with the news Carter brought back with him that Kim Il-sung accepted the idea of an inter-Korean summit and that he would welcome Kim Young-sam's visit to Pyongyang in July. Negotiations to prepare for the inter-Korean summit were already under way when the news came on July 8, 1994, that Kim Il-sung had died, thus scuttling Kim Young-sam's opportunity to hold an historic summit in Pyongyang.

However, even more complicated for Kim Young-sam and the South Korean government was the question of how to respond to Kim Il-sung's death. On the one hand, Kim Il-sung was Kim Young-sam's prospective negotiating partner; on the other hand, he was the perpetrator of a war that had cost millions of lives. In deciding how to handle the South Korean government's official response to Kim Il-sung's death, the South was greatly sensitive as usual to the potential political uses to which North

Korea might put any South Korean statement. In the end, Kim angered the North by not offering condolences, but perhaps even more serious was his characterization of North Korea after Kim Il-sung as a "broken airplane," suggesting that the North's collapse was inevitable. The downturn in inter-Korean relations following Kim Il-sung's death added to tensions between the United States and South Korea over the Agreed Framework and implementation of the light-water reactor project when North Korea attempted to marginalize South Korea's involvement in the project.

In 1995, Washington was able to reassure Seoul to some extent with the U.S. Department of Defense policy document *United States Security Strategy for the East Asia-Pacific Region*, which stopped the troop drawdown in South Korea.[65] In 1996, after the U.S. troop drawdown had stopped, Kim changed his stance toward North Korea and laid out three principles: "(1) South Korea would not take advantage of the North's trouble; (2) it would not try to isolate the North; and (3) it would not seek unification by absorbing the North."[66]

Reports of famine in North Korea were another factor that softened Kim Young-sam's policy toward North Korea. These reports began to have a serious impact on South Korean public attitudes toward the North, especially as reports and refugees began to trickle out through northeastern China. Public concerns about the human situation in North Korea outstripped and ended up shaping government policy as South Korea's church community began to launch major humanitarian drives to send food and money to starving North Koreans. The groundswell of public concern ultimately led the South Korean government to negotiate the shipment of 150,000 tons of grain to North Korea in 1996, and the government of Japan also agreed to provide an additional 500,000 tons of surplus rice. The negotiation of food assistance provided a way of thawing the atmosphere that had developed following North Korea's outrage at Kim Young-sam's refusal to send condolences following Kim Il-sung's death in 1994. In essence, South Korea had already begun a shift toward a policy of engagement toward North Korea even before Kim Dae-jung came to power in 1998.[67]

For North Korea, the Agreed Framework of 1994 to freeze and eventually dismantle North Korea's nuclear program in exchange for U.S.

leadership of an international consortium to build proliferation-resistant light-water reactors in North Korea and to improve U.S.-DPRK relations was the first success it had had in directly engaging with the United States after decades of failed efforts to reach over South Korea's head and split the alliance. Nevertheless, the negotiations also revealed the unanticipated costs of failure for not fully implementing cross-recognition, which would potentially depoliticize and reduce South Korea's sensitivities to such a dialogue. In the end, the fact that the dialogue was bilateral proved to be a major source of tension that dogged the negotiations and their outcome, especially in that the U.S.-DPRK Agreed Framework in the end insisted on multilateral involvement and cooperation to build proliferation-resistant light-water reactors in North Korea in return for a freeze on North Korea's nuclear program.

KIM YOUNG-SAM AND GLOBALIZATION

Kim Young-sam successfully built on Roh Tae-woo's efforts to take advantage of a benign international security environment to extend South Korea's reach internationally through a policy that became known as *segye-hwa*, "globalization."[68] This policy was important both as an expression of South Korea's expanding capacity and as a precursor to subsequent efforts to enhance South Korea's profile and leadership internationally. The theme of globalization was reinforced by South Korea's foreign minister, Han Sungjoo, who noted in May 1993 that South Korean diplomacy "will no longer become hostage to [North Korea]" and emphasized South Korea's internationalization as a central objective of its "New Diplomacy," whereby it would pursue more active contributions to global peace and security issues, international development, and environmental protection.[69] The setting out of these themes provided an early reflection of South Korea's growing sense of responsibility to the rest of the world that derived from its growing economic capabilities and represented the seeds of an approach more fully developed more than a decade later under Lee Myung-bak's Global Korea policy.

Although the vision for globalization presented under the Kim Young-sam administration was comprehensive, it took concrete form when South Korea attained the economic capabilities and credentials necessary to join the OECD, which was regarded as a club of developed nations, so that membership in it was an affirmation of South Korea's modernization. Unfortunately, Kim's drive to achieve developed-country status was tarnished as a result of the "IMF crisis" that engulfed the country in 1997 as many of South Korea's leading companies became trapped in a financial quagmire. South Korea's economic growth prior to the crisis had been sustained largely by the expectation that major companies would be able to constantly service mounting debts that doubled or tripled the worth of their assets. This financing strategy was aided by the easy availability of short-term loans denominated in dollars that aided the companies in managing short-term cash flows despite their indebtedness. However, when the value of local currencies plummeted in the context of the Asian financial crisis that began in 1997, Korean companies were caught in a financial crunch that exposed their inefficiencies and overreliance on short-term dollar loans. The debts were suddenly deemed too large and unsustainable for many Korean companies to repay, requiring action by the Korean government to negotiate with international lending institutions in an effort to save companies whose asset valuations priced in won had dropped precipitously.

These developments played out in the waning months of the Kim Young-sam administration and led to criticisms that the administration had pushed too hard to achieve globalization, putting at risk South Korea's financial standing. Politically, these developments tarnished the ruling party's reputation and were probably decisive in aiding the electoral victory of opposition candidate Kim Dae-jung in 1997, setting up South Korea's first ever power transition from conservative to progressive control of government.

NORDPOLITIK AND THE EVOLUTION OF SOUTH KOREA'S FOREIGN POLICY

By pursuing Nordpolitik, Roh Tae-woo astutely took advantage of the changing strategic environment in Northeast Asia; South Korea's growing prowess, symbolized by the Summer Olympics in 1988; and the end of the Cold War, marked by U.S.-Soviet and Sino-Soviet rapprochement. The

Olympics provided networking opportunities with representatives of Eastern bloc countries, who returned home with a newfound awareness of South Korean industrial accomplishments.

The end of the Cold War generated opportunities to reap the fruit of prior South Korean efforts both to establish relations with the former Communist world, particularly with China and the Soviet Union, and to reduce tension with North Korea. South Korea's economic successes enabled a more confident policy toward a North Korea that was in the process of losing valuable sources of support from the former Soviet Union and China, developments that indirectly catalyzed high-level inter-Korean dialogue and paved the way for both Koreas to separately enter the United Nations. Nordpolitik integrated many progressive elements and even foreshadowed elements of the engagement policies of Roh's successors. In fact, some South Korean scholars would dispute whether the main elements of Roh's policy were truly conservative, even though he came from a strictly conservative political lineage.[70]

Nordpolitik also signaled a South Korean vision for multilateral cooperation through Roh Tae-woo's willingness to adapt and support a flexible six-nation "consultative conference for peace" in Northeast Asia in his speech before the UN General Assembly in September 1988.[71] The idea represented the seed of what would become a perennial theme of Korean diplomacy in the post–Cold War period: the desirability of a cooperative security approach within Northeast Asia that could contribute to confidence building, tension reduction, and regulation of regional behaviors by neighboring great powers according to commonly accepted norms. As sensible as the idea seems, however, it has proven difficult to achieve in practice despite continuous efforts by successive South Korean administrations.

Even as South Korea reached out to its former adversaries and began to envision a broader role for itself in the region, the U.S.-ROK alliance remained robust. U.S. support for South Korea's efforts to expand the scope of its diplomatic activities to include the Soviet Union, the People's Republic of China, and formerly Communist countries in eastern Europe proved to reinforce rather than to fray the U.S.-ROK alliance. The United States also took cautious steps in close coordination with South Korea to remove nuclear weapons from South Korean soil and to engage North Korea on nuclear issues.

At the same time, South Korea's democratic transition generated new opportunities and constraints for South Korean diplomacy. It removed a significant obstacle that had proven to be a headache for U.S. relations with Roh's authoritarian predecessors. But South Korean domestic sectors that had long been suppressed under authoritarian leaders emerged as a factor that had the potential to complicate and constrain South Korean policy. Kim Young-sam's efforts to manage rising public expectations for South Korea's policy toward North Korea generated new tensions in its overall foreign policy. U.S.-ROK relations would require more careful management in both Washington and Seoul as public opinion became a more important factor. Domestically, South Korea's democratization proved to be a boon for the U.S.-ROK alliance, despite criticisms of the United States from South Korean democracy activists, who could no longer be muffled. To be sure, the United States paid a price for the perception that it had a hand in perpetuating the South Korean government's authoritarianism. This notion led to the establishment of a small, but professional anti-American cadre within South Korean society and the alienation of a generation of democratization activists who had fought against Park Chung-hee and Chun Doo-hwan. In the long term, however, democratization removed a major source of tension in U.S.-ROK relations.

But Kim Young-sam, despite his commitment to domestic democratic reforms, experienced great friction in coordinating with the Clinton administration over policy toward North Korea. Ironically, this friction occurred against the backdrop of a benign international security environment, in which South Koreans desired a central role in policy toward the North, even while maintaining strong ties with the United States. In the end, however, the Agreed Framework of 1994 was inked as a bilateral U.S.-DPRK agreement.

The agreement revealed the divergence in the relative weight that the United States and South Korea accorded to the urgency of the risk of North Korean nuclear development and proliferation, the implications that a bilateral dialogue between South Korea's primary patron and its primary adversary had for South Korean security, and the question of how to respond to signs of North Korea's internal instability that accompanied both its generational leadership transition from Kim Il-sung to Kim Jong-il and the famine. On each of these issues, a benign international environment and a democratizing South Korea generated pressures on Kim Young-sam to assert South Korea's desires for autonomy despite its continued need to maintain a strong security alliance with the United States.

The unexpected impact of the Asian financial crisis both required U.S. intervention to save the South Korean economy and laid the groundwork for a surprising political transition and dramatic policy reset in inter-Korean relations under Kim Young-sam's rival and South Korea's most well-known progressive pro-democracy activist, Kim Dae-jung.

4

KIM DAE-JUNG AND THE SUNSHINE POLICY

THE ELECTION OF Kim Dae-jung in 1998 as South Korea's first progressive opposition candidate to become president marked a decisive shift in its domestic politics from conservative to progressive control for the first time in its history. Moreover, South Korean progressive forces were able to test their ideas and implementation of foreign policy for the first time against the backdrop of a relatively benign international environment. As a result, domestic political factors played a major role in shaping South Korean foreign policy, especially during the first half of Kim's term. During decades of opposition to authoritarian conservative rule, Kim had advocated a liberal approach toward North Korea that was a dramatic departure from the anti-Communist thinking of the mainstream conservatives who had historically guided South Korean foreign policy.

As a democracy activist against South Korea's authoritarian governments and as a progressive who also had international experience, Kim Dae-jung developed a unique profile within South Korea's truncated political spectrum. Unlike many homegrown South Korean democratic activists, Kim was in exile in the United States during the Chun Doo-hwan administration's rule, which enabled him to develop an international network of pro-democracy supporters, including prominent U.S. congresspersons and former U.S. government officials. The network of contacts Kim gained while in exile at Harvard also meant that he had many friends and supporters in the United States who sympathized with his desire for democracy in South Korea. However, despite his credentials as a fighter for democracy, he also had deeply held views regarding the need for inter-Korean reconciliation and a tenacious desire to take leadership toward that end.

Kim Dae-jung also had a free hand to pursue a new approach toward North Korea in an environment that was relatively unconstrained by international tensions. South Korea's advantage over the North had grown following the collapse of the Soviet Union, but the Asian financial crisis temporarily settled the government's debate over whether to pursue unification through absorption by putting that prospect out of reach for the time being. In this respect, the advent of the financial crisis provided a double benefit for Kim Dae-jung: it aided his election and enabled a South Korean domestic consensus over the desirability of pushing back the timeline for achieving Korean unification.

South Korea's increasing capacity relative to the North put Kim Dae-jung in a better position than ever to achieve inter-Korean reconciliation and reunification, despite the fact that the financial crisis had delayed or removed the immediacy of expectations regarding unification. The building of a domestic consensus around the idea of a delayed Korean unification was a particularly striking development given the heightened expectations for early unification that had developed following German unification in 1990, Kim Il-sung's death, and North Korea's growing economic difficulties in 1994, which had generated speculation in South Korea regarding a "soft landing" or possible collapse of the northern regime.

However, even though South Korea's economic growth had outstripped that of the North, Kim Dae-jung recognized that he needed support from his U.S. allies and from the international community to effectively implement his policies. Given the limits of its relative power compared to its great-power neighbors, South Korea still valued the alliance with the United States. To secure South Korea's defense against North Korean provocations, Kim Dae-jung continued to recognize and acknowledge the decisive role of the United States as an essential element in achieving inter-Korean reconciliation. As a result, Kim was sorely disappointed to see the foundations for his reconciliatory approach to North Korea crumble as the United States shifted from support to criticism of this approach as part of the transition in U.S. leadership from Bill Clinton to George W. Bush, which painfully exposed the limits of South Korea's autonomy in setting its own policy course.

KIM DAE-JUNG'S WORLDVIEW AND THE OBJECTIVES OF THE SUNSHINE POLICY

Although Kim Dae-jung came into office facing a financial crisis that required his own and his advisers' full engagement immediately following his election, the major strategic issue that defined his administration was his commitment to abandon South Korea's policy of containment toward the North in favor of a policy of economic and political engagement, known as the Sunshine Policy.

Among all of South Korea's presidents since Syngman Rhee, Kim Dae-jung was the leader who had thought the most deeply prior to becoming president about South Korean foreign policy and who brought with him a clearly defined philosophy to the Blue House. He had begun to formulate his "three-stage" approach to Korean unification and foreign policy in the early 1970s. His philosophy on Korean unification was based on "self-reliance, peace, and democracy" and on a "three-stage" approach that envisioned a confederal arrangement between the two Koreas, leading first to a federated political union in which the Koreas had a shared foreign policy but maintained autonomy over domestic political affairs and then to a unified Korean political system over time. Kim published his views in English a year prior to his successful election in a book titled *Kim Dae-jung's "Three Stage" Approach to Korean Reunification*.[1] Alongside his approach to unification, Kim espoused "open nationalism, positive pacifism, and global democracy" as principles underlying his foreign policy.[2] He argued for a positive approach to international cooperation, sought to build a proactive peace with neighbors through enhanced cooperation, and preferred mechanisms that would promote democratization of international relations by giving smaller countries equal voice with larger countries in international affairs.

Kim Dae-jung's policy toward North Korea had elements in common with Roh Tae-woo's Nordpolitik. Both policies nominally sought peaceful coexistence with the North rather than pursuing containment and perpetuating legitimacy competition with the North as a top priority. In fact, Roh had already incorporated some of Kim's ideas in Nordpolitik in an effort to bridge ideological divisions and create a coherent base of national support for an effective policy toward North Korea. For instance, under the leadership of Roh's minister of unification, Lee Hongkoo, the Korean National Community Unification Formula emerged as a broad-based policy that intentionally sought to garner support from both the opposition and the ruling party.[3] Nevertheless, Kim Dae-jung's Sunshine Policy marked a major departure in foreign policy for several reasons. First, it emphasized the centrality of inter-Korean engagement and sought to align international forces behind that policy rather than focusing on normalization of relations with North Korea's patrons as a means to open dialogue with North Korea.[4] In other words, whereas under Nordpolitik the road to Pyongyang led through Moscow and Beijing, under the Sunshine Policy South Korea placed relations with the North at the center and relations with its great-power neighbors in a supporting role.

Second, the Sunshine Policy sought to use expansion of economic relations as a tool for transforming the security environment on the Korean Peninsula and in the region, in contrast to past policies that had sought to reduce tensions first as a prerequisite for the development of economic exchange. Kim Dae-jung argued that economic engagement would be a force that would transform North Korea, justifying the idea of unilateral generosity that would pay dividends later as North Korea recognized that it could not do without the material benefits of integration with the outside world.

Third, the Sunshine Policy reflected a high level of confidence in South Korea's ability to drive change inside North Korea and to induce the global community and by extension the North to support inter-Korean rapprochement. In the process, South Korea positioned itself both as an intermediary between North Korea and the global community and as an advocate-lobbyist for international engagement with North Korea. According to Lim Dong-won, Kim Dae-jung's chief of the National Intelligence Service, the policy sought to replicate what the Europeans had done with the Helsinki Accords of 1975, which Lim believed eventually produced Mikhail Gorbachev and peaceful German unification. He felt that North Korea "will have no other choice but to gradually open itself and pursue a market economy to survive. . . . If threatened from the outside or constantly contained, North Korea will find it difficult to open up and reform."[5]

To some extent, these differences between Nordpolitik and the Sunshine Policy stemmed from the radically different alignment of forces in Northeast Asia that developed with the end of the Cold War. The Soviet Union collapsed; Russia became a secondary power in the region; China normalized its relations with South Korea; and North Korea suffered a massive famine. The confluence of these factors made South Korea well positioned to step in as a lead player in an effort to reshape the dynamics on the Korean Peninsula.

In support of his policy, Kim Dae-jung presented three fundamental principles in his inauguration speech on February 25, 1998: "we will not tolerate any military provocation of any kind"; "we do not have any intention to undermine or absorb North Korea"; and "we will actively pursue reconciliation and cooperation between [the] North and [the] South."[6] Based on these principles, Kim Dae-jung's first step in pursuit of inter-Korean reconciliation was to emphasize the "division of economics and politics." This approach enabled South Korea to reach out to North Korea and propose various forms of inter-Korean economic cooperation as a means of inducing "trust" that would establish the basis for development of higher forms of exchange and cooperation.[7]

THE SUNSHINE POLICY IN PRACTICE

INTER-KOREAN RELATIONS

The initial objective of Kim Dae-jung's Sunshine Policy following his inauguration as president was to win the trust of the North Koreans by showing the North that South Korea's new policy was beneficial to

Pyongyang through the "separation of the economy from politics."[8] To achieve this objective, Kim pursued an approach to North Korea that frontloaded economic and other benefits to the North with the expectation that the North might reciprocate later.[9] He elucidated his expectations in his address to a joint session of the U.S. Congress during his visit to Washington, D.C., in June 1998: "We are going to promote cooperation in a wide range of areas under the principle of separation of politics and economics. . . . We hope such an approach gives North Korea psychological room to open its mind and its doors."[10] A corollary to this approach was that South Korea could afford to give more and that North Korea might not be expected to reciprocate fully. This sort of generosity reflected South Korea's hopes and desires for peaceful coexistence as well as the idea that economic interaction with the North could be transformative.[11]

The main manifestations of Kim Dae-jung's policy toward the North came in the form of governmental support for renewed economic exchanges led by Hyundai chairman Chung Ju-young. Chung had a long-standing interest in the North, having been born in an east coast village there. He had pursued economic cooperation with the North about a decade earlier, including preliminary discussions regarding development of Mount Kumgang as a potential site for South Korean tourism to the North; however, the Kim Young-sam government had blocked those discussions because of the North Korean nuclear issue and the downturn in inter-Korean relations.

With the South Korean government's support for Chung Ju-young's visit, including a humanitarian offering of 501 cows that he brought with him on one of his visits in return for the cow he had reportedly brought with him to the South as a child, Chung was able to meet with Kim Jong-il and to ink agreements on two North Korean projects: the Kumgang tourism plan and a plan to build a business complex near the city of Kaesong. As part of the deal, Chung agreed to pay $12 million per month for access to Mount Kumgang, and the two sides worked out all arrangements necessary for Hyundai to build a tourist hotel and for the two Koreas to put into place customs arrangements necessary to support South Korean tourism to the North. This project was controversial because it put cash directly into the hands of the North in return for limited access to the North in the designated project areas. In addition, Hyundai committed to provide substantial infrastructure to the North to support both projects, which ultimately required the approval and financial support of the South Korean government.[12]

The Sunshine Policy succeeded in opening the door to greater South Korean exposure to and understanding of some parts of North Korea. Between 1989 and 1997, only 2,408 South Koreans had visited North Korea for economic, social, and personal reasons, but during the first eighteen months of Kim Dae-jung's administration that number more than tripled to 8,509. Moreover, the opening of the Mount Kumgang resort enabled an additional 200,000 South Koreans to visit North Korea in its first year of operation.[13]

But then North Korea tested the Sunshine Policy in its initial phases with a series of military provocations against South Korea. First, a small North Korean submarine alleged to have been involved in espionage and infiltration operations was captured in the net of a South Korean fishing boat along South Korea's east coast on June 22, 1998.[14] The Kim administration downplayed the incident and returned the crew to the North without deviating from the commitment to engagement with North Korea through the Sunshine Policy, in contrast to the major manhunt and chill in inter-Korean relations stemming from a similar incident on the east coast of South Korea under Kim Young-sam only two years earlier. Second, the two Koreas were involved in military clashes in the Yellow Sea, first in 2001 and then in 2002 near the disputed maritime border in the sea, Northern Limit Line, as South and North Korean military vessels protected fishermen on both sides.[15] Although the second clash resulted in an exchange of fire and casualties on both sides, Kim insisted on avoidance of escalation so as to avoid a "cold war mentality" in handling relations with the North. According to *New York Times* correspondent Don Kirk, Kim "had told the defense ministry [*sic*] to order commanders not to fire warning shots, to fire only in self-defense, forcing the South Korean navy to rely on loudspeakers and visual signals."[16]

Despite these incidents, Kim Dae-jung argued that South Korea's provision of economic benefits to the North would eventually generate political trust or at least that the policy had provided momentum for the initiation of political dialogue in 2000, when the North expressed interest in further talks. On March 9, 2000, Kim gave a speech at the Free University in Berlin, the contents of which were prebriefed to the North Koreans, in which he pledged support for North Korea's economic recovery, advocated for the end of the Cold War on the Korean Peninsula and the achievement of peaceful coexistence between the two Koreas, called for resolution of the issue of separated families, and proposed direct inter-Korean talks in preparation for a summit.[17] Following the Berlin speech, through a series of meetings with Kim Dae-jung's longtime political colleague Park Chi-won as well as with the chief foreign-policy architect and head of the National Intelligence Service Lim Dong-won, the North Koreans agreed to allow Kim Dae-jung to travel to Pyongyang to meet with Kim Jong-il.

Upon the conclusion of the summit on June 15, 2000, the two leaders announced a North-South joint declaration, which consisted of the following points:

1. The North and the South agreed to solve the question of the country's reunification independently by the concerted efforts of the Korean nation responsible for it.

2. The North and the South, recognizing that a proposal for federation of lower stage advanced by the North side and a proposal for confederation put forth by the South side for the reunification of the country have elements in common, agreed to work for the reunification in this direction in the future.

3. The North and the South agreed to settle humanitarian issues, including exchange of visiting groups of separated families and relatives and the issue of unconverted long-term prisoners, as early as possible on the occasion of August 15 this year.

4. The North and the South agreed to promote the balanced development of the national economy through economic cooperation and build mutual confidence by activating cooperation and exchanges in all fields, social, cultural, sports, public health, environmental and so on.

5. The North and the South agreed to hold dialogues between the authorities as soon as possible to implement the above-mentioned agreed points in the near future.[18]

Although the summit was a huge success that riveted South Koreans' attention, with a live television feed to Seoul showing Kim Jong-il and Kim Dae-jung together that transformed public thinking in the South about possibilities for inter-Korean cooperation, it was subsequently revealed that Hyundai had channeled up to $500 million in cash payments to the North in order to facilitate the summit. Kim Dae-jung later confessed in a televised speech that he was aware of illegal payments to North Korea before the summit, and he apologized: "The government allowed it [Hyundai's transfer] out of the belief that it would help peace between the two Koreas and promote the national interest, despite the problems it had legally."[19] The perception that the summit was bought and paid for rather than being a sincere response to the South Koreans' offers of goodwill severely tarnished Kim Dae-jung's accomplishment. The Korean Supreme Court subsequently ruled that $400 million was justifiable as a payment by Hyundai for future concessions, but the additional $100 million constituted a bribe in connection with the summit.[20] This legacy of cash-for-summit payments has had a largely negative effect on South Koreans' views of prospects for and suitable tools by which to pursue engagement with the North.

In addition, the summit proved to be a polarizing move in that South Korean conservatives were never comfortable with the idea, nor were many elderly Koreans, who had grown up seeing the North as an existential enemy. Although the conservatives acknowledged that the summit was an historic moment, they continued to see the North as an untrustworthy adversary intent on taking advantage of Kim Dae-jung's naïveté. As one lawmaker from the conservative Grand National Party put it, "Kim Jong Il is very good at putting on a show. . . . But he is an old-line Communist leader who believes that he can make the South his own at any time, and that is very dangerous."[21] Other conservative National Assembly members generally ridiculed the president; the Grand National Party even accused him of using the summit for political purposes, arguing that "announcing the summit talks just three days before the elections is aimed at changing the circumstances in the ruling party's favor."[22] A party spokesperson stated: "No regime in history has turned to such a blunt and shameless trick to win an election."[23] The leader of the party, Lee Hoi-chang, feared that the summit would lead to reduced support for U.S. forces remaining on the Korean Peninsula.[24]

The joint declaration led Kim Dae-jung to proclaim upon his return to the South that the summit precluded the threat of renewed military conflict between the two Koreas. In a postsummit briefing, he stated, "There will no longer be a war. South and North Korea should co-prosper and co-exist to make Korea a first-class nation of the world in the 21st century. The four powers [the United States, China, Japan, and Russia] are no longer imperialists but our markets."[25] Many conservatives thought that this statement went too far, and a heated debate on almost all aspects of the joint declaration ensued. The summit ironically precipitated *nam-nam kalteung*, or "South-South divide," over almost every aspect of Seoul's North Korea policy. The issues of contention included whether the landmark joint statement overemphasized unification rather than peace and security, the nature of the respective versions of federation and confederation, who should be included as part of "separated families," whether "balanced development of the national economy" would truly be balanced or just be a cover for wealth transfers to the North, and when and whether Kim Jong-il would indeed attend a return summit in South Korea. By the end of the year, however, the two Koreas had made unprecedented progress in promoting social and cultural exchanges, including the holding of emotional family reunions in Pyongyang and Seoul, the North's hosting of a media tour for South Korean newspaper and broadcasting company presidents, the holding of inter-Korean defense ministerial talks and other high-level exchanges, and South Korean pledges of humanitarian aid and assistance to protect historic sites in the North.[26]

U.S.-ROK RELATIONS AND THE SUNSHINE POLICY: THE CLINTON PERIOD

In the United States, Democrats and Republicans alike welcomed Kim Dae-jung's election as president of South Korea. Kim's long-standing reputation as a dissident under South Korean authoritarian rule and as a fighter for democracy was buttressed by the bipartisan efforts that had occurred as part of the transition from Jimmy Carter to Ronald Reagan to save his life and assure his exile to the United States in 1980. As Richard V. Allen explained when Kim was elected, the United States had secured Kim's exile to the United States in return for holding an early summit for Chun Doo-hwan at the beginning of the Reagan administration.[27] While in the United States, Kim had the opportunity to meet many congresspersons, several of whom were still around to greet him in June 1998 during his first official visit as president of the Republic of Korea, when he addressed a joint session of Congress.

Like the United States, Kim Dae-jung recognized the importance of denuclearization on the Korean Peninsula, but when he inaugurated the Sunshine Policy in 1998, he was able to pursue reconciliation with North Korea under the widespread assumption at the time that the nuclear issue was under control and that the U.S.-DPRK Agreed Framework of 1994 was being implemented faithfully. Under the surface, however, there were problems.

First, because the Clinton administration wanted to win support from congressional Republicans for the small financial outlays necessary to implement the Agreed Framework, U.S. implementation of the agreement was constantly delayed. As a result, the political components of the Agreed Framework involving improvement of U.S.-DPRK relations never progressed, raising North Korea's doubts about U.S. political commitment to the deal. The U.S. commitment to reduce trade and investment barriers within three months, to work toward normalization of relations, and to build two light-water reactors faced constant challenges from a Republican Congress, particularly during the first few years after the agreement was signed. As a result, the first concrete for the light-water reactors promised under the Agreed Framework was not poured until August 7, 2002.[28] The Clinton administration faced constant criticisms for the Agreed Framework amid speculation that it had been signed only because the administration expected North Korea, as one of the last remaining Communist dictatorships, to collapse after the death of Kim Il-sung the year the agreement was negotiated.[29]

Second, North Korea, frustrated by the slow progress of the agreement's implementation, launched what it claimed was a satellite, which flew over the Japanese mainland on August 31, 1998, raising alarm in the

United States and its allies about North Korea's missile-development efforts. The purpose of the launch, according to Kim Jong-il himself, was to recapture U.S. political attention, but the incident instead only eroded political support for the Agreed Framework in the United States.[30]

Third, U.S. satellite evidence in 1998 identified suspicious activities in North Korea around a site called Kumchang-ri, stimulating an American debate over the direction of the Clinton administration's Korea policy. A visit to the site by U.S. inspectors in May 1999 eventually determined that the activities were not nuclear related, but the suspicions and negotiations over access to the site damaged U.S.-DPRK relations and again raised skepticism on Capitol Hill about the effectiveness of the Agreed Framework.[31]

Fourth, human intelligence gathered by South Korea as early as 1998 on North Korean physicists' visit to Islamabad, Pakistan, may have already pointed to covert efforts to pursue a new pathway to the development of a nuclear device: the development of a uranium-enrichment program alongside the capped- and frozen-plutonium program that had been set aside because of the Agreed Framework.[32]

In response to these growing challenges to the implementation of the Agreed Framework, the Clinton administration launched what came to be known as the "Perry process" to review policy toward North Korea, named after former secretary of defense William Perry, who was put in charge of its coordination. While conducting his review of U.S. policy toward North Korea, Perry held a series of conversations with Kim Dae-jung as well as with senior Japanese officials on how to deal with North Korea; he also made a trip to Pyongyang for meetings with the North Korean leadership. After the meetings, the Perry team was divided over whether North Korea had responded positively to Perry's message encouraging North Korea to come back to talks or face consequences.[33] Nevertheless, Perry's trip and consultations as well as the inauguration of the Trilateral Coordination and Oversight Group, consisting of the United States, South Korea, and Japan, were important factors that ultimately facilitated the creation of an atmosphere in which inter-Korean dialogue could continue.

Despite the Clinton administration's own troubles in securing bipartisan political support for implementation of the Agreed Framework, Kim

Dae-jung aligned his emphasis on engagement with the thrust of the Clinton administration's policy toward North Korea. In fact, a more robust South Korean engagement of North Korea eased the friction in U.S.-ROK coordination over North Korea, which had been a constant source of irritation between the United States and South Korea under Kim Youngsam. With Kim Dae-jung's election, the Clinton administration had a willing South Korean partner in pushing for engagement with the North.

In fact, Kim Dae-jung was prepared to take over and autonomously drive policy toward the North, leaving the Clinton administration to play a supporting (if still critical) role. In other words, Kim sought to restore the centrality of South Korea in managing both the peninsular and regional aspects of the Korean problem.[34] Clinton, for his part, was only too happy to oblige and remarked during his meeting with Kim, "In view of your stature and experience, I would encourage you to lead on the issue of the Korean Peninsula. You take the driver's seat, and I will take the seat beside to help you."[35] On the one hand, this approach made sense because South Korea had the greatest stake in improved relations with North Korea, both as a means by which to enhance South Korea's security and because of its interest in Korean reunification. The fact that both the Kim and Clinton administrations were temperamentally aligned in the same direction initially made coordination relatively easy.

However, as the momentum for improved inter-Korean relations gained speed, one issue that came up was the extent to which South Korea had briefed the United States on the developments in inter-Korean relations. Given the secrecy of the talks in advance of the announcement on April 10, 2000, of the inter-Korean summit and the rapidity of developments in the run-up to the summit, which would take place in June, the United States expressed the wish that South Korean officials provide more adequate briefings to their U.S. counterparts. Although the Clinton administration did not show inordinate concern about South Korea being in the lead in dealing with North Korea, it did have concerns about being kept in the loop, particularly given the long-standing U.S. commitment to South Korea's security and the fact that U.S. policy toward North Korea remained deeply controversial due to ongoing concerns about suspected North Korean efforts to pursue additional nuclear program activities. In particular, U.S. ambassador to the ROK Stephen Bosworth conveyed these concerns to South Korea's intelligence chief, Lim Dong-won, who provided periodic briefings to Bosworth following secret trips to Pyongyang.[36]

Another concern for American observers was that Kim Dae-jung sought to dismantle "the Cold-War structure" surrounding the Korean Peninsula, but this description was often left ambiguous.[37] Kim's primary goal appears to have been the normalization of U.S.-DPRK relations as a show of support for inter-Korean reconciliation and normalization of North Korea's international relations. He believed that, "more than anything, dialogue between North Korea and the United States is the key to a solution."[38] Despite his clear expressions of support for continuing an alliance with the United States even after Korean reunification, however, Kim did not address in specific terms how or in what form the alliance might be perpetuated. This ambiguity sowed doubts among some analysts about his intentions, especially given North Korea's long-standing insistence on U.S. withdrawal as a prerequisite for unification. Despite Kim Dae-jung's assurances following the inter-Korean summit in June 2000 that Kim Jong-il accepted the necessity of a continued U.S. military role on the Korean Peninsula over the long run, Kim Jong-il's subsequent joint statement with Russian president Vladimir Putin about the need for U.S. troops to leave the peninsula raised questions about what North Korea really thought and intended.[39]

U.S.-ROK RELATIONS AND THE SUNSHINE POLICY: THE GEORGE W. BUSH PERIOD

Kim Dae-jung's drive to achieve inter-Korean reconciliation and to mobilize the global community in support of inter-Korean reconciliation eventually ran into two major obstacles. The first was the election of George W. Bush as the president of the United States in 2000, resulting in a shift of U.S. policy from engagement with to "skepticism" and eventually hostility toward the North. Second, the Bush administration's discovery of North Korea's covert efforts to develop an alternative path to nuclear weapons capability through a uranium-enrichment program after the Agreed Framework blocked the plutonium pathway put the Bush administration at odds with Kim Dae-jung. The consequence of the revelation was that the United States effectively withdrew its support for inter-Korean engagement, and the task of U.S.-ROK policy coordination toward North Korea became extraordinarily contentious.

Bush saw a totalitarian regime in North Korea, which had been engaged in serious repression of its own people, and was personally disgusted by that inhumane treatment. Kim Dae-jung, having convinced the world to support his Sunshine Policy, an approach validated when he was awarded a Nobel Peace Prize, sought an early meeting with Bush to convince him to support the Sunshine Policy. Instead of winning Bush over, however, the summit served to reveal a deep divergence between Kim and Bush that could not be bridged.[40] Without U.S. support, Kim Dae-jung was unable to pursue a second summit with Kim Jong-il in part because he could no longer deliver on promises that such a summit would also generate benefits for DPRK-U.S. relations. Kim failed to gain the international recognition from his main ally that was necessary to bring North Korea to fully integrate with the global community. Following the terrorist attacks on New York and Washington, D.C., on September 11, 2001, the gap between the United States and South Korea was papered over by Korean support for the U.S. focus on the war on terror, but the existence of the gap also meant that there were practical limits on prospects that North Korea's integration into the global community would be facilitated by further advancements in inter-Korean relations. When Bush accused Kim Jong-il of all the atrocities that he and his regime had committed, Kim Dae-jung responded by arguing, "You can have dialogue with evil if it is necessary. It's not for making friends; it's for pursuing your national interests. Even as President Reagan called the Soviet Union an evil empire, he also had dialogue. So then, why can't you have dialogue with North Korea? If you do not pursue the option of dialogue, the only viable option here can be war."[41] In contrast, Vice President Dick Cheney famously said of North Korea, "We don't negotiate with evil; we defeat it."[42]

Another factor hindering inter-Korean cooperation was the reemergence of the North Korean nuclear issue, with U.S. assistant secretary of state for East Asian and Pacific affairs James A. Kelly confronting North Korea with the knowledge of its covert uranium-enrichment program in 2002. In fact, concern about North Korea's nuclear development was the main instrument that enabled the Bush administration to hold South Korea's engagement efforts toward North Korea in check and to pursue a strategy based on pressure. The United States demanded that inter-Korean economic cooperation be limited as a source of leverage by which to pressure North Korea on its nuclear weapons program. Kim Dae-jung, however, was adamantly against heavy-handed tactics and believed sanctions would in fact lead to loss of leverage vis-à-vis North Korea: "What I firmly believe is that [the nuclear weapons issue] should be settled through dialogue, not economic sanctions or war. Scrapping the Geneva agreement [the Agreed Framework] through economic sanctions would only result in North Korea being freed from the restraints of the agreement concerning the nuclear issue."[43] He saw dialogue as the best means to persuade North Korea because "pressuring and isolating communist countries have never been successful—Cuba is one example . . . [whereas] inducing such countries to open up through dialogue has always been successful."[44]

Exacerbating the already fraught U.S.-ROK relations was anti-Americanism in South Korea, which was in part a consequence of frustration with the idea that the United States was standing as an obstacle to improvement of inter-Korean relations. In this respect, Korea scholar Bruce Cumings points out that powerful anti-Americanism during this period was really anti-Bushism.[45] Koreans were not necessarily anti-American but were against the Bush administration's hawkish foreign policy. Indeed, during this time many South Koreans perceived a dichotomy between support for North Korea and support for the U.S.-ROK alliance. A spike in anti-American expressions toward U.S. servicemen in Korea occurred simultaneously with the end of the inter-Korean summit, suggesting that some South Koreans felt that inter-Korean reconciliation would likely enable even greater Korean autonomy and might eventually bring about the end of the U.S.-ROK alliance. A Gallup Korea poll in November 2002 showed that only about 4.7 percent of South Korean respondents believed that there was a serious possibility of North Korea starting war, 28.1 percent that there was a slight possibility, 26.5 percent that the possibility was low, and 31.4 percent that the possibility was totally zero.[46]

As it became clear that a Bush administration turn toward hard-line policies was constraining progress in inter-Korean relations, some in South

Korea interpreted these policies as self-interested U.S. interference because such improvement would likely weaken the rationale for continued U.S. troop presence in South Korea.[47] Kim Dae-jung himself had always stressed the importance of the U.S.-ROK alliance to South Korea's broader security interests, but he and his colleagues were perceived as slow to defend the alliance in the face of South Korean public expressions of anti-Americanism and to respond to or refute many of these expressions.

Moreover, emotional and sensationalistic media coverage of a number of accidental but serious errors committed by U.S. servicemen aggravated the situation. A mentally ill Korean man stabbed an American military pediatrician to death. Koreans assaulted American soldiers in public areas and in one case forced an American soldier to publicly apologize for American military misdeeds.[48] Other incidents arose involving threats to or confrontations with American soldiers at late-night drinking establishments in a district near Hongik University frequented by university students and foreigners. In response, USFK instituted a 9:00 p.m. curfew for its personnel and took a much lower public profile in public areas of downtown Seoul. Another incident that drew strong Korean public criticism involved a case in which U.S. forces once inadvertently dumped toxic chemicals into the sewers, which might have eventually flowed into the Han River.[49] This series of incidents, including an incident during the Winter Olympics of 2002 in which South Koreans believed that an American short-track skater, Anton Ohno, won unfairly at South Korean ace Kim Dong-sung's expense.[50] These incidents contributed to perceptions of rising anti-Americanism in South Korea, but Koreans' demands for respect and criticisms of USFK for being heavy-handed and for failing to adapt to Korea's rapid modernization suggest that another underlying issue was South Koreans' changing self-perception: many saw their country as having grown in its own capabilities and willingness to take responsibility as a partner in co-managing the Korean Peninsula's political and security issues. Yet the United States in policy and attitude did not appear to give South Korea any deference or to treat it as a full partner in the course of U.S. policy formulation toward the peninsula.[51]

In this atmosphere, a traffic accident in which a U.S. military vehicle ran over and killed two South Korean middle school girls in June 2002 became the straw that broke the camel's back, setting off massive protests in South Korea. U.S. handling of the incident and prosecution of the vehicle operators received close public scrutiny in South Korea. When in November the USFK acquitted the two soldiers, a wave of emotional public candlelight protests began in central Seoul.[52] By the end of 2002, a Korean Gallup poll reported that 53.7 percent of South Koreans had "unfavorable" and "somewhat unfavorable" views of the United States; the number was at 80 percent among college students.[53] In terms of generations, 26 percent of middle-aged South Koreans at the time had negative views of the United States compared to 76 percent of those in their twenties and 67 percent of those in their thirties; the formative years of these youth had been shaped by experiences of U.S. support for South Korea's authoritarian leaders.[54] The public outrage stemmed in part from the perception that the U.S. military was acting with impunity, that the soldiers should have been subject to Korean law, and that the USFK was operating by old rules that did not recognize the advances Korea had made over the decades. The explosion of public protests was categorized as "anti-American," but the main motive behind them was a feeling that the United States was not treating Korea with deserved respect. At the same time, as Victor Cha notes, many South Koreans still seemed to support the U.S.-ROK alliance even while disagreeing with U.S. policies.[55]

Furthermore, Katharine Moon points out that holding a negative attitude toward the United States during this period was not unique to Koreans; it was a widespread phenomenon around the world. In Canada, for example, 44 percent of Canadians younger than thirty had negative views of the United States, but only about 20 percent of those in the fifty- to sixty-four-year-old age group did, according to a Pew Survey taken in 2002.[56] In 2003, millions of Europeans took to the streets to protest the U.S. war in Iraq.[57]

THE SUNSHINE POLICY AND REGIONAL RELATIONS

For the Sunshine Policy to succeed, winning international support for inter-Korean reconciliation from the four major powers in Northeast Asia (the United States, China, Russia, and Japan) was important. Following the inter-Korean summit in 2000, mobilization of international support became even more important. One consequence of Kim Dae-jung's efforts was that in the initial stages of his administration he successfully achieved the feat of having a positive relationship with all four of the major powers at the same time. In the process, he raised the profile of South Korea as an independent actor that used its influence to involve the global community— large and small countries—in Korean affairs in ways that would support his goal. In this regard, the Sunshine Policy was an expression of South Korean autonomy.[58] Nevertheless, the success or failure of Kim Dae-jung's policy toward North Korea continued to be entirely dependent on his ability to win support for the policy from the United States.

Kim presented to the world the international dimensions of his Sunshine Policy in a CNN interview in May 1999. He made five points that reflected his hope that South Korean engagement would be a catalyst not only for inter-Korean reconciliation but also for greater international contact with North Korea, with the effect of bringing North Korea out of isolation into the global community as a normal nation: (1) inter-Korean confrontation and distrust must be converted into reconciliation and cooperation; (2) the United States and Japan must improve their relations with North Korea; (3) the world community must create favorable conditions for North Korea to join it; (4) weapons of mass destruction and nuclear weapons must be controlled and eliminated; and (5) a cease-fire regime should be replaced by a permanent peace regime.[59]

Kim Dae-jung's campaign to win support for the Sunshine Policy was comprehensive and highly effective around the globe, especially during the first three years of his administration. By the time of the Asia-Europe Meeting held in Seoul following the inter-Korean summit, Kim had encouraged thirteen of fifteen European nations to normalize relations with North Korea.[60] Progress in inter-Korean relations became an effective platform from which Kim engaged with the world in an effort to sustain inter-Korean reconciliation. The policy was dependent in part on his ability to bring along the four major powers to engage with Kim Jong-il's regime sufficiently so that North Korea not only would see the rewards and benefits of engagement with South Korea but also would be enmeshed economically with other countries in East Asia. The logic behind the policy was that a North Korea economically integrated in the region would have sufficient economic stakes to maintain stable and favorable relationships with other Northeast Asian countries and would cease provocations as a result. According to Lim Dong-won, this idea was also partially based on the European integration model, developed to create prosperity and prevent war.[61]

As part of this effort, Kim Dae-jung sought to strengthen regionalism in East Asia as part of establishing "global democracy" and leveling the field between small countries and larger powers.[62] At his first Association of Southeast Asian Nations (ASEAN) Plus Three meeting in 1998, Kim proposed the formation of the East Asia Vision Group with intellectuals from each of the member countries, the purpose of which would be to suggest ways "to nurture East Asia into a single community of cooperation."[63] Former South Korean foreign minister Han Sungjoo led the establishment of this group of "wise men," and the group developed recommendations that led to the establishment of the East Asia Study Group and ultimately to the establishment of the East Asian Summit.[64] At the same time, Kim supported the establishment of a "Plus Three" gathering among Chinese, Japanese, and South Korean leaders on the sidelines of the ASEAN meetings from 1999 on.[65] The regularization of this gathering eventually led to the establishment of the Trilateral Coordination Secretariat and the plan for the three countries to hold regular trilateral summit meetings on a rotating basis.[66] Kim was in favor of efforts to promote Asian "solidarity" on the model of the European Union and the North American Free Trade Agreement, arguing in an English publication that "Asia should, on the one hand, work for balanced benefits and development among its countries and, on the other hand, prepare for cooperation and competition with other leading communities."[67]

SOUTH KOREA–JAPAN RELATIONS

A notable regional dimension of Kim Dae-jung's Sunshine Policy was his expectation for the United States and Japan essentially to complete the cross-recognition process that had been envisioned in the early 1990s at the time of South Korea's normalization of relations with China and the

Soviet Union. For this to occur, Japan–South Korea relations needed to improve, and Kim had already laid the groundwork through successful visits to Washington in May 1998 and to Tokyo in October 1998. Japan–South Korea relations improved for a time with Kim's efforts, but U.S.–Japan–North Korea relations did not because Pyongyang continued to engage in provocations, notably the launch of the Taepodong-1 missile in 1998. And despite Japan's attempts to reach out to North Korea to solve abductee issues (discussed later), Japan–South Korea relations began deteriorating again as new history controversies arose.

During Kim Dae-jung's visit to Japan, he and Japanese prime minister Obuchi Keizo signed a landmark joint partnership agreement, the New Partnership for the Twenty-First Century, which included Obuchi's expression of "remorseful and heartfelt apology" and Kim's acceptance of the apology and commitment on both sides to pursue "future-oriented relationship." Both Japan and South Korea stated their willingness to "squarely face the past and develop relations based on mutual understanding and trust" and to expand their cooperation in bilateral exchanges and participation in international efforts. [68] For example, Japan and South Korea showed their alignment in security interests as North Korea test-launched the Taepodong-1 missile in 1998. As a sign of their commitment to the joint declaration, they held their first bilateral six-day naval search-and-rescue exercise the following year and joined the United States in the Trilateral Coordination and Oversight Group.[69]

But the Japan–South Korea bilateral relationship soon soured when the Japanese Society for History Textbook Reform endorsed in 2001 a series of new Japanese textbooks that omitted or downplayed many of the atrocities committed by imperial Japan. Following the Japanese Ministry of Education's certification and authorization of these new textbooks, widespread protests took place in South Korea, drastically straining the relationship. Further deterioration occurred after a visit by Japanese prime minister Koizumi Junichiro to the Yasukuni shrine, which honors the spirits of Class A war criminals from World War II, among others. South Koreans perceived the visit as a sign that Japan was backtracking on the spirit, if not the letter, of the joint declaration.[70] They grew increasingly frustrated with Japanese actions on these issues, constraining Kim Dae-jung's efforts to put Japan-ROK relations on a path to reconciliation. Although the two countries attempted to restore their ties to some degree by holding joint military exercises, by hosting the World Cup together in 2002, and by expanding their trade relations, relations continued to grow worse under the weight of negative Korean public opinion toward Japan.[71]

Meanwhile, Koizumi took a bold path in Japan's relations with North Korea when he met with Kim Jong-il directly in 2002.[72] This meeting resulted in Kim Jong-il's admission of past abductions of Japanese citizens to North Korea in the 1970s and 1980s to be used as part of North Korean spy-training operations; in the release of five Japanese abductees; and in the signing of the Pyongyang Declaration, which identified outstanding issues to be resolved to improve relations between the two countries.[73] These developments, however, further estranged Japan and North Korea rather than putting them on a track supportive of the need to improve North Korea's relations with other Northeast Asian countries and to continue inter-Korean reconciliation efforts. When Kim Jong-il admitted to the kidnappings, Koizumi came under pressure to do more to resolve the issue, effectively putting a brake on any progress in Japan–North Korea relations.[74] The negative turn in Japanese public opinion on the abduction issue pushed Japan's policy closer to that of the United States, further straining Japan–South Korea relations and leading to the abandonment of the Trilateral Coordination and Oversight Group process, which had seemed promising as a means to promote trilateral policy coordination toward North Korea among the United States, Japan, and South Korea.

SINO–SOUTH KOREAN RELATIONS

In dealing with North Korea and preventing a new cold war in Northeast Asia, Kim Dae-jung saw China's role as critical. Under Kim, China–South Korea relations grew rapidly. In 1998, Kim visited China and forged a "cooperative partnership" with Beijing.[75] The two countries also initiated the China-ROK defense ministers' meetings.[76] In 1999, South Korea refused to become part of the U.S.-led theater missile defense out of the concern that joining it might antagonize relations with China.[77] In 2000, Seoul and Beijing upgraded their relationship again to a "full-scale cooperative partnership."[78]

China reciprocated by fully supporting Kim Dae-jung's Sunshine Policy. Beijing had every reason to welcome the policy, not least because it promised to reduce some of the burden of providing humanitarian support for North Korea and to reduce pressure on China by decreasing conflict between Seoul and Pyongyang and contributing to a more peaceful Korean Peninsula, which had been a long-standing Chinese priority.[79] Moreover, China and South Korea began to move toward greater familiarity with each other's positions through periodic Four-Party Talks (the United States, China, and the two Koreas) on the possibility of replacing the armistice with a permanent peace regime, although the talks did not make substantive progress.[80] China remained a major supporter of North Korea, but Beijing's and Seoul's respective interests in integrating and promoting economic reform in North Korea were converging during this period.

Sino–South Korean relations were not without friction during the Kim Dae-jung presidency. For instance, a major economic dispute with China over garlic imports threatened to spill out of control. South Korean garlic farmers sought protection from low-cost Chinese imports. When Kim restricted Chinese garlic imports to provide relief to Korean farmers, the People's Republic of China escalated the dispute by restricting South Korean firms' access to the far larger Chinese telecommunications and electronic equipment sector. China's entry into the World Trade Organization the following year, however, provided a far more equitable dispute-settlement mechanism by which the two countries were able to pursue cases in various sectors involving allegations of unfair dumping and countervailing duties. China's membership in the organization also provided the legal protections that opened the way for major trade and investment flows to China from South Korea's large conglomerates, launching a decade of 20 percent year-on-year growth in bilateral exports and significant investment inflows from South Korea. South Korea's decades of development experience and its relatively rapid recovery from the Asian financial crisis provided opportunities to build an economic relationship with China given China's interest in utilizing the South Korean experiences as a model for charting its own economic development.[81]

RUSSO–SOUTH KOREAN RELATIONS

During the 1990s, Russia was in political, social, and economic turmoil and thus not a major player in Korean affairs. Nevertheless, Kim Dae-jung also sought to ensure that South Korea had beneficial relations with Russia, which held a seat on the UN Security Council. Initially, however, a spy scandal involving South Korean efforts to gather intelligence about North Korea in Russia became public in Kim's first year, getting the relationship off to a rocky start. Second, South Korea and Russia were still struggling to find ways to settle Russian repayment of the loan package that Roh Tae-woo had offered to Mikhail Gorbachev at the time of normalization with the Soviet Union in 1990. Third, the Russians' lobbying of Kim to sign a joint statement criticizing theater missile defense only weeks prior to his first summit meeting with George W. Bush proved to be an irritant.

Despite these setbacks, Kim sought to build a cooperative relationship with Russia, especially around the expansion of regional transportation and railway networks that would enhance connections between the Korean Peninsula and the Russian Far East and promote inter-Korean reconciliation. Kim personally supported the idea of an "iron silk railroad," which not only would extend through the two Koreas but would involve relinking the Korean Peninsula with Europe through Russia's Trans-Siberian Railway.[82] As inter-Korean exchanges and cooperation increased following the inter-Korean summit, the prospect of a web of region-wide cooperation that might draw in Russia and China became more attractive. However, these efforts were cut short as a result of the shift in U.S. policy toward North Korea under the Bush administration and the reemergence of the nuclear issue as an obstacle to North Korea's regional integration.

LIMITS OF KIM DAE-JUNG'S FOREIGN POLICY

Kim Dae-jung's approach ran into two obstacles, one domestic and one international, which ultimately led to the failure of his efforts. Domestically, his policy ended up changing South Korea more than it changed North Korea. One manifestation of that change was a deepening polarization in the public debate on the policy toward the North. The greater the apparent success in inter-Korean reconciliation, the stronger the backlash from South Korean conservative groups, who opposed Kim's engagement policy. Second, the election of George W. Bush in the United States in 2000 and his extreme skepticism regarding the efficacy of dealing with the North removed a fundamental pillar of support for Kim's policy because a critical goal for North Korea in its dealings with the South was a transformation of the South's political relationship with the United States. The transition from Clinton to Bush was a jarring reversal for Pyongyang as North Korea went from hosting Clinton's secretary of state Madeleine Albright and wooing Clinton himself to make a visit Pyongyang to dealing with Bush, who despised North Korean human rights practices and characterized North Korea as a member of the "axis of evil" by January 2002.

SOUTH KOREAN DOMESTIC DEBATES OVER THE SUNSHINE POLICY

The progressives greeted with enthusiasm Kim Dae-jung's engagement policy toward North Korea and perceived the security-oriented conservative focus on ideology as creating needless obstacles to the pursuit of national unification based on brotherhood and ethnic unity. Conservatives were cautiously skeptical of Kim Dae-jung's approach even though it overlapped and built on aspects of conservative engagement with North Korea symbolized by Nordpolitik. Despite some similarities, the differences between conservative and progressive views of North Korea ran deep, in part because progressives had always been outsiders to governing power exercised by conservative authoritarian leaderships and had in many cases suffered persecution for their links to or sympathy for North Korea. Thus, the further Kim Dae-jung went in his implementation of engagement with North Korea, the more divisions between conservatives and progressives came to the fore. Following the inter-Korean summit in June 2000, these divisions came to be known within South Korea as the *nam-nam kalteung*, or "South-South divide."

South Korean progressives and conservatives differed over many issues related to North Korea despite the fact that both progressive and conservative South Korean presidents sought dialogue and summit opportunities with North Korean counterparts. Roh Tae-woo had sought summit opportunities as part of Nordpolitik, and Kim Young-sam's opportunity for a summit meeting with Kim Il-sung brokered by Jimmy Carter had been stolen away by Kim Il-sung's untimely death in the middle of summit preparations. Thus, some conservative criticism of Kim Dae-jung's policies and of his success in realizing a summit with Kim Jong-il contained an element of sour grapes; however, this did not mean that there were not real and deeply felt differences between conservatives and progressives regarding respective strategies toward North Korea and the desired outcomes of improved relations between the two Koreas.

One major gap between South Korean conservatives and progressives involved divisions over the viability of an approach that involved trust or mutual respect or both for North Koreans as counterparts in a negotiation and reconciliation process. Based on both ideology and the memory of a fractious and devastating conflict that North Korea had initiated, conservatives harbored doubts about North Korea's intentions. They also knew that acceptance of North Korea as a negotiating counterpart implied that the injustices inflicted on South Korea by the North had to be set aside and that both sides would have to pursue negotiations based on trust and cooperation rather than on unilateral pursuit of victory and the absorption of one Korea by the other. A negotiated inter-Korean reconciliation process implied that it would no longer be possible to hold North Korean leaders to account or brought to justice for atrocities committed during or after the Korean War.

A second major gap between South Korean conservatives and progressives involved differences over whether accommodation of North Korea could lead to reform within North Korea as implied and anticipated by Kim Dae-jung. This dispute revolved around differences over the question of whether closer economic cooperation with North Korea through the "separation of economics from politics" or the provision of economic benefits first in order to yield returns from North Korea later could lead to transformative change within the North Korean system. Many progressive supporters of Kim Dae-jung's policy believed that exposure to capitalism would be a transformative factor that would undermine North Korean state policies and bring about political reconciliation by giving North Korea a stake in cooperation with South Korea and making it dependent on the South for its economic well-being to some degree. But conservatives remained skeptical that inter-Korean interaction would erode North Korea's power, instead believing that such an approach was naive and would ultimately strengthen a North Korean leadership that would never accept the principle of reciprocity or abandon confrontation with the South. Divisions between progressives and conservatives emerged most sharply following the inter-Korean summit as South Koreans grappled with the domestic social consequences of the shift from enmity to cooperation with North Korea, including how to update and revise South Korean school textbooks so as not to demonize the North, the implications of possible inter-Korean reconciliation for Korean defense needs, and even the most appropriate way to refer to North Korean leaders.

Ultimately, one of the biggest shortcomings of Kim Dae-jung's execution of the summit with Kim Jong-il involved a failure to reach across the political aisle and gain participation from conservatives as part of the South's delegation in Pyongyang. This failure gave North Korea room to maneuver within South Korean domestic politics both by cooperating with progressives and by demonizing conservative critics of engagement.

One reason for Kim Dae-jung's failure to bring conservatives to the summit involved the timing of the announcement of the summit three days prior to National Assembly elections, suggesting to some that the administration was trying to use the summit to promote his party's standing in the National Assembly. Regardless of whether this motivation existed or not, the summit announcement proved not to have such an effect as the opposition Grand National Party emerged as the largest party in the National Assembly.

The failure to gain conservative participation in the delegation to Pyongyang indirectly served to deepen political divisions over a policy of engagement with North Korea, sharpening the South-South divide. It left space for Pyongyang to exploit political differences between conservatives and progressives and to try to play them off against the other. Even North Korea's willingness to cooperate with progressive political leaders while stonewalling conservative media outlets such as *Chosun Ilbo* was a clear attempt to exploit political differences between the two sides. However, the failure to make inter-Korean reconciliation a bipartisan project in the South ultimately generated a conservative backlash against a perceived one-sided inter-Korean cooperation in which South Korea provided resources and access to the North, but North Korea did not reciprocate.

Despite the initial euphoria following the inter-Korean summit in June 2000 at the end of the Clinton administration, friction between the Kim Dae-jung administration and the George W. Bush administration over how to deal with North Korea contributed to a sharpening of South Korea's own internal debates over the direction of policy toward North Korea. These developments reinforced conservative criticisms of Kim Dae-jung's policy and contributed to a deepening polarization over how to deal with the North. One of the most powerful criticisms of Kim's engagement policy at the time was that it failed to improve the security situation around the peninsula. As a result, "North Korea fatigue" began to swallow up "North Korea euphoria" in South Korea.[83]

Perhaps the most damaging critique of the Sunshine Policy among conservative critics of Kim Dae-jung revolved around the question of how North Korea was using the foreign exchange earned from South Korean largesse to build nuclear weapons that would eventually pose a threat to the South.[84] One immediate effect of those criticisms was that the South Korean government came under pressure to shift, to the extent possible, from cash to in-kind payments to the North for cooperation. The critique of cash payments to North Korea became sharper as the second North Korean nuclear crisis unfolded and as the North showed continuing advances in its nuclear and missile programs.[85]

Another polarizing issue between conservatives and progressives was the question of human rights in North Korea. Especially when President Bush shone the spotlight on the human rights situation by hosting North Korean defectors such as Kang Chol-hwan at the White House, South Korean conservatives questioned why Kim Dae-jung, a democracy activist and former human rights victim of South Korean authoritarian regimes, would fail to stand up and criticize the North Korean system for its egregious human rights practices.[86] In South Korea's domestic politics, liberals preferred a quiet approach to human rights so as not to endanger the potential for inter-Korean reconciliation, whereas conservatives tended to use human rights as a club by which to mount a powerful attack on North Korea's legitimacy.[87]

KIM DAE-JUNG IN THE DRIVER'S SEAT, BUT ON A MADE-IN-THE-USA CLOSED COURSE

Kim Dae-jung's attempt to shape South Korean foreign policy was a bold effort. It represented the first time that a South Korean president had put forward a progressive agenda with respect to North Korea and the world, drawing opposition from conservatives within South Korea. To succeed, Kim sought to win South Korea's domestic debate with the conservative political establishment, which had long dominated South Korean politics. In addition, Kim took advantage of a relatively benign international environment as he evangelized the major powers to support his efforts to achieve inter-Korean reconciliation. The policy was bold both because it required Kim Dae-jung to show leadership domestically and internationally and because the success of the policy depended on Kim Jong-il's cooperation. The policy took advantage of South Korea's relative economic strength vis-à-vis North Korea but attempted to use that strength to offer North Korea a helping hand as a means by which to achieve reconciliation rather than perpetuating competitive relations with the North. However, the policy ultimately failed to induce North Korea to respond in kind.

The Asian financial crisis notwithstanding, South Korea's democratization and its rising capacity vis-à-vis an increasingly diplomatically isolated and bereft North Korea provided Kim Dae-jung with a window of opportunity to shift South Korean policy toward North Korea from one based on containment and pursuit of tactical advantage to one that leveraged rising South Korean diplomatic influence both in the region and on the peninsula in support of inter-Korean reconciliation and cooperation. The Sunshine Policy was rooted in Kim Dae-jung's confidence that he could persuade both Kim Jong-il and the global community of the benefits of inter-Korean reconciliation and North Korea's political integration with the outside world. In this respect, Kim Dae-jung attempted to take advantage of a benign international environment to build momentum in inter-Korean relations that he hoped would in turn generate domestic political support and transform North Korea from adversary to partner. Although this approach had much in common with Roh Tae-woo's Nordpolitik policy, in the first three years of Kim Dae-jung's administration the Sunshine Policy's inter-Korean and international components did a remarkable job of working as coordinated tracks designed in tandem to draw North Korea into contact with the outside world in the hope that this greater international and peninsular integration would lead to transformation.

Kim Dae-jung's Sunshine Policy influenced the alliance with the United States in a number of ways. First, Kim's assumption of leadership on North Korea policy was an expression of limited autonomy that tested the tolerance of the United States, and the alliance partially evolved from the historic patron–client relationship into a relationship in which South Korea chose its own clear direction and sought U.S. support rather than seeking space for autonomous actions through consultations with the United States. Under the Clinton administration, the United States was tolerant of Kim Dae-jung's efforts to lead within a context of broad consensus on the desirability of greater engagement with North Korea, but the United States still expected South Korea to consult closely and in a timely fashion on the substance and progress of South Korean efforts to engage with the North.

Second, the United States and South Korea faced some difficulties in managing the domestic effects of the Sunshine Policy due to the South Korean public's perceptions that reconciliation with North Korea would diminish South Korean dependency on the U.S.-ROK alliance to provide for South Korea's security. Although Kim Dae-jung himself argued that the U.S.-ROK alliance should be sustained even after Korean unification, some Koreans saw inter-Korean reconciliation as a factor that would win South Korea even greater autonomy from the United States and possibly even bring about the end of the alliance. One manifestation of these views was a rise in local-level incidents between Koreans and members of USFK.

Third, the withdrawal of U.S. support for Kim Dae-jung's engagement policy toward North Korea under the Bush administration revealed the limits of Korean autonomy within the context of the U.S.-ROK alliance. Despite Kim Dae-jung's best efforts, Clinton's successor, George W. Bush, harbored skepticism toward North Korea and withdrew U.S. support for Kim's efforts to achieve reconciliation with the North. Without U.S. support, Kim was unable to proceed. Moreover, U.S. opposition to the Sunshine Policy also created a polarizing feedback loop in Korean domestic politics, emboldening critics and weakening the South Korean public's support for the policy. At the same time, the United States made itself the main obstacle to Kim Dae-jung's efforts, thus feeding negative South Korean perceptions of the United States and generating heavy-handed restraints on Korean space to pursue an autonomous policy. Although Kim Dae-jung may have harbored bitterness at the obstacles imposed by the Bush administration's policy toward North Korea, there was no serious effort in his administration to pursue autonomy outside of the alliance. That debate would occur during the upcoming Roh Moo-hyun administration.

5

ROH MOO-HYUN'S
BALANCER POLICY

OUTH KOREA'S PRESIDENTIAL election in 2002 occurred at the height
of a public debate about the future of the country's alliance with the
United States. Implicit in that debate was the question of whether
the structure of alliance relations between the United States and South
Korea had evolved to take into account growing South Korean capabilities
and desires for greater autonomy in foreign policy. Amid public candlelight protests over the death of two schoolgirls killed by a U.S. military
vehicle in June and a USFK-administered trial in November that resulted
in the acquittal of the vehicle operators, policy debates during the election
campaign were infused with emotion and volatility. The main issue that
drew public concern was whether the U.S. military had shown respect in
its treatment of Korea commensurate with Korea's societal progress, democratization, and rise as a middle power. Another aspect of the debate
was the question of how much autonomy South Korea should rightly be
able to exercise in setting its own foreign policy as a result of its rising capacities and the appropriate role of the U.S.-ROK alliance versus South
Korean aspirations for greater autonomy. In light of the George W. Bush
administration's aggressive antiterrorism policies after September 11, 2001,
in this case especially with respect to North Korea, the South Korean public expressed increasing concern that the alliance might end up being an
instrument that would entrap South Korea in a cycle of confrontation with

North Korea. In addition, South Koreans felt that the alliance was generating burdens for South Korea through U.S. requests for support in Iraq,
which was peripheral to South Korea's immediate interests. Likewise, the
United States undertook its own evaluation of the long-term strategic importance of the alliance as part of its strategic planning toward Asia.

The political debate around the presidential election in 2002 was fueled
by decentralization within South Korea's governing structure, the diffusion of political power resulting from democratization, and the rise of a
nebulous coalition of interest groups that organized around a broad set of
issues and grievances deriving from past mistreatment or injury associated
with the establishment of U.S. bases in South Korea and the lack of appropriate channels for compensation for the inconvenience or distress caused
to nearby local communities. In the context of a closely fought campaign,
views on South Korea's relationship with the United States became politicized to an unprecedented degree. The U.S.-ROK alliance had been formed
in the aftermath of the Korean War primarily through direct negotiations
by Syngman Rhee and had been off-limits as a subject of debate under
authoritarian rule during the Cold War. Although tensions over anti-
Americanism arose during South Korea's transition to democratization
and on the sidelines of the Seoul Olympics in 1988, the election in 2002
was the first genuine instance that the U.S.-ROK alliance became a subject of broad public debate in a democratic setting.

The two main candidates hailed from radically different backgrounds
that reflected the divergent experiences and points of view that epitomized
conservative versus progressive experiences in South Korea's transition
from authoritarianism to democracy. The conservative candidate was Lee
Hoi-chang, a former prosecutor and former prime minister in the Kim
Young-sam administration who had graduated from Seoul National University. Lee was a prototypical representative of South Korea's conservative
elite in both reputation and performance. His major flaw as a candidate
revolved around the issue of whether he had helped his sons gain a medical
exemption from military service, which indirectly served as a further indication of his elite status.

The progressive candidate was Roh Moo-hyun, a self-educated human
rights lawyer who had never graduated from college and who had been

active in promoting democratization and labor rights. Roh had no experience abroad, was not captive to South Korea's vested elite interests, and exploited anti-American sentiments during the campaign, although his main election platform emphasized anticorruption and his desire to achieve a more equitable social structure within South Korea. In this respect, Roh's experience as a progressive was parochial, but he was able to ride rising public sentiment that insisted on greater respect for South Korean autonomy both within the context of the alliance with the United States and as a reflection of South Korea's rising international profile. Although Roh had been a reformist challenger to traditional South Korean elite interests throughout his career, his election as president in 2002 placed him at the center of power in South Korea and forced him to reconcile his ideals with reality. In foreign policy, the central challenge of this reconciliation revolved around how to expand South Korea's autonomy while recognizing the necessity to maintain the alliance with the United States.

Moreover, domestic public opinion played a major role in Roh Moo-hyun's foreign policy. Roh's national security strategy directly acknowledged the impact of both South Korea's democratic consolidation and its rising capacity in the following statement: "Our people, with the rapid growth of national power, successful democratization, and enhanced perception of peoples' rights, now want more cooperative and horizontal foreign relations."[1] This statement encapsulates South Korea's expectations of greater autonomy in the management of its foreign relations and of a more egalitarian approach based on mutual respect within the U.S.-ROK alliance.

Yet the Roh administration discovered that it faced a mismatch between its relative ability to conduct an autonomous and relatively balanced foreign policy through the ongoing development of political relations with China and Russia, on the one hand, and the realization that the U.S.-ROK security alliance was a necessary source of constraint because South Korea remained heavily dependent on the United States for security, on the other. This dependency manifested itself primarily as friction over institutional arrangements, wherein South Koreans, instead of focusing on larger, strategic issues, decided on pushing the United States to take a more respectful approach on technical and tactical-level issues such as the

Status of Forces Agreement or management of other local issues between the USFK and local communities in South Korea. These attitudes catalyzed Future of the Alliance talks, including implementation of the Land Partnership Plan initiated in the late 1990s and negotiations on U.S. consolidation of its presence on the peninsula around Camp Humphreys near the Osan-Pyongtaek area. Overall, the tight U.S.-ROK defense relationship also was a source of constraint on Roh's multilateralist vision for peace and prosperity in Northeast Asia. The argument manifested itself most often in the realization that South Korea had limited capability to prevent tensions over North Korea from driving the region into a new cold war in Asia.

ROH MOO-HYUN'S VISION: THE PEACE AND PROSPERITY POLICY

Roh Moo-hyun rose to the presidency on a groundswell of populist discontent with the United States but also with a wide range of social inequities that had bubbled up in Korean society. Roh and his associates were supported by progressive dissidents, human rights lawyers, and members of the vaunted "386 generation," the group of South Koreans who were in their thirties during the 1990s, attended university during the 1980s, and were born in the 1960s. This generation had cut their teeth by mobilizing street protests against South Korea's authoritarian rule at university campuses around the country during the 1980s. Many backed by the 386 generation rose to become influential officials and policy makers under the Roh presidency. In 2004, they made up approximately 20 percent of the South Korean National Assembly.[2]

Reflecting conflicting feelings about the U.S.-ROK alliance, however, the Roh administration was split into two factions—the alliance faction representing the conservative approach toward foreign policy and the independence faction representing the progressive approach—that fought over the direction of the administration's foreign policy. Both factions sought greater autonomy for South Korea as a responsible and central actor in managing its security needs and in charting its foreign relations. The alliance faction, however, sought greater autonomy for South Korea *within* the context of the U.S.-ROK alliance, whereas the independence faction openly advocated for South Korea to pursue an independent foreign policy *outside* the context of the U.S.-ROK alliance. A major difference between the two groups revolved around whether the alliance was the foundation for deterrence against North Korea or a fundamental obstacle blocking the path toward inter-Korean reconciliation. The struggle between these two factions was intense and bitter, and each faction's relative influence fluctuated during the course of Roh's administration based on specific issues and personnel placements. At the same time, the two factions were also integrated in the administration and had to work with each other, resulting in a foreign policy that reflected an uneasy coexistence and compromise between these contending forces. The administration's national security strategy contained several distinctive themes that embodied these internal contradictions.

First, despite the reemergence of the North Korean nuclear issue, the administration retained a strong commitment to pursue cooperative and peaceful management of existing tensions through dialogue, a commitment that generated tension between peace versus security as a priority. In his Inaugural Address on February 25, 2003, Roh Moo-hyun stated that "in order to bring about a genuine Age of Northeast Asia, a structure of peace must first be institutionalized on the Korean Peninsula."[3] This approach became a lightning rod for differing and often self-contradictory approaches between the Roh administration's and the Bush administration's respective declaratory policies. South Korea was unconditionally committed to a peaceful settlement of disputes through dialogue; the United States insisted that all options be on the table even as it sought multilateral dialogue as the preferred means for addressing the North Korean nuclear issue. According to Roh, "North Korea's claim that their [*sic*] nuclear missiles are measures for self-protection from outside forces has a point," but the United States criticized his remark and emphasized that "North Korea's nuclear weapons are a threat to the alliance and other allied nations."[4] Many of Roh's supporters from the left also believed that the North Korea problem ultimately resulted from the estrangement between Pyongyang and Washington. Despite the renewal of U.S.-DPRK tensions over the nuclear issue, the Roh administration expressed its firm commitment to a process of tension and arms reductions through a dialogue process, the result of which would be the replacement of the armistice system with a permanent peace regime on the peninsula. In light of the seriousness with which the Bush administration perceived the North Korean nuclear threat, Washington regarded Roh's stance as unrealistic. In the end, the United States pursued negotiations through Six-Party Talks as the main avenue for addressing the North Korean nuclear challenge, while South Korea scrambled to show that it was playing a "central role" in the talks.

Second, the Roh administration sought to pursue "balanced and pragmatic diplomacy" designed to address competing goals and demands in a flexible and integrated fashion. In particular, it sought to achieve a balance between "values and national interest," between the alliance and multilateral cooperation, between globalization and national integrity, as well as between Koreans and others.[5] Lee Ju-heum explains the balancing policy as a strategy that "1) seeks to avoid a state's diplomatic strategy from being overly tilted toward one specific state and thus becoming rigid while 2) adhering to a flexible diplomatic position in inter-state relations."[6] This idea was the precursor to Roh's controversial "balancer" concept, introduced in early 2005, which called for South Korea to be a "balancer" for peace and stability by introducing a new set of norms, principles, and rules.[7]

Third, while continuing to uphold the importance of the U.S.-ROK alliance, the Roh administration gave equal emphasis to the need for South Korea to develop a "cooperative, self-reliant defense system" that would enable it to play the leading role in defending the Korean Peninsula under close cooperation with the United States.[8] Roh's initiative to revise wartime operational control arrangements demonstrated his desire for South Korea to play a more responsible, autonomous defense role on the peninsula while the United States played a supporting role. Although one motivation for pursuing these talks might have been the pursuit of greater autonomy from the U.S.-ROK alliance, another might have been the acquisition of the sorts of capabilities that would enable South Korea to replace the old patron–client model with a more "horizontal" partnership to achieve "the harmony of interdependence and autonomy."[9] At the same time, the Roh administration sought to develop regional multilateral security cooperation through stepped-up military exchanges with Japan and China that would be developed in parallel and at the same pace with each other.[10]

Fourth, the Roh administration strongly desired to provide regional leadership for Northeast Asian cooperative security, in which South Korea would serve as the "hub of Northeast Asia."[11] Roh proposed the Northeast Asian Cooperation Initiative, which aimed to transform the region into a community with South Korea at the center. In part, the desire to play a larger, central role in the region represented an early stage of South Korea's efforts to cast itself as a middle power. Roh's Presidential Commission on Policy Planning labeled South Korea a "strong middle power."[12] Roh himself labeled South Korea a "strong nation,"[13] holding a view that starkly contrasted with Koreans' traditional self-perception of their nation as a shrimp among whales. Roh proclaimed: "The Korean peninsula is a bridge between China and Japan. . . . Even though this geopolitical stance had given us pain in the past, it is giving us new opportunities today. The era of Northeast Asia in the 21st century is demanding Korea to play a central role in the region."[14] He initially emphasized this idea in his Liberation Day speech in 2003 and made it a centerpiece for the administration's thinking with regard to how a rising South Korea might proactively transform the region alongside its own national development and efforts to pursue peace and prosperity on the Korean Peninsula. Roh believed that the expansion of cooperative security arrangements would complement South Korea's alliance with the United States in the near term and that regional community-building efforts might one day supersede the stabilizing role of the U.S.-ROK alliance and become the main mechanism for guaranteeing regional security in Northeast Asia.[15]

Fifth, the Roh administration actively sought to play an autonomous and central role in management of Korean Peninsula issues, with the expectation that South Korea would be the driver of forward constructive regional relations and that other parties would respond positively to its initiative. However, as noted earlier, the question of whether South Korea should pursue autonomy from the constraints imposed by the U.S.-ROK alliance or pursue autonomy within the alliance was contested within the administration. The pursuit of a "balanced" two-track approach that simultaneously emphasized self-defense and cooperation within the alliance pointed to a key question: Did South Korea have the diplomatic and military capabilities to effectively balance its reliance on the alliance with its efforts to promote multilateral security cooperation? The Roh administration believed that such multilateral cooperation, if realized, would then serve in part as a hedge against the perceived risks that the United States might entrap South Korea in conflict with the North.

With regard to North Korea, the Roh administration actively pursued a coprosperity concept that intended to build on the idea of "balanced economic development of the Korean peninsula" mentioned in the inter-Korean declaration of June 15, 2000.[16] A resulting source of tension in U.S.-ROK relations throughout the Roh administration was how far inter-Korean economic cooperation under the banner of coprosperity could go without running into limitations imposed by the Bush administration's desire to freeze economic cooperation with North Korea pending satisfactory progress on denuclearization. Indeed, Roh lamented, "No matter how much we want to carry out the inter-Korean economic cooperation on our own at our own pace, we are under U.S. scrutiny for every item that is brought into the Kaesong [Industrial] Complex [north of the DMZ]."[17]

Under the Roh administration, efforts to achieve autonomy in defense and foreign relations as well as the robust effort to promote multilateral security dialogues coexisted with efforts to evolve the U.S.-ROK alliance. Measures to bolster the alliance included tangible South Korean troop contributions to postconflict stabilization operations in Iraq (South Korea sent the third-largest foreign contingent) and the negotiation of a bilateral Korea-U.S. free-trade agreement (FTA). Despite the politicized nature of the debates regarding the U.S.-ROK alliance and open differences with the Bush administration on a number of issues, Roh laid the foundation for the strengthening of the alliance in several important areas and sought to develop new defense capabilities, most notably through his efforts to procure a blue-water naval capability, which have subsequently become the basis for even stronger U.S.-ROK cooperation.[18]

ROH MOO-HYUN'S BALANCER CONCEPT
AND NORTHEAST ASIAN SECURITY

One of Roh Moo-hyun's distinctive policy initiatives that grew directly out of the principles enumerated in the previous section was his proposal that South Korea play an active role as the "balancer" in Northeast Asia. By proposing the idea, Roh sought to highlight the geopolitical significance of the Korean Peninsula and the influence Seoul might potentially be able to wield as a growing middle power occupying a strategic position: "Depending on what choice we will make in future, the power structure in Northeast Asia will change."[19] The idea was that South Korea can and should be "balancing on its own," doing more to assert itself, and actively shaping the events in the region instead of being swept along by history, as it had always been.[20]

Roh Moo-hyun first unveiled his balancer concept in a National Assembly speech on February 25, 2005. Although the concept appears to have been directed primarily at finding a way for South Korea to manage rising tensions between China and Japan, it also drew close attention in the context of the rapidly developing Sino–South Korean relationship. Many of Roh's advisers also sought greater independence from the United States. The concept implied that South Korea wanted to be free from entrapment in any hypothetical military conflict between the United States and China as part of U.S.-ROK discussions regarding "strategic flexibility." It would allow the United States to deploy its forces from the Korean Peninsula to regional hot spots rather than having U.S. forces dedicated solely to a North Korean contingency.[21] In concrete terms, an important component of the balancer concept was the plan Defense Reform 2020, which called for greater modernization and professionalization of the South Korean military, greater focus on air and naval power, and a transition into a more rapid, precision-based military using extensive command, control, communications, computers, intelligence, surveillance, and reconnaissance capabilities, thus moving away from a static, defensive posture.[22]

Roh Moo-hyun's balancer concept had three effects on the implementation of South Korean foreign-affairs and defense policy. First, South Korea aimed to pursue a roughly parallel development of defense relations with both Japan and China, as suggested in its defense white papers. These relations included high-level exchanges of defense officials, educational exchanges, and establishment of military cooperation arrangements. For example, in 2005 Seoul raised the level of military exchanges with Beijing to the same level as its exchanges with Tokyo.[23] Because of the obstacles stemming from history-related disputes between Japan and South Korea as well as from South Korea's quasi-alliance relationship with Japan, however, this approach in practice elevated the objective of strengthening security ties with Beijing but put a damper on development of security ties with Tokyo.

Second, South Korea resisted U.S. pressure to strengthen trilateral coordination with Japan in order to put more pressure on North Korea. As discussed in chapter 4, the approach of strengthening of trilateral coordination had emerged in the late 1990s under Kim Dae-jung as an important method for drawing North Korea's attention and showing resolve against its development of nuclear weapons. Roh, however, hesitated to take this approach in part as a way of showing his administration's disagreement with the Bush administration's coercive diplomacy toward North Korea.

Third, after articulating the balancer concept, the Roh administration resisted both the idea of "strategic flexibility" that would allow U.S. forces to deploy to regional conflicts—with a hypothetical Taiwan Strait conflict being the main area of concern—as well as the extension of war planning to include an operational plan for responding to North Korean contingencies or internal instability scenarios, known as Plan 5029. The Roh administration's disagreement with this plan leaked, and it insisted on agreeing to 5029 only as a concept plan but refused to allow it to become an operational plan.[24]

Despite all these initiatives to pursue a more independent foreign policy, Roh Moo-hyun later toned down his rhetoric and stated, "In order for us to successfully carry out balancer diplomacy in Northeast Asia, it is necessary to establish a solid US-Korean alliance."[25] According to Lee Ju-heum, "The balancer theory is not aimed at reorganizing the power structure in Northeast Asia. Rather it seeks to surmount the national and ideological chauvinism of Northeast Asian countries and build a new economic community and multilateral security cooperative system based on the existing U.S.-ROK alliance."[26] By means of an "independent, pro-American" posture, Roh wanted South Korea to be more assertive and to play a larger role while retaining the full benefits and assurances from an alliance with the United States.[27]

Nevertheless, a fierce debate erupted in South Korea almost immediately after Roh unveiled the balancer concept. South Korean conservatives and centrists argued that pursuit of autonomy, or "independent diplomacy," would only "isolate Korea from its neighbors."[28] Most media criticism of Roh's balancing idea—using phrases such as "delusion of grandeur," "coming out," and "challenge to a duel"—centered on the questions of whether it might unduly weaken South Korea's alliance with the United States. Whether greater South Korean autonomy or independence would indeed involve a dominant Chinese role in regional relations and what China's relationship would be to the alliance were additional questions.[29] Conservative South Korean newspapers argued that South Korea was losing political backing from the United States that it needed for China to take it seriously and that South Korea on its own could not generate sufficient influence in the region.[30] Many scholars have also criticized the balancer concept by comparing it to a "mirage," questioning whether South Korea has the capacity to become a balancer in the region and whether such a role would even be accepted among the region's nation-states.[31] The most striking bit of criticism came from Roh's predecessor and political mentor, Kim Dae-jung, who said, "It's best that our diplomatic relations operate within the three frameworks of a strong Korea-U.S. relationship, the tripartite alliance and cooperation between the region's four Great Powers. . . . This is not a choice, but a position we have to accept fatalistically, our destiny."[32]

By the end of its term, the Roh administration more or less seemed to have abandoned the balancer concept and was struggling to come up with an alternative. The publication by the Presidential Commission on Policy Planning stated in 2008 that Seoul "cannot become a dominating balancer for Northeast Asian peace. Even so, it must not play the role of attaching itself to stronger nations and reinforcing the structure of confrontation in Northeast Asia. . . . The role that the Republic of Korea must play for Northeast Asian peace and prosperity is that of a facilitator and shaper of peace."[33] In the end, the Roh administration never clarified what role South Korea was supposed to play, if not as a balancer, or how South Korea could realistically be a "facilitator" and "shaper of peace."

ROH MOO-HYUN'S NORTHEAST ASIAN COOPERATION INITIATIVE: PROMOTING MULTILATERALISM

The Roh administration sought to take advantage of "the era of Northeast Asia" by harnessing Asia's economic dynamism and South Korea's own activism to "make a new order of cooperation and integration in Northeast Asia."[34] It sought to harness regional integration initiatives to promote cooperation and overcome sources of tension that might lead to conflict and risk regional prosperity. Toward this goal, the Roh administration established a presidential committee focused on cooperation in Northeast Asia as a component of its policy of peace and prosperity, the purpose of which was to generate synergy between inter-Korean and multilateral security cooperation initiatives. In order to be the catalyst in promoting regional cooperation while also promoting inter-Korean peace and prosperity, however, the Roh administration needed to overcome bilateral difficulties and win support for multilateral cooperation from each of South Korea's immediate neighbors.

The Northeast Asian Cooperation Initiative envisioned an open, networked, participatory Northeast Asian regional community and identified historical issues, "exclusive nationalism," and the need to develop pluralistic cultural exchange and cooperation as the main challenges to be overcome to achieve the long-term objective of establishing that community.[35] However, the committee never gained traction or support from neighboring countries. For instance, China objected to early formulations of the initiative that described South Korea rather than China as the "hub of Northeast Asia."[36] The Roh administration, despite its desire and belief that it was well positioned to be an effective mediator of regional cooperation, simply did not have the capability to overcome the entrenched historical, territorial, and security-based sources of distrust among more powerful neighbors that had prevented and continues to prevent the institutionalization of multilateral security cooperation in Northeast Asia.

JAPAN–SOUTH KOREA RELATIONS

In the initial stage of his presidency, Roh Moo-hyun sought a positive tone for Japan–South Korea relations by emphasizing the future during his visit to Tokyo on June 6, 2003.[37] Roh and Prime Minister Koizumi Junichiro affirmed that both South Korea and Japan "[will] not allow North Korea to possess nuclear weapons nor [sic] [a] nuclear development program and have to solve this issue in a peaceful and diplomatic manner."[38] Both leaders also agreed to cooperate in concluding the ROK-Japan FTA as well as promoting people-to-people exchanges.[39] As a sign of his willingness to preserve warm relations with Japan, in July 2004 Roh Moo-hyun responded to a Japanese reporter's question by stating: "I will not talk that much about Takeshima. I don't feel that it is necessary to re-discuss the Dokdo islets."[40] He used the Japanese name for the islets, Takeshima, and clearly did not want this territorial issue to hamper Japan-ROK relations. In 2005, however, a declaration by the Shimane prefecture in Japan that it would celebrate "Takeshima Day" to mark the one hundredth anniversary of the disputed islands' annexation by Japan roiled the South Korean public.[41] Soon after this declaration, Roh warned that Seoul would declare "diplomatic war" against Tokyo, and the progress in bettering their relationship was once again halted.[42]

The island dispute in particular became tense in 2006 when Tokyo decided to conduct a maritime survey in the seas around the Dokdo/Takeshima Islets.[43] In addition to the territorial issue, other problems, including the history books and Koizumi's visits to the Yasukuni shrine, made it impossible for the Roh administration to improve relations with Japan.[44]

The downturn in relations with Japan had reverberations for U.S.-ROK relations as well. As South Korea was seeking greater diplomatic independence from Washington, Japanese prime ministers Koizumi and Abe Shinzo were working to strengthen the U.S.-Japan alliance by highlighting the difficulties in the U.S.-ROK alliance by comparison. When Roh Moo-hyun complained about Japan's behavior during summit meetings with President Bush, his comments were considered perplexing and were poorly received.[45]

SINO–SOUTH KOREAN RELATIONS

Roh Moo-hyun also began his presidency on good terms with China, upgrading China-Korea relations from a "cooperative partnership" to a "comprehensive cooperative partnership" during his visit to Beijing in 2003.[46] Moreover, the bilateral relationship appeared to receive a boost from Roh's strategic focus on the "age of Northeast Asia" (even though Beijing ultimately dismissed the Roh administration's claim that South Korea could serve as the region's "hub").[47] Another helpful factor was the burgeoning trade between the two countries, which grew by more than 20 percent per year to a level of $118 billion by 2006, especially as South Korean conglomerates sought a manufacturing foothold in China and actively incorporated Chinese-based factories that benefited from low Chinese labor costs into their U.S.-centered supply chains.[48] China's new role as host of Six-Party Talks and the idea among the independence faction that South Korean diplomatic independence would be buttressed by a stronger relationship between Seoul and Beijing as a counterweight to excessive dependency on the U.S.-ROK alliance also contributed to the growth in the bilateral relationship. In 2004, 55 percent of South Korea's newly elected National Assembly members regarded China as more important than the United States.[49]

However, a dispute over the nature of Goguryeo, an ancient Korean kingdom that encompassed what is today's North Korea and large portions of Manchuria, put a damper on the development of Sino–South Korean relations. In 2002, the state-sponsored Chinese Academy of Social Sciences began the Northeast Project to investigate and confirm that Northeast China had always been under Chinese control and later to include an UN Education, Scientific, and Cultural Organization application to declare Goguryeo tombs in Northeast China as China's own historical heritage site.[50] In 2003, a Communist Party of China journal, *Guangming Ribao*, claimed that "Koguryo [Goguryeo] was an ancient nation established by a Chinese minority tribe."[51] Making matters worse and causing consternation and outrage in South Korea, the Chinese Ministry of Foreign Affairs deleted Koguryo/Goguryeo from a summary of Korean history on its website in 2004.[52]

The South Korean government and the public perceived Chinese claims over Goguryeo as a direct attack on Korea's sovereignty. After the controversy broke out, the Korean Broadcasting System took an opinion poll, in which 58.2 percent of South Koreans indicated that they did not "like" China. South Korean displeasure toward China became clear in this public-opinion poll by Dong-A Ilbo, in which only 29 percent of respondents considered China a country important to South Korea, a drastic decrease from 61 percent in 2004.[53]

In addition to the intrusion on Korean sovereignty, there was also the concern in South Korea that China might use the narrative to claim and encroach on North Korea if it were to collapse.[54] The Chinese, for their part, expressed concerns that Korea's own Goguryeo narrative could one day be used to claim Chinese territory in northern Manchuria. Nevertheless, Beijing and Seoul worked through the dispute in a relatively low-key manner and reached a verbal agreement in 2004. To prevent the issue from affecting their bilateral relations, China agreed not to assert sovereignty over Goguryeo or to make historical claims and to stop provincial and local governments from doing so.[55] Yet China never explicitly acknowledged Goguryeo as a fully independent Korean state.[56] As a consequence, the controversy continued until 2007, when the Northeast Project officially ended. However, the fact that the Roh administration did not let the Goguryeo issue derail China-ROK relations is notable, especially in comparison to its handling of history disputes with Japan. Moon Chung-in and Li Chun-Fu write that the South Korean Foreign Ministry argued for a low-key approach to dealing with the Goguryeo controversy because of China's role in dealing with the North Korean nuclear issue and because of Beijing's growing importance in Northeast Asia.[57]

There were other thorny issues in China-ROK relations, including the repatriation of North Korean refugees. For example, the Chinese government repatriated seventy North Korea refugees in 2004, eight of whom were stopped as they tried to go over the wall around the South Korean embassy to claim asylum in South Korea.[58] Despite these sensitive issues, however, the ballast from a rapidly growing economic relationship kept Sino–South Korean relations on an even keel.

RUSSO–SOUTH KOREAN RELATIONS

Russia figured into South Korea's vision of peace and prosperity in Northeast Asia primarily in the context of restored transportation and energy connections that would integrate North Korea and better connect South Korea to the wider Eurasian economy. The Roh Moo-hyun administration shared Kim Dae-jung's vision of a reconstituted Trans-Siberian Railroad and potential connection of oil and gas pipelines from the resource-rich Russian Far East to the Korean Peninsula. In addition, Russia remained relevant as a participant in Six-Party Talks and as an actor with ties to North Korea. South Korea's bilateral trade with Russia remained relatively low, at around $10 billion in 2006.[59] Nevertheless, Roh was able to upgrade bilateral ties with Russia to a "comprehensive partnership of mutual trust" during his visit to Moscow in September 2004.[60] Beyond these developments, the South Korea–Russia relationship did not develop any traction as a strategic relationship of significance under Roh.[61]

ROH MOO-HYUN'S FOREIGN POLICY, INTER-KOREAN RELATIONS, AND THE ALLIANCE WITH THE UNITED STATES

With the reemergence of the North Korean nuclear issue, Roh Moo-hyun embraced an ambitious three-pronged approach: (1) no nuclear North Korea, (2) peaceful resolution through dialogue, and (3) South Korea as a central player in the process. This approach faced serious challenges as Roh's ambitious policy goals were blocked by circumstances that South Korea did not control.

North Korea's breakout from the Agreed Framework of 1994 and the decision to conduct its first nuclear test in October 2006 directly challenged Roh Moo-hyun's Peace and Prosperity Policy. The test generated much pressure on the Roh administration from both domestic and international sources to limit or condition inter-Korean economic cooperation on the bringing of North Korea's nuclear program under control. The issue was initially reflected in differences between U.S. and South Korean intelligence assessments regarding the advancement of and intentions behind North Korea's nuclear weapons development—differences that were partially but not fully erased when North Korea conducted its first nuclear test. These differences also spilled over into disputes between the United States and South Korea regarding the scope of inter-Korean economic cooperation that should be allowed to go forward in a context where North Korea's nuclear weapons development was continuously progressing. Moreover, North Korea's insistence that the nuclear issue could be discussed only with the United States directly challenged Roh's efforts to exert a more autonomous and influential diplomatic role for South Korea on the peninsula and within the region.

Because the Roh Moo-hyun administration saw the nuclear issue primarily as a conflict between Washington and Pyongyang and because Roh insisted on resolving the conflict by peaceful means, constraining the United States from pursuing coercive approaches toward North Korea became South Korea's primary objective. First, Roh established a declaratory policy that eschewed coercive measures toward North Korea in line with the objectives of his Peace and Prosperity Policy. Second, the Roh administration pursued issue linkage by seeking greater autonomy over policy toward North Korea in return for a positive response to the U.S. request that Korean forces be dispatched on postconflict stabilization missions in Iraq. Third, South Korea asserted its "centrality" as part of the Six-Party Talks process to avoid charges that such a forum would marginalize its diplomatic influence and role. Fourth, Roh continued to pursue peace and economic cooperation initiatives despite the nuclear issue, as best exemplified by the broad and ambitious scope of the inter-Korean summit declaration on October 4, 2007.

INTER-KOREAN RELATIONS UNDER ROH MOO-HYUN

Although the broad thrust of Roh Moo-hyun's Peace and Prosperity Policy built on the foundations laid by Kim Dae-jung's Sunshine Policy, the two policies differed in practice. In fact, Roh's decision early in his administration to allow a judicial investigation into cash-for-summit allegations surrounding the summit in June 2000 led to the embarrassing indictment of several of Kim's senior aides and elicited a vituperative response from Pyongyang. In addition, the North Koreans initially refused to meet with Roh's chief adviser, Lee Jong-seok, when he accompanied Lim Dong-won on a visit to be introduced as the new South Korean official in charge of South-North relations in early 2003. As a result, there was almost no political continuity at senior levels between South Korean administrations, and North Korean senior officials had to take time to get to know their new counterparts in the Roh administration.

Despite this initial setback, the Roh Moo-hyun administration set about building on the foundation laid by Kim Dae-jung by pursuing the two primary objectives of "enhancing peace on the Korean peninsula" and "co-prosperity of North and South Korea" on the basis of four principles: (1) solving problems through dialogue, (2) prioritizing mutual trust and reciprocity, (3) marshalling international cooperation based on the principle that North Korea and South Korea are the main parties in the peace process, and (4) implementing policies based on the consensus of the people.[62]

However, achieving these objectives remained dependent on progress in North Korea's denuclearization. Here, the Roh administration faced a constant tension between its stated desire to play a leading role in Six-Party Talks and the multilateral negotiation framework initiated by the Bush administration and hosted by the People's Republic of China. On the one hand, South Korea sought a central role in denuclearization talks through its coordination efforts. To achieve this purpose, the Roh administration wanted to moderate the Bush administration's tough stance and to promote negotiations. On the other hand, it acknowledged that the nuclear issue depended primarily on progress in U.S.-DPRK relations, implicitly admitting its own incapacity to play a central role on the issue that served as an essential prerequisite for its efforts to achieve peninsular peace and prosperity. The contradictions inherent in this approach showed themselves from the very inception of the Six-Party Talks, which started with an unprecedented trilateral meeting among China, the United States, and North Korea in Beijing in April 2003. Although Roh Moo-hyun had acquiesced to the talks, South Korea started off outside the talks, where it was clearly not positioned to play a "central role."

Another source of tension between South Korea and the United States had to do with the preferred set of instruments for bringing North Korea to the negotiation table. The Bush administration sought to increase coercive actions; pushed for sanctions and the early implementation of the Illicit Activities Initiative, designed to stop North Korean drug-trafficking, counterfeiting, and money-laundering activities; and achieved unexpected success in paralyzing North Korea's external economic relations by means of a U.S. Treasury advisory targeted at the Banco Delta Asia, a Macao-based bank where North Korea had substantial deposits. The Roh administration was fundamentally opposed to coercive measures. Roh had stated in advance of his inauguration, "I am willing to differ with the United States if that helps prevent war. An attack on North Korea could trigger a war engulfing the entire Korean peninsula."[63] This concern went much beyond the desire to pursue a more autonomous foreign policy in that the Roh administration genuinely feared that U.S.-DPRK tensions might lead to another war on the peninsula. Roh once said, "As a nation that has built the Korea of today from the ashes of yesterday, we simply cannot be asked to relive the traumatic experience."[64]

Although Roh Moo-hyun promised not to pursue major new avenues of inter-Korean economic cooperation in light of the renewed North Korean nuclear crisis, his administration continuously pursued implementation of the first phase of the Kaesong Industrial Complex from June 2003. The two Koreas opened the complex and invited South Korean companies to begin on-commission manufacturing using materials from the South and labor from the North. In addition, there was a steady stream of inter-Korean ministerial talks on various forms of humanitarian aid, economic cooperation, and military talks on measures necessary to reduce tensions in the Yellow Sea. Alongside steady subsidies for South Korean tourists visiting the Mount Kumgang resort in North Korea, the expansion of the Kaesong Industrial Complex during the Roh administration provided a steady flow of cash payments to North Korea and helped to double inter-Korean trade relations from $642 million in 2002 to $1.349 billion in 2006.[65] Moreover, the level of assistance to North Korea for various projects during the Roh administration more than doubled to 16 billion won (approximately $14.3 million), from 8.5 billion won (approximately $7.6

million) spent during the Kim Dae-jung administration. As a result, despite pressure from the Bush administration to limit inter-Korean economic cooperation, inter-Korean trade experienced some of its most rapid growth under Roh. As figures 5.1 and 5.2 show, inter-Korean economic and personnel engagement expanded significantly under his presidency.

In addition, the Roh Moo-hyun administration relied heavily on the idea that North Korea's nuclear program was a bargaining chip for negotiating and extracting economic concessions. As a result, a major unification initiative under the Roh administration featured efforts by the unification minister, Chung Dong-young, to provide alternative energy supplies to North Korea as part of the resolution of the nuclear issue, including a proposal to provide up to 2 million kilowatts of energy to North Korea by connecting the North to South Korea's energy grid.[66] The North Koreans, however, appeared wary of the possibility of becoming dependent on South Korea.

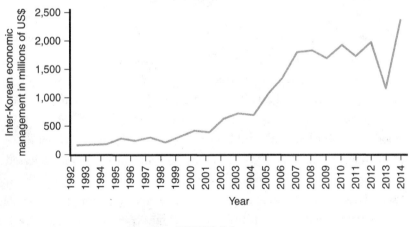

FIGURE 5.1

Inter-Korean Economic Engagement, 1992–2014

Source: Ministry of Unification 통일부, Republic of Korea, "Inter-Korean Trade Cooperation" "남북교류협력," n.d., http://eng.unikorea.go.kr/content.do?cmsid=3103; Korea Statistical Information Service 국가통계, "North Korean Statistics: Total Trade" "북한 통계: 무역총액," n.d., http://kosis.kr/statHtml/statHtml.do?orgId=101&tblId=DT_1ZGA91&vw _cd=MT_BUKHAN&list_id=101_101BUKHANB01_AA15&seqNo=&lang _mode=ko&language=kor&obj_var_id=&itm_id=&conn_path=E1#.

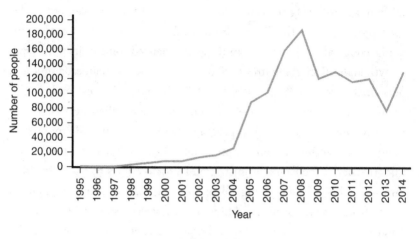

FIGURE 5.2

Inter-Korean Personnel Flows and Exchanges, 1995–2014

Source: Ministry of Unification 통일부, Republic of Korea, "Inter-Korean Exchanges of People and Goods" "남북 인적 물적 왕래," n.d., http://eng.unikorea.go.kr /content.do?cmsid=3103.

Despite the overhanging North Korean nuclear issue, the Roh administration made periodic efforts to achieve a second inter-Korean summit. It was only after the Six-Party Talks had established a new modus operandi for addressing North Korea's denuclearization following its nuclear test in 2006 that Roh Moo-hyun could pursue a summit meeting with Kim Jong-il on October 3–4, 2007. The second inter-Korean joint declaration released on October 4, 2007, in conjunction with progress in the Six-Party Talks, comprised an ambitious laundry list of inter-Korean economic projects and attempted to lay the groundwork for further tension-reduction measures in the Yellow Sea.

Nevertheless, the summit suffered from a number of shortcomings. First, it occurred in the waning days of the Roh administration, a time when the Korean public's attention had already turned to the next presidential election. As a result, some observers felt that it was held in part to mobilize support for another progressive presidential candidate. Second, the summit outlined extensive inter-Korean economic-cooperation projects but without consideration of or negotiations on the budget necessary to carry them out. In this respect, the road map generated unrealistic expectations regarding the price and likely benefits of cooperation. Third, the potential impact of the summit was eclipsed by the fact that the presidential election of December 2007 brought to power a conservative president, Lee Myung-bak, whose own campaign plan for inter-Korean relations—the Denuclearization and Opening 3000 plan—insisted on more direct reciprocity: North Korea must denuclearize in return for an ambitious pledge to raise North Koreans' per capita annual income to $3,000.

U.S.-ROK RELATIONS IN THE ROH–BUSH ERA: BRIDGING DIFFERENCES

The Roh Moo-hyun administration came into office seeking to redefine the alliance with the United States on a more horizontal basis in an effort both to reduce South Korea's dependency on the United States and to gain greater respect from Washington and greater autonomy over Korean af- fairs. The specific differences arose over how to respond to North Korea's nuclear development, institutional arrangements governing the U.S.-ROK security relationship on issues such as operational control and troop readjustments, the U.S. interest in "strategic flexibility," and debates over North Korean human rights.

First, the Roh Moo-hyun administration recognized the necessity of bringing the North Korean nuclear issue under control, but there remained a visible gap between its focus on "peace and prosperity" and the Bush ad- ministration's focus on denuclearization. The Roh administration in fact exhibited two minds on the North Korea issue. Roh clearly opposed North Korea's pursuit of nuclear weapons, but many of his advisers from the inde- pendence faction saw U.S. hostile policies as the root cause of the conflict on the Korean Peninsula and viewed North Korea's use of the nuclear issue as a bargaining chip. In this respect, this faction's view converged with North Korea's view that South Korea needed to pursue autonomy from the alliance with the United States. The alliance faction, however, pushed for South Korea to seek greater influence within the alliance, desiring to strengthen its influence in forging policies toward North Korea, both to temper the Bush administration's hard-line policies and to channel U.S. support for South Korean leadership. In any case, both approaches conflicted with the Bush administration's North Korea policy.

As a result, there were constant tensions between Roh administration and Bush administration policies, despite continuing efforts by both governments to manage their differences through regular consultation. At times, Roh himself appeared to discount the level of North Korea's nuclear weapons potential and capabilities and publicly stated his disagreement with the United States regarding this issue on several occasions.[67] Based on these disagreements, an early Council on Foreign Relations assessment of U.S.-ROK ties reported that the Bush administration regarded the Roh administration's policies toward North Korea as "naïve and injurious to the alliance."[68]

Ironically, North Korea's first nuclear test in October 2006 had the effect of bringing the Bush administration to more active pursuit of dialogue with North Korea, a development that also brought the United States and South Korea back into closer alignment. The test catalyzed greater leadership from the United States but potentially at the expense of South Korea's efforts to play a more central role. The test also created an environment in which the Roh administration had little choice but to cooperate more closely on implementation of sanctions on North Korea. In addition, it generated greater public criticism within South Korea of the Roh administration's policy toward the North, hardened South Koreans' attitudes regarding North Korea's intentions, and reduced South Koreans' support for assistance to North Korea. With the rapid return to the Six-Party Talks, the main challenge for the Roh administration was to show that it still had a central role to play in the talks, which ultimately were dependent on bilateral understandings between the United States and North Korea.

During this period, the Bush and Roh administrations worked relatively well with each other, fashioning pragmatic understandings in an attempt to draw North Korea into a process that might lead to the freeze and abandonment of North Korea's nuclear program. However, as the denuclearization process moved forward, Roh also sought to win the United States over to exploration of a prospective peace regime, which the Bush administration regarded as premature in the absence of a more developed effort to draw North Korea into a verified regime involving the monitoring of its nuclear facilities.

Second, the Bush and Roh administrations had to manage tensions resulting from military issues in the U.S.-ROK alliance, including the U.S. request for the deployment of South Korean troops to Iraq, negotiations over revised command-and-control arrangements, as well as plans for a reconfigured U.S. troop presence on the Korean Peninsula. The conflict in Iraq in particular generated two distinct challenges that had ramifications for alliance management.

The first challenge had to do with the U.S. decision in 2003 to deploy a U.S. Army mechanized brigade of the Second Infantry Division from the Korean Peninsula to Iraq to pacify the country following the U.S. invasion. This request coincided with anti-American protests in Korea in the run-up to the election of Roh Moo-hyun and was the first reduction in U.S. troops on the Korean Peninsula in decades. The U.S. troop withdrawal came on the heels of candlelight demonstrations and growing South Korean perceptions that U.S. unilateralism and hard-line policies toward North Korea might entrap South Korea in an unwanted conflict with the North. At the same time, it raised questions about the durability of the American security commitment to South Korea and possible abandonment.

Furthermore, the United States requested South Korean security assistance in Iraq as part of a multinational UN-sponsored effort to stabilize Iraq following the U.S. invasion. This request became a major issue in South Korea as Roh Moo-hyun himself opted to meet the U.S. demand despite street demonstrations by his core constituents, who saw his decision as kowtowing to the United States. In 2002, only about 15 percent of South Koreans considered terrorism to be a priority issue, and 72 percent opposed Bush's war on terror; 81 percent opposed the U.S. invasion of Iraq, and only 10 percent supported it; 76 percent opposed sending South Korean troops in support of the war, and only 16 percent supported it. A striking 88 percent of South Korean college students believed that the war against Iraq was without any justification, in contrast to the mere 5 percent who believed the United States had a justification.[69] To justify his decision and to garner support to authorize the deployment, Roh told his party leaders, who are immensely powerful in Korean politics, "I made the decision for the national interest because we may get a bigger say in dealing with the United States by sending noncombat troops."[70] Despite his campaign rhetoric, Roh went to great lengths to maintain and support the alliance despite the risks of losing public support and becoming entangled in a conflict not directly tied to Korean interests. To pass the bill to authorize sending troops, Roh's Yeollin Uri Party took the unusual step of freeing its members to vote their conscience and relied on support from the opposition Grand National Party. The South Korean National Assembly ended up passing the Roh administration's request to send troops despite public protests.

South Korea dispatched the third-largest contingent of troops to Iraq (the largest and second largest being from the United States and the United Kingdom, respectively), approximately 3,600 soldiers, even after a Korean hostage was beheaded in the country.[71] Nevertheless, the view among American observers that Seoul only very reluctantly sent troops and the extended domestic debate over the dispatch detracted from South Korea's agreement to honor its American ally's request.[72] A further source of conflict between the United States and South Korea arose as the Roh administration sought a quid pro quo from the United States in the form of a more moderate Bush policy toward North Korea as part of bargaining over the dispatch of South Korean troops to Iraq.

Even as South Korea agreed to send its soldiers to Iraq, the Roh and Bush administrations held a series of security dialogues, the Future of the Alliance and the Security Policy Initiative, which were designed to hash out a long-term strategy for managing revised command-and-control arrangements and a consolidated troop presence for USFK.[73] Coming on the heels of South Korean demonstrations against USFK, the redeployment of a mechanized army brigade from the Korean Peninsula to Iraq, and a broader U.S. strategy that emphasized flexible deployments against a diverse range of threats rather than a permanent deployment of U.S. forces along the DMZ dedicated solely to deterring the North Korean threat, the revised arrangements were perceived as the first step toward reduced U.S. commitment and perhaps eventual withdrawal of U.S. forces from the Korean Peninsula. When Roh raised the topic of revised operational control arrangements, U.S. secretary of defense Donald Rumsfeld reportedly told him that he was "pushing an open door."[74] However, the results of the talks also met both countries' multiple mutual needs. The United States sought a more flexible and multifaceted strategy and a consolidated presence on the peninsula that would reduce potential conflicts at the local level and would be less obtrusive to the Korean citizenry.[75] South Korea sought greater autonomy in, responsibility for, and a leading role in its own defense, but it also continued to seek support from the United States in areas where it still depended on U.S. capabilities as part of its defense. The Roh administration showed a special interest in recovering a perceived loss of sovereignty by seeking to assert full operational control over its own forces. The United States could support this aim, especially if it meant greater Korean investment in critical self-defense capabilities that had previously been inadequate or excessively dependent on capabilities provided by the United States. The result of the negotiations was that the United States would consolidate its presence around an expanded Camp Humphreys in the Osan-Pyongtaek area and provide a supporting role to the South Korean lead in providing for South Korea's defense once South Korea acquired the capabilities to lead. The original target date for establishing the new operational control arrangements was October 2012, with the completion of the move to Camp Humphreys by 2015.

Third, the United States and South Korea established a new high-level strategic consultation between their foreign ministries designed to discuss shared threat perceptions and work out coordinated policy responses. In this context, one U.S. security objective was to secure South Korea's understanding regarding "strategic flexibility," which stemmed from the Bush administration's Global Posture Review of 2004 to allow the U.S. forces in South Korea to be deployed off peninsula in the event of a regional crisis.[76] South Koreans worried about being entrapped in a conflict caused by an overaggressive United States, particularly after the invasion of Iraq in 2003. The Roh administration worried most that South Korea might become involved in a hypothetical cross-strait conflict between the United States and China over the issue of Taiwan. In the end, Seoul and Washington agreed in a joint statement issued in January 2006 that "the ROK, as an ally, fully understands the rationale for the transformation of the U.S. global military strategy, and respects the necessity for strategic flexibility of the U.S. forces in the ROK. In the implementation of strategic flexibility, the U.S. respects the ROK position that it shall not be involved in a regional conflict in Northeast

Asia against the will of the Korean people."[77] Roh also stated that Seoul would reserve the right to veto any deployment of U.S. forces based in South Korea in the case of any contingencies outside of the Korean Peninsula.[78]

Fourth, the issue of North Korean human rights became an area of tension between the United States and South Korea following the passage of the North Korean Human Rights Act in the U.S. Congress and the Bush administration's appointment of a special envoy for human rights. The Roh administration had been cautious in its handling of North Korean human rights issues in the UN Human Rights Council, generally preferring to abstain rather than go on the record as opposing North Korea's practices. Roh Moo-hyun did so intentionally to keep inter-Korean dialogue on track and perhaps to hold a summit with Kim Jong-il.[79] This approach, however, was contrary to the instincts of George W. Bush, who was personally offended by the failure of the North Korean leadership to respect basic standards of human rights and governance. In contrast to the Roh administration's seeming allergy toward the North Korean human rights issue, Bush welcomed North Korean refugees at the White House and allowed the newly appointed UN human rights representative to speak out against North Korea's practices.

Despite disagreements with the Bush administration in many areas, the Roh and Bush administrations were able to point to a number of practical accomplishments. And despite Roh's relative inexperience and his desire to play to the progressive 386 generation that helped elect him, he took several actions that helped strengthen and broaden the U.S.-ROK relationship and move it toward an equal partnership.

MELDING AUTONOMY AND ALLIANCE: ROH MOO-HYUN'S COOPERATIVE SELF-RELIANT DEFENSE

The Roh Moo-hyun administration sought to remake Korean foreign policy based on principles of autonomy and multilateral cooperation. Its efforts were notable in several respects.

First, the administration attempted to maximize its autonomy and responsibility for South Korea's security within the context of the U.S.-ROK alliance. The desire for autonomy challenged the traditional structures of the long-standing U.S.-ROK patron–client relationship and laid the foundation for revising forms of institutional cooperation to define the relationship on a more egalitarian basis than had previously existed. This approach resulted in visible tensions between the United States and South Korea over how to best manage policy toward North Korea, but it was also accompanied by a robust bureaucratic consultation process that, despite facing choppy waters and clear differences in ideological orientation between the two leaders, performed admirably and maintained cooperation.

Second, domestic politics played a major role in shaping South Korea's foreign-policy orientation. Most notably, the internal struggle between pro-alliance and pro-independence factions created new challenges for U.S.-ROK alliance managers. The independence faction toyed for the first time with the idea of a more independent Korean orientation from the United States, although the Roh administration ultimately decided to embrace the U.S.-ROK alliance while fighting for greater independence within the context of the alliance rather than pursuing diplomatic strategies independent of the alliance.

Third, the United States recognized South Korea's increasing capacity and made efforts to show respect for South Korea's political and social progress, despite the fact that the emotional manifestations of frustration toward the United States were initially confusing and off-putting. American flexibility had two sides to it. On the one hand, the United States responded to South Korea's push for autonomy by working with South Korea. On the other hand, there were clear differences in ideological and policy inclination, especially on how to deal with North Korea. The respective U.S. and South Korean responses to North Korea's first nuclear test eventually pushed the two countries toward closer cooperation with each other. In the end, given the magnitude of the North Korean nuclear challenge, the two countries and their leaders had no choice but to work together closely while reserving their differences.

Fourth, South Korea articulated a more autonomous foreign policy, but ultimately its interests as an outward-oriented, trade-dependent economy meant that there remained a broad convergence of South Korean and U.S. interests. Although Roh Moo-hyun resisted acknowledging the depth of South Korea's structural ties to the United States because of his own ideological and domestic political inclinations, U.S. and South Korean interests remained so closely tied with each other that South Korea could pursue autonomy only within the context of the U.S.-ROK alliance; a true independence option was not politically or practically feasible.

Finally, despite Roh Moo-hyun's desire to forge a Korean peace regime and a multilateral regional peace regime, it was not possible to make significant progress due to the obstacles posed by the North Korean nuclear program. However, South Korea's support for the Six-Party Talks—and the vision of a Northeast Asia peace and security mechanism as a potential lasting outcome of these talks—showed South Korea's interest in complementing the bilateral U.S.-ROK alliance with a regional cooperative security mechanism to moderate conflict and promote greater institutional cooperation.

6

LEE MYUNG-BAK'S GLOBAL KOREA POLICY

L EE MYUNG-BAK'S presidency beginning in 2008 marked a dramatic shift in the rhetoric, priorities, and thinking behind South Korea's foreign policy, even as it built on the country's growing capabilities and confidence in its ability to influence foreign affairs, which had become apparent under Roh Moo-hyun and Kim Dae-jung. Lee's landslide victory in the presidential contest marked a return to conservative leadership following ten years of progressive rule. Shortly after his election, Lee described South Korean efforts to court North Korea under his predecessors as a "lost decade" and pledged to restore the loss of trust in the U.S.–South Korea alliance that the conservatives perceived as having languished because of excessively high expectations for and misplaced emphasis on expanded inter-Korean cooperation.[1] Lee also promoted South Korea's international profile and leadership by hosting a variety of gatherings among international leaders and promoting his Global Korea policy, which magnified South Korea's international profile to a greater degree than accomplished by any prior administration.

Lee Myung-bak's North Korea policy, Denuclearization and Opening 3000, was considered a "thorough and flexible approach" because it promised to provide comprehensive economic support to raise North Korean per capita GDP to $3,000 per year in exchange for the North's denuclearization and integration with the international community.[2] Roh Moo-hyun's liberal approach had provided greater economic benefits with less conditionality, although the ultimate objective was the same, denuclearization. However, Lee's approach imposed limits on economic exchanges in the absence of denuclearization. As long as North Korea maintained its commitment to nuclear development and pursued conventional provocations, Lee's conditional policy removed long-standing tensions with the Bush administration in U.S.-ROK relations over the degree of acceptable economic engagement with a nuclearizing North Korea, but it also resulted in a gradual deterioration of both the economic and political dimensions of the inter-Korean relationship.

In dealing with the United States, Lee Myung-bak set out to reverse perceived mistrust and mutual recriminations between Washington and Seoul that had existed under Roh Moo-hyun. Lee fully embraced the U.S. objective of North Korea's denuclearization and expanded consultations with Washington on a wide range of issues, while broadening the scope of the alliance to include regional and global security issues. Lee's perception that a close relationship with the United States was invaluable to raising South Korea's international profile and contributions to the international community enabled a dramatic transformation in the alliance. The bilateral relationship moved from a condition of uncertainty to a state in which the United States came to consider South Korea a "lynchpin" in regional security and a reliable contributor to regional and global security.[3] Lee led the establishment of the Joint Vision Statement of 2009, which described an alliance that not only provided for South Korea's security but also enumerated regional and global security activities beyond the Korean Peninsula for the first time. For Lee, a strong U.S.-ROK alliance served as the platform enabling greater autonomy for South Korea but in directions that highlighted and leveraged common interests with the United States. Lee desired to apply South Korea's expanded capabilities in tandem with shared U.S.-ROK objectives in a fashion that reinforced and expanded the scope of the bilateral partnership.

LEE MYUNG-BAK'S GLOBAL KOREA POLICY

The distinctive element of Lee Myung-bak's policy compared with his predecessors' policies was its embrace of the notion of "Global Korea."

Global Korea built on Kim Young-sam's emphasis on "globalization" in the 1990s by emphasizing South Korea's potential to contribute to global leadership. As Lee declared at the UN General Assembly in September 2009, "We are striving to become a 'Global Korea' harmonizing our interests with others and making our well-being also contribute to the prosperity of humanity."[4] This approach to foreign policy recognized that South Korea's success as a market economy and a democracy had given the country not only global reach but also responsibilities to play a leadership role on the international stage. Lee personally embraced this narrative by acknowledging the help South Korea had received from the international community during and after the Korean War and by espousing its duty to give back to the international community as part of "contributing diplomacy" and appreciation for the country's achievements.[5] Lee's view on foreign affairs reflected his experience as a businessman in emphasizing "creative pragmatism," networking with international leaders, and forging cooperation based on mutual interests and common values for success.[6]

Lee's national security strategy identified his administration's main interests and security challenges as synonymous with efforts by the global community to "forge and disseminate a consensus on freedom and democracy, humanitarian values, and market economy."[7] Thus, South Korea highlighted its interests in upholding the existing liberal international order by declaring the shared need to respond to diversified functional challenges to international order, such as nuclear proliferation, environmental threats, "extreme nationalism," and economic problems, among other issues. In grappling with these complex global challenges, the Lee administration identified itself as a responsible and leading member of the liberal international order.[8]

On this basis, Lee Myung-bak's national security strategy stated that Global Korea is "a Republic of Korea that not only cooperates actively, but also offers solutions for dealing with common issues facing the world community." South Korea would be a "state that combines the strengths of an advanced welfare economy and self-reliant defense capability with significant educational, cultural, and artistic potential, and is accordingly needed and respected by the international community."[9] The national security strategy identified national security objectives in four broad categories: (1) pursuit of mutual benefits and common prosperity in inter-Korean relations; (2) cooperative network diplomacy, including strengthening the U.S.-ROK alliance along with commitments to regional and global cooperation; (3) comprehensive result-oriented foreign policy, including energy diplomacy, expanded FTA networks, and heightened Korean contributions to international public goods; and (4) defense modernization through future-oriented and advanced security commitments.[10] These objectives built on traditional priorities in South Korea's foreign policy, such as relations with North Korea and the alliance with the United States, but they also envisioned South Korea as a capable actor with interests that extended to a wide range of global issues.

Distinctive characteristics of South Korea's foreign policy under Lee Myung-bak include the following elements. First, to the extent possible, the Lee administration refused to treat North Korea as a special or exceptional priority. This meant a dramatic reduction in unconditional humanitarian assistance and treatment of the country as a normal state rather than prioritizing inter-Korean relations as an all-consuming focus and interest.[11] Lee believed that the nuclear issue could be resolved only by North Korea rejoining the world as a nonnuclear state and normalizing relations with the United States. The Lee administration also desired to provide long-term economic aid for improving North Korea's living standards and economic structure, but only after denuclearization.[12] Following the killing of a South Korean tourist at Mount Kumgang, the North Korean mountain resort, in 2008, North Korea's missile and nuclear tests in 2009, and further provocations in 2010, the Lee administration's approach also included demands for a joint investigation and assurances of civilian safety as preconditions for resuming the Mount Kumgang tourism project, support for tougher UN sanctions against North Korea, and pursuit of unilateral economic sanctions in response to the conclusion of an international investigation led by the South Korean Ministry of National Defense that a North Korean torpedo sank the ROK warship *Cheonan* in an unprovoked attack in 2010. All of these steps required North Korea to accept accountability for its actions rather than defining itself as exceptional or not bound by international norms of behavior. By the end of Lee's presidency, the Kaesong Industrial Complex became the sole surviving venue for inter-Korean economic cooperation.

Second, Lee Myung-bak's refusal to treat North Korea as a special priority meant that South Korea's global interests and diplomacy with the rest of the world seemed to eclipse inter-Korean relations and unification as a priority of South Korean foreign policy. Despite the continuation of the inter-Korean standoff, South Korea took on global security obligations for the first time. (This shift to encompass off-peninsula objectives may also provide a glimpse, however limited, of how South Korea might approach foreign policy after unification.) However, this shift was vexing for North Korea because it had become used to having disproportionate influence and attention as a top South Korean policy priority[13] and because it meant fewer tangible benefits from South Korea. It also reflected an inevitable adjustment stemming from the South Korean public's frustration over past governments' failure to gain leverage with North Korea so that it would reciprocate South Korea's financial contributions and political efforts by curbing the most dangerous aspects of its behavior.

Third, Lee Myung-bak's emphasis on reenergizing the U.S.-ROK alliance based on enhanced trust, shared values, and commitment to preserving peace stabilized and deepened the framework for U.S.-ROK cooperation and elevated the value that the United States placed on South Korea as an ally. Lee sought to improve and strengthen the alliance with the United States "based on the historical trust built upon the two countries."[14] He actively coordinated with the United States in response to the global financial crisis in 2008–2009, volunteered to host the Nuclear Security Summit in March 2012, and actively sought to play a constructive role on global issues such as climate change, energy security, international peacekeeping, and postconflict stabilization in Afghanistan. The U.S.-ROK Joint Vision Statement in 2009 followed a similar statement between Lee and Bush in 2008 and built on the foundations of dialogue between the two militaries under the Roh and Bush administrations to articulate more clearly the vision and purposes of the alliance.[15] The Joint Vision Statement reaffirmed a common focus on the denuclearization of North Korea as a primary objective, broadened the scope of the alliance cooperation beyond the peninsula and extended it to address a wide range of nontraditional security issues, reiterated U.S. extended deterrence commitments to

South Korea, and reaffirmed the two countries' political commitment to joint actions to deter North Korean provocations.[16]

Fourth, Lee Myung-bak saw South Korea's leadership as a responsibility derived from its having been a recipient of past international development assistance at a time when it was weak and defined its international contributions as a way to give back. He described South Korea's bid for greater global responsibility in his observation that "the World can be split into two groups: One group sets global rules, the other follows. South Korea has successfully transformed itself from a passive follower into an active agenda-setter."[17] South Korea pledged to enhance its contributions to international development both by growing its program and by hosting the OECD Development Assistance Committee in Busan in 2011. In his opening speech at the Busan committee meeting, Lee proclaimed: "Our citizens and I believe it is time that the Republic of Korea 'moves forward with the world.' ROK wants to be a partner that shares our experiences of success and failure with developing countries."[18] In addition, Lee's efforts to support "green growth" as an adaptive approach to climate change, putting reduction of carbon emissions at the center of a business-oriented approach, built on his personal experience. This initiative led to the establishment of the Global Green Growth Institute as an international organization and enabled South Korea to become the host of the UN Green Climate Fund.[19]

GLOBAL FINANCIAL CRISIS, FTAS, AND ENERGY DIPLOMACY

The major successes of the Lee Myung-bak administration's Global Korea policy came through promotion of "cooperative network diplomacy" in two functional areas: (1) economic diplomacy, including contributions to G20 leadership in dealing with the global financial crisis as well as the ratification of the South Korea–European Union and South Korea–U.S. FTAs, and (2) energy diplomacy, including international recognition for Lee's promotion of green-growth policies and South Korea's successful bid to build four South Korean–designed nuclear power plants in the United Arab Emirates (UAE).[20] Both the FTA strategy and nuclear diplomacy involved deft negotiations based on efforts to leverage South Korea's relations with the United States to obtain FTA terms in Europe and with the UAE to enhance South Korea's bargaining power in entering the nuclear plant export sector. In addition, South Korea was able to use its international economic profile and capabilities to negotiate and open new markets for Korean goods. In these respects, South Korea's FTA and energy diplomacy represents its ability to achieve progress in issue areas that would not have been possible even a decade earlier. Lee announced in a radio speech in 2012 that South Korea is "the world's 4th largest energy-importing country and the 10th largest energy consuming country. . . . The government will aim to reach 35% of energy self-sufficiency by 2020 for our nation's stable energy security."[21]

Lee Myung-bak actively sought to promote South Korea's experience and leadership as part of a response to the global financial crisis. Early in the crisis, Lee urged a standstill on trade protectionism and stood against competitive currency devaluations, which, he argued, could result in a trade war. He offered lessons from Korea's financial crisis in the late 1990s as a constructive guide to global recovery. In an article he wrote for the *Wall Street Journal* in March 2009, he offered recommendations for how to deal expeditiously with bad debts and recapitalize financial institutions, how to minimize moral hazards and share burdens among financial stakeholders, and how to establish a clear exit strategy and active participation from the private sector.[22] In a follow-up *Financial Times* piece jointly authored with Australia's prime minister Kevin Rudd, he recommended the importance of implementing financial reforms and modernizing international financial institutions as steps toward stabilization of the global economy.[23] As the first non-G8 host of a G20 leaders meeting in November 2010, South Korea managed an agenda that promoted international financial institution reform, attempted to bridge gaps between the United States and China on currency "rebalancing," and added development to the G20 agenda in an effort to play an active bridging role between developing and developed countries.[24]

Regarding South Korea's FTA strategy, which had been initiated under Roh Moo-hyun, Lee said in his seventy-sixth speech on the radio in 2011, "Lacking resources and market for domestic demand, we cannot maintain our growth without FTAs. We are currently the only country in the world that concluded FTAs with the U.S., 27 nations of the EU, and all 10 ASEAN countries. This means that 61% of the whole world has become our economic domain."[25] In 2004, South Korea negotiated its first FTA with Chile, opening the door to a trade-liberalization strategy that allowed South Korea to take full advantage of its strengths in exports and the relative trade dependency of its economy. Given the small size of the country's domestic economy and the aspirations and comparative advantages of its largest companies, trade liberalization made a great deal of sense for South Korea. It enabled continuation of export-led growth, albeit on the narrowing foundations of a conglomerate base that enhanced competitiveness by taking advantage of globalizing supply chains and by moving hiring out of Korea to other countries with more competitive labor and manufacturing costs. The benefits for South Korea's burgeoning exports and trade over the past decade are clear, but perhaps at a cost to its domestic economy, which has failed to replace manufacturing jobs with high-value-added jobs in the service sector. However, export growth kept its economy afloat, so that it narrowly avoided recession even at the height of the global economic crisis in 2008–2009.

Lee Myung-bak's energy diplomacy proved to be equally successful in the area of leadership on behalf of green growth. Lee articulated a philosophy that put carbon-emissions mitigation at the heart of a business strategy, incentivizing countries to adapt in the search for more efficient growth. To promote such strategies and offer consulting services to governments seeking climate-change solutions, the Lee administration established the Global Green Growth Institute, which has since become an international organization and leader in the field of climate adaptation.[26] Likewise, Lee's emphasis on reducing carbon emissions enabled Seoul to attract and host the UN Green Climate Fund, which is set to become a major international lender for global business projects that seek to reduce carbon emissions. These thought contributions capitalized on South Korean strengths in business and innovation; however, Lee's policies were less successful in mobilizing South Korea to adapt renewable-energy sources as part of its energy mix.

Closely related to green growth as a strategy for reducing carbon emissions is the adoption of nuclear power. Over decades, South Korea has gained experience with nuclear power by successfully mastering the domestic construction and management of nuclear plants. The securing of South Korea's first overseas contract in the UAE was initially celebrated in South Korea as a major achievement, and the construction of the plants has thus far gone smoothly, raising the prospect that successful construction will yield more contracts in other parts of the world.[27] However, the drop in global oil prices, the dramatic rise in shale oil and gas production, and the fallout from the Fukushima disaster in 2011 has slowed the global growth of the nuclear sector, limiting the advantage South Korea has been able to gain from this effort.

REVIVAL AND FORGING OF JOINT VISION FOR THE U.S.-ROK ALLIANCE

Lee Myung-bak's emphasis on revitalization of the U.S.-ROK alliance and embrace of a partnership arrangement through the forging of a global and regional vision for the alliance no doubt expanded and restored the strength of that relationship. However, despite this success, the tension between South Korea's desire for autonomy and its need for the alliance persisted and manifested itself in new ways.

One effect of North Korea's provocations in 2010 and heightened inter-Korean tensions was the decision to delay transfer of wartime operational control negotiated under Lee Myung-bak's predecessor, Roh Moo-hyun, from December 2012 to 2015. Seoul had already signaled a possible postponement of the transfer in early 2010 even before the *Cheonan* and the Yeonpyeong Island incidents.[28] Under Lee's successor, Park Geun-hye, the deadline was pushed back indefinitely. Grand National Party and Democratic Party members were "nearly unanimous" in deciding that the planned transition of wartime operational control to the ROK should be delayed because they felt "uneasy" about the transfer given continued provocations from North Korea.[29] The Korean public also believed that the transfer would mean decreased U.S. commitment to South Korea's defense, calling for the government to "calm public concerns."[30] The delay in transfer may have been an understandable effect of an expanding North Korean nuclear weapons capacity, but it has also slowed South Korean acquisition of capabilities necessary to independently exercise operational control because of continued dependence on the United States.

However, another lesson of the North Korean provocations in 2010 revolved around South Korea's decision to review its doctrines related to defense against North Korean aggression. A South Korean civilian panel recommended in December 2011 that South Korea pursue a doctrine of proactive deterrence in which it would pledge to undertake stronger responses and even potentially take preemptive action in response to an imminent North Korean military threat. USFK officials worried that such a doctrine might enhance the potential for miscalculation or accidental escalation of tensions on both sides. As a result, USFK and South Korea's Ministry of National Defense negotiated a counterprovocation plan in 2012 designed to clarify levels of decision making and scope of retaliation at each rung of the conflict-escalation ladder.[31] These issues suggest potential for tensions between autonomy and alliance at an operational level, especially if the U.S. and South Korean governments were to begin to diverge over aims of military action: to uphold deterrence and reinforce the status quo or to induce action-forcing events with the objective of ultimately reunifying the Korean Peninsula.

REGIONAL RELATIONS UNDER LEE MYUNG-BAK

Unlike Roh Moo-hyun and Kim Dae-jung, Lee Myung-bak did not have a flagship policy focused on Northeast Asia or East Asia. However, his administration was able to claim some important accomplishments with regard to trilateral cooperation among China, Japan, and South Korea by holding the first stand-alone trilateral summit meeting in 2008. Although trilateral summit meetings had previously been held in conjunction with the ASEAN Plus Three meetings, the independent trilateral summit marked an advance for regional cooperation in Northeast Asia.[32] Building on the regularization of annual summits, the three countries established the Trilateral Cooperation Secretariat in 2010 with an office in Seoul. Staffed by officials from the three countries with a rotating chairmanship, the secretariat coordinates a wide range of functional cooperation on energy and the environment and promotes enhanced cooperation and people-to-people ties.[33] Moreover, Lee Myung-bak sought to go beyond South Korea's traditional focus on Northeast Asia and expand its multilateral diplomacy globally. In line with the idea of Global Korea, the Lee administration included Central Asia, Southeast Asia, and Oceania in his New Asia Initiative.[34] One of the initiative's goals was for South Korea to sign FTAs with every state in East Asia in order to turn Seoul into a regional trade hub.[35]

SOUTH KOREA–JAPAN RELATIONS

Lee Myung-bak's national security strategy toward Japan called for a "principled and consistent approach to the history issue" while acknowledging that the relationship "rests on a common strategic consensus that recognizes the need to cooperate in dealing with North Korea and to serve stability and progress in Northeast Asia."[36] He also initially pronounced: "South Korea and Japan should build a future-oriented relationship with a pragmatic attitude. . . . [W]e cannot give up on future relations, bound by the past forever."[37] Although the relationship between Seoul and Tokyo at this time seemed to start on a rather optimistic note, it took a nosedive at the end of Lee's presidential term as various conflicts arose.

In the early part of Lee's term, Japanese politics was in flux, with the Democratic Party of Japan taking political leadership for the first time in 2009 following a shocking defeat of the Liberal Democratic Party.[38] Prime Minister Hatoyama Yukio, the Democratic Party's candidate, sought to improve Japan's relations with Asia, but his policies generated strains with the United States, especially when he attempted to renegotiate the Futenma base-relocation issue.[39] U.S.-Japan relations, however, would nonetheless remain tight as Japan's relations with China deteriorated rapidly over the Senkaku/Diaoyu dispute. After less than a year in office, Hatoyama resigned in 2010 and was replaced by Kan Naoto, who made some conciliatory gestures toward South Korea, including a comprehensive statement of regret for the colonization of Korea on the one hundredth anniversary of Japan's annexation of the Korean Peninsula.[40] The relationship remained cordial but cool.

On the eve of his trip to Seoul for a Japan-ROK summit meeting in 2011, Japanese prime minister Noda Yoshihiko explained Japan's unchanging position that "the issue of the comfort women was legally resolved in 1965" and that he would not bring it up during the meeting because "it has already been settled."[41] Then in August 2011 a Korean Constitutional Court ruling judged that South Korea had not been sufficiently diligent in seeking compensation on behalf of the "comfort women," Korean sex slaves who were forced to service Japanese imperial soldiers during World War II.[42] As a result, this issue displaced other issues, including the establishment of a bilateral information-sharing agreement, as the main subject of discussion between Lee Myung-bak and Noda in December of 2011.[43] Lee strongly urged Japan to resolve long-running grievances over this issue, calling it a "stumbling block" in relations between the two countries,[44] and this "tense" summit talk was widely regarded as a disaster.

In May 2012, following South Korea's National Assembly elections, the two governments tried to enact the General Security of Military Information Agreement.[45] The agreement, which South Korea has with twenty-four other countries, including Russia, was directed primarily at North Korea and would have given South Korea access to Japanese satellite intelligence in return for South Korea's human intelligence.[46] Yet the South Korean public's resistance to the agreement was considerable, and some South Korean civic groups and politicians argued that it was a way for Japan and the United States to push South Korea into a coalition against a rising China.[47] In the end, with only months left before the end of his term, Lee canceled the agreement, sacking one of his senior advisers in the process.[48]

Then, in August 2012, Lee made an ill-advised personal visit to Dokdo/ Takeshima, a group of small islets that are being disputed between Japan and South Korea.[49] This visit was greeted negatively in Japan, with Prime Minister Noda responding, "The visit is incompatible with Japan's position and therefore unacceptable," also adding that the islands belong to Japan "historically and by international law."[50] The visit also raised the Japanese public's consciousness regarding the dispute. After Lee's visit, the Japanese government filed a complaint with the International Court of Justice and sent Noda's letter of protest to South Korea.[51] Lee responded firmly by stating that Japan's complaint was "not worth any attention" and returned the letter to the Japanese government.[52]

CHINA–SOUTH KOREA RELATIONS

The China-ROK relationship advanced to the level of a "strategic cooperative partnership" under Lee Myung-bak. This level of partnership signified close consultations and negotiations for matters on the Korean Peninsula and was supposed to support a strategic communication system between the two countries.[53] The bilateral relationship, however, ended up deteriorating during the Lee presidency for a number of reasons.

First, differences over the status of the U.S.-Korea alliance remained between China and South Korea. On the day of Lee Myung-bak's visit to Beijing in May 2008, a Chinese Foreign Ministry spokesman, Qin Gang, said, "The Korean-U.S. alliance is a historical relic. The times have changed and Northeast Asian countries are going through many changes and transformations. We should not approach current security issues with military alliances left over from the past Cold War era."[54] He was clearly referring to the shifting balance of power in East Asia. The South Koreans were understandably apprehensive with regard to the Chinese position, given Lee's desire to maintain good relations with both China and the United States.[55]

Second, despite the attempts by both Beijing and Seoul to develop their relations, they could not agree on how to deal with North Korea. When North Korea sank the South Korean warship *Cheonan* in 2010, Beijing refused to partake in an international investigation of the sinking, claimed that the international report was inconclusive, and prevented the incident from being discussed at the UN Security Council, responses that were easily seen as protecting Pyongyang.[56] China even protested U.S.-ROK military exercises aimed at deterring North Korea.[57] From China's perspective, extensive economic ties with South Korea did not outweigh the geostrategic concerns and historical closeness of the relationship between Beijing and Pyongyang.[58] As a result, South Korea's expectations of Chinese political support were dashed, and its views of China began to take a downturn. According to the Asan Institute for Policy Studies annual survey, 72.1 percent of two thousand respondents in 2011 thought that China would go to war on behalf of North Korea, and that number peaked at 75.9 percent in 2012.[59]

Third, incidents involving illegal, aggressive intrusions by Chinese fishermen in South Korean territorial waters in the Yellow Sea began to increase during Lee Myung-bak's presidency. In 2010, two Chinese fishermen died in a collision between a Chinese trawler and a South Korean Coast Guard ship.[60] Although the incident occurred while the trawler was engaged in illegal fishing, Beijing demanded that "South Korea . . . do its best to search for the missing crewman," "severely punish those responsible," "compensate for damage done to the Chinese fishermen[,] and take thorough measures to prevent recurrence of similar incidents."[61] In October 2011, South Korea's Coast Guard seized three Chinese boats fishing illegally, and a South Korean Coast Guard crewmember died during an attempt to board a Chinese fishing boat in December 2011.[62] In April 2012, four South Korean fishing inspectors were wounded when they attempted to board a Chinese boat.[63] These incidents seemed to signal a general increase in China's assertiveness in the region in the aftermath of the economic crisis of 2008–2009.

Fourth, although China–South Korea trade growth remained robust with the launching of FTA negotiations in May 2012, the nature of the economic relationship began to shift as well.[64] Not only did South Korean firms face stiffer competition from state-protected local Chinese companies in the domestic market, but China also became more competitive in the international market, showing a rapid expansion of its global market share in middle- to high-tech items, a trend that many South Korean analysts saw as increased competition with the Korean high-tech industry.[65]

Lee Myung-bak had said in March 2008, "I don't agree with such concepts as pro-American or pro-Chinese policy."[66] He came into office seeking to restore South Korea's relations with the United States, but he also never intended for the China-ROK relationship to deteriorate as it had by the end of his presidency. Yet the series of events described here and China's increasing assertiveness led precisely to what he sought to avoid.

RUSSIA–SOUTH KOREA RELATIONS

In 2008, Lee Myung-bak made a visit to Russia and had a summit meeting with President Dmitry Medvedev, during which they agreed to move their nations' bilateral relationship to a "strategic cooperative partnership" and to make progress in railway connection, energy and resources cooperation, and Far East and Siberia development.[67] Both sides also agreed to regularly hold vice-minister-level strategic talks to boost exchanges in military and defense fields.[68] Lee's diplomacy toward Russia combined his economic interest in energy cooperation and his policy toward North Korea. Russia-ROK trade surged from $190 million in 1992 to $22.5 billion in 2012, with South Korea ranking third among East Asian countries trading with Russia by 2012.[69] Plus, because South Korea is a state devoid of domestic natural resources, it was keen on developing joint efforts and cooperation with Russia in the energy sector—such as the laying of the gas pipeline to the Korean Peninsula. Pursuing the possibility of building energy pipelines through North Korea, however, also showed that South Korea considered cooperation with Russia in dealing with North Korea important.[70]

For its part, Moscow had shown continuous interest in using energy diplomacy as a tool for bringing together the two Koreas. With governmental encouragement, the Russian energy company Gazprom and Korea Gas Corporation held preliminary talks to explore the possible construction of an energy pipeline between the Russian Far East and South Korea through North Korea in 2010.[71] Under the contract, Russia was to send South Korea at least 7.5 million tons of natural gas annually for thirty years, amounting to an estimated 20 percent of South Korea's annual natural gas consumption.[72] Medvedev also held a meeting with Kim Jong-il during Kim's visit to Russia in August 2011, during which they discussed North Korea's nuclear program and prospects for the pipeline project.[73] Lee also followed up with Medvedev on the pipeline project in St. Petersburg the following November.[74] As a result, talks between Korea Gas and Gazprom heated up, but both sides were unable to come to a final decision on pricing and on liability for supply disruptions in the event of noncooperation from North Korea. In the end, the energy deal went nowhere despite Russian efforts and Lee's interest in using energy cooperation with

Moscow as part of a package of inducements to secure North Korea's return to nuclear talks.

LEE MYUNG-BAK'S NORTH KOREA POLICY

Despite Lee Myung-bak's initial attempts to make North Korea a secondary priority, the increasing capabilities of the North Korean nuclear weapons program forced him to focus more on the North toward the end of his administration.

Following a decade of inter-Korean economic engagement but no commensurate reduction in inter-Korean tensions, most South Koreans felt frustrated that their efforts had failed to generate reciprocity or cooperation from North Korea. Instead, North Korea seemed ever ready to collect on South Korean largesse. A white paper published by the Ministry of Unification in 2010 summed up its judgment of the results of a decade of progressive-led inter-Korean engagement: the policies of previous administrations "did not meet the expectations and demands of the Korean people." Over time, South Korea's payments for economic projects and investment in infrastructure inside North Korea—at Mount Kumgang and at the Kaesong Industrial Complex—benefited North Korea but "did not make positive changes" in the two Koreas' relationship.[75]

Yet the pursuit of "inter-Korean relations that advance mutual benefits and common prosperity" remained Lee Myung-bak's first strategic objective.[76] South Korea pursued these objectives by insisting on North Korea's denuclearization, envisioning the foundation for an inter-Korean economic and sociocultural community, and promoting humanitarian cooperation, including pursuit of family reunions and improvement of human rights conditions in North Korea.[77]

Lee Myung-bak's approach to North Korea sought to correct for perceived policy failings under a decade of engagement framework pursued under Kim Dae-jung and Roh Moo-hyun. First, Korean conservatives were concerned that North Korea had taken advantage of South Korean generosity and had invested some of South Korean resources in building its military capabilities, including its nuclear program. Second, they believed that human rights concerns had been swept under the rug by progressive administrations for the sake of engagement. Third, they felt that inter-Korean cooperation came at the expense of the U.S.-ROK alliance. Fourth and most importantly, they perceived a gap between South Korea and the United States as well as a vast limitation in the potential for inter-Korean economic cooperation in the absence of denuclearization.

As a result, North Korea's nuclear breakout and ongoing development of nuclear weapons had become a fundamental obstacle in the way of improved relations during the Lee Myung-bak presidency. An official of the Lee administration claimed that "inter-Korean business projects should be linked to progress over the North's nuclear issue."[78] Lee's Denuclearization and Opening 3000 proposal was premised on the idea that in exchange for denuclearization and opening South Korea was prepared to promote large-scale trade and investment that would substantially raise the average North Korean's standard of living.[79]

North Korea greeted Lee Myung-bak's proposal with hostility from the outset. In response to this hostility, the Lee administration dramatically curtailed assistance to North Korea, even restricting aid that had previously been given for ostensibly humanitarian purposes. North Korea was aware of the divisions among South Korean conservatives, including within the Lee administration, over whether South Korea should work to bring about the demise of the North or use economic aid as a tool for the regime's subversion. North Korea showed greater skepticism toward South Korean conservatives' intentions than toward the progressives' aims, thus constraining prospects for sustaining inter-Korean economic cooperation. In such a situation, North Korea could foment domestic divisions in the South over policy toward the North by taking a hard line and engendering progressive criticisms that the conservative policy was shutting the door to inter-Korean reconciliation. By August 2008, Kim Jong-il's health problems had intervened to preoccupy North Korea, ultimately resulting in a decision by Pyongyang to abandon Six-Party Talks and to pursue additional nuclear and missile tests in the spring of 2009.

A further complication that soured the atmosphere in the months following Lee Myung-bak's assumption of the presidency was a North

Korean soldier's shooting of a South Korean tourist who had taken a walk in an off-limits area near the resort at Mount Kumgang on July 11, 2008.[80] The news of the incident coincided directly with Lee's speech on inter-Korean relations to the National Assembly, at which he was set to unveil a number of new initiatives and proposals for inter-Korean economic cooperation, which emphasized pursuit of "mutual benefits and common prosperity."[81] The news of the tourist's death ruined the prospects for renewed inter-Korean economic cooperation. Instead of pursuing mutuality and reciprocity, the Lee administration suddenly faced the challenge of seeking North Korea's accountability for the tourist's death. Lee expressed his dismay and suspended the tours of Mount Kumgang, urging Pyongyang to "actively cooperate" in the investigation.[82] But efforts to establish a joint investigation foundered as North Korea refused to allow South Korean officials to visit the area of the shooting.[83] In the absence of apologies or assurances from North Korea that the lives of South Korean tourists would be safeguarded, the project was suspended indefinitely.

With inter-Korean dialogue virtually stalled, the focus shifted to Six-Party Talks and the question of whether U.S. assistant secretary of state for East Asia and the Pacific Christopher Hill would be able to push forward North Korea's implementation of its initial steps toward denuclearization under the Six-Party agreement. Despite successful (albeit reversible) steps toward dismantlement at Yongbyon, North Korea's major nuclear complex, further steps foundered over the North's unwillingness to allow verification of its declaration regarding nuclear facilities. Hill held last-ditch negotiations in Beijing in December 2008, but those negotiations failed.

With the election of Barack Obama as the next U.S. president in November 2008, South Korean conservatives worried that the United States might move too fast in pursuit of diplomatic outreach to North Korea. Those fears proved unfounded, however, as it became clear that North Korea had made a decision to move away from denuclearization and toward additional long-range missile and nuclear tests. It blocked early feelers from the Obama administration that sought a delay on North Korea's long-range rocket-launch preparations, and it ultimately refused an offer by Special Representative Stephen Bosworth to make an early visit to

North Korea if the rocket launch, scheduled for early April, were canceled. Instead of an exploration of rapprochement between Pyongyang and Washington, North Korea's missile test brought on UN condemnation, which was followed by the Pyongyang's outrage at the condemnation and a second nuclear test in June 2009.

This series of actions pushed the Obama and Lee administrations closer together as they pursued joint efforts to punish and impose a measure of accountability on North Korea through the establishment of UN Security Council Resolution 1874, which imposed sanctions on North Korea and established a panel of experts to investigate its violations of the resolution.[84] In addition, South Korea closed ranks with the United States by announcing that Seoul would join the Proliferation Security Initiative, a move that the Roh Moo-hyun administration had refused to make for fear of alienating Pyongyang, although the Lee administration was also hesitant in providing full material support for the initiative for fear of unnecessarily aggravating North Korea.[85] South Korea also gained enhanced extended deterrence guarantees from the United States as part of the U.S.-ROK Joint Vision Statement of June 2009, which also envisioned the goal of Korean unification under a democratic, market-led system (i.e., South Korean–led Korean unification).

An emerging element of the Lee Myung-bak administration's strategy following North Korea's second nuclear test involved multilateralization or internationalization of South Korean efforts to pressure North Korea. This strategy involved stepped-up international policy coordination to pressure North Korea into accepting denuclearization. The diplomatic face of internationalization was presented in the form of a "Grand Bargain" approach that Lee presented in a speech to the Council on Foreign Relations in September 2009.[86] It involved strengthened policy coordination toward North Korea among Six-Party members, a combination of rewards and punishment in pursuit of denuclearization, and a package-deal exchange of denuclearization for economic prosperity. At an Economist Business Roundtable in 2009, Lee proclaimed, "Our government has proposed the Grand Bargain strategy within the context of the objective of resolving North Korea's denuclearization. It is an approach to dissolve the core of the North's nuclear program and concurrently provide the North with economic aid and guarantee of security."[87] North Korea rejected this proposal by reiterating that its nuclear program was a response to the U.S. hostile policy toward North Korea.

Adding to the challenge posed by the cancellation of the Kumgang tours and the imposition of new UN Security Council resolutions condemning North Korea's nuclear and missile programs, South Korea faced a new provocation in March 2010 with the sinking of the naval corvette *Cheonan*, resulting in the loss of more than fifty South Korean soldiers and the vessel itself. The Lee administration launched a Ministry of National Defense–led international investigation into the cause of the sinking, which concluded that a North Korean shell had struck the vessel.[88] The Lee administration then responded to the investigation by imposing "May 24" sanctions on North Korea, effectively shutting down all inter-Korean trade, exchanges, and investment, with the exception of operations at the Kaesong Industrial Complex. Lee proclaimed in his address on May 24, "We have been patient with the North's intolerable behavior until now, and that was only because we were longing for peace on the Korean peninsula. But things will change. [From this point on,] North Korea will have to pay the price that corresponds to its actions."[89] Following the unilateral imposition of economic sanctions, South Korea sought UN condemnation for North Korea's attack on the *Cheonan*, but the UN Security Council was divided and failed to take further actions to pressure North Korea.

Then, the North Koreans created yet another crisis in 2010. Despite apparent improvement in inter-Korean relations in the fall of 2009, including inter-Korean talks on possible resumption of family reunions in advance of South Korea's hosting of the G20, South Koreans were shocked to witness North Korea's shelling of Yeonpyeong Island in November. The shelling resulted in casualties, including the death of two civilians. Due to Chinese opposition, it was not even possible for South Korea to request UN condemnation of the North Korean shelling, so South Korea conducted a major military exercise near Yeonpyeong Island instead and launched a civilian commission to review South Korean military doctrine and strategy toward North Korea. This deterioration in inter-Korean relations underscored the fragility of the relationship and the near impossibility of taking actions that would successfully hold North Korea accountable for its actions.

Even following these setbacks, though, the Lee administration met secretly with the North Koreans in Beijing in search of a formula for resumption of inter-Korean dialogue, but the talks reached an impasse, revealing the extent of the gap between the two sides. To add insult to injury, the North Korean National Defense Commission, in an attempt to humiliate the Lee administration, exposed the talks in a statement in June 2011 and accused South Korea of begging for a summit. Finally, the North Korean side let loose with vitriolic statements condemning the Lee administration, perhaps hoping that South Korea's next election would bring a power transition back to a progressive government.

In dealing with North Korea, the Lee administration initially demanded greater reciprocity and mutuality from North Korea, ending unilateral assistance. However, Lee's Denuclearization and Opening 3000 policy and its variants were unappealing to North Korea, and South Korea's placing of the nuclear issue as an obstacle in inter-Korean relations became an ever-deepening source of difference, especially as North Korea moved to abandon Six-Party Talks in April 2009 and to conduct further nuclear and missile tests. Lee declared that "North's nuclear program must be dismantled through Six Party Talks" and that "Seoul should play a major role in helping the North dismantle its nuclear program through inter-Korean dialogue."[90] Furthermore, North Korea continued to see the nuclear issue as a proper subject for discussion with the United States and so rejected South Korea's efforts to add it to the agenda of any inter-Korean dialogues.

All in all, North Korea's provocations revealed South Korea's failure to hold Pyongyang accountable for its actions and drove South Korea increasingly to pursue international isolation strategies against Pyongyang, further inciting North Korean frustration. This vicious cycle led to an unraveling of all forms of inter-Korean cooperation by the end of the Lee presidency, with the notable exception of the Kaesong Industrial Complex.

EVOLUTION OF DOMESTIC PUBLIC OPINION
TOWARD FOREIGN POLICY UNDER
LEE MYUNG-BAK

Despite steadily rising South Korean public support for the U.S.-ROK alliance during Lee Myung-bak's term, a number of incidents served as reminders of the South Korean public's sensitivities to the need to protect South Korean autonomy even in the context of strengthening U.S.-ROK alliance cooperation. The first reminder came only months into Lee's five-year term with the emergence of public demonstrations over concerns that the United States had pressured South Korea to import beef that might have come from cows at risk of contracting mad cow disease.

Although the protracted confrontation primarily reflected South Korean public anxieties that Lee Myung-bak, in his enthusiasm for restoring the alliance, might compromise South Korea's national interests for the sake of preserving cooperation, it also revealed the difficulty of securing domestic consensus in support of presidential leadership in foreign policy. A ban on American beef imports was first imposed in 2003 after a case of mad cow disease was detected in the United States. The Obama administration expressed discontent at the import ban, claiming that it was inconsistent with standard international practice and with South Korea's commitments under the U.S.-Korea FTA.[91] In response to the Lee administration's agreement to resume U.S. beef imports, nearly ten thousand South Koreans staged candlelight protests calling for their government to scrap the agreement. Lee's approval ratings plunged to less than 20 percent after the incident, and presidential spokesperson Lee Dong-kwan accused some Internet sites of spreading false allegations about the safety of U.S. beef.[92] Lee Myung-bak later apologized on national television for the agreement and backed away from it, although he had personally approved the deal in April 2008.[93] U.S. ambassador Alexander Vershbow expressed his disappointment in the retrenchment, arguing that "there is no scientific justification to postpone implementation."[94] In the end, the Lee administration reversed its stance again and eventually lifted a ban on imports of U.S. beef despite overnight protest rallies by thousands of people in which hundreds were injured, and Lee's reputation sank to an all-time low.[95]

A second sensitive alliance issue on which the South Korean public's predispositions influenced the U.S.-ROK alliance was related to South Korean efforts to secure U.S. approval to extend the limit on ballistic missiles' range from 300 to 800 kilometers under the Missile Technology Control Regime.[96] The public's sensitivities to protection of sovereignty came into play on this issue following the *Cheonan* sinking and the artillery attack on Yeonpyeong Island in 2010. South Korea argued that "while North Korea has the capability to launch a direct strike on the Korean Peninsula and surrounding countries such as Japan . . . with a firing range of 3,000 km," North Korea was not even within South Korea's firing zone, which had a range of only 180 to 300 kilometers.[97] Whenever North Korea held test launches of mid- and long-range missiles, South Korean conservatives and the Ministry of National Defense claimed that South Korea should also extend the range of its missiles to cover all of the North.[98] The United States had long restricted South Korean missile development by bilateral agreement to ranges even more restrictive than those required under Missile Technology Control Regime. Following difficult negotiations, however, the Obama and Lee administrations arrived at a consensus that enabled South Korea to expand its ranges but continued to impose restrictions on size of payload.

A third sensitive issue that revealed tensions between the South Korean public's desire for autonomy and restrictions imposed by the alliance came in the context of the renegotiation of an expiring U.S.-ROK nuclear cooperation agreement. During the negotiations that began in late 2010, the Lee administration sought U.S. "advance consent" for South Korea's right to enrich or reprocess U.S.-origin nuclear material.[99] These demands were fed in part by worries that North Korea's nuclear breakout might leave South Korea vulnerable to nuclear blackmail by the North. This issue also elicited public calls by influential Korean opinion leaders for "nuclear sovereignty," which could be interpreted in different ways but in general meant that South Korea be allowed to pursue its own nuclear program without restriction.[100] South Korean national security adviser Chun Yung-woo rationalized the idea that South Korea should have enrichment and reprocessing rights by arguing that the country was now one of the world's top-five nuclear power producers.[101] He further emphasized that public opinion would not tolerate the perception that South Korea was being discriminated against in comparison to Japan, which had been granted enrichment rights and had been allowed to construct a reprocessing facility in its nuclear cooperation agreement with the United States. The other driver catalyzing South Koreans' interest in obtaining the capacity to enrich and reprocess was the country's entry into the global nuclear reactor export market and its desire to emerge as a full-service provider capable of handling every facet of the nuclear fuel cycle. South Korea claimed that renegotiating the agreement would facilitate cooperation with the United States for utilization of nuclear energy and help make energy "another pillar in bilateral economic cooperation along with the South Korea-U.S. free trade agreement."[102]

GLOBAL KOREA AND A COMPREHENSIVE STRATEGIC ALLIANCE WITH THE UNITED STATES

Although *globalization* had been a buzzword in South Korea since the mid-1990s under Kim Young-sam, the Lee Myung-bak administration was the first to back up the slogan with capabilities by actually making significant contributions to the international agenda. A successful element of Lee's strategy was "hosting diplomacy," through which South Korea brought more global leaders to Seoul for international meetings than ever before, such as the G20 in 2010 and the Nuclear Security Summit in 2012.[103] These successful ventures gave South Korean officials the opportunity to guide the international agenda for the first time on critical financial and security issues of global importance. They provided tangible evidence of a South Korea fully capable of making significant contributions to global leadership but best positioned to do so in areas supporting and reinforcing American-led structures, institutions, and initiatives. In hosting both the G20 and the Nuclear Security Summit, Lee Myung-bak took leadership initiatives at the request of and with the support of the United States. South Korea's success in hosting these initiatives marked a high point in its international reach and the influence of its foreign policy.

South Korea's hosting of the OECD Development Assistance Committee meeting in Busan in 2011 exploited its rising reputation as a successful modernizer that had graduated from aid recipient to donor. During the meeting, South Korea attempted to add emerging voices to the debate over best practices in international development. Lee Myung-bak made a mark in the debate over climate change by advocating the incorporation of business-oriented adaptation strategies and by creating an international institution, the Global Green Growth Institute, dedicated to providing advice on best practice for states interested in reducing carbon emissions. The Lee administration paid close attention to the global financial crisis of 2008–2009 and utilized the expansion of South Korea's FTA commitments to take leadership in trade liberalization and to expand opportunities for its export sector. All of these efforts expanded the country's profile and interests beyond the Korean Peninsula and Northeast Asia. However, although the advent of Global Korea did not mean abandoning the pursuit of Korean unification or regional security, an emerging stalemate on inter-Korean issues prevented the Lee administration from achieving anything significant in the South's policy toward and relationship with North Korea.

Additional observations are important in assessing the Lee administration's impact on the development of South Korea's foreign policy. First, the administration capitalized on close relations with the United States to enhance its autonomy and its influence even as it attempted to play a bridging role between the developing and the developed world on many global issues. South Korea consciously played up this role in advance of its hosting the G20, the Nuclear Security Summit, and the OECD meetings. Although South Korea was capable of independently making contributions to international leadership, Lee Myung-bak smartly chose areas where he was best positioned to work autonomously from but in tandem with the United States in areas where South Korea and the United States clearly shared common interests and objectives.

Second, the Lee Myung-bak administration identified a set of overlapping niche areas where South Korea could arguably make the case that it was uniquely positioned to make international contributions. South Korea's rapid development experience argued for its presenting itself as a model for emulation in international development. Lee's adaptation approach to climate change nicely applied attributes of South Korea's development experience, but with a focus on carbon-emission reductions through green growth. South Korea promoted trade liberalization and used it as an effective strategy to minimize the impact of a global recession, becoming the first non-G8 country to host a G20 meeting at a time when the G20 seemed poised to take leadership in coordinating international financial policies. South Korea's contributions to development, mitigation of carbon emissions, and global trade liberalization were independent initiatives that manifested the maturity of South Korean policy and served to broaden the scope and breadth of the U.S.-ROK alliance beyond peninsular security-focused initiatives.

Third, Lee Myung-bak's efforts to revitalize the U.S.-ROK security alliance based on shared values of trust, security, and peace paid big dividends for the alliance as it became an effective platform that enabled South Korea to raise its international profile and to contribute to international public goods in close coordination with the United States. Lee's embrace of close relations with the United States also brought South Korea and the United States into sync on denuclearization as the main priority in dealing with North Korea. Yet these initiatives also had the effect of reversing and reducing inter-Korean cooperation, with the notable exception of the continuation of the Kaesong Industrial Complex.

Fourth, Lee Myung-bak's exclusive and conditional focus on denuclearization had the effect of greatly reducing prospects for inter-Korean cooperation, and South Korea's resort to internationalization of responses to North Korean provocations both greatly antagonized the North Korean leadership and exploited the extent to which South Korea had become reliant on international cooperation while North Korea became increasingly isolated. Although Seoul offered Pyongyang a helping hand and made offers to promote North Korea's economic integration with the rest of the world, Pyongyang perceived these offers as hostile efforts to isolate, outflank, and absorb the North. In this respect, a relatively vulnerable North Korea was dealing with a South Korea that continued to grow in its relative power vis-à-vis the North and that had a tougher, conditions-based policy that the North found to be deeply threatening. Ironically, the Achilles heel of South Korea's globalization efforts turned out to be the fact that North Korea refused to allow Lee Myung-bak to look past the inter-Korean stalemate and instead continued to serve as both a hindrance and a growing threat to South Korea's security and prosperity.

7

PARK GEUN-HYE'S ASIAN PARADOX

A S A CANDIDATE for president in 2012, Park Geun-hye correctly assessed South Korea's security environment when she described "Asia's Paradox," the cracks in the foundations underlying Asia's remarkable economic growth.[1] Among the most serious threats to Asian regional stability she identified were the absence of trust-based inter-Korean relations, Japan's failure to reckon fully with its imperialist past, and the prospect that a major arms race could be set off in Northeast Asia in the event that Sino-U.S. relations turned adversarial. However, Park's experience as president showed that although the business of identifying Asia's problems is relatively easy, the search for effective solutions to those same problems is frustrating and fleeting. In fact, rising regional rivalries caused the security situation to deteriorate much more rapidly during Park's term than many had anticipated, generating obstacles that thwarted her efforts to identify and implement effective solutions or even effectively to manage rising tensions and keep them from metastasizing. Then, Park's own personal scandal resulted in extended domestic political paralysis and impeachment, further undermining South Korea's capacity to maneuver against a backdrop of growing uncertainty. The country's worsening regional security environment highlighted the reality that despite South Korea's growing capacity the alliance with the United States remained a valuable and necessary tool for preserving both its security and its autonomy.

Park's strategy for managing these issues, based on a strong alliance with the United States, adopted essentially the same template that had been used by her predecessor, Lee Myung-bak. During her first visit to Washington in May 2013, Park and President Obama affirmed a joint statement on the sixtieth anniversary of the establishment of the U.S.-ROK alliance that was a virtual carbon copy of the U.S.-ROK Joint Vision Statement issued during Lee's visit to Washington in June 2009. However, despite South Korea's growing commitment to expanding its international impact and contributions, Park took a more narrow approach to foreign affairs that focused first on the peninsula and the neighborhood of Northeast Asia while capitalizing but not necessarily expanding on diplomatic opportunities afforded by South Korea's global reach. In some respects, Park's personality, history, and working style proved to be more insular than Lee's, although a worsening regional environment characterized by Sino-Japanese tensions and North Korea's nuclear advances provided good reason for Park to focus on challenges associated with South Korea's immediate neighborhood.

Park's most significant challenge in addressing the core issues she identified as part of Asia's Paradox was that efforts to address each problem she identified required diplomatic cooperation from her counterparts in order to achieve progress. In addition, she expected those partners to acknowledge and accept the principles behind her diagnosis of the problem and be willing to work with her on her terms. In these respects, Park's policies reflected a principled approach to foreign policy and (over)confidence in South Korea's ability to influence its neighbors. Her implementation of Trustpolitik, or trust-based relations, with North Korea required Chairman Kim Jong-un to act in a way that lived up to Park's standards and expectations of what it means to be trustworthy. By making the issue of how Japan might properly express responsibility for its treatment of "comfort women," Korean sex slaves placed into the service of the Japanese military during World War II, the central problem inhibiting South Korea's relationship with Japan, Park placed the burden on Abe to show a "correct understanding of history" and to address the issue as part of efforts to achieve a "grand reconciliation" among China, Japan, and South Korea.[2] Moscow generated major obstacles to Park's pursuit of the Eurasia Initiative as a result of its military aggression in Ukraine and the subsequent downturn in U.S.-Russia relations, which made the initiative unfeasible.[3]

As president of South Korea, Park promoted three signature initiatives designed to counter Asia's Paradox and to further South Korean diplomatic objectives of maintaining security on the peninsula while building frameworks for regional peace and prosperity. These three initiatives were Trustpolitik (applied to both North Korea and the region in general), the Northeast Asia Peace and Cooperation Initiative, and the Eurasia Initiative, which sought to expand cooperation with Russia to build energy and transit networks that would enmesh North Korea and integrate it into Northeast Asian economies.[4] In addition, Park sought improved relations with China as a source of leverage on North Korea and as a means of deepening regional cooperation. Her pursuit of better relations with China, however, was firmly rooted in greatly expanded alliance cooperation with the United States. But Park's only foreign-policy accomplishment turned out to be the stabilization of Japan–South Korea relations through a settlement on the comfort women issue; even that accomplishment was domestically contested as the Park administration became engulfed in scandal and impeachment.

PARK'S NATIONAL SECURITY STRATEGY

In her inauguration speech on February 25, 2013, Park Geun-hye identified South Korea's economic vulnerability in the midst of global economic uncertainty and North Korea's growing nuclear threat as major challenges for her administration. She identified four guiding principles for realizing her national vision: economic revival, the people's happiness, cultural enrichment, and the establishment of a foundation for national unification.[5] Park's national security strategy presented three fundamental objectives to uphold these principles: safeguarding South Korea's territory and sovereignty and ensuring the people's safety; establishing sustainable peace on the Korean Peninsula and preparing for an era of unification; and promoting cooperation in Northeast Asia and contributing to world peace and development. The strategy applied the concept of trust building as the administration's main diplomatic approach, both with regard to North Korea and as a precept for how the administration would conduct its international relations.

Several main themes stand out in Park's national security strategy. First, the strategy started with a pledge to maintain a "robust defense posture" and to develop "future-oriented defense capabilities." The U.S.-ROK alliance was considered an instrument for achieving those goals, and the United States a valuable partner to South Korea as both countries forged a "comprehensive security alliance," but South Korea was also presented as an autonomous actor with primary responsibility for its own security and with aspirations to promote peace and cooperation regionally and globally, when, in fact, South Korean autonomy stands on the platform provided by the U.S.-ROK security alliance. Second, the national security strategy presented the pursuit of trust-based relations with North Korea as a parallel objective to preparation for national unification. This was consistent with the idea that the Park administration aimed for peaceful unification based on dialogue and cooperation. However, the North Korean nuclear threat was clearly presented as intolerable to South Korea's national security and North Korea's denuclearization as a prerequisite for the achievement of a trust-based inter-Korean relationship. Third, the Park administration presumed that it would make positive contributions to peace and stability by promoting cooperation regionally and globally, underscoring the scope of South Korea's aspirations to have a global impact and to be a leader in the world.

Each of these three themes suggests an evolution in South Korea's foreign policy that builds on prior themes. South Korea continued to view the security alliance with the United States as the foundation for its security by building on Lee Myung-bak's pro-alliance policy. Park also conceived of the establishment of a "comprehensive alliance" as a basis for partnership to pursue both peninsular and global security objectives. Her assertion of the need for trust in inter-Korean relations built on Roh Tae-woo's Nordpolitik strategy and suggested that South Korea had the ability to take the lead in inter-Korean relations, despite the persistence of the nuclear problem as a central issue requiring the involvement of the United

States. Her emphasis on cooperation in Northeast Asia built directly on the themes of Roh Moo-hyun's Northeast Asia Cooperation Initiative, and she incorporated Lee Myung-bak's Global Korea policy as a given for South Korea's foreign policy.

NORTH KOREA POLICY: FROM TRUSTPOLITIK TO UNIFICATION

PARK GEUN-HYE'S VISION

In advance of her campaign for the presidency of South Korea, Park Geun-hye wrote a *Foreign Affairs* article in which she unveiled a policy toward North Korea she termed "Trustpolitik." The article identified the absence of trust-based interactions as the main obstacle hindering progress in inter-Korean relations. She called for North Korea to keep its agreements with the South and the international community and pledged "assured consequences for actions that breach the peace." The strategy essentially called upon North Korea to show itself trustworthy in inter-Korean relations and in its international interactions as the essential ingredient necessary to build a positive relationship. Park pledged to pursue a policy of "alignment" of peninsular and international efforts toward North Korea as a primary source of leverage designed to pressure Pyongyang to respond and reciprocate in its relations with the outside world.[6] The alignment policy was reaffirmed in Park's national security strategy.

Park presented a second element of her policy toward North Korea in a speech she gave during a visit to Dresden, Germany, in March 2014, a year after she became president. The Dresden speech laid out a phased process of inter-Korean integration that started with humanitarian cooperation, then introduced "co-prosperity through the building of infrastructure that supports the livelihood of the people," and finally promoted "integration between the people of North and South Korea."[7] Although Park did not explicitly mention denuclearization, she repeatedly emphasized in other remarks elsewhere that any large-scale inter-Korean economic cooperation would be conditioned on North Korea's denuclearization. The Dresden speech was advertised as a major statement by the president that would build on Trustpolitik; however, it was criticized sharply by the North Koreans and did not seem to gain traction as a framework driving South Korea's implementation of policy toward the North.

A third prong of Park's policy toward North Korea came in her emphasis on the need to prepare for Korean unification. Although unification was clearly not a new theme in South Korean policy, Park prioritized the issue through the establishment of the Presidential Committee on Unification Preparation to devise a strategy to comprehensively address the security, political, legal, economic, and social implications of unification.[8] Park highlighted unification in her New Year's press conference at the start of 2014 by stating that it would be a "bonanza" for the Korean people and highlighting the central importance of unification as a strategic objective of her administration.[9] The establishment of the committee identified unification preparation as a priority, but once again the government struggled to bring about concrete and lasting results in its implementation, and the unification-preparation committee came to be seen as a source of irritation and suspicion among North Korean counterparts.

NORTH KOREA POLICY IN PRACTICE

Despite Park's apparent intent to build inter-Korean relations based on gradually evolving trust and cooperation, inter-Korean dialogue during her term was characterized by wild swings and developed in fits and starts. These swings occurred in part as a result of North Korea's efforts to test the inter-Korean relationship and Park's leadership, but the more fundamental failure of inter-Korean relations, despite periodic fluctuations driven by the search for tactical gains, was driven by the gap between Park's insistence on North Korea's denuclearization and Kim Jong-un's drive to make North Korea a permanent nuclear weapons state.

The first test of wills between Park and Kim came in the aftermath of North Korea's third nuclear test, which was staged to occur only weeks prior to Park's inauguration. However, the main confrontation occurred as a result of North Korea's shutdown of the Kaesong Industrial Complex in

March 2013 and a weeks-long negotiation over the terms under which the complex might be restarted. The negotiation involved a test of wills over protocol, principles, and terms of operation, in which North Korea employed all of its favorite tactics: threats, brinkmanship, and extortion-like demands for greater financial support. However, South Korea had leverage in the form of the inputs of money and materials that made the complex work and in the fact that tens of thousands of workers in North Korea remained idle during the shutdown. In a preview of the prevailing pattern of inter-Korean negotiations under her administration, Park controlled the negotiation closely from behind the scenes, tenaciously adhered to principle until the North Koreans backed down, and, as a result, gained domestic public approval for her leadership. In return for the resumption of complex operations and pledges of South Korean efforts to "internationalize" it by bringing in foreign companies, South Korea gained pledges of joint management over the complex through a newly established inter-Korean advisory committee.[10] Alongside the resumption of Kaesong, Park gained agreement for a one-time resumption of family reunions. However, the mood turned nasty again as North Korea let loose a rhetorical barrage against Park, calling her a whore and other nasty names in late 2013. Despite the North's personal invective toward Park, the family reunions eventually occurred in February 2014.[11]

The North Koreans responded negatively to Park's Dresden speech and her characterization of Korean unification as a "bonanza" in early 2014, criticizing Park bitterly and contrasting her speech, which appeared hostile to North Korea's future given the symbolism of the location of its delivery in the former East Germany, with the Berlin speech that Kim Dae-jung gave in spring of 2000, which had sent positive signals of inter-Korean reconciliation in advance of the summit that June. Negotiations to have a cheering squad at the Incheon Asian Games in September 2014 also failed. Nevertheless, North Korea surprisingly and with little advance notice sent three leading officials to the games' closing ceremonies in October 2014, apparently to celebrate the North Korean athletes' better-than-expected performance.[12] South Korea accepted the three senior officials' attendance and probed opportunities for improvement of inter-Korean relations, but no signals of a wider opening were forthcoming.

In August 2015, a crisis erupted when the explosion of landmines alleg-edly planted by North Korea near a guard post on the South Korean side of the DMZ seriously injured two South Korean soldiers. The incident resulted in a series of escalatory measures on both sides, including South Korea's resumption of propaganda broadcasts through large speakers near the DMZ, an ultimatum from North Korea and pledges to retaliate for South Korea's resumption of the broadcasts, and an exchange of fire near the DMZ. But North Korea's surprising offer of talks at the DMZ halted further escalation, and three days of marathon negotiations among, on the South Korean side, National Security Adviser Kim Kwan-jin and Minister of Unification Hong Yong-pyo and, on the North Korean side, top advisers to Kim Jong-un, director of the Korean People's Army Hwang Pyong-so, and secretary for United Front Department Kim Yang-gon re-sulted in a five-point agreement to deescalate and to prepare for a round of inter-Korean family reunions, to be held in October.[13] However, further working-level talks on steps to expand inter-Korean political and economic exchange stalled in December over South Korea's insistence on North Ko-rea's denuclearization. Moreover, the death of Kim Yang-gon, the experi-enced and longtime hand in South Korea affairs, in an apparent car crash in December marked North Korea's turn to a harsher approach toward the South as responsibility for South Korean affairs passed to chairman of the Reconnaissance General Bureau Kim Yong-chol, who had allegedly been responsible for the North's provocations toward the South in 2010.

In January 2016, North Korea conducted its fourth nuclear test, draw-ing strong responses from Park Geun-hye, whose foreign minister, Yun Byung-se, had referred the previous April to the prospect of a fourth North Korean nuclear test as a "game changer."[14] Park argued for strong measures to prevent more nuclear tests and decided to close the Kaesong Industrial Complex, to impose additional unilateral measures, and to push for implementation of strong international measures, which were eventu-ally contained in UN Security Council Resolution 2270, adopted in March 2016.[15] Following North Korea's fifth nuclear test in September, the UN Security Council passed even more stringent sanctions on North Korea through UN Security Council Resolution 2321, passed in December 2016. The Park administration continued to insist on the necessity of North

Korea's denuclearization and seemed intent on changing North Korea's strategic calculus through pressure, leading a campaign for strict implementation of sanctions and publicizing group defections of North Korean restaurant workers at various locations in China. Park continued to state categorically that North Korea's nuclear program was an intolerable threat to South Korea's survival, while Kim Jong-un declared at the seventh DPRK Worker's Party Congress North Korea's intent to pursue *byungjin*, or simultaneous economic and military development, as a permanent state strategy.[16] In response to this series of events, the Park administration eventually responded by approving the deployment of the Terminal High-Altitude Area Defense (THAAD) System in South Korea over Chinese objections and by laying out a massive retaliation and decapitation doctrine designed to preempt the North if it were to be seen as moving toward using nuclear weapons. All these measures suggested that Trustpolitik, which had originally focused on the desirability of renewed dialogue and peaceful coexistence between the two Koreas, had been swept under the rug and replaced by diametrically opposed positions over the imperative of North Korea's denuclearization.

ASIA'S PARADOX IN NORTHEAST ASIA

While dealing with North Korea, Park Geun-hye also sought to bring about a more cooperative regional strategic environment and find a path to solve Asia's Paradox. The elements of her regional policy in this regard included pursuit of multilateral initiatives, notably the Northeast Asia Peace and Cooperation Initiative (NAPCI) and the Eurasia Initiative; improved relations with China to manage regional tensions and the North Korean problem; reconciliation with Japan based on an understanding of history; and a strong U.S.-ROK alliance based on a broad trust-based partnership.

NAPCI AND THE EURASIA INITIATIVE

The NAPCI was the primary policy prescription for Asia's Paradox and Park's second signature foreign-policy priority behind Trustpolitik. The initiative's logic and vision of strengthened multilateral cooperation was firmly in line with similar initiatives by both Roh Tae-woo and Roh Moo-hyun, but the NAPCI encountered many obstacles and proved difficult to implement, and its incremental accomplishments were limited.

The first challenge the NAPCI faced was lukewarm support from the United States. Despite Park's invitation to the United States to join the NAPCI as a "coarchitect" of multilateral cooperation in Northeast Asia, the Obama administration had already prioritized its commitment to the East Asia Summit as its primary norm-building initiative in East Asia and worried that a duplication of effort in Northeast Asia would prove diversionary and counterproductive. The United States also wondered whether the NAPCI would survive the Park administration, despite the fact that a generation of South Korean presidents had pursued subregional multilateral cooperation initiatives in one form or another.

Americans also showed skepticism over the initiative in the context of a seeming tilt in South Korean diplomacy toward China and away from Japan. In fact, it was clear that the NAPCI would not be able to make progress as long as South Korea–Japan relations were hobbled by history or to provide the Park administration with a strong incentive to achieve a solution that would restore normality to those relations (described in greater detail later in this chapter). Without enthusiastic support from the United States and Japan for the initiative, it was unlikely that China would endorse a new forum for multilateral cooperation in the region. In general, China showed little interest in supporting other countries' initiatives, which it seemed to feel would distract from its own leadership of new initiatives that might serve to put Beijing at the center of regional cooperation.

Nonetheless, South Korean diplomats methodically attempted to enhance working-level cooperation and to encourage pursuit of practical functional cooperation initiatives under the NAPCI framework. NAPCI showed some success in promoting experts meetings on nuclear safety and promoted information sharing and technical cooperation in environmental and maritime areas, while patiently pushing officials from the countries concerned to raise the level of their official representation at NAPCI meetings to higher levels. With time, South Korean diplomats were able to show incremental progress, although enhanced functional cooperation continued to remain dependent on a cooperative political environment and therefore was vulnerable to risk from spiraling tensions or regional rivalries.

Park Geun-hye launched the Eurasia Initiative in a speech at the "Global Cooperation in the Era of Eurasia" conference in October 2013. The South Korean Foreign Ministry presented the Eurasia Initiative as "a cooperation initiative and a grand national strategy put forward by the Korean government to achieve sustainable prosperity and peace in Eurasia." The initiative prioritized connecting Eurasia, promoting creativity as the "new growth engine of Eurasia," and facilitating peace and prosperity on the Korean Peninsula through a trust-building process. It attempted to promote transportation, information and communication technologies, and energy networks as well as to strengthen partnership through the establishment of the Korea–Central Asia Cooperation Secretariat and cooperation between the two Koreas and Russia and China.[17] However, Russia's invasion of Crimea and Ukraine and the failure of Trustpolitik in dealing with North Korea rendered most of the envisioned projects inactive. For instance, the only concrete effort associated with the Eurasia Initiative involved cooperation to promote the Rajin–Khasan logistics project with Russia and North Korea in which coal would be shipped from the border town Khasan in Russia to the Rajin port in North Korea and from there to South Korean companies, but that project was suspended following North Korea's fourth nuclear test in early 2016.

IMPROVED RELATIONS WITH CHINA

Recognizing the need to improve their bilateral relationship and to overcome tensions under Hu Jintao and Lee Myung-bak, the Chinese and South Korean governments took advantage of simultaneous power transitions to Park Geun-hye and Xi Jinping to strengthen high-level political relations. Park showed interest in improved relations with China and generated public interest and admiration among the Chinese public as a Chinese speaker and the daughter of a former South Korean president. Both sides successfully managed the exchange of high-level envoys prior to Park's inauguration, leading to an unprecedentedly intense exchange of visits between Park and Xi, who seemingly abandoned meetings with North Korea's Kim Jong-un in favor of regular exchanges with Park Geun-hye.

Park's first visit to China in July 2013 was a lovefest, generating hopes in South Korea for close cooperation on North Korea, while China signaled the desire for closer cooperation with South Korea to isolate Japan. China responded positively to South Korean requests for Beijing to honor South Korean patriot Ahn Jung-geun, who had assassinated Ito Hirobumi, Japan's governor general in South Korea, in Harbin in 1910. In place of the requested plaque to mark the location, China offered a small museum in honor of Ahn. During Xi's return visit to Seoul in July 2014, his efforts to split South Korea from Japan appeared to intensify, introducing a delicate point of diplomacy for South Korean diplomats, who remained hopeful of enhanced Chinese cooperation to pressure North Korea.[18] A public speech by Xi highlighting Japan's colonial aggression against South Korea while ignoring innumerable Chinese aggressions against the Korean Peninsula soured South Korean public opinion and led to the elite's criticisms of Xi's seeming heavy-handedness.

Nevertheless, perhaps the most diplomatically complex challenge Park Geun-hye faced involved her decision to participate in Beijing's seventieth anniversary commemorations of the end of World War II in September 2015. Park's attendance at the ceremony seemed out of place because most democracies declined to participate, and her presence on the podium with top Chinese leaders and Russian president Vladimir Putin sparked criticism.[19] However, in South Koreans' eyes, Park had symbolically replaced Kim Jong-un on the platform. In addition, she won Chinese consent to resume the long-delayed China-Japan-ROK trilateral summit in Seoul, which brought Chinese and Japanese leaders Li Keqiang and Abe Shinzo to Seoul to meet for the first time since 2012. The trilateral summit paved the way for Park's first bilateral summit meeting in Seoul with Abe.

Park Geun-hye's view was that a rising China and the Obama administration's rebalance to Asia, a policy of bringing greater diplomatic, economic, and military focus on Asia, were not "mutually exclusive" and that South Korea's ties with both countries were "not premised on choosing one over another." South Korea instead attempted to play the role of constructive convener between the United States and China. In one instance, it thwarted Chinese attempts to maneuver it into an anti–U.S. alliance position by objecting to an anti-alliance statement from China at the Conference on Inter-action and Confidence-Building Measures in Asia held in

Shanghai in the summer of 2014.[20] But in another instance it decided to join China's Asian Infrastructure and Investment Bank in the spring of 2015 following the United Kingdom's and Australia's decisions to join. Then in the following year, after North Korea's fourth nuclear test, South Korea deployed the THAAD System despite China's vociferous objections.

However, both China's and South Korea's efforts to achieve a closer relationship unraveled in 2016 following North Korea's fourth and fifth nuclear tests. First, Park Geun-hye's efforts to improve relations with China became subject to public criticism when Xi Jinping refused to take Park's calls and failed to coordinate a joint response to the fourth test. Second, South Korea's push for tougher sanctions on North Korea and China's reluctance and failure to properly follow through on its commitments to strictly reinforce the sanctions emerged as an important gap in China–South Korea relations. Third, China launched a concerted effort involving diplomatic protest and economic retaliation to reverse the decision by the United States and South Korea to deploy the THAAD System because Beijing viewed the system as part of a broader strategy of containment, even though it was clearly initialized in response to North Korean actions.[21]

THE DEBATE OVER SOUTH KOREA'S "TILT" TOWARD CHINA

The imbalance between South Korea's improved relations with China and the stalemate in its relations with Japan during the first three years of the Park administration led to speculation that South Korea would inevitably fall into China's orbit over the long term. This speculation was particularly strong in Japan due to the fact that worsening Japan–South Korea relations had coincided with South Korea's effort to improve relations with Beijing. Nevertheless, such speculation neglected to take into account the fact that South Korea's efforts to improve relations with China were firmly rooted in a strengthening alliance relationship between the United States and South Korea. The Obama administration's rebalance-to-Asia policy further raised the U.S. stake in ensuring that allies of Washington also have good relations with each other.

Moreover, U.S. and South Korean policies toward China under the Obama and Park administrations were parallel to each other, with both countries committed to simultaneous pursuit of active engagement with China and of hedging strategies in the event of negative consequences that might result from China's rise. For the United States, the strengthening of security alliances across Asia as part of the Obama administration's rebalancing policy constituted the hedge, and for South Korea the U.S.-ROK alliance provided a solid foundation upon which it could pursue more active engagement with China. South Korea's strategic interest in engaging with China was focused primarily on securing cooperation to contain North Korea, whereas the U.S. engagement efforts were more broadly gauged across the region, including both Northeast Asia and Southeast Asia.

Another factor that mitigated the negative effects of South Korea's use of the U.S.-ROK security alliance as a hedge that enabled engagement with China was South Korea's profound interest in pursuing strategies designed to dampen rather than encourage strategic rivalries in East Asia. Concerns about the possibility of great-power rivalry between the United States and China in the region were one of the specific issues Park cited as part of Asia's Paradox—namely, the possibility that China and the United States might pursue an arms race in Asia or that the Sino-U.S. relationship might come to be dominated by strategic rivalry.

Such a rivalry was clearly against South Korea's interests in part because it would force South Korea to make choices between the United States and China and would block it from continuing to benefit simultaneously from flourishing economic relations with China and the security benefits that flowed from the U.S.-ROK alliance. South Korea instead sought to promote cooperative relations across Asia through its promotion of the NAPCI. However, poor Japan–South Korea relations stood in the way of South Korea's ability to achieve that objective, generated tension in U.S.-ROK relations, and ultimately thwarted its interest in promoting cooperative relations in East Asia. Thus, based on a strong U.S.-ROK alliance, it was in South Korea's interest to promote the institutionalization of multilateral cooperation within Northeast Asia. The hope was that such cooperation would become sufficiently strong to inhibit tension and raise the tangible costs of overt rivalry among South Korea's larger neighbors.

Xi Jinping's failure to consult with Park Geun-hye in the aftermath of North Korea's fourth nuclear test, which followed the agreement between

Japan and South Korea regarding the comfort women issue by only a week, proved to be the trigger for South Korea's reversion to its traditional foreign-policy orientation, in which its cooperation with Japan, although uneasy, was greater than its cooperation with China. The emergence of the THAAD issue as a point of political tension in China–South Korea relations further unraveled any seeming progress between Seoul and Beijing during the first three years of the Park administration.

RECONCILING WITH JAPAN

Whereas the Park administration actively promoted its relations with China, relations with Japan under Abe Shinzo remained at an impasse. Park had emphasized in her presidential campaign the necessity that Japan take a "correct view of history" and acknowledge state responsibility for the Imperial Army's exploitation of Korean "comfort women" during World War II, and her administration stiff-armed Japanese overtures to send Abe to her inauguration. Abe's envoy to the inauguration, Aso Taro, bungled efforts to set a positive tone for South Korea–Japan relations and then a few months later led a parliamentary delegation to the Yasukuni shrine (which remains sensitive to South Koreans because spirits of class "A" war criminals from World War II are enshrined there), further straining the relationship. Abe's visit to Yasukuni in December 2013 and the Diet investigation in 2014 into the history behind the statement from Japan's chief cabinet secretary Kono Yohei in 1993 indirectly acknowledging the enslavement of Korean and other women to meet the sexual needs of the Japanese military during World War II further roiled the waters. However, U.S. efforts to stabilize the environment for improved Japan–South Korea relations through President Obama's hosting of a trilateral summit with Park and Abe on the sidelines of the Nuclear Security Summit in March 2014 resulted in the establishment of a regularized series of director-general-level meetings between Japan and South Korea to resolve the comfort women issue.[22]

Both South Korea and Japan gradually took steps to improve bilateral relations in the run-up to the fiftieth anniversary of diplomatic normalization. Cabinet-level relations were normalized, and Park and Abe appeared at parallel receptions held in Tokyo and Seoul to commemorate the anniversary.

Following Abe's speech commemorating the seventieth anniversary of the end of World War II on August 14, 2015, Park sent conciliatory signals, setting the tone for her to host Abe at a summit on the sidelines of the China-Japan-ROK trilateral summit on November 1.

The Japan-ROK summit generated backchannel negotiations that led to the announcement on December 28, 2015, of an agreement on the comfort women issue. The government of Japan issued a statement in the name of the prime minister that took responsibility for causing pain to the victims and pledged payment to the government of South Korea to establish a foundation dedicated to providing restitution to these Korean women and their families. The ROK acknowledged settlement of the issue as "final and irreversible" and pledged to open discussions with its nongovernmental organizations about moving the memorial statue honoring the comfort women from its location outside the Japanese embassy in Seoul.[23] Park Geun-hye's public statement to the Korean people indicated that "the Korean government made every effort to have the Japanese government acknowledge its responsibility and officially express remorse and apologies for the comfort women. And based on the judgment that sufficient progress was made within the boundaries of feasibility, we reached agreement." She called on the Japanese government "to squarely face history while faithfully implementing the agreement" and called on the Korean public and the victims to "view the agreement with largeness of heart and to stand together for the future of our nation."[24]

The South Korean public initially responded skeptically to the agreement. More than half of all South Koreans opposed the agreement days after its announcement, although the level of opposition was gradually reduced as the South Korean government methodically set about establishing the amount of restitution, receiving funds from the Japanese government for the Healing and Reconciliation Foundation, and securing the acceptance of the funds by the surviving comfort women and their families. However, South Korean public opinion remained strongly in support of keeping the memorial statue in its original location in front of the Japanese embassy in Seoul despite the Park administration's pledge in the agreement to discuss relocation to another, less-sensitive location. This would remain a sensitive political issue for the Park administration because opposition to the agreement fell largely along partisan lines. In the end, Park's involvement in a political scandal and impeachment prevented her from carrying out her pledge, leaving the issue a future sticking point in Japan–South Korea relations.

STRENGTHENING THE ALLIANCE WITH THE UNITED STATES

Park Geun-hye signaled the fundamental importance of the U.S.-ROK alliance by making the United States her first overseas destination following her election as president. Her summit with President Obama at the White House in May 2013 coincided with the sixtieth anniversary of the U.S.-ROK alliance. The subsequent joint statement reaffirmed both sides' commitment to a "comprehensive strategic alliance" that echoed themes first unveiled in the U.S.-ROK Joint Vision Statement of June 2009. In her press conference with President Obama, Park affirmed that the "alliance has been faithfully carrying out its role as a bulwark of peace and stability on the Korean Peninsula and in Northeast Asia, and . . . should continue to serve as a linchpin for peace and stability on the Korean Peninsula and in Asia."[25] Both leaders highlighted joint efforts to oppose North Korea's nuclear program as the core mission of the alliance, and President Obama cited global dimensions of cooperation with South Korea on development assistance for Afghanistan, bilateral development cooperation around the world between the American Peace Corps and its South Korean counterpart, and cooperation to support the opposition in Syria. By the time Park visited Washington again in October 2015, the list of global cooperation efforts had grown. The two sides successfully completed politically difficult agreements on military cost sharing and nuclear cooperation that had appeared likely to generate considerable bilateral tensions prior to their conclusion. In addition to development and humanitarian cooperation in Afghanistan and efforts against the Islamic State in Syria, President Obama identified "new frontier" efforts to enhance cyber defense against North Korea, to expand clean-energy investments, and to promote health and global development through anti-Ebola efforts, poverty reduction in Southeast Asia, and coordinated global education- and health-promotion efforts for girls.[26]

The U.S.-ROK alliance constituted an important foundation for South Korean foreign-policy efforts in several ways. First, senior-level administration officials expressed confidence and appreciation for Park Geun-hye's steadfast opposition to North Korea's nuclear weapons development. In addition to President Obama's public expressions of support for Park, senior administration officials expressed confidence in Park's understanding of and coordination to respond to the expanding threat posed by North Korea. Senior-level South Korean officials touted that they were not only on the same page as the United States but also on the same paragraph in their coordination regarding North Korea.[27]

Second, senior South Korean officials consulted closely with the United States on South Korea's regional diplomacy, including efforts to improve relations with China and efforts to manage differences with Japan. South Korea was responsive and proactive in its support for Obama administration initiatives—for instance by hosting follow-on meetings on nuclear security and global health.

Third, North Korean provocations and nuclear and missile tests drove closer U.S.-ROK political and security cooperation, including at the United Nations and through consultations between USFK and the ROK Ministry of National Defense on how to counter these provocations. The tests also catalyzed U.S.-ROK consultations on missile defense, including the joint announcement of the deployment of the politically sensitive THAAD System on July 8, 2016. U.S.-ROK security consultations evolved to include extended deterrence and cybersecurity.

IMPEDIMENTS TO PUBLIC SUPPORT FOR PARK ADMINISTRATION POLICIES

Park Geun-hye was domestically hampered from the start in her ability to pursue many of the objectives laid out in her inauguration speech. First, the National Assembly had passed a law prior to her administration that required 60 percent of National Assembly support before a bill could be put up for a vote in plenary session, effectively requiring a supermajority as a prerequisite for passage of new laws. This rule generated prolonged periods of paralysis within the legislature because it provided the opposition party with the capacity to block many bills that would pass the National Assembly if they were brought to a vote. The law resulted in a one-month delay in National Assembly approval for Park's plans to reorganize the government and strengthen economic planning, and it generated several prolonged stalemates during which the National Assembly failed to convene.

Second, the sinking of an overloaded cargo ferry between Incheon and Jeju Island on April 16, 2014, resulted in 304 casualties, including 250 high school students and 11 teachers on a school trip. The incident became a national tragedy that paralyzed the government and the Korean economy for months and revealed serious omissions in South Korea's disaster-response capacity and safety and regulatory standards. Park fired senior officials and ordered a reorganization of South Korea's maritime management. Responsibility for the cascading failures at every level of government ultimately became Park's responsibility and a major tool of criticism used by the opponents of her administration.[28] The administration bounced back after the initial shock of a second unexpected crisis hit in the summer of 2015 with the introduction of the Middle East Respiratory Syndrome to South Korea. The disease initially spread through South Korea's hospital system, but an aggressive diagnosis and quarantine system brought it under control within months, after 166 people had been diagnosed with it and 35 had died.[29]

Third, Park Geun-hye made a series of mistakes with regard to nomination of key officials in her administration, resulting in delays to critical appointments. Her first nomination for prime minister was held up as a result of the nominee's connection to embarrassing real estate deals and ethical lapses that gave the opposition grounds for attack and generated negative public perceptions, resulting in the nominee's withdrawal from the process. Then later, after having to fire her prime minister as a way to take responsibility for the *Sewol* ferry disaster in April 2014, she was embarrassed again by impolitic comments the replacement nominee made during the confirmation process. These repeated errors left the impression that Park and her close associates did not have the ability to scout, vet, and recruit the best talent in Korea to lead her administration. Although stewardship of defense and foreign-policy issues was not directly influenced by these failures, these incidents posed a distraction and a limitation for Park and influenced the public's judgment of her capability to achieve her economic and foreign-policy objectives.

Fourth, Park's support base in her election as president revealed the persistence of serious generational cleavages that reinforced the long-standing political divide between conservatives and progressives. These generational differences had first showed themselves in the surprising strength of support and turnout among younger voters for Roh Moo-hyun in the presidential election of 2002. However, the defining factor shaping Park's successful election victory in 2012 was a nearly 90 percent turnout rate among voters older than fifty.

Sagging support for Park and a major setback in the National Assembly elections in April 2016 that put the ruling party in a secondary position proved to be a foreshadowing of her fall from power. A series of scandals emerged in the summer and fall of 2016 that quickly led to her downfall: it became known that her closest confidant and family friend, Choi Soon-sil, had secretly been deeply involved in government affairs and had used Park's support and influence to establish a foundation and solicit tens of millions of dollars from Korean conglomerates. Public outrage and the discovery that Park was an accomplice led to extended political paralysis and ultimately to Park's December 2016 impeachment by the National Assembly, upheld unanimously by the Constitutional Court in March of 2017.

PARK'S FOREIGN-POLICY FAILURES

The phrase "Asia's Paradox" aptly describes the dilemmas that have long characterized South Korean foreign policy. Nevertheless, in the face of rising regional rivalries and despite South Korea's increased capabilities, Park proved largely unable to implement solutions to the foreign-policy challenges she aspired to address. Trustpolitik could not work if North Korea was unwilling to meet the standards for trust-based relations that Park insisted on. In fact, the intensified frequency of North Korea's nuclear tests only enhanced peninsular and regional tensions as Kim Jong-un flouted Park's insistence on denuclearization as a foundation for improved inter-Korean relations.

Likewise, South Korea had few practical tools with which to buffer Sino-Japanese or Sino-U.S. tensions in the region or to induce regional cooperation in Northeast Asia. Park sought to promote functional cooperation on technical issues through the NAPCI, but that effort fared little better than a similar effort made by Roh Moo-hyun. In her efforts to improve South Korea's relations with China and to induce greater Chinese cooperation on North Korea, Park fortunately risked little by standing on the U.S.-ROK alliance, but she came home empty-handed as a result of China's geostrategic mistrust of the United States and Xi's focus on Chinese objectives vis-à-vis Japan and because of an insufficient consideration of the fact that Beijing could develop a strategic relationship with Seoul only at the expense of its relationship with Pyongyang. If the NAPCI proved idealistic and unfeasible in its implementation, Park's Eurasia Initiative was even more so in the aftermath of Russia's invasion of Crimea.

Park's fundamental concerns and focus remained tied to the growing challenges to peninsular stability from North Korea's nuclear program. South Korea pursued its foreign policy autonomously but in close concert with the United States, relying firmly on the alliance as the primary foundation and partnership guaranteeing the success of South Korean foreign policy and security strategies at the peninsular, regional, and global levels. Park Geun-hye's foreign policy showed great comfort with the coexistence of autonomy and alliance.

Ironically, Park Geun-hye's main diplomatic achievement turned out to be the stabilization of relations with Japan as a result of the agreement with Prime Minister Abe Shinzo on the comfort women issue on December 28, 2015. The agreement—a "final and irreversible" but domestically contested effort to resolve the issue between the two governments—restored a veneer of normalcy to the Japan–South Korea relationship and promised to remove a serious diplomatic impediment from the two countries' bilateral agenda. However, despite stabilization and marginal improvement between the two publics regarding the state of the bilateral relationship, their relationship remained contested domestically in South Korea, especially following

Park's impeachment, and subject to renewed risks of misunderstanding over historical and territorial issues.

These developments raise important questions about how and whether South Korea's rising capacity can be effectively applied to expand its maneuvering room as long as its strategic environment is shaped by the needs and interactions of larger powers. The remaining chapters review the strategic considerations shaping the approaches South Korea has taken and should take, whether its rising capabilities can provide it with new options for securing autonomy apart from the alliance with the United States, and how these capabilities might evolve in the event that China becomes the most powerful global actor and in the context of Korean aspirations for national unification.

8

THE PARADOX OF SOUTH KOREA'S
MIDDLE-POWER STATUS

S OUTH KOREA'S EMERGENCE as a middle power has generated a bedev-
iling paradox for South Korean strategic thinkers. Its increased
capabilities have indeed given the country the basis upon which to
play unprecedented constructive roles as a leader in international affairs
and contributor to global security and prosperity. They have also generated
expectations within South Korea that the country will have more leverage,
both with the United States and with its neighbors, especially on the issues
that matter to it the most. However, South Korea's options in managing
regional affairs within Northeast Asia are still constrained by the complex
regional security environment it faces and by expanding threats from
North Korea. As a result, South Korea finds that its flexibility to act as a
middle power is inversely proportional to its priorities: it faces the greatest
limits on its capacity to act on existential security issues that involve hard
power. In addition, it remains less powerful than all of its immediate
neighbors with the exception of North Korea. Realist scholars such as
John Mearsheimer would conclude that the country cannot escape its fate
as a weak victim with little space for strategic maneuver in a world shaped
by great-power politics.[1]

Thus, the dilemma for South Korean strategists is how to effectively
utilize the capabilities the country has to enhance its importance as a
global leader while navigating a regional environment in which it faces

serious constraints on its ability to determine its own fate. Despite South Korea's expanded autonomy on global issues, its comparative vulnerability in a regional context still dictates the need to work with a patron that is able to guarantee the strategic environment necessary to ensure its security and prosperity. This chapter defines the concept of middle power in terms of the specific roles to which South Korea aspires, outlines South Korea's contributions to specific areas of global governance, and analyzes its regional deficit in relative power to illustrate how regional constraints have limited its ability to take full advantage of its relative capacity on a global scale or of its decisive advantages in relative power vis-à-vis North Korea.

SOUTH KOREA AS A MIDDLE POWER

South Korean strategic thinkers have historically thought of the country as a weak state with few means available to shape its own strategic environment. But by the 1990s South Korean leaders expected that the country's economic accomplishments would make space for it to pursue a more expansive and multifaceted foreign policy from the early 1990s, when President Kim Young-sam adopted the concept of *segyehwa*, or globalization. Roh Moo-hyun administration officials referenced South Korea as a middle power and considered a level of autonomy and agency that assumed a middle-power status for South Korea. But it was not until the inauguration of Lee Myung-bak in 2008 that South Korean academics and government officials began to actively debate the foreign-policy implications of South Korea as a middle power. The main assumption underlying this idea is that South Korea is an actor that has the capacity to influence and contribute to world affairs.

Based on South Korea's membership in and hosting of the G20 and on its efforts to contribute constructively to environmental protection by hosting multilateral initiatives to promote nuclear security, development cooperation, and "green growth," Vice Minister for Foreign Affairs Kim Sung-han argued in early 2013 that "South Korea is well poised to take the initiative in middle-power diplomacy with several other like-minded countries."[2] Jongryn Mo and G. John Ikenberry argue that diffusion of power within the context of the liberal international order provides middle powers such as Korea with new opportunities to play important agenda-setting roles and that "a power shift from the developed to the developing world places middle powers in strategic and pivotal positions."[3]

Lee Myung-bak's "hosting diplomacy" role as a convener of international gatherings on important governance issues generated interest among Korea scholars and policy makers in South Korea's adoption of middle-power diplomacy as a new framework that might be used to evaluate and guide its foreign policy.[4] Andrew O'Neil characterizes middle powers as "those states . . . that possess the material capabilities to shape outcomes in niche areas in the global governance sphere when acting in concert with like-minded states."[5] According to this definition, middle powers are countries with the capacity and willingness to play the role of catalyst, facilitator, and/or manager in support of peace and conflict management, multipolarity, and rule building within the international system.[6] South Korean scholars have utilized these characteristics as measures by which to judge South Korea's effectiveness in pursuing "middle-power diplomacy."[7] The East Asia Institute's Middle Power Diplomacy Initiative identifies four primary roles that middle powers such as South Korea should aspire to play as part of that diplomacy: early mover, bridge, coalition coordinator, and norm diffuser. These roles respectively involve leading by example, mediating differences in international negotiating settings, building coalitions of like-minded states, and helping to diffuse international norms and standards.[8]

A major feature of South Korea's middle-power debate is about South Korea trying to escape the curse of geography that has sandwiched it between major powers and their often conflicting interests. However, in order to effect this escape, it needs to capitalize on its unique advantages and position, usually defined by networking capability or capacity, to contribute to a specific issue using the capabilities it has developed from its unique experiences with modernization, democratization, or specific functional issues. By defining middle power relationally as a node or center of attraction among like-minded parties or as an actor that is able to use catalytic or networking roles as a means of exerting influence, South Korea seeks to escape from the geographic limitations that have historically defined its situation. Sohn Yul argues that South Korea's positional role as a "node" in a network enables a "middle power diplomacy" that exploits Korea's connectedness, bridging capabilities, and niche diplomacy as a rule setter in international institutions.[9] Andrew Carr suggests that middle powers "must have some reasonable capacity to protect their core interests, including through military means—not necessarily to be able to defeat a great power, but certainly to raise the costs such as to provide a significant discouragement of attacks on themselves or their core interests." He also argues that middle powers have the "ability to alter a specific element of the international order through formalized structures, such as international treaties and institutions, and informal means, such as norms or balance of power."[10]

South Korea has carved out a niche role and made contributions to international order by building on nontraditional security issues such as green growth, development, nuclear nonproliferation, and international financial governance. In each of these areas, it has earned a place at the table through its expression of interests, its ideas, and its capabilities. However, its contributions in nontraditional security areas have not broken down the regional constraints that accompany the power deficit it faces as a middle power in comparison with its larger neighbors.

SOUTH KOREA ON THE GLOBAL STAGE

South Korea has increasingly contributed to international leadership through participation in and hosting of international gatherings. It has made contributions in areas that have demonstrated its soft power, has provided a system-reinforcing role, and has played a bridging role between developed and developing countries.[11] Its efforts to assume the attributes of a middle power as a source of leadership in the international system are a departure from its past diplomatic profile in that these efforts have established it as a country that desires to be a net security producer after having spent many decades as a net security consumer. The Lee Myung-bak administration pursued global efforts alongside peninsula security efforts in four primary areas that reflected South Korea's relative strength in the context of global capabilities: global financial governance, international development cooperation, green growth and climate change, and international security, with a focus on nuclear security.

GLOBAL FINANCIAL GOVERNANCE

In response to the global financial crisis of 2008–2009, South Korea took a leadership role in financial governance through its contributions to the G20 process. First, in September 2009 Lee Myung-bak and Australian prime minister Kevin Rudd advocated for countries to avoid protectionism and address macroeconomic imbalances by promoting more active macroeconomic policy coordination. As leaders of non-G7 countries that aspired to have an impact on the international agenda by discouraging protection and advocating for macroeconomic policy coordination, Lee and Rudd offered constructive guidance at a moment of international crisis.[12]

Second, South Korea became the first non-G7 country to host a G20 summit in 2010, a time when the bridging of global differences on a number of issues was critical to fostering a global economic recovery. In the role of diplomatic host and caretaker of the G20 agenda, South Korea was called upon to mediate Sino-U.S. tensions over currency and sought to rebalance the governance structure of the IMF to reflect the relatively greater weight of China and other developing countries in international finance. South Korea also sought to promote its role as a bridge between developed and developing countries through its efforts to push forward the idea of building a global financial safety net to protect developing-country economies from external shocks, to promote a more inclusive approach to international development, and to promote green growth as an adaptive approach to addressing climate-change issues.[13] South Korea's efforts to support the G20 process included the deployment of an impressive array of bureaucratic talent and resources in the establishment of an interagency committee responsible for diplomatic and logistical preparations for the meeting, staffed with a leadership that reflected decades of international experience in international financial governance.[14]

Third, South Korea has been a leader in promoting trade liberalization through the negotiation of FTAs since it negotiated its first FTA with Chile in 2004. After that, reflecting the export-dependent nature of South Korea's economic growth, the country aggressively pursued FTAs around the world, concluding new FTAs with India, the European Union, the United States, and China, among others. Its efforts in this area provided momentum for the country's trade liberalization at the bilateral and regional level at a time when worldwide momentum for trade liberalization through pursuit of global agreements had come to a standstill.[15]

INTERNATIONAL DEVELOPMENT COOPERATION

South Korea came to the task of leadership in international development with high aspirations despite its relatively small contributions to international development (although those contributions were rapidly growing) and a small share in the overall international development-assistance pie. However, South Korea did bring unique experience as a former consumer of international development assistance that had experienced rapid development and become a new international donor within two generations. The living memory of being on the receiving end of development assistance combined with South Korea's successful economic-development experience has made South Korea an attractive model for developing countries and has provided it with a unique claim to a potential bridging role between developing and developed countries.

South Korea's international development program remains modest, although it aspired to grow the size of the program rapidly beginning in 2008. The program has expanded from 0.086 percent of the gross national income in 2008 to 0.139 percent of gross national income in 2016, but South Korea still faces limitations in its ability to effectively monitor development impacts. South Korea has also successfully built the Korean Volunteer Program to send Korean overseas to support international development efforts. That program has become the second-largest government-run volunteer program in the world, behind the U.S. Peace Corps. Cooperation between U.S. and Korean development agencies has also taken hold in recent years, with a Memorandum of Understanding signed in 2011.

South Korea's primary impact on approaches to international development came in the context of its hosting the OECD Development Assistance Committee in Busan in 2011. At that time, South Korea led an effort to bridge the thinking of established donors and new donors by adjusting their focus from the idea of aid effectiveness to the concept of development effectiveness. This approach marked a shift toward the idea that the main metric for judging the impact of development assistance should be less the effectiveness of particular projects as defined by donors than the broader impact of assistance on national development, thereby incorporating aid recipients' aspirations to a greater degree.

South Korean contributions to international development have increasingly been reflected as a new dimension of U.S.-ROK alliance relations and as an opportunity for expanded cooperation between the two countries. This was the case in the context of South Korea's willingness to respond to public-health crises, such as the Ebola crisis in Liberia and Sierra Leone. In addition, South Korea has made entrepreneurial contributions to job creation in postcrisis situations, such as the earthquake in Haiti in 2010, where a South Korean textile producer worked with American private-sector efforts to establish an employment center and create jobs in Haiti in the aftermath of the crisis.

GREEN GROWTH AND CLIMATE CHANGE

The Lee Myung-bak administration developed unique intellectual leadership on behalf of green growth, so that South Korea's contributions had an impact disproportionate to the size of its stake in the issue. President Lee promoted domestic and international efforts to respond to the effects of climate change by persuading government and industry to join in pursuit of an adaptive model that would incorporate green growth as an essential element of national energy and development strategies. Toward this end, the Lee administration established the Global Green Growth Institute as an international organization dedicated to consulting with government, industry, and international financial institutions on how to incorporate green growth as part of a clean-development model. In part because of this emphasis, South Korea's Songdo city was selected as the global headquarters of the Global Climate Fund, a new international institution for climate finance established through the UN Framework on Climate Change. The Global Climate Fund is projected to be the main player in financing climate-change adaptation and mitigation efforts and seeks through a new governance model to combine private and public financing sources toward this end.

INTERNATIONAL SECURITY AND THE NUCLEAR SECURITY SUMMIT

South Korean efforts on nuclear security came about primarily in the context of the U.S.-ROK alliance but provided South Korea with an opportunity to build experience and ties internationally in an area directly related to its accumulated technical experience and capabilities in peaceful production of nuclear power and its direct interest in countering nuclear weapons proliferation on the Korean Peninsula.

South Korea has likewise made development contributions in the context of UN efforts to promote postconflict stabilization in war-torn areas such as Afghanistan, where it established a field hospital that became a leading provider of health services to local Afghans from 2010 to 2015. In addition, South Korea contributed to multilateral antipiracy efforts in the Gulf of Aden and successfully recovered a South Korean ship from pirate control in 2012. It has also stepped up its contributions to UN peacekeeping operations in recent years, with active efforts to respond to the situations in Sudan and Lebanon.

* * *

Since 2010, South Korea's desire and capability to become an international leader have taken concrete form in its efforts with respect to the G20, international development, climate change, and international security issues. These developments show South Korea's enthusiasm to play a middle-power role in contributions to international governance and in efforts to form global networks designed to tackle specific issues. However, the manifestations of these contributions have occurred primarily far from the

Korean Peninsula rather than within the region. Therefore, it is necessary to examine more closely South Korea's situation in a regional context to understand the constraints on its ability to use its middle-power capabilities and aspirations.

REGIONAL CONSTRAINTS ON SOUTH KOREAN ACTION

In contrast to South Korea's growing global contributions, its relative weakness compared to its neighbors constrains its freedom of action to shape its own strategic environment.

Figure 8.1 shows the impact of Asia's modernization in terms of relative GDP. The graph shows that the United States has remained the most powerful economy in the world by size and compared to the leading countries in Northeast Asia. The graph also shows clearly Japan's economic gains deriving from its postwar recovery and the fact that through the 1990s Japan was the dominant source of economic growth and the largest economy in East Asia. Although South Korea followed Japan's model as a late-developing country, the smaller relative size of its population and economy mean that its economic gains have not registered as large an increase in GDP relative to the increase in Japan's GDP. Because of China's larger overall scale, the size of China's economy surpassed the size of South Korea's in the early 1990s despite the fact that South Korea's modernization began two decades earlier. Moreover, by 2008 China's rise in GDP had clearly outstripped that of Japan despite the fact that Japan remains a relatively rich country in per capita GDP terms. Nonetheless, the size of China's GDP has clearly surpassed and nearly doubled Japan's GDP in a relatively short period.

South Korea's national GDP has remained the smallest among the countries of Northeast Asia (with the exception of North Korea), despite its economic success. Its economy is among the top-twenty national economies in the world, but the size of its GDP when viewed in a regional context remains relatively small. Although South Korea's GDP, as shown in figure 8.1, is now equivalent to Russia's GDP, that is due to Russia's

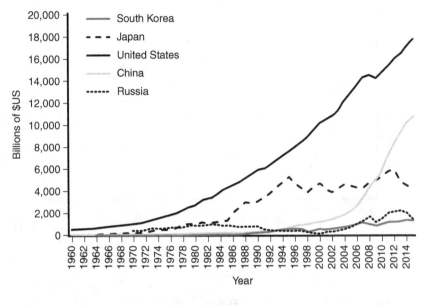

FIGURE 8.1

Gross Domestic Product of Northeast Asian States, 1960–2014

Source: World Bank, "GDP (Current US$)," updated 2015, http://data.worldbank.org
/indicator/NY.GDP.MKTP.CD; "GDP and Its Breakdown at Current Prices in
U.S. Dollars," United Nations National Accounts Main Aggregate Database,
updated December 2015, http://unstats.un.org/unsd/snaama/dnllist.asp.

economic mismanagement rather than to South Korea's success. Figure 8.2 shows that although South Korea's share of GDP in Northeast Asia has continued on an upward trajectory, that share is relatively small and has never been larger than the 11 percent that it achieved in 2007. Thus, despite South Korea's relative economic growth, its economic capacity remains the weakest in the region, with the exception of North Korea's.

South Korea has likewise emerged in recent years as one of the top-fifteen countries in defense expenditures, a measure that can be used as an indicator of relative military power. Historically, South Korea's defense spending has always been relatively high given the scale of the threat that the country faces from North Korea, but it is also useful to view its defense expenditures in a regional context. Once again, these expenditures are

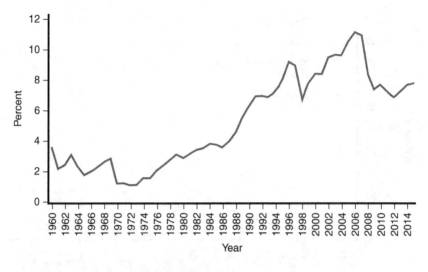

FIGURE 8.2

South Korea's Share of Northeast Asian States' Gross Domestic Product (Excluding the United States), 1960–2014

Source: World Bank, "GDP (Current US$)," updated 2015, http://data.worldbank.org /indicator/NY.GDP.MKTP.CD; "GDP and Its Breakdown at Current Prices in U.S. Dollars," United Nations National Accounts Main Aggregate Database, updated December 2015, http://unstats.un.org/unsd/snaama/dnllist.asp.

small when viewed as a proportion of overall defense expenditures in Northeast Asia. Figure 8.3 shows that the United States still remains the dominant investor in military capability on a global scale when compared to other regional actors such as China, Russia, and Japan. However, even when the United States is removed from the equation, as shown in figure 8.4, South Korea's defense spending in overall terms severely lags China's rapid growth in military spending as well as Russia's. In absolute terms, defense expenditures in South Korea are approaching the level of defense expenditures in Japan, which have steadily declined due to Japan's domestic informal commitment not to spend more than one percent of its GDP on defense. Figure 8.5 shows that South Korea's share of regional defense spending remains relatively small, at around 4 percent of overall defense expenditures in Northeast Asia.

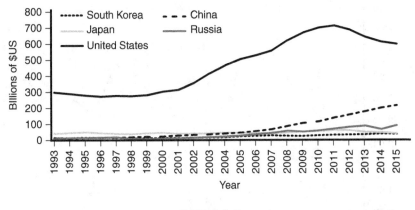

FIGURE 8.3

Defense Expenditure in Northeast Asia, 1993–2015

Source: "Data for All Countries from 1988–2015 (Current US$)," Stockholm International Peace Research Institute Military Expenditures Database, updated 2015, https://www.sipri.org/databases/milex.

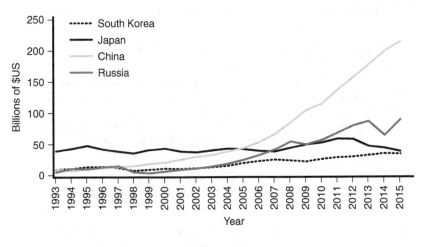

FIGURE 8.4

Defense Expenditure in Northeast Asia (Excluding the United States), 1993–2015

Source: "Data for All Countries from 1988–2015 (Current US$)," Stockholm International Peace Research Institute Military Expenditures Database, updated 2015, https://www.sipri.org/databases/milex.

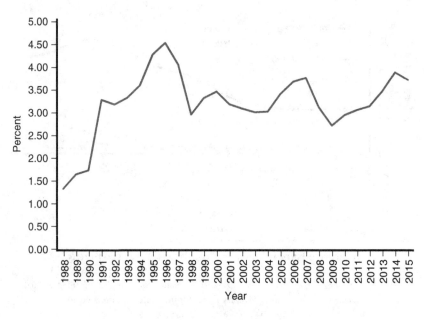

FIGURE 8.5

South Korea's Share of Regional Defense Expenditures, 1988–2015

Note: Estimates before 1988 omit several states, including China and the Soviet Union/Russia due to lack of information. More recent figures of Chinese and Russian expenditures are estimates.

Source: "Data for All Countries from 1988–2015 (Current US$)," Stockholm International Peace Research Institute Military Expenditures Database, updated 2015, https://www.sipri .org/databases/milex; Chung-in Moon and Sangkeun Lee, "Military Spending and the Arms Race on the Korean Peninsula," *Asia Pacific Journal* 8, no. 2 (2008), http://apjjf.org/-Chung-in-Moon/3333/article.html.

What do these trends mean for South Korea's status as a middle power in Northeast Asia? First, they show that its economic and military capacity within the regional context remains constrained by the gap between its resources and its immediate neighbors' relatively larger economic and military resources. Second, as explored in chapter 9, they help to explain why South Koreans increasingly view regional security issues through the lens of Sino-U.S. relations. With China's continued rise, the increasingly tense regional environment, and the growing North Korean threat, South Korea may potentially face even more constraints in the future.

These factors, combined with the fact that the Korean Peninsula is sandwiched between the world's first-, second-, and third-largest economies in the world, mean that South Korea faces immense constraints at the regional level. In addition, the trajectory of South Korea's GDP and defense spending as a share of the regional total may raise questions about its ability to sustain its middle-power status in the Northeast Asian regional context.

PENINSULAR IMPACT OF SOUTH KOREA AS A MIDDLE POWER

South Korea's growing capabilities vis-à-vis the North are dramatically different from its capabilities in a regional context. As shown in figure 8.6 and 8.7, its economic growth and defense expenditures have far outstripped those of the North, leaving an isolated Pyongyang with little choice other

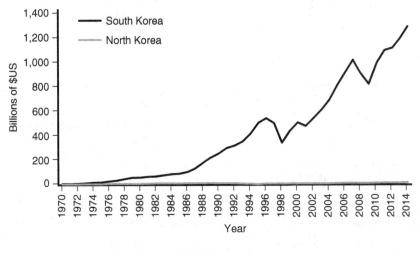

FIGURE 8.6

Gross Domestic Product, South Korea and North Korea, 1970–2014

Source: "GDP and Its Breakdown at Current Prices in U.S. Dollars," United Nations National Accounts Main Aggregate Database, updated December 2015, http://unstats.un.org/unsd/snaama/dnllist.asp.

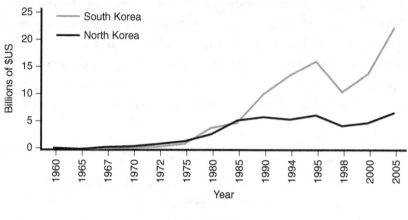

FIGURE 8.7

Defense Expenditures, South Korea and North Korea, 1960–2005

Source: "Data for all Countries from 1988–2015 (Current US$)," Stockholm International Peace Research Institute Military Expenditures Database, updated 2015, https://www.sipri .org/databases/milex; "Pre-1988 Military Expenditures (Constant USD Beta)," Stockholm International Peace Research Institute Extended Milex Database Beta, updated 2015, available on request from the institute; Chung-in Moon and Sangkeun Lee, "Military Spending and the Arms Race on the Korean Peninsula," *Asia Pacific Journal* 8, no. 2 (2008), http://apjjf.org/-Chung-in-Moon/3333/article.html.

than to utilize asymmetric strategies as a way to level the peninsular playing field and to defend itself against a more powerful South Korea. Moreover, South Korea's access to international technology makes its weapons systems superior to those of the technologically backward North, despite North Korea's advantages in manpower, special-operations forces, and unconventional weapons.

South Korea has utilized its comparative advantages vis-à-vis North Korea and its growing reach through its middle-power diplomacy in seeking to cut off international sources of economic and political support for North Korea. South Korea's increased capacity relative to North Korea has enabled it to influence international perceptions and make its case on issues involving North Korea's conventional provocations, nuclear pursuits, and human rights practices. This influence has three implications. First, on the basis of its considerably greater international influence compared to that of North Korea, South Korea has come to see itself as the main intermediary between North Korea and the international community. Second, to the extent that North Korea takes actions inimical to South Korean interests, South Korea sees itself as capable of using international pressure to enhance North Korea's further isolation. And third, South Korea's middle-power capabilities will most likely affect the structure of the U.S.-ROK alliance.

SOUTH KOREA AS INTERMEDIARY BETWEEN NORTH KOREA AND THE INTERNATIONAL COMMUNITY

South Korea's growing capacity, international connections, and relative influence vis-à-vis North Korea have led to the belief in South Korea that North Korea's opening to the international community will be effective only when it involves cooperation and facilitation from South Korea. Its engagement-oriented governments sought to play this role by establishing South Korea as an economic intermediary for trade and investment in North Korea first by promoting tourism at Mount Kumgang in the early-2000s and later through establishing the Kaesong Industrial Complex in the mid-2000s. Despite the eventual failure of the complex, South Koreans expect that they will be the de facto window through which the international business community is best placed to pursue business opportunities in North Korea in the event of the North's economic integration, reform, and opening. Although Beijing remains the de facto entrepôt and transit point for interactions with Pyongyang, many South Koreans believe that it would be difficult for North Korea to pursue effective economic relationships with the outside world (with the exception of Sino-DPRK relations) independent of South Korea's tacit support and cooperation. The Kaesong Industrial Complex, despite its failure, provided a clear indication of South Korea's expectations and willingness to be the primary conduit for the rehabilitation of North Korea and its integration with the South as part of a process of national unification. The view of North Korea as a market is a major factor shaping the Moon Jae-in administration's (2017–) efforts to restore inter-Korean relations. The conservative government of Lee Myung-bak also endorsed such an approach with his government's pledge that it would invest in business and development in North Korea to roughly triple North Korea's per capita annual income to $3,000, but implementation of Lee's approach was clearly conditioned on North Korea's denuclearization. South Korea has clearly and consistently shown its willingness to invest the lion's share of resources required to achieve North Korea's rehabilitation to achieve the objective of a unified Korean state.

SOUTH KOREA AS AN INTERNATIONAL SOURCE OF PRESSURE ON NORTH KOREA

North Korea's relationships with international humanitarian aid and emergency assistance organizations increasingly depend on South Korean government attitudes. North Korea's efforts to threaten South Korea's security by pursuing nuclear weapons have resulted in South Korea's efforts to mobilize international pressure to punish and isolate Pyongyang. The Park Geun-hye administration's unilateral closure of the Kaesong Industrial Complex following North Korea's fourth nuclear test in January 2016 set an example that helped generate momentum toward the adoption of UN Security Council Resolution 2270. Likewise, Park's main regional initiative, the NAPCI, sought to strengthen functional cooperation in Northeast Asia, on the one hand isolating North Korea but on the other hand giving it the opportunity to join in cooperation if it was willing to do so.

The South Korean government is also capable of influencing UN member states' attitude and generosity with respect to international organizations that provide humanitarian aid to North Korea. Moreover, South Korea has been a leading contributor of funds for humanitarian assistance to North Korea via UN organizations. Many countries are likely to ensure that their plans for humanitarian assistance to North Korea do not run afoul of South Korean wishes, given the likelihood that South Korean trade with almost any nation in the world is larger than that country's trade with North Korea. South Korea's globalized and vibrant trade relationships provide a source of leverage that it can use to North Korea's disadvantage in the context of efforts to strengthen UN sanctions following North Korean nuclear and missile tests.

SOUTH KOREA'S RELATIVE POWER VIS-À-VIS NORTH KOREA AND THE U.S.-ROK ALLIANCE

South Korea's increasing military capabilities vis-à-vis North Korea have provided the basis for some cogent arguments that the United States should reduce its presence on the Korean Peninsula and turn over the main responsibilities for deterrence to South Korea. These pressures were particularly strong in the mid-2000s, at which time South Korea expressed the desire for greater autonomy during Future of the Alliance Talks. The two countries negotiated steps toward the consolidation of the U.S. presence on the Korean Peninsula and envisioned a shift from a combined wartime command structure under U.S. control to an institutional structure in which the United States would provide air and intelligence support to South Korean–led operations. Both governments set in place a planning process that envisioned a new structure for the relationship by 2012. In 2010, however, the U.S. and South Korean presidents decided to delay implementation of these arrangements in light of provocations by North Korea (the sinking of the *Cheonan* and shelling of Yeonpyeong Island) that led to concerns about possible weaknesses in deterrence and defense.

A second factor that has emerged to push off implementation of a revised command structure indefinitely is the steady, slow improvement in North Korea's asymmetric nuclear and missile capabilities, which have required a redoubling of U.S. commitment to the peninsula. Concerns over North Korea's ongoing nuclear development also resulted in strengthening of U.S.-ROK alliance dialogues on how to deal with the issue as well as on the mechanisms by which the United States intends to implement extended deterrence.

South Korea's enhanced capabilities both vis-à-vis North Korea and within the alliance raise questions about whether and under what circumstances South Korea might seek greater autonomy from its current alliance relationship with the United States. Alternatively, one might wonder whether the United States might conclude that South Korea is strong enough to defend itself or that the alliance with South Korea is no longer essential to U.S. security interests in the region. This set of questions appeared to motivate efforts by South Korea and the United States in the mid-2000s to critically evaluate the future of the alliance based on the extent to which the two countries continued to share a common assessment of the regional threats. Therefore, it is worth evaluating the conditions under which such a debate might reemerge in the future.

In 2005, several factors stimulated skepticism among U.S. alliance planners about the long-term future of the alliance. First, the United States and South Korea differed in terms of their priorities and threat assessments regarding North Korea. The South Korean leadership appeared to downplay the dangers associated with North Korea's nuclear development, whereas the United States continued to regard North Korea's breakout from its commitments to denuclearization as a serious threat not only to the region but also to the global nonproliferation regime. Although the U.S.-ROK alliance did not dissolve at this time, it did suffer considerable tensions.

Second, the United States and South Korea focused on different regional threats. South Korea focused on Japan, particularly with regard to the history and territorial issues, whereas the United States focused on China and saw Japan as a crucial ally. Although the problems in the Japan-ROK relationship were not the main source of difference between Washington and Seoul, these differences were a source of secondary tensions between the two countries.

Third, although progressive Roh Moo-hyun and conservative George W. Bush differed in their ideological predispositions, the institutions that bound the alliance held, and the relationship did not dissolve, just as although U.S. relations with many European allies during the period suffered due to differences over the Iraq War under George W. Bush, these alliances, too, survived.

GLOBAL, REGIONAL, AND PENINSULAR IMPACT OF SOUTH KOREA AS A MIDDLE POWER

South Korea's growing capabilities have enabled it to have an impact at the global level in specific areas where it is able to make contributions based on its own experiences with development and democratization. However,

South Korea has not been able to translate those capabilities into its regional context, where the power gap between it and its larger neighbors continues to impose constraints on its capacity to maneuver and influence those neighbors. At the same time, South Korea's capabilities have outstripped those of North Korea, contributing to a peninsular imbalance that South Korea has sought to exploit by leveraging its international influence to increase pressure on the North. To the extent that South Korea's capabilities continue to grow within the alliance or to the extent that U.S. capabilities and commitment are perceived as weakening in the context of China's rise, there may be greater willingness to consider alternatives to the alliance within South Korea and greater desire within the United States to reduce risk of entrapment or to pare down U.S. commitments to the defense of South Korea. For instance, statements made by Donald Trump during the U.S. presidential campaign in 2016 generated close scrutiny within South Korea regarding the possibility that the United States might withdraw from its long-standing commitments to South Korea's defense. These developments could lead to a crisis for the alliance in the future.

South Korea's aggregate conventional capabilities will continue to outstrip those of the North. However, North Korea's emphasis on development of asymmetric capabilities, in particular its unchecked nuclear and missile development, is likely to remain a convincing argument for a continued U.S. force presence on the Korean Peninsula. In the longer term, South Korea's strategic choices will continue to face constraints in the context of rising regional rivalries, despite its relative dominance compared to the North. The paradox between South Korea's limited capability to shape its own security environment and its growing ability as a leading global economy to contribute on specific niche issues will continue to vex South Korean strategists for the foreseeable future.

9

KOREA BETWEEN THE UNITED STATES
AND CHINA

ROM ITS ESTABLISHMENT in 1948, the Republic of Korea has faced limited strategic options and has needed its security alliance with the
United States in order to survive. The withdrawal of U.S. forces from
South Korea prior to the Korean War and North Korea's surprise attack
revealed South Korea's vulnerability and need for a protector. Since the
Korean War, South Korean leaders have relied on the alliance to guarantee its security, enable its prosperity, and, it is hoped, achieve Korean unification. No viable alternative to the U.S.-ROK alliance exists.

However, China's rapid rise, increasing weight on the international
stage, and geographic proximity to the Korean Peninsula have stimulated an active debate within South Korea over whether it faces a transformed strategic environment. Koreans are increasingly considering the
need to make trade-offs among its fundamental objectives and the high
costs and consequences of making a wrong strategic choice between the
United States and China as a possible alliance partner capable and willing to play the role of security guarantor for South Korea. The parameters of this debate will be influenced more and more by a range of factors,
including the relative power, influence, and commitment of the United
States and China; the extent to which the relationship between the
United States and China is cooperative or confrontational; and the South

Korean public's comparative level of satisfaction with the relative level of autonomy and respect that their country receives from the United States and China.

As an example of the consequences of choosing the wrong partner to guarantee security of the nation, Korean scholars recall the disastrous failure of Korean leaders to switch their allegiances in response to the power transition from the declining Chinese Ming dynasty to the rising Manchus, the rulers of the succeeding Qing dynasty, in the 1600s. References to this sobering historical experience are used to underline the importance of being an early adapter in the midst of a power transition from the United States to China as the dominant global or regional actor or both. In the case of the Ming–Qing transition, Korea's Joseon dynasty leader Gwanghaegun initially sought to stay out of the conflict, but he was eventually overthrown by pro-Ming officials. Korea ended up paying a heavy price when the Manchus subdued Joseon Korea through force. The decision to challenge the Manchus had catastrophic consequences; it is estimated that as much as 10 percent of Korea's population was taken to Shenyang as slaves of the new Qing leadership.[1]

However, even if China were to emerge as an alliance partner for South Korea, would it be an adequate and credible replacement of the United States in providing security guarantees on the peninsula and at what cost? These questions require convincing answers before South Korea can attempt to pursue China as an alternative security guarantor to the United States. Another set of considerations involves the means available to South Korea to deal with the evolving strategic environment in East Asia. The questions include under what conditions South Korea might plausibly pursue its security needs in an independent and autonomous manner, whether an alliance with a larger power is still necessary to ensure South Korean security objectives, the extent to which South Korea's aspirations for security and unification may involve contradictory pathways or means, and whether unification is perceived as a strategic dead end or as a pathway that will lead to a broader set of strategic options for securing an independent and prosperous Korea.

EVOLUTION OF SOUTH KOREAN POLICY TOWARD CHINA AND THE EMERGENCE OF DEBATES OVER STRATEGIC CHOICE

During and after talks that led to diplomatic normalization in 1992, South Korea primarily pursued a strategy of accommodation with China. South Korea's main strategic objective in pursuing normalization of relations with China was to further Roh Tae-woo's Nordpolitik (as described in chapter 3) through the establishment of diplomatic relations with Beijing and Moscow. However, Roh's eagerness to normalize relations with China by the end of his term led him to accommodate China's strategic goal of marginalizing Taiwan, and South Korea failed to convince Beijing to favor Seoul over Pyongyang.[2]

Another factor leading South Korea to pursue an accommodation strategy toward China was the tremendous growth in trade relations with China. Sino–South Korean trade relations grew at double digits consistently for almost two decades, emerging as a primary driver for a closer relationship between Seoul and Beijing. The desire to keep mutually beneficial trade relations on track led both Seoul and Beijing to minimize or proactively manage political crises. The burgeoning of the China–South Korea economic relationship was not regarded as a threat to the U.S.-ROK security alliance in the 1990s or early 2000s, but when China surpassed the United States as South Korea's number one economic partner in 2004, the apparent divergence between South Korea's economic opportunities with China and the security alliance with the United States began to draw attention in South Korean policy circles. A "China lobby" within South Korean business circles emerged that sought to protect South Korea's relations with China because they had long considered China a low-cost production base at which intermediate goods might be assembled and produced for the U.S. consumer market.

South Korea's views of relations with China remained remarkably benign, even despite the "garlic wars" of the late 1990s, which involved China's barring of high-value South Korean electronics and telecommunications exports in retaliation for South Korea's failure to open agricultural markets to imports of Chinese garlic. The "garlic wars" sensitized South Korea to the potential leverage China could utilize to damage South Korea's economy in the event of Sino–South Korean conflict.[3] However, China's entry into the World Trade Organization in 2001 provided a framework that incorporated China into the global economy, mitigated the prospect of trade retaliation by establishing an international mechanism for resolving disputes, leveled the playing field for addressing economic disputes, and catalyzed large-scale investment in China by South Korean conglomerates. As a result, South Korean trade and investment with China increased by nearly 30 percent per year following China's entry into the World Trade Organization.[4]

The dispute in 2004 over the origins of the Goguryeo dynasty dramatically shifted the South Korean public's attitudes and spurred South Korean policy makers and strategists to publicly discuss the possibility that the divergence in South Korea's economic interests in cooperation with China and its security interests reflected by the alliance with the United States might come into conflict with each other.[5] Much of this discussion revolved around South Korea's economic exposure to the Chinese market and its implications for South Korea's ability to win China's cooperation on political and security matters, including the handling of North Korean refugees who sought safe passage to South Korea by entering Korean diplomatic facilities inside China and strategies for enhancing cooperation with China through Six-Party Talks on North Korea. The Goguryeo dispute stimulated more active strategic thinking among Korean specialists about South Korea's future options and strategic choices between Washington and Beijing.

In 2005, Roh Moo-hyun introduced the "balancer" concept, which generated considerable debate over South Korea's strategic choice between China and the United States. Roh's initial reference to the "balancer" concept was intended to raise the possibility that South Korea could play a constructive role in the context of rising Sino-Japanese tensions. Nevertheless, the concept was interpreted as part of a discussion about whether South Korea should exercise relative autonomy from the United States while seeking to improve relations with China.[6] South Korea's negotiations with the United States regarding "strategic flexibility" for USFK involved its concerns about entrapment in a potential conflict between the

United States and China and seemed to emphasize its autonomy at the expense of U.S.-ROK alliance cooperation.[7]

The Roh Moo-hyun administration showed sensitivity to its growing economic dependence on China by negotiating a bilateral FTA with the United States. Although the negotiation of this FTA was part of a broader South Korean strategy designed to capitalize on export competitiveness and globalization, the decision to pursue it was also driven in part by the desire among senior Korean officials to find an economic counterbalance to growing dependency on China. Ratification of this FTA was also important in 2011 as a catalyst for U.S. pursuit of an even more ambitious multilateral trade agreement with Asian partners in the Trans-Pacific Partnership. While seeking to maximize its advantage as a leading exporter in the global trading system, South Korea under Roh Moo-hyun used both hedging and efforts to promote a multilateral framework to support multilateral cooperation under the Northeast Asia Cooperation Initiative.[8]

The Lee Myung-bak administration continued to build on the foundation of a thriving Sino-Korean trade relationship, but it also raised the profile of U.S.-ROK alliance cooperation in part as a form of hedging against China's rising regional influence. Just prior to Lee's first visit to Beijing in 2008, the Chinese Foreign Ministry spokesperson referred to the U.S.-ROK alliance as a "historical relic . . . left over . . . from the Cold War era,"[9] publicly signaling China's desire to see South Korea loosen its security ties with the United States and move closer to Beijing. The Lee administration staked out a very different approach from the Roh administration on both inter-Korean relations and the relative importance of the U.S.-ROK alliance, an approach that clearly disappointed counterparts in Beijing. It strengthened and broadened the scope of the U.S.-ROK security alliance through adoption of the U.S.-ROK Joint Vision Statement in June 2009 and reversed policies of engagement, thus heightening tensions with North Korea. In response, China showed greater skepticism regarding Lee Myung-bak's approach to North Korea. In the aftermath of North Korea's sinking of the Korean naval vessel *Cheonan* in waters near North Korea and North Korea's shelling of South Korea's Yeonpyeong Island in 2010, Beijing protected Pyongyang from South Korea's international drive to hold North Korea accountable at the United Nations, a choice that strongly disappointed the South Korean public.

In contrast to the relative stagnation of the Sino-ROK relationship under Lee Myung-bak, a positive relationship between the two countries was restored in the initial stages of Park Geun-hye's and Xi Jinping's terms in office. Park emphasized her Chinese-language study to establish a positive image with the Chinese public, and Xi continuously met with Park at various international and bilateral forums and refused to meet with Kim Jong-un. The warm personal relationship between the two leaders led many analysts to suspect a South Korean tilt toward China, especially following Park's participation in a parade and ceremonies in Beijing in September 2015 to commemorate the seventieth anniversary of the end of World War II. Despite warming relations, however, neither Park's efforts to win China's support for South Korean policy toward the North nor Xi's efforts to bring South Korea in line with China in opposition to Japan appeared to make much progress. Moreover, Park's efforts continued to maintain strong U.S.-ROK alliance cooperation so as to avoid getting stuck in a strategic rivalry between Beijing and Washington. As described in chapter 7, Park also pursued the NAPCI to strengthen functional multilateral cooperation in Northeast Asia as a way of promoting both regional and Sino-U.S. cooperation.

In her campaign statements and administration policies, Park raised concerns about the quality of the relationship between China and the United States and its potential impact on South Korea's security environment as a component of her assessment of South Korea's security environment as "Asia's Paradox." During the presidential election campaign of 2012, she expressed apprehension about the possibility that an arms race led by China and the United States would increase regional tensions and heighten the possibility of conflict, a development that would have clear negative consequences for South Korea.

Thus far, South Korea has made little effort to exploit Sino-U.S. strategic rivalries or to play Washington and Beijing off against each other. Foreign Minister Yun Byung-se made a statement in a meeting with senior South Korean officials in March 2014 that South Korea may also benefit from a certain amount of competition between China and the United States,[10] but this statement became a lightning rod for public criticism in South Korea, and further discussion of such an idea was quickly muted.

However, South Korean responses regarding the existence of the Sino-U.S. competition and its implications for South Korean interests have been self-contradictory and ambivalent. Such ambivalence is only likely to increase as a result of the mix of costs and benefits associated with almost every aspect of China's rising influence on South Korea's economic, political, and strategic context. At the same time, public perceptions of China and the United States have shifted in favor of the United States as China's relative power has increased.

DEBATES ON THE STRATEGIC CHOICE BETWEEN WASHINGTON AND BEIJING

South Korean debates on how to deal with China have revolved primarily around the following options: (1) accommodating China so as to maintain cooperation and avoid costs that might derive from antagonism with China as a larger power; (2) balancing to counter potential negative effects on South Korean security from China's rise by strengthening alliance cooperation with the United States; (3) avoiding or deferring strategic choices between the United States and China, including hedging against a potential negative impact from China's rise; (4) making efforts to maintain freedom of action by taking measures to promote or expand areas of common interest and forestall the spread of a conflict between Washington and Beijing; and (5) pursuing an independent foreign policy that capitalizes on Sino-U.S. rivalry so as to maximize South Korean freedom of action by playing off larger-power interests against each other. These options are not necessarily mutually exclusive, and South Korea has often debated and pursued them in combination with each other.

ACCOMMODATION WITH CHINA

South Korean progressives, who had long sought to lessen South Korean dependency on the U.S.-ROK alliance, have seen strengthened ties with China as a means of enhancing South Korean autonomy, especially during the Roh Moo-hyun administration. In 2006, Robert S. Ross viewed South Korean policies toward North Korea under Roh as bringing South Korea closer to China than to the United States and considered South Korea's approach to "strategic flexibility" as part of a strategy of accommodating China at the expense of the U.S.-ROK alliance.[11] These developments led to questioning within security circles about the future of the U.S.-ROK alliance in light of China's rise. In 2009, David C. Kang argued that both South Korea and the United States have not been balancing China but have been accommodating Beijing's peaceful rise.[12] More recently, a *Mainichi* editorial in 2015 warned that "[President] Park's observation of the military parade in Beijing could give Tokyo and Washington the false impression that Seoul is siding with China in security issues" and called on her to "proactively adopt a well-balanced form of summit diplomacy."[13] This statement exemplifies the argument that South Korea will somehow tilt toward China, away from the United States and Japan.

Chinese analysts have floated the idea that South Korea might accommodate China by forging an alliance with it that has equal status to the alliance with the United States. According to Yan Xuetong of Tsinghua University, Beijing and Seoul have a number of important mutual interests: "the Japan threat, North Korea's nuclear threat, and maintaining peace in East Asia."[14] Chen Dingding argues that these interests might lead South Korea to form an alliance with China over the long run.[15]

South Korean proponents of accommodation argue that the economic opportunities represented by the China market are too valuable to pass up and that antagonism of China in areas that it perceives as in its core interests will entail great costs that would ultimately damage South Korean interests. The magnitude of economic gains made by the two countries as a result of two decades of double-digit growth in trade relations has promoted accommodationist approaches as a way of maximizing mutual economic opportunity. The implicit judgment underlying a Korean strategy of accommodating Chinese interests is that South Korea cannot afford conflict with China because of the risks and dangers of retaliation and the ensuing costs to South Korean economic and strategic interests. Some supporters of South Korean accommodation of Chinese interests also perceive closer relations with China as a strategic opportunity to loosen South

Korea's long-standing dependence on the United States for its security in ways that will enable it to increase its autonomy and freedom of action.

Moreover, as South Korean economic interests have grown, a "China lobby" has emerged in the South Korean business community. This group benefits immensely from doing business with China, particularly by taking advantage of the low cost of manufacturing in China, and tends to prefer accommodation with China out of the concern that Beijing might use its economic leverage to coerce Seoul. One risk to South Korea of relying solely or excessively on a strategy of accommodation of China is that the strategy indirectly supports assumptions among Chinese strategists that South Korea will eventually and inevitably be pulled into China's strategic orbit as a consequence of China's rise and South Korea's economic dependency on China.

BALANCING

South Korea could balance against China, but South Korean experts have yet to make strong recommendations urging this option. Many in the South Korean foreign-policy community and newspaper editorials have argued in favor of taking a principled stance on defending national interests on issues such as the deployment of the THAAD system and illegal fishing by Chinese in South Korean waters, but there has yet to be a call to shift South Korea's overall posture from hedging to balancing China's rise.[16] Indeed, Seoul has not pursued a clear balancing policy against China since the 1960s, when Park Chung-hee supported U.S. efforts to counter Chinese aggression in Asia. This is understandable, given that attempts to push back against China might spur Beijing to double down in supporting Pyongyang, while leaving South Korea at the frontline of the U.S.-China competition.

HEDGING OR CHOICE AVOIDANCE

A popular strategy favored by South Korean analysts is hedging or, arguably, choice avoidance. Within this strategy, there are a wide range of views in and out of South Korea regarding how best to hedge so as to avoid making strategic choices between China and the United States. Generally speaking, however, hedging means South Korea must maintain good relations with both countries and avoid taking sides in any conflict in order to escape entrapment.

Seoul National University professor Chung Jae Ho has recommended that South Korea "*not . . .* make any specific choice prematurely, lest it should limit the range of strategic options available to itself." This option does not mean South Korea should reject choosing but simply that Seoul should not make choices *prematurely*. Chung acknowledges that "South Korea may find it increasingly difficult to locate a suitable middle ground between the United States and China without offending either of the two."[17]

Ellen Kim and Victor Cha argue that South Korea could choose two alternative ways to avoid taking sides. First, it could maneuver back and forth between China and the United States and make choices on individual issues. Second, South Korea could consider its relations with China and the United States to be not mutually exclusive and thus avoid choosing as long as U.S.-China-ROK relations remain cooperative. Choice avoidance in this context is a passive approach that exploits but does not try to actively encourage Sino-U.S. cooperation. [18]

Han Sukhee of Yonsei University has described South Korean policy toward the United States and China as dual hedging or "strategic hedging." Han argues that "the major objective of Korea's strategic hedging in contrast to dual hedging is not aimed at balancing the two powers, but aimed at accommodating or to some degree bandwagoning with the counterparts. Since the major goal of Korea's strategic hedging is to maintain favorable relationships with both [the United States] and China, Korea tends to emphasize the bilateral cooperation in the fields with comparative advantages for mutual development, respectively."[19] An alternative version of hedging, as a U.S.-China Economic and Security Review Commission report sees South Korea pursuing, is "cultivating its security relationships not only with the U.S. but with China as well."[20]

According to Gilbert Rozman, South Korea is not engaging in "heavy-hedging" toward China, as Japan is doing with the United States to increase security cooperation against China, but in "light-hedging," understandably focusing on the more immediate North Korean threat. Hence, in this approach China is seen as a necessary strategic partner.[21] Park Jin believes that the Park Geun-hye government not only practiced "heavy-hedging" in the security field, with a degree of ambiguity because China is an increasingly assertive power, but also pursued a more even-handed hedging in political relations and accommodation in economic relations.[22] As strategic competition between Beijing and Washington intensifies, however, dual hedging may be harder for South Korea to sustain.

Since the 1990s, South Korea has pursued hedging by maintaining a strong alliance with the United States while developing strategic and economic cooperation with China. To achieve this, it has, at least until 2016, shied away from entering into closer security cooperation with Japan, remained outside of the U.S.-led regional missile defense network, remained quiet on territorial disputes in the East and South China Seas, and made China the largest trading partner, all the while pushing for closer ties with the United States as well. Yet this hedging policy might not be sustainable over the long-run.

COOPERATIVE SECURITY

Another possible strategy is one that actively attempts to encourage and expand space for cooperation between the United States and China, primarily by encouraging institutionalization of multilateral regional cooperation. This strategy builds on the premise that South Korea benefits from cooperative relations between the United States and China but suffers from competitive relations between the two countries by attempting to lock in and expand cooperative Sino-U.S. relations. South Korean multilateral initiatives such as the NAPCI would be an example of South Korean efforts to promote functional cooperation in the region as a buffer against the possibility of heightened regional tensions or major power conflict. Moon Chung-in, the former chairman of Roh Moo-hyun's Presidential Committee on Northeast Asian Cooperation, argued in 2005 that South Korea should "mediate the chronic feuds and dissonance that have plagued this region through open diplomacy, and to establish a new order of cooperation and integration."[23] As shown in previous chapters, almost every South Korean president since Roh Tae-woo has pursued the goal of achieving some kind of a cooperative security mechanism. None of these ideas, however, came to be realized. South Korea simply does not seem to hold enough leverage throughout Northeast Asia to achieve such a vision.

INDEPENDENT FOREIGN POLICY

Last, another option available to South Korea is pursuing an independent foreign policy by playing larger powers off against each other in order to maximize its room to maneuver and to avoid excessive dependency on a single great power. North Korea used this strategy in the past, seeking both aid and autonomy from the Soviet Union and China during the Cold War. Thus far, South Korea has not pursued such a strategy. Nevertheless, there has always been a strain of idealism within Korean strategic thought that imagines the possibility of an independent or neutral Korea that does not align itself with great-power interests. The desire for autonomy will remain a powerful influence in South Korean discourse on strategic choices, especially in the event that South Korea faces an environment in which no great power can provide an absolute security guarantee to it. This prospect is most likely to present itself if there is an extended period in which U.S. and Chinese power are in rough parity with each other, and South Korea has sufficient capacity to provide for its own defense.

As South Korea's own capacity has grown, pursuit of greater autonomy vis-à-vis great powers has already begun to play a larger role in its strategic discourse. South Korean foreign minister Yun Byung-se hinted at the idea of taking advantage of great-power competition when he said that "some local critics portray South Korea as suffering a side blow in a fight between big powers or sandwiched in between them. . . . [I]t could not be a headache or dilemma to receive love calls from both the U.S. and China. It could be, so to speak, a blessing."[24] Yun, however, faced criticism from South Korean experts, who said that he was probably too gleeful in portraying South Korea's dilemma as a blessing.[25]

Yoon Sukjoon at the Korea Institute for Maritime Strategy, however, agrees with Yun Byung-se and argues that "South Korea's current position offers new opportunities: it is a great blessing, not an intractable dilemma."[26] Hwang Byung Moo also suggests that "prospects for both rivalry and co-operation between the US and China, and between Japan and China, would allow greater space for South Korea to pursue its own national objectives, rather than put it in a position where it is forced to choose sides."[27] Kim Seong-kon, writing for the *Korea Herald*, suggests, "Perhaps, Korea, once a powerless piece on the board, can now play the players off against each other. For example, using THAAD as leverage, we can demand that China exert its influence on North Korea. At the same time, when things go awry and the time comes when THAAD is imperative in Korea, we can demand the U.S. to deploy it at their own expense, arguing that ultimately it is a game between the two players."[28]

Nevertheless, South Korea remains a weak power compared to its neighbors, making a balance-of-power strategy risky. Writing in 1972, Hahm Pyong-choon, then special assistant on foreign affairs to Park Chung-hee, mentioned

the dangerous game of playing the three powers [China, Japan, and Russia during the late nineteenth and early twentieth century] off against one another. The failure to play this age-old game with any degree of finesse may have been due to an innate clumsiness of the Korean people. However, the real reason seems to have been again the weakness of the Korean polity. The game only intensified the mutual distrust and belligerence among the three powers and encouraged the fear that Korea might at any time undermine the position of one in the peninsula by snuggling up to one of the others. Moreover, the game helped Koreans to earn a reputation among their neighbors for being tricky and deceitful, thus reinforcing their [neighbors'] desire to extinguish Korea's political independence.[29]

South Korea certainly has greater capacity today than it did in the late nineteenth and early twentieth centuries or in 1972, but its relative capacity remains less than that of all of its neighbors except North Korea, leaving in place inherent limits on its capability to independently shape its own environment.

LOOKING FORWARD: DETERMINANTS OF KOREAN STRATEGIC CHOICE BETWEEN CHINA AND THE UNITED STATES

An evaluation of the determinants underlying South Korean strategic choices between China and the United States ultimately must focus on three primary factors as likely influences. First, South Korea is sensitive to the relative power of the United States and China, especially as determined by these two countries' relative ability to provide leadership in shaping the international environment and global rules of the international order. South Korea ultimately must live in and seek opportunities to enhance its security and prosperity based on the established rules of the international order as shaped by the predominant global power or the dominant norms that characterize the global order. Its current policies maximize its ability to exploit global trade rules based on transparency, free markets, and rule of law, a regime that up to now has been shaped primarily by the United States. Second, South Korea must be attentive to the respective intentions of the U.S. and Chinese foreign policies. How the United States deals with China's rise, whether by seeking to contain or to accommodate it, and whether China will use its increasing capabilities to modify the U.S.-led global order are important factors. South Korea is sensitive to the relative level of cooperation and conflict between the United States and China in aligning their interests and policies and in enjoying greater cooperation. Greater alignment will lessen the degree of pressure that South Korea might face to choose between these great powers. Sino-U.S. cooperation will expand the space in which South Korea might try to facilitate cooperative efforts that enlist the respective strengths of the United States and China to establish an environment most conducive to South Korean strategic interests and goals. Conversely, a higher degree of conflict between the two sides will constrain South Korea's maneuvering room and generate an environment in which South Korea feels compelled to maneuver between the United States and China. Under such circumstances, South Korea may feel compelled to make strategic choices to align with one or another of the larger powers, to play the larger powers against each other to maximize its freedom to maneuver, or to seek neutrality so as to avoid making a strategic choice to the extent possible. Third, South Korea is sensitive to the tone and approach taken in the respective major powers' interactions with Seoul and is particularly focused in interactions with great powers that show respect for and provide standing to Seoul. This factor reflects South Korea's long-standing sensitivity to the fact that it has long been dominated and subjugated as a consequence or outcome of rivalries among major powers. Based on South Korea's strategic position, desire for respect, and potential to contribute capabilities that may be increasingly valuable to larger powers in close competition with each other, an effective major-power strategy to win South Korea's support may be characterized less by coercive or dominating behavior toward it and more by strategies that explicitly recognize and appreciate its strategic position and contributions. An assessment of these three factors provides a basis upon which to understand the international factors influencing South Korea's strategic choices as it considers its own external environment.

THE RELATIVE BALANCE OF POWER BETWEEN CHINA AND THE UNITED STATES

As South Korean analysts consider their strategic environment, a major factor influencing South Korea's strategic choices is the relative balance of power between China and the United States. Korea's historic preference has been to accommodate the country with the greatest influence on Korea while seeking to preserve Korea's security and sovereignty. When China's power was dominant, South Korea naturally aligned itself with the Middle Kingdom and adopted many Chinese cultural norms, even as Koreans also maintained their distinct culture. The tributary relationship between Korea and China involved economic trade that symbolically reinforced relationships of protection and loyalty. China's dominant influence on Korea during this period meant that China was the provider of the normative order and the hierarchy in relationships through which order and stability were perpetuated. Korea accepted China's status and protection, but, even more important, it accepted Chinese thought as a normative foundation for regulating international relations. David Kang characterizes this situation as a critical element of Asia's traditional Sino-centric order, characterized by well-understood hierarchical and power relationships between China and its periphery that also proved to be a source of peace and stability for hundreds, if not thousands, of years.[30]

Thus, China's recent reemergence as East Asia's potential hegemon has triggered a Korean debate for the first time in Korea's modern history over which country is best suited to serve as its protector and benefactor. The task of determining the components of power that are likely to be most salient as factors shaping South Korea's strategic choices, especially in the event that Chinese power challenges or possibly even eclipses U.S. power, is more complicated than simply placing China and the United States on a scale and measuring what the Chinese refer to as "comprehensive national power." As South Koreans anticipate that China may surpass the United States as the dominant regional actor in Asia, a wide range of forms of influence must be taken into account, including South Korea's relative geographic proximity to China, the Sino-U.S. regional competition within Northeast Asia, and the respective U.S. and Chinese influence on the norms that compose the global order.

SINO-U.S. RELATIVE ECONOMIC POWER

China's economic rise has been at the center of South Korean debates over whether such economic interdependence might somehow undermine previously existing security alliances as a result of divided allegiances between economic and security partners. As figure 9.1 shows, South Korea's trade with China has outstripped its trade with the United States and Japan combined. However, its dependence on trade and investment with China has not had a discernible effect on the strength of the U.S.-ROK alliance. In fact, the alliance has grown stronger since the mid-2000s despite South Korea's increasing economic exposure to China. Liberal theorists have also cited increasing economic interdependence as a factor that arguably reduces the prospect of military conflict, especially given that Sino–South Korean economic interdependence exists in parallel with deep economic interdependence between the United States and China. The primary counterargument to this claim is that levels of economic interdependence in

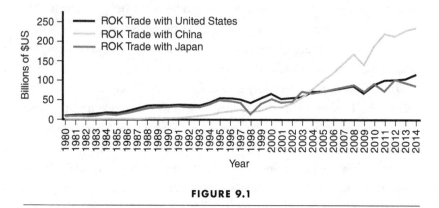

FIGURE 9.1

South Korea's Trade with China, Japan, and the United States, 1980–2014

Source: Korean Statistical Information Service 국가통계, *Trade Statistics Yearbook* 무역통계연보, http://kosis.kr/statHtml/statHtml.do?orgId=360&tblId=DT_1R11006_FRM101&vw
_cd=MT_ZTITLE&list_id=360_36002&seqNo=&lang_mode=ko&language
=kor&obj_var_id=&itm_id=&conn_path=E1#.

Europe prior to World War I, particularly between Great Britain and Germany, did nothing to prevent the outbreak of war.

South Korea's increasing trade dependency on China has not thus far resulted in increased Chinese political leverage on Seoul's strategic choices, especially as related to security. It appears to have influenced primarily private-sector choices rather than state concerns. South Korean corporate desires to manage political risks, pursue diversification, and respond to rising costs of doing business in China stimulated South Korean companies to look for alternative investment destinations, but the influence of government-driven strategic considerations appears to have been a secondary influence on economic patterns in the relationship. In addition, Chinese investment in South Korea has sparked fears that it comes with excessive Chinese influence. Nevertheless, South Korean private-sector concerns serve as an autocorrective instrument that diminishes the possibility that China will be able to derive decisive political leverage from trade and investment flows.

Conversely, in the aftermath of North Korea's sinking of the *Cheonan* and shelling of Yeonpyeong Island, South Koreans witnessed the limits of increased economic ties with Beijing regarding their country's ability to affect Chinese political decisions. Many South Koreans observed that although the volume of South Korean trade with China was at least thirty times the volume of North Korean trade with China, Beijing still protected Pyongyang from international condemnation. Figure 9.1 shows South Korea's trade ties with China relative to those with the United States and Japan.

SINO-U.S. RELATIVE MILITARY POWER

If economic power proves to be a relatively limited influence on South Korean strategic choice, what about the relative military power of the United States and China? As China modernizes its military, this factor will likely have a direct influence on South Korean assessments of the credibility of the United States as an ally. In fact, if China were to usurp the U.S. role as the dominant political and military power in East Asia, such a development would no doubt shake South Korean confidence in the capacity of the United States to provide for South Korea's defense. Given South Korea's historic preference to align itself with the dominant regional or global power, active debates over whether to abandon the alliance with the United States in favor of an understanding with China are not hard to imagine in the long run. History suggests that South Korea is more likely to align with the most powerful actor rather than try to join with others to restrain or balance against a hegemonic regional or global actor; however, the involvement of the United States as a factor in the East Asian equation is historically unprecedented. In fact, South Korea's anticipation of the impact of China's rise and its implications for the U.S. security guarantee could become a source of friction in the U.S.-ROK alliance as the gap in relative military power between the United States and China diminishes. South Korea arguably is already employing a hedging strategy against the prospect of U.S. decline, on the one hand, and against the negative consequences of China's rise, on the other.

For the time being, the United States remains the dominant global and regional security actor. China's capacity to challenge the United States in a direct military confrontation is limited. However, China's asymmetric strategies that challenge American credibility and expose American weaknesses are a political concern that could prematurely do damage to Korean confidence in U.S. capability to meet its commitments to defend South Korea. However, South Korean pragmatism and realpolitik assessments are likely to keep the country on the side of the United States until South Korea is able to find a clear alternative to the U.S.-ROK alliance as a primary means for achieving security.

SINO-U.S. RELATIVE POWER TO SHAPE INTERNATIONAL NORMS

A third component of relative U.S. and Chinese power that will likely be an important influence on South Korean strategic choice is the two powers' relative ability to set the rules and conventions that shape the global order. The United States still maintains a significant advantage in this area, and South Korea's relative success in building its own capabilities and international standing derives directly from its ability to adapt to and thrive in a normative environment that has been led by the United States since World War II. The United States has set the international economic and security rules of the global order, and South Korea, to a greater extent than many other countries, is dependent on a global, rules-based, liberalized economic order for its survival and prosperity because its dependence on trade for its economic growth is disproportionately high: approximately half of the country's GDP comes from exports.

However, China's rising influence has increasingly attracted South Korea's attention. More and more South Koreans are spending time in China, and South Korea represents the largest source of foreign-language students in China. The choice of increasing numbers of South Koreans studying Chinese is a reflection of South Korea's recognition of China's growing importance, but the United States will continue to be seen as South Korea's most reliable partner as long as it is the dominant influence shaping the norms of the global order.

In this respect, South Korea's response to China's attempts to enhance its share of influence as a contributor to the global order bears scrutiny.

South Korea decided to join the Asian Infrastructure and Investment Bank and is proud to have a major initial stake in the institution. Membership in this bank provides South Korea with an opportunity to scrutinize China's efforts to enhance its influence as the founder of a multilateral financial institution as well as an opportunity to influence management of this institution. Ultimately, however, South Korean attitudes toward the Asian Infrastructure and Investment Bank and other such institutions will be profoundly affected by the extent to which China emerges as an alternative to the United States in leadership and global rule setting.

RELATIVE POWER OF THE UNITED STATES AND CHINA AND SOUTH KOREAN STRATEGIC CHOICE

The most important factor likely to influence South Korea's fundamental strategic preferences will ultimately be tied to the relative ability and willingness of the United States and China to help South Korea achieve its primary objectives: security, prosperity, and unification. Among these three objectives, the most important priority will remain security, and South Korean judgments regarding a partner's ability to provide security will be tied primarily to which country is the most powerful global rule setter and which country has the greater military capability. Economic power will be important but is unlikely to be decisive by itself in South Korea's strategic calculus.

As the relative power differential between the United States and China narrows, South Korea will be increasingly tempted to hedge against the prospect that China may replace the United States as the most powerful state in East Asia. However, several factors will impede the pace of South Korea's willingness to adapt to China's rise.

The most intense debates within South Korea over whether it should align itself with the United States or with China are likely to occur under circumstances in which the two great powers are in rough parity with each other in their military capacity and global influence. In a situation where the dominant global and regional power is indeterminate, South Korea may seek to weaken its alliance ties with the United States yet not be willing to embrace China. Under these circumstances, there will also be voices in South Korea that show interest in neutrality—that it not rely on either the United States or China for its security. South Korea's ability to pursue sustained neutrality is likely to depend on the duration of the rough parity between the United States and China and on South Korea's relative capability to pursue autonomous options for guaranteeing its self-defense. In the event of a more gradual or prolonged transition between the United States and China, South Korea may perceive greater freedom of action to pursue neutrality and may likely be tempted to examine carefully the feasibility of military self-strengthening options, potentially including a push for its own nuclear deterrent, as an independent option to secure both autonomy and security simultaneously. In a situation where both Beijing and Washington are competing for Seoul's allegiance, preventing South Korea, as a critical pivot state, from building its own nuclear deterrent will likely be difficult, especially because such considerations will occur against the backdrop of a debate over the sustainability of the U.S.-ROK alliance.

Although the U.S.-ROK alliance is likely to come under strain in such conditions, Suh Jae-jung points to factors that may prevent South Korea from quickly distancing itself from the United States or from aligning with China. First, the sunk costs that have already been invested in U.S.-ROK alliance ties will likely delay South Korea's decisions to rapidly shift to another partner until it is clear that the alliance is no longer capable of assuring South Korea's security. Second, the degree of institutionalization of the U.S.-ROK alliance serves to bind the two countries together even in the face of political factors that may challenge the alliance. Third, South Korean democratic values will likely keep Seoul aligned with Washington for the time being and serve as a brake on a rapid embrace of Beijing as a primary guarantor of South Korean security.[31] If South Korean neutrality or alignment with China does occur, it will be a gradual, cautious, and reluctant process.

U.S. AND CHINESE FOREIGN-POLICY INTENTIONS AND RELATIVE LEVEL OF TENSION AND COOPERATION IN SINO-U.S. RELATIONS

Some South Korean analysts have pointed to South Korea's ability to strengthen economic ties with China while maintaining a strong U.S.-ROK alliance and have noted South Korea's desire to avoid situations that require it to make a choice between the United States and China.

Nevertheless, South Korea can avoid choosing between the United States and China only in an environment where the United States and China are willing and able to work with each other. Hence, U.S. and Chinese foreign-policy intentions and the resulting cooperative or conflictual dynamic are major factors that need to be taken into account.

The U.S.-China relationship is a complex one that is characterized by a mix of conflict and cooperation and that prioritizes cooperation to effectively manage potential conflicts. South Korea is banking on Sino-U.S. economic interdependence as the buffer that will inhibit conflict and preserve space for South Korea so that it can avoid having to choose between the two great powers. Yet there are still important questions with regard to how the United States will deal with China's rise. Amid rising tensions, calls have been growing in the United States, notably by Donald Trump's Asia advisers, to pursue a tougher policy on China in areas of both trade and security. Meanwhile, China has been increasingly assertive in seeking to erode the U.S.-led world order. If Washington and Beijing should get caught up in a cycle of rising tensions and overt competition, South Korea would face inordinate pressure to make a strategic choice between its economic partner and its security ally.

If the United States and China see value in moderating competition and in preserving space for cooperation, South Korea does not necessarily have to choose and compromise its ability to exploit both its economic interests with China and its security alliance with the United States. This means that South Korea has a stake in encouraging Sino-U.S. moderation and in supporting multilateral mechanisms that institutionalize Sino-U.S. cooperation.

South Korea, however, lacks the capability to act as a mediator between Washington and Beijing because neither great power is likely to see itself as in need of help from Seoul. Its efforts to mediate could instead result in China and the United States exerting greater efforts to compete for South Korea's support in the event of confrontation. Therefore, attempts by South Korea to become a mediator would entail unnecessary risk.

THE SOUTH KOREAN DESIRE FOR RESPECT AND IMPLICATIONS OF GREAT-POWER COMPETITION FOR INFLUENCE IN SOUTH KOREA

The third factor likely to influence the strategic choices South Korea makes between Washington and Beijing is its sensitivity to great-power coercion in the tone and substance of interactions with these great powers. South Korea's desire for respect from the great powers and its resistance to being taken for granted will ironically mean that Washington and Beijing should compete to consult with South Korea and to take Seoul seriously as part of their respective efforts to win influence over it and gain its support. Nevertheless, such efforts to give attention to South Korea are likely to be contradictory with a broader environment in which great-power competition or tensions between China and the United States lead both sides to pursue competitive strategies against each other. Nonetheless, both Washington and Beijing will need to show consideration for South Korea's interests in order to win its confidence and support.

THE UNIFICATION WILD CARD

The fourth factor that has influenced and will continue to influence Korean strategic choices is the issue of national unification. Unification could potentially transform Korea's domestic makeup in unpredictable ways. For instance, politics in a unified Korea would be dramatically transformed even if a unified Korea were to have a democratic political system. The population of North Korea is about twenty-five million, half that of the South, so one-third of the citizens of a unified Korea would be able to make their preferences felt for the first time despite having had a drastically different history and experience with government for more than six decades. In a democratic, unified Korea, northern Koreans would thus undoubtedly have a major voice, but it is impossible to have advance knowledge of their preferences and the implications of those preferences for governance of a unified Korean state.

Another factor that would potentially influence the strategic orientation of a unified Korea is Korean perceptions of whether the United States and China will play a helpful or impeding role in the process of national unification. Finally, in the absence of North Korea, the security priorities of a unified Korea might shift in unpredictable ways depending on whether it chooses to align with China or the United States.

THE FUTURE OF SOUTH KOREA BETWEEN CHINA AND THE UNITED STATES

For the time being, South Korea will continue to rely on the alliance with the United States, seek reassurances regarding the reliability and durability of the alliance, and continue hedging to avoid limiting its own choices. It is unlikely that South Korea will pursue an independent foreign policy. If the regional environment deteriorates, or if U.S. support for the alliance declines, however, South Korea will face increased pressure to make choices. For example, increasing friction over the South China Sea could push U.S. policy makers to determine that South Korea has to do more to maintain freedom of navigation in that sea. These pressures could start to make themselves felt before China is able to attain parity with the United States. Alternatively, rising uncertainty regarding U.S. commitment to the defense of South Korea might push South Korea toward greater self-help or even toward more serious consideration of stronger security ties with China. To the extent that South Korea sees Chinese power increasing to the point that China replaces the United States as the region's dominant power, South Korea may pursue a dual-hedging strategy by distancing itself from overt alignment with the United States and alliance responsibilities while also using the alliance as a counterweight to Chinese efforts to increase its influence on the Korean Peninsula. This approach will likely be unsustainable, however.

To the extent that the relative U.S. and Chinese positions and power move toward parity with each other, South Korean debates over strategic choices are likely to intensify. However, the sunk costs of the U.S.-ROK alliance, the institutional binding between the two allies, and the credibility gap likely to result from system and values differences between South

Korea and China are factors that will make it difficult for South Korea to abandon its alliance with the United States in favor of China. In addition, South Korean desires for autonomy may make themselves felt most strongly in an environment where the United States and China are at parity with each other; the temptation to play off larger powers against each to maximize autonomy would likely be greatest in the context of an extended standoff between roughly equivalent larger powers.

10

UNIFICATION AND KOREAN STRATEGIC CHOICES

T HE HISTORY OF South Korea's foreign policy since the country's establishment following World War II has featured an unwavering focus on national unification as an essential strategic objective, alongside the objectives of enhancing national security and economic prosperity that are common to almost every state. However, South Korea's policies toward the North for decades have been developed against the backdrop of the perception that the likelihood of achieving national unification is low. As a result, South Korean leaders have tended to prioritize security and prosperity, seeming to hold national unification more as an aspiration than as a strategic objective. Despite periodic recurrence of tensions and vicious competition, neither Korea has perceived that renewed military conflict would have any better chance of achieving unification than existed during the Korean War, nor has mistrust faded sufficiently to imagine that negotiations would lead to the unification of the two opposing systems on the peninsula. National unification has been a holy grail for both Koreas, a strategic objective that lies just beyond reach, an unattainable and all-consuming yet, for Koreans, seemingly essential strategic goal that promises to fundamentally transform Korean power, priorities, and strategic options within Northeast Asia.

South Korean unification strategies arguably must influence or take into account interaction among the following four primary factors: (1) South Korea's domestic debates over Korean unification, (2) North Korea's policy choices and nature of interaction with South Korea, (3) the balance of power on the Korean Peninsula and, more recently, North Korea's relative vulnerability to instability or regime collapse, and (4) the policy preferences and influence of relevant major powers, in particular China and the United States.

First, because unification policy is about Korea's national identity and is a powerful political instrument for building domestic political support for national leadership, it encompasses both domestic policy and foreign policy. Thus, Korean administrations inevitably develop and pursue strategies to achieve national unification as a touchstone for leadership and as a calling card by which to prove their legitimacy. The formation and pursuit of national unification strategies is driven by domestic political imperatives and is a factor that consumes significant time and attention in Korean foreign policy. Second, the nature of inter-Korean relations (i.e., the degree to which inter-Korean relations has been conflictual or cooperative) has influenced South Korean debates over both the feasibility and the likely mode of Korean unification (i.e., whether unification can be achieved by a negotiated settlement or will be achieved because the weaker party's vulnerability leads to instability or collapse or both). In this respect, feasibility of national unification depends in part on North Korea's policy choices and preferences as well as on South Korea's ability or willingness to influence or accommodate them or on both. Alternatively, it depends on whether North Korea's vulnerability turns into an inability to assert preferences in the event of instability or collapse of the North Korean system.

Third, a powerful influence on the unification policies of both Koreas has been the balance of power on the Korean Peninsula. Figures 8.6 and 8.7 in chapter 8 show the shifting balance in the size of the South and North Korean economies over the course of the past several decades. The relative economic power and perceived durability of North and South Korea have influenced perceptions regarding whether unification should be treated as an imminent or long-term strategic objective. In the early stages following the Korean War, South Korea had no choice but to rely on its security alliance with the United States as the main factor that provided security against a relatively more powerful North Korea. Likewise, Park Chung-hee's primary concern as he faced a strong and aggressive North Korea was the possibility that the United States would abandon its security commitment to South Korea. To the extent that Park saw U.S. security commitments as wavering in the early 1970s following Nixon's announcement of the Nixon Doctrine, he sought self-help internally, including independent, covert pursuit of a nuclear weapons capability. The prospect of unification on South Korean terms was unimaginable.

As the relative power gap between South and North Korea began to move in favor of Seoul, domestic debates in South Korea over unification and the mode by which South Korea might achieve this objective began to evolve. South Korea had achieved a sense of confidence that the country was relatively stronger than the North but did not feel strong enough to absorb the costs of unification. As the gap has widened further over the past decade, South Korea has begun to see itself as powerful enough vis-à-vis the North that the benefits of an eventual—and in the minds of many—inevitable Korean unification are considered to far outweigh the costs. However, the shift in power in Seoul's favor by itself has provided only a necessary but not sufficient condition for Korean unification to become real. Ironically, as South Korea has become more powerful vis-à-vis the North and as the prospect of a South Korean–led unification process has become more likely, domestic divisions over the benefits of unification appear to have deepened.

The fourth variable that has influenced the feasibility of national unification has been the relative degree of support or opposition and capability to intervene that exists among the relevant major powers, especially China and the United States. Korean unification is likely to be feasible only with the acquiescence of both Beijing and Washington, yet China and the United States have directly conflicting interests over the preferred outcome of Korean unification.

SOUTH KOREAN DOMESTIC DEBATES OVER UNIFICATION: BRIDGING THE IDEOLOGICAL GAP

The relative balance of power between the two Koreas, the direction of inter-Korean relations (toward cooperation or toward continued competition), and perceptions of a weak Korea's vulnerability to either external or internal forces have sharpened the intensity of South Korea's domestic debate over unification. A seemingly insuperable challenge besetting South Korea's political leaders is the task of uniting its factionalized, ideologically charged domestic politics through a common vision of Korean reunification achieved by a gracious, peaceful, just, and decisive victory over the North. In South Korea, the conservatives hold a Darwinian vision of reunification by absorption as the natural and preferred pathway leading to national unification. The progressives hope that a gradual, negotiated unification will result in a progressive polity that prizes ethnic unity and finally achieves peninsular autonomy from excessive foreign influence. South Korean unification debates must overcome these deep ideological divisions for South Korea's leaders to effectively provide the Korean people with a single unification vision, shape the parameters and direction of government policy, and impose limits on the direction of a unified Korean government.

Within South Korea, there have arguably been four periods when progressive–conservative debates over unification have intensified because they have coincided with moments when the feasibility of Korean unification seemed within reach. During the period of Nordpolitik, Roh Tae-woo sought to compensate for his domestic unpopularity and take advantage of North Korea's loss of international support by incorporating the opposition's progressive ideas into his unification policy, as described in chapter 3. One manifestation of this effort was the adoption in South Korea of the Korean National Community Unification Formula, which posited a cooperative, three-stage process leading to unification. Another moment of internal division followed the death of North Korean leader Kim Il-sung, when South Korea debated the possibility and implications of a North Korean hard landing—in other words, a collapse of North Korea's ruling system. As described in chapter 4, during the historic inter-Korean summit between Kim Dae-jung and Kim Jong-il in June 2000, South Korea's pursuit of cooperation and exchanges with North Korea induced deep political divisions within South Korea over whether a just and morally satisfying unification could be achieved through incremental inter-Korean accommodation. Finally, Park Geun-hye's comments in 2014 referring to unification as a jackpot stimulated new preparations for Korean unification amid growing skepticism and foreboding among younger-generation Koreans.[1] Each of these periods has revealed both the deep domestic divides within South Korea over the best approach to unification and the impact of changes in the international context and evolving perceptions of North Korea. The different periods also reveal the complex evolution of interaction between government circles and the Korean public during South Korea's democratic transition and consolidation, when public and civil society voices were becoming more influential in the formation of strategies and policies toward unification.

SOUTH KOREAN UNIFICATION DEBATES, DEMOCRATIC TRANSITION, AND THE END OF THE COLD WAR

South Korea's transition from authoritarianism to democracy and the end of the Cold War generated a broadening of South Korean debates on national unification. As discussed in chapter 3, on July 7, 1988, Roh Tae-woo announced the Special Declaration for National Self-Esteem, Unification, and Prosperity, which sought to promote an improved inter-Korean relationship through expanded exchanges of Korean leaders in various fields, the promotion of "balanced development of the national economy" through enhanced inter-Korean trade, and support for improved North Korean relations with Japan and the United States in parallel with efforts to normalize South Korea's relations with China, the Soviet Union, and Eastern European countries.[2] Roh followed this declaration with a forward-leaning UN General Assembly speech the following October in which he proposed a political conference on peace in Northeast Asia among the United States, China, Japan, the Soviet Union, and the two Koreas; an inter-Korean summit to adopt a nonaggression declaration and to replace the armistice with a permanent peace arrangement; and the construction of a "city of peace" in the DMZ.[3] North Korea's speech at the UN General Assembly that year also proposed a tripartite conference among the United States and the two Koreas to discuss transforming the armistice into a permanent peace treaty, phased withdrawal of U.S. military forces and nuclear weapons from the peninsula, and mutual arms and equipment reductions by the two Koreas.[4]

In pursuing unification, the Roh Tae-woo administration sought to take advantage of momentum generated by international developments in favor of South Korea and adverse to the North and to generate domestic public support by integrating ideas from opposition leaders as components of his policy toward North Korea. The administration's effort recognized that, despite Roh's weak public standing and the expansion of freedom within South Korea that accompanied democratization, a successful unification policy would require support from Roh's conservative supporters, the opposition elites, and the broader South Korean public. Roh's unification minister Lee Hong-koo led the development of a unification formula that, to the surprise of opposition leaders, borrowed elements from Kim Dae-jung's campaign proposals rather than denigrating them as being sympathetic to the North.[5] The Korean National Community Unification Formula presented by Roh to the National Assembly on September 11, 1989, envisaged a three-phase process of mutual confidence building, establishment of a national commonwealth consisting of two separate states, and, finally, establishment of a unified democratic state. The formula was the product of a consensus-oriented approach that drew on both conservative and progressive thinking and attempted to bridge gaps and build trust between the two Koreas at a moment when tectonic shifts in international politics were making themselves felt on the Korean Peninsula.[6] The success of the Korean National Community Unification Formula can be judged by its longevity; it has survived both conservative and progressive South Korean leaderships for two and a half decades and has remained the official unification formula of the government of the Republic of Korea regardless of the extent of North Korea's cooperation or vulnerability.

At the same time that Roh Tae-woo took the initiative in pursuing unification at perhaps the most propitious moment since the end of World War II, international events in the early 1990s put North Korea on the defensive. Kim Il-sung reacted poorly to Mikhail Gorbachev's decision to normalize relations with Seoul; to German reunification, which occurred in breathtakingly rapid fashion; and to China's signal that it would not oppose South Korean membership in the United Nations, which prompted Pyongyang to change its position and accept dual UN membership. These developments probably generated serious concerns in Kim Il-sung's own mind about North Korea's prospects for survival.

At the same time, a number of factors signaled an unprecedented easing of global tensions in ways that Pyongyang presumably deemed favorable. The United States and South Korea cooperated to provide assurances to North Korea regarding the removal of U.S. nuclear weapons from the Korean Peninsula, announced the cancelation of Team Spirit combined U.S.-ROK military exercises, and showed some willingness to improve relations with North Korea.[7] In this context, North Korea accepted Roh's outreach with proposals for dialogue and unification and agreed to the establishment of a high-level inter-Korean dialogue at the prime ministerial level in September 1990 through early 1992. The United States and North Korea also held an unprecedented meeting between Undersecretary of State Arnold Kanter and Chairman of the International Division of the Korean Workers' Party Kim Young-sun in New York in 1991. At the fifth round of dialogue in December 1991, the two Koreas announced the Inter-Korean Agreement on Reconciliation, Non-aggression, and Exchanges and Cooperation (or Basic Agreement).[8] The two sides reached the agreement within months following German reunification and established an elaborate framework for pursuing confidence-building, economic exchanges, and cultural and social exchanges. For North Korea, the most important element of the agreement may have been that it established mutual recognition of each other's systems, implying peaceful coexistence during a period of North Korean psychological vulnerability.

Despite the consensus-based development of the Korean National Community Unification Formula and the negotiation of the Basic Agreement, which envisaged a gradual confidence-building process leading to peaceful coexistence and eventual unification, South Korean domestic debates over unification became more intense with the onset of democratization and revealed fundamental divisions between the progressives and the conservatives over the issue. South Korea's democratization generated greater space for private dialogue among South Korea's opinion leaders and civil society than had existed in the authoritarian era. On the one hand, euphoria from German unification spilled over into Korean debates, heartening the conservatives, who assumed North Korea's collapse would open the way to unification on South Korean terms, and giving pause to the progressives in South Korea, who saw a political negotiation as a way to remake a truly autonomous and powerful unified Korea that would be unshackled from imperial influence and U.S. military presence. German unification gave hope to Koreans that their own unification was feasible, but it also deepened divisions between the conservatives and progressives over the desired mode of unification. The conservatives touted the likelihood of North Korea's collapse, whereas progressive thinkers such as Han Sangjin argued that the German model "would be unthinkable in the near future" for the two Koreas and advocated for a "third way" that the two Koreas could take simultaneously.[9]

During this period of rapid opening in the context of democratization, the Roh Tae-woo administration expanded the space for South Korean public knowledge and debates about North Korea by curtailing strict bans on literature sympathetic to socialism and North Korea. Roh had to manage South Korean activists who had developed an infatuation with the North and had even sought to reach out to Pyongyang directly. Even as the Roh administration softened its position toward the North, leftist student activists and progressives demanded U.S. troop withdrawals, more active exchanges with the North, and repeal of South Korea's National Security Law.

SOUTH KOREA'S DEBATE OVER WHETHER NORTH KOREA WOULD MAKE A "HARD" OR "SOFT" LANDING

The second period of debate was during the Kim Young-sam administration following North Korean chairman Kim Il-sung's death on July 8, 1994, at which time the South Korean government and civil society debated the possibility and implications of a "hard landing" for North Korea and pursued policies designed to achieve a "soft landing" through the approval of humanitarian aid for the North. The emotional complexities and self-contradictions of South Korean thinking about unification during this period were well captured by Kim Young-sam's roller-coaster reactions to the developments in North Korea as well as the mixed signals North Korea was sending during this period.

Kim Young-sam came into office with the idea of reaching out to North Korea by unilaterally releasing prominent prisoners held in South Korea for decades who had refused to renounce support for the North Korean regime. This gesture was intended to be an olive branch that would gener-ate continued inter-Korean cooperation, but North Korea's failure to recip-rocate and revelations of the existence of a North Korean spy ring in South Korea killed early momentum for progress in inter-Korean relations. A further complication came within weeks of Kim Young-sam's inaugura-tion when North Korea declared that it would leave the NPT within ninety days, generating an international crisis and opening the way for Pyong-yang to bypass Seoul and talk directly to Washington. The opening of bi-lateral dialogue between Washington and Pyongyang on security issues that directly affected South Korea was a concern for Kim.

However, South Korean ambivalence, emotionalism, and ideological divisions over policy toward North Korea came into relief in the days fol-lowing Kim Il-sung's death. Kim's death came at a moment of promise in inter-Korean relations. Jimmy Carter, during his trip to Pyongyang in June as part of private efforts to defuse rising nuclear tensions between Wash-ington and Pyongyang over North Korea's decision to unload fuel rods containing weapons-grade plutonium from its facility at Yongbyon, had secured a pledge from Kim Il-sung to meet with Kim Young-sam. How-ever, Kim Il-sung's sudden passing removed the prospect that he would be a negotiating partner and raised questions about whether South Koreans should mourn or celebrate the passing of a long-time archenemy. His death also raised questions about North Korea's capacity to survive the loss of its founder. Many North Korea watchers assessed that North Korea would not survive a leadership transition from father to son, Kim Jong-il. More-over, the leadership transition occurred against the backdrop of extraordi-nary stresses inside North Korea resulting from the loss of external patrons and the emergence of a devastating famine in 1994–1998 that killed approxi-mately one million of North Korea's twenty million people. Moreover, Kim Jong-il was virtually absent from public view for more than three years when he observed the traditional mourning period as an expression of fealty to his father.

Perceptions of North Korea's fragility during this period led to an active discussion about prospects for and implications of a North Korean hard landing. North Korea's dire economic circumstances induced a vigor-ous debate within South Korea over whether a North Korean hard landing was something to be desired or avoided and whether the humanitarian crisis was so serious that South Korea should focus first on saving lives by providing humanitarian assistance and put political considerations in the background. North Korea's circumstances also raised questions in South Korea over whether the South was prepared to take on the tremendous financial burdens associated with unification.[10]

THE INTER-KOREAN SUMMIT DECLARATION AND THE "SOUTH-SOUTH DIVISION"

The third period of debate occurred in the aftermath of the inter-Korean summit in June 2000, revealing deep social cleavages over the Sunshine Policy and its goal of a gradual, consensus-based unification as well as over the trustworthiness of the North Korean leadership.

The inter-Korean summit provided powerful symbolism in support of the proposition that North Korea and South Korea might abandon confrontation and pursue a wide range of exchanges and cooperation. It opened the door to a wide range of inter-Korean exchanges, including a joint symphony orchestra performance broadcast live in both Koreas, a series of soccer and other sports exchanges, expanded visits to North Korea by South Koreans, the expansion of family reunion programs, the expansion of a tourism zone at Mount Kumgang through which hundreds of thousands of South Koreans would have the opportunity to visit the North, and plans to build and operate the Kaesong Industrial Complex by combining South Korean capital, goods, and infrastructure with North Korean land and labor. However, despite Kim Dae-jung's assertion that because of the inter-Korean summit he had confidence that there would be "no more war" on the Korean Peninsula,[11] the summit declaration did not in fact improve the conventional security situation between the two Koreas.

The clauses of the North-South Joint Declaration that stirred the most controversy focused on the question of whether there might be a future confederal or federal structure if economic and cultural cooperation were to proceed far enough to bring about discussions of closer inter-Korean political cooperation. Nevertheless, debate over these clauses was a pretext for discussing the change in mood brought about because of the summit, through which North Korea was seen among the public less as an enemy than as a distant brother. [12]

The deepened division between the progressives and conservatives following the inter-Korean summit in the summer of 2000 came to be known as *nam-nam kalteung*, "South-South divide." Conservative opposition critics of Kim Dae-jung remained skeptical about the prospect for a negotiated unification and that exchanges and cooperation would lead to real tension reduction between the two Koreas. These critics were frustrated in part by the feeling that Kim Dae-jung had claimed that his policies would bring about great change in North Korea, when his policies seemed to have a bigger impact on promoting change in South Korea, which, in the view of many conservative critics, ran the risk of sacrificing South Korea's democratic values or whitewashing North Korea's unsatisfactory human rights record for the sake of illusory and expensive cooperation that generated little return from North Korea. For instance, inter-Korean economic and people-to-people flows increased greatly after 2000, but the increase was consistently one way; North Koreans were not coming south. Critics came to refer to the Sunshine Policy as "one-sided love" and to see the exercise as an elaborate ploy by Kim Dae-jung to secure a Nobel Peace Prize.[13] The criticism deepened when it became known that in advance of the summit Hyundai had made cash payments of at least $100 million to North Korea as part of a larger payment of up to $500 million in return for the right to develop a variety of businesses in the North.[14]

Kim Dae-jung himself genuinely believed that North Korea's exposure to South Korean people, products, and practices would eventually have a transformational effect on North Korean society. He believed that the opening and integration of North Korea into the regional community would alter North Korea's strategic calculations and that the lure of profit and development would transform the society. However, while complaining that South Korea's strategies of engagement were like a Trojan horse, North Korea's leadership appears to have calculated that it would be able to gain desperately needed hard currency from the South while restricting any politically liberalizing effects of greater contact with South Korea on the North Korean populace. Kim Dae-jung's policy gained much momentum from 1998 to 2000. As a result of the election of George W. Bush in

the United States in 2000 and of his skeptical view of North Korea, however, as well as Kim Dae-jung's inability to deliver in full the promised
international benefits of engagement to Kim Jong-il slowed the engagement policy, especially following outbreak of the second North Korean
nuclear crisis.

THE UNIFICATION "JACKPOT"

During the Park Geun-hye administration, the fourth period of debate
emerged, in part because of Park's comments in January 2014 that realization of Korean unification would be a "bonanza" or "jackpot" for Korea.[15]
Her statement reflects the idea that there are clear benefits to be reaped from
unification. She established the Presidential Committee on Unification
Preparation on the premise that, regardless of when unification comes, it is
necessary to be ready for unification. The emergence of this theme as an
element of Park's North Korea policy represented a relative hardening
of her approach to North Korea over the course of her administration,
primarily as a response to North Korea's continued emphasis on nuclear
development.

During her election campaign, Park Geun-hye's initially dubbed her
North Korea policy "Trustpolitik" because she emphasized the importance of building trust between the two Koreas as the central missing element of the relationship.[16] This policy appeared to be designed to bridge
differences between the conservatives and progressives because it emphasized the importance of dialogue with the North for the ostensible purpose of building trust. In practice, however, it appears that the main intent
behind Trustpolitik was to suggest that the North Koreans needed to
show themselves worthy of trust as a prerequisite to expanded inter-
Korean cooperation. Park's subsequent Dresden declaration in 2014 suggested a three-phase process of cooperation with North Korea that would
commence with humanitarian issues, progress to large-scale economic cooperation, and eventually include social and political cooperation.[17] These
statements initially seemed to be somewhat more pragmatic and open-
minded toward the North than statements made under the Lee Myung-
bak administration.

Park's approach to negotiations with North Korea over North Korea's unilateral closure of the Kaesong Industrial Complex in the spring of 2013 was unyielding as she insisted that she would not sacrifice her principles. She deflected many extraneous North Korean demands and won an agreement that promised marginal improvements in the structure of the complex's operation. Park also proved to be a tough negotiating counterpart during the marathon talks in August 2015 held at Panmunjom to ease military tensions following a North Korean mine detonation near a South Korean security outpost on the southern side of the DMZ. South Korea had turned on its propaganda speakers, and North Korea had mobilized and threatened to shoot at the speakers, but the negotiating session reversed the spike in tensions. In the end, Park gained North Korea's statement of regret and a pledge to conduct two rounds of divided family reunions; in turn, she made a statement that pledged to turn propaganda speakers back on in the event of "unusual activity" from the North.[18] Following a fourth North Korean nuclear test and missile launch, Park ordered propaganda speakers back on and unilaterally suspended operations at the Kaesong Industrial Complex.

Park Geun-hye's tough approach may have been premised on intelligence reports that anticipated North Korean instability during Kim Jong-un's consolidation of political power might lead to regime collapse. Her "jackpot" statement reportedly was directed toward younger-generation South Koreans, who are increasingly apathetic about Korean unification according to some opinion polls. The remarks also reflect her consistent view that North Korea's nuclear pursuit is dangerous and cannot be tolerated. Park took resolute and tough unilateral measures in response to North Korea's fourth nuclear test.

Park's suspension of the Kaesong Industrial Complex removed the last vestige of Kim Dae-jung's engagement policy. Supporters of the project were critical of this move. However, perhaps more striking was Park's shift from dialogue to a resolute approach that strove at all costs to turn around North Korea's nuclear development and did not sweep the magnitude of the threat under the rug. In response to North Korea's fourth nuclear and missile tests in 2016, Park appeared prepared to pursue financial strangulation and to risk North Korea's destabilization to achieve that objective.

NORTH KOREAN POLICY CHOICES AND IMPLICATIONS FOR UNIFICATION: PROSPECTS FOR CONVERGENCE

Aside from the necessity of managing South Korea's domestic debates over unification, South Korean strategists must devise tactics for managing and influencing the direction of North Korea's policy or, alternatively, to devise effective counterstrategies to deal with elements of North Korean policy that oppose South Korea's preferred pathway to unification. The major challenges the North Korean leadership presents are defined primarily by the question of North Korea's relative openness and willingness to cooperate with South Korea and by its economic choices (i.e., whether to continue to pursue isolation and autarky or to expand economic relations with the outside world, including with South Korea, even in limited forms). Table 10.1 shows how North Korean economic policy preferences and political orientations toward South Korea influence the prospects for the modality and timing of unification.

TABLE 10.1 NORTH KOREA'S STABILITY AND PROSPECTS FOR KOREAN UNIFICATION

		STABLE NORTH KOREA	
		ECONOMICALLY LIBERALIZING	AUTARKIC
Nature of North Korean Leadership	Peaceful	Peaceful existence possible; ultimately economy trumps nukes in North Korean policy; economic integration possible, leading to long-term unification; South Korean dream unification scenario	Peaceful coexistence possible; unification unlikely
	Hostile	North Korean–led unification objective; continued tension between economic and security objectives; continued inter-Korean competition	North Korean–led unification objective; heightened inter-Korean tensions; continued inter-Korean competition

To enhance the prospect of achieving a peaceful unification, South Korean leaders need to influence the evolution of North Korea's policies in a direction that affirms peaceful coexistence as an interim step toward unification and that is economically liberalizing. Essentially, these were the fundamental premises and objectives that characterized Kim Dae-jung's approach under the Sunshine Policy. This sort of approach would likely return as the main framework for South Korea's strategy if the North Korean leadership were perceived as cooperative and willing to pursue limited steps toward economic liberalization.

The benefits of a North Korean leadership that is cooperative with South Korea are obvious given South Korea's relative dominance compared to the North and the economic and political opportunities that South Korea would derive from peaceful coexistence. North Korea would no longer be inclined to hold at risk the benefits of economic progress with South Korea, and South Korean business might begin to reap opportunities for enhanced growth through cooperation with North Korea. South Korea would benefit from a growing and liberalizing North Korea because these changes would reduce the economic gap between the two sides and be a potential source of growth for South Korea, making a gradual economic convergence imaginable and reducing the likely public-sector costs that would ensue if the South Korean government were to take financial responsibility for facilitating a rapid integration, either to reduce the prospect of southward migration or to meet North Korean citizens' political expectations.

Although South Korea has an interest in working with a cooperative North Korean leadership that is economically liberalizing, such a scenario appears to be the one that North Korean elites are likely to perceive as the most threatening to their own interests. They would consider it reunification by absorption, much like the German reunification process, promising few benefits and many risks for North Korean elites, who would lose their status in a unified Korea. Therefore, North Korean leaders prefer to maintain an atmosphere of hostility toward the South while pursuing North Korean–style economic reforms and to resist economic reforms from the outside while pursuing political isolation. This means that the biggest task for South Korean policy makers who seek gradual unification with the North is to induce political cooperation from North Korea, together with enhanced economic cooperation and even economic integration measures. Nevertheless, this task is fraught with challenges if indeed North Korea's leaders perceive that their self-preservation requires either economic cooperation with South Korea combined with political isolation or political cooperation with South Korea combined with economic autarky. If South Korea cannot depend on voluntary cooperation from North Korea's leadership to move in a direction conducive to gradual economic integration, then it has no choice but to rely on marketization to penetrate and gradually transform North Korea.

Either North Korean opening without reform or reform without opening requires South Korea to pursue countermeasures in order to create an environment conducive to the desired goal of national unification. If the North Korean leadership were autarkic but not hostile, South Korea might face a difficult choice between peaceful coexistence and unification. However, such an approach would leave the North Korean people under a leadership that would likely make only marginal improvements in the quality of life of the average North Korean even while promising South Korea that as long as Seoul does not pursue subversion, North Korea will not revert to overt inter-Korean hostilities.

The type of North Korean leadership that would be the most impervious to influence from South Korean policies would be one that combines hostility toward the South with economic autarky. Such policies would blunt South Korean policy instruments aimed at integration and cooperation, thereby lessening North Korea's exposure to the South that would potentially undermine the legitimacy of the North Korean leadership domestically or would contribute to collapse of the North Korean system.

Because of the divided nature of South Korea's domestic debates over North Korea, a progressive leadership might not be able gain support for the level of cooperation and mutual engagement with North Korea needed for North Korea to let down its guard. Such an approach would face domestic opposition from South Korean conservatives, who prefer to subvert or transform the North Korean regime. The prospect of a North Korean leadership devoted to both peace and cooperation with the South is unlikely because North Korea remains vulnerable and isolated and because conservative South Koreans would continue to seek near-term unification rather than allow peaceful coexistence as an interim stage in the quest for national unification.

NORTH KOREAN INSTABILITY, SOUTH KOREA'S RESPONSE, AND PROSPECTS FOR UNIFICATION

If South Korea is unable to influence the North Korean leadership in a direction that opens up new possibilities for cooperation, the only possible pathways toward national unification depend on South Korea's ability to exploit North Korea's vulnerability and on North Korea's potential vulnerability to internal instability. South Korea has limited capacity to push North Korea past the point of no return, in part because of the North's tight internal control. Moreover, North Korea's systemic vulnerability may possibly manifest in early stages in some sort of violence, whether internally directed if Kim Jong-un's rule becomes contested or externally directed against the United States or South Korea. Indeed, history has shown that heavily centralized states, such as Romania, Syria, and Libya, have experienced violence if internal instability develops as a result of contested leadership. Other factors that could influence the prospects for Korean unification in the event of instability include the pace and nature of political developments inside North Korea, a newly consolidating replacement leadership's openness to external support or cooperation with South Korea, and whether the process by which unification occurs is peaceful or violent. Table 10.2 shows the range of scenarios that would be influenced by the pace and nature of North Korean instability. The orientation and direction (isolating or integrating) of North Korea's internal policies and their impact on the nature of inter-Korean interactions (i.e., whether the nature and pace of the Korean unification process are likely to be peaceful or violent, rapid or slow) are also shown.

Most South Koreans hope for peaceful and gradual Korean unification. Nevertheless, South Korean policy planners must be prepared to recognize and respond to an array of different possibilities that stem from uncontrollable circumstances within North Korea. South Korea has

TABLE 10.2 INSTABILITY FACTORS, NORTH KOREA

NATURE OF INSTABILITY

		EXPLOSION	IMPLOSION
Timing and Pace	Gradual	Periodic provocations designed to obscure or slow the loss of domestic political control	Progressive manifestations of the central government's limited ability to assert political control (e.g., humanitarian crisis)
	Sudden	North Korea lashing out, conflict escalation, war, and defeat	Tipping point or cascade effect of internal failures to manage multiple crises

devised military strategies together with the United States designed to deter North Korea from lashing out and to respond in the event of North Korean instability, but the ultimate decisions to intervene in the event of internal instability are political. Such decisions will be influenced both by alliance consultations regarding thresholds and conditions for intervention and by the degree of tangible spillover effects on South Korea (or on China or on both countries) that might influence South Korea's domestic political environment and generate pressures for intervention to stanch the spillover effects (e.g., refugee flows) likely to result from North Korean instability.

Although national unification has been a consistent and long-held strategic priority for successive South Korean administrations, security and prosperity, in the end, have been higher priorities. Yet unification potentially threatens South Korea's security and prosperity. Hypothetically, South Korea may be tempted to pursue unification even at a cost to security and prosperity, but such a temptation would exist only under circumstances where unification is directly achievable and would carry enormous risks to a political leadership in South Korea that responds incorrectly to internal developments in North Korea. For this reason, although unification has been a long-standing and persistent South Korean strategic objective, it is likely to remain a secondary concern unless conditions develop in such a way that it becomes clearly achievable at manageable cost.

THE INTERNATIONAL ENVIRONMENT AND KOREAN UNIFICATION: LEADING FROM A POSITION OF RELATIVE WEAKNESS

South Korean strategists face an enormously challenging international context in which they must find sources of leverage and cooperation with larger neighbors that may have directly opposing policy preferences and objectives toward the Korean Peninsula. For instance, China and the United States have widely divergent preferred end states in the event of Korean unification, as discussed in the previous chapter. Although South Korea's relative capacity to influence the United States, China, Japan, and Russia has increased, it remains comparatively weaker than any of its neighbors, both politically and militarily.

Moreover, there is the complicated question of how South Korea can influence the situation when the neighboring powers' policies conflict with each other or are not conducive to the establishment of a reunified Korea consistent with South Korea's own strategic priorities. What is the best strategy for South Korea to win acquiescence to, if not support for, unification from China, the United States, Japan, and Russia? Moreover, South Korean domestic debates influence the tone and scope of options in both inter-Korean relations and in managing regional relations, and there are linkages between inter-Korean relations and the regional security context. In order to pursue Korean unification as a strategic objective, South Korea must simultaneously manage the regional environment, domestic politics, and its own interactions on the peninsula.

Effective management of regional relations in a way that is conducive to progress toward national unification is probably one of the most daunting diplomatic and strategic tasks that South Korean policy makers will face. The main challenge derives from South Korea's limited capacity vis-à-vis its larger neighbors and the worry that great powers may prioritize management of their relations with each other over relations with South Korea. Great-power management of peninsular issues risks turning Korea into one among many issues on the agenda and makes major-power policies toward the Korean Peninsula contingent upon the regional context rather than anchored or fixed. This is why Koreans are continuously sensitive to the possibility not only that excessive cooperation among the great powers will minimize Korean influence on the process of managing a Korean transition but also that excessive conflict among them may result in continuation of national division.

With regard to Korean unification, all the major powers have clearly defined strategic preferences regarding the ultimate outcome or end state. The formation of a South Korean strategy in pursuit of unification must inevitably take into account these major-power preferences and make a calculation regarding which preferences South Korea must accommodate and where it might have the capacity to influence the situation in a direction that coincides with its needs and objectives. On the one hand, South Korea is best positioned to respond to developments on the ground; on the other hand, it will need to win support from the United States and acquiescence from China if unification is to be realized.

Thus, it is necessary to review the primary policy objectives and preferences of the major powers regarding Korean unification (see table 10.3) and South Korea's desired unification objectives in its relations with each of its neighbors. American preferences regarding the main objectives of Korean unification have been formally and publicly aligned with those of South Korea since both sides promulgated the U.S.-ROK Joint Vision Statement in June 2009. This statement defines the alliance objective as the realization of a unified, democratic Korean state that embraces free-market principles. China has stated that it is also supportive of eventual independent Korean unification achieved gradually through peaceful dialogue. The key word in Chinese policy toward unification of the Korean Peninsula is *independent* because it is clear that China seeks a Korean Peninsula that is friendly or at least not hostile to China.[19] Although Japanese statements are less clear, Japan presumably sees a friendly, denuclearized Korea as critical to its security and would generally be supportive of a continued U.S.-ROK security alliance as the primary means by which to ensure that a unified Korea remains nonthreatening to Japan's security.[20] Russia's interest in the Korean Peninsula has been primarily commercial, focused on access to potential future energy- and transportation-sector projects. Russia has the potential to play a spoiler role if it chooses to use the Korean Peninsula as a point of leverage against the United States in the ongoing geopolitical struggle in

TABLE 10.3 INTERESTS AND PREFERENCES WITH REGARD TO KOREAN UNIFICATION

U.S.-ROK Alliance	• Included in the U.S.-ROK Joint Vision Statement of June 2009 • A unified, democratic, and denuclearized Korea that embraces free-market principles
China	• A unified, denuclearized Korea that is friendly or at least not hostile to China • Preferably an end to the U.S.-ROK alliance or at least a reconfigured alliance with a much smaller role on the Korean Peninsula
Japan	• Presumably a denuclearized Korea tied to the U.S.-ROK alliance to ensure it is not hostile to Japan
Russia	• A unified, denuclearized Korea • Limited ability to affect the outcome of unification but an interest in energy and transportation projects on the Korean Peninsula

Europe, but Moscow's capacity to assert its interests vis-à-vis a potential Korean unification process is limited.[21]

Based on this thumbnail sketch of major-power interests and views toward Korean unification, what are South Korea's fundamental objectives toward the major powers with respect to its unification policy? First, an atmosphere of cooperation among the major powers would enhance the prospects for Korean unification. The road to Korean unification will likely be more complicated, if not wholly obstructed, in an atmosphere of regional competition or rivalry among major powers, particularly between the United States and China. South Korea is unlikely to be able to control the quality and nature of regional relations among major powers, but Seoul still has an interest in promoting regional cooperation and multilateral mechanisms that can serve to modulate competition and insulate the region from rising rivalries or full-blown regional conflicts.

Second, South Korea has an interest in maintaining good diplomatic relationships with all four powers surrounding the peninsula and in continuously representing its own interest in and desire for support for a unification process. Seoul needs to reduce prospects for regional conflict or to inhibit the likelihood that the Korean Peninsula might once again be the epicenter of rivalry among larger neighbors. At the same time, the U.S.-ROK alliance remains the central platform by which South Korea's security and economic prosperity have been guaranteed. In addition, South Korea also has an interest in ensuring that alliance aims and objectives are not perceived as contrary to the objective of unification, which means working hard to manage potential conflicts between stability and unification priorities within the U.S.-ROK alliance. Squaring all these objectives, in particular the tension between management of great-power rivalries and maintenance of a strong U.S.-ROK alliance, will be a herculean task.

Third, with regard to South Korean desires for the U.S. role in unification, South Korean strategists should presumably want to ensure that the Korean Peninsula remains a high U.S. policy priority and that the United States is prepared to provide strong political support for South Korea when the Korean unification process unfolds. A reunifying Korea will remain intensely interested in continuing alliance benefits that have aided in securing Korean security and prosperity during the process of unification. South Korean strategists will also seek U.S. support for international and multilateral financing mechanisms to help manage the economic costs of unification.

South Korea recognizes both China's interest in a friendly Korean Peninsula and its "veto power" or capability of preventing Korean unification by continuing to promote a policy that privileges stability and prefers the certainties of the status quo to the uncertainties that Korean unification would likely entail. At the very least, it will be important for China to acquiesce to unification as a fait accompli rather than continue to generate obstacles by continuing to prop up a separate North Korean state. South Korea and China share an interest in seeing a peaceful unification process and in seeing North Korea abandon provocations and embrace peaceful existence as an essential prerequisite to enhancing regional stability. South Korea has sought to reassure China that a unified Korea would be in China's interest, but the future of the U.S.-ROK alliance is clearly a big sticking point and inhibitor to the development of China-ROK relations. China has an interest in ensuring that the peninsula does not become hostile toward China. China also fears that the current North Korean threat provides a rationale for the U.S.-ROK alliance to grow and eventually pose a threat to China as well.

If Korean unification becomes feasible, a mechanism for promoting regional stability that includes the United States, China, Japan, Russia, and the two Koreas will be an important ingredient. In fact, the ongoing informal framework of consultations among regional actors in Northeast Asia that derives from the Six-Party Talks plays a de facto role in enabling consultation on regional issues. Another challenge for Korean strategists is how to support efforts to ensure that China and the United States are on the same page regarding North Korea. The Park Geun-hye administration floated the idea of a trilateral U.S.-ROK-China dialogue on North Korea, but this consultation format has not yet gained real traction. Given the complexity and breadth of the U.S.-China relationship, it is increasingly difficult for the two governments to prioritize North Korea in the bilateral dialogue. This may be an area where South Korean diplomatic persistence and focus might pay off by drawing the two most important outside powers together as part of an effort to encourage them to cooperate on critical issues involving the future security situation on the Korean Peninsula. It remains to be seen whether South Korea, a junior partner to these two major powers, can draw them in sufficiently to coordinate and deconflict their respective short- and long-term policies on issues related to Korean unification.

Finally, South Korea needs to secure support from Japan and Russia to ensure that neither acts as a spoiler with regard to Korean unification. The best way of consulting with and securing support from these two countries is likely to continue ongoing consultations in the context of the Six-Party framework and in the case of Japan by means of U.S.-Japan-ROK security consultations. Such consultations should aim to secure support for a Korean unification process and to secure regional buy-in to new security arrangements designed to support and buffer a Korean unification process.

IMPACT OF UNIFICATION POLICIES ON SOUTH KOREAN STRATEGIC CHOICES

South Korea has consistently pursued national unification as a wish and a political objective that has absorbed a great deal of attention and strategic thinking ever since the end of the Korean War. However, despite the unification issue's constant presence as an essential element of Korean domestic political discourse and national strategy, and even though the South is now considerably more powerful than the North, South Korea has thus far simply not had the means to achieve this objective. Unless North Korea either cooperates or collapses, unification is likely to remain distant and unfeasible.

South Korea's preoccupation with the strategic objective of national unification clearly has had several important implications for its foreign policy. First, its national unification strategies have clearly had significant impact on the objectives and implementation of its foreign policy, as has been evident throughout this book. Second, its national strategies toward unification have had spillover effects on its diplomatic goals and strategies vis-à-vis all of its neighbors, and the ongoing competition with North Korea has permeated South Korean global foreign-policy strategies. Third, the South Korean pursuit of unification requires a combination-lock or Rubik's cube strategy: it is necessary for domestic, peninsular, regional, and global forces to align for Korean unification to be feasible, but the likelihood of such an alignment remains low. Finally, a powerful motivation behind the Korean focus on national unification is directly related to the enduring tension between autonomy and alliance in the following way; many Koreans' dreams of national unification anticipate that unification will augment national strength sufficiently that a unified Korea will finally be able to autonomously shape its own security environment. However, as implied in chapter 8, the idea that national unification will enhance Korea's national power sufficiently to allow it to break out of the geographic constraint of being surrounded by larger powers is illusory.

For South Koreans, national unification remains secondary to security and prosperity. In fact, a good reason for caution regarding the pursuit of national unification has been the possibility that unification can be achieved only at significant cost to the relative security and prosperity that South Korea has already obtained. Indeed, the desire for peaceful unification is at odds with scenarios in which unification occurs because of internal instability in North Korea, and even internal instability in the current regime may not necessarily result in a full-scale collapse of the state or system. Periods of North Korean cooperation or perceived instability have heightened South Korea's interest in and focus on pursuit of Korean unification, but those moments appear to have been accompanied by deepening polarization in South Korean domestic debates.

Moreover, South Korea will seek the support of the United States and the acquiescence of China for Korean unification, but both countries continue to have contradictory preferences regarding the type of unification and the diplomatic and political orientation of a unified Korean state. These contradictory preferences inhibit prospects for dialogue on unification-related sensitive issues where the United States and China share an interest in cooperation. South Korean strategists should continue to prioritize this matter of concern and seek ways to bridge the gap between its Chinese and American counterparts.

EPILOGUE

South Korean Strategic Choices and
the U.S.–South Korea Alliance

HIS BOOK HAS chronicled the evolution of South Korea's foreign policy as the country has navigated between its desire for autonomy and its need for alliance in the pursuit of security, prosperity, and national unification. Throughout its history, South Korea's strategic choices have been constrained by its relative weakness as a country surrounded by larger powers. Its clear need for external help to assure its security and prosperity has necessitated its reliance on assistance from a powerful external patron, the United States, to achieve its security objectives. Those needs were particularly acute following the Korean War, when the country faced direct threats of renewed military infiltration from a more powerful, hostile North Korea, backed by the Soviet Union and China. Successive South Korean leaders sought to carve out space within the alliance to assert their own autonomous interests. As South Korean capacities grew, and as the Cold War ended, the scope of the country's interests has become less parochial and more internationalized, especially as South Korean economic interests and influence became tied to relationships with new countries through international trade driven by South Korea's own modernization. South Korean capabilities have also changed the nature and distribution of roles and responsibilities within the U.S.-ROK security relationship. South Korea's strategic options have expanded, but not to the extent that South Korea no longer needs the alliance with the United

States to assure its security. The democratization of South Korea strengthened the role of domestic public opinion on foreign policy and spurred debates over its strategic choices between well-established progressive and conservative factions in its society.

As South Korea's capacity has expanded, the alliance has evolved from one in which South Korea tried to enhance its utility to U.S. interests so as to avoid abandonment to one in which South Korea was able to pursue greater autonomy through self-help but within the context of the country's continued need for the alliance as a bulwark against threats from major powers. South Korea's ability to catch up to and surpass North Korea in economic and military terms has made it more confident in its dealings with the North and has enabled it to take a more active role in pursuit of unification. The alliance has evolved to support Korean unification but has consistently placed South Korea's security, stability, and prosperity above unification. At times, South Korea has been tempted to pursue autonomous roles beyond the framework provided by the U.S.-ROK alliance, both to deal with a declining North Korea and to manage China's rise. However, South Korea's need for the United States as the enabler of its success, as its best insurance policy, and as its primary security guarantor has tempered its moves toward an independent foreign policy.

To a greater extent than ever before, South Korea stands at a potential turning point as it evaluates the direction of its foreign policy and evaluates its strategic choices. Its long-standing reliance on the alliance with the United States is likely to come under increasing scrutiny. As China continues to grow in regional power and influence, South Korea will find itself under greater pressure to consider alternatives to its reliance on the United States as the primary guarantor of its security. Pressure on South Korea to reevaluate its long-standing strategic choice to ally with the United States would become particularly acute if China were to surpass the United States in economic influence, military power, and capability to shape global norms; however, it is far from certain that China will be able to sustain its economic growth or become a trusted provider of regional security in East Asia, much less emerge as a regional and global rule maker. In addition, the gap in relative power between South and North Korea continues to grow, but the pathway to achieving national unification and that unification's potential impact on South Korean strategic choices remain unclear. Although South Korea's growing capability and willingness as a middle power to lead on international issues might suggest wider flexibility in pursuing strategic options, its relative weakness in comparison with its major-power neighbors continues to necessitate its dependence on the United States to protect its security and prosperity.

South Korea faces a paradox as it considers its strategic choices. On the one hand, its growing capabilities and emergence as a middle power mean that it has the capability to make its own choices, a capability that it historically did not enjoy when it had to rely on the United States as a matter of necessity borne of weakness. For South Koreans not used to having a choice or resentful that the choice to rely on the United States has been locked in for so many decades, the opportunity exists to have a vibrant, contentious, and potentially consequential debate over alternative futures that will have real consequences for South Korea's security and prosperity. On the other hand, rising tensions in South Korea's security environment and greater competition among great powers for South Korea's favor and allegiance will generate increasing pressure to make a strategic choice even though it may be against South Korea's desires and interests to make such a choice. At the same time that South Korea now enjoys sufficient capabilities to choose for itself about whether to sustain the alliance with the Unites States, to seek an alternative security guarantor such as China, or to try to strengthen independent self-defense capabilities, it remains premature for South Korea to pursue any other choice but continued reliance on the United States for the foreseeable future. Despite China's rising economic and political influence in East Asia, the United States remains the country that is most capable, committed, and strategically aligned with South Korea. Moreover, the United States remains more powerful than China and continues to guarantee an open and liberal global order under which South Korea as a leading exporter has thrived. China does not have the commitment or capability necessary to be an alternative security guarantor for South Korea, especially in an environment where China continues to provide backing to North Korea. Nor would South Korea be able to assure its security or prosperity on its own, given its relative weakness compared to its major-power neighbors.

THE DURABILITY OF THE U.S. COMMITMENT TO SOUTH KOREA IN A TRUMP ADMINISTRATION

Even as South Korea's debates over its strategic options have been growing more active, a potential accelerant to the salience of these debates was added during the U.S. presidential campaign in 2016, when Republican candidate Donald J. Trump cast doubts on the durability of U.S. alliance commitments to South Korea and argued that a country as rich as South Korea should be paying more to sustain U.S. commitment to its defense. In the hours following Trump's victory in the U.S. election, the South Korean government called an emergency national security meeting to discuss the implications of a Trump administration for South Korea.

South Korea's fear of abandonment by the United States is hardly new to discussions of the future of the U.S.-ROK alliance. In fact, as discussed in chapter 2, Park Chung-hee's fears of U.S. abandonment in the wake of the Nixon Doctrine and Jimmy Carter's pledges to withdraw U.S. troops from North Korea in the 1970s resulted in South Korea's efforts to enhance its self-defense, including the launching of a secret nuclear weapons program. In the mid-2000s, South Korean expressions of anti-Americanism and ideological differences between the Roh Moo-hyun and George W. Bush administrations led some Pentagon strategists to conclude that the U.S.-ROK alliance should no longer be viewed as central to long-term U.S. strategy in the Asia-Pacific region. But the U.S.-ROK alliance survived these difficulties, and public support for the alliance in both the United States and South Korea has rebounded strongly since that time. As described in chapter 8, both countries have deepened and broadened coordination on security issues in the face of a growing threat from North Korea while also cooperating to promote international stability in other parts of the world.

South Korea's responses to U.S. efforts to retrench or curtail the scope of its defense commitments are likely to unfold along three distinct paths. First, its initial response is likely to involve a redoubling of efforts to seek assurances and to convince the United States to maintain its alliance commitments to South Korea. These efforts would likely involve intensive public and private lobbying of constituencies deemed friendly to South Korea, including bureaucratic partners within the U.S. government, academic specialists and university professors, friends in the U.S. Congress, and the broader American public, including American veterans of the Korean War and members of the U.S. military who have served in Korea since that time. The South Korean government would mobilize official and informal ties with counterparts in the United States in an attempt to argue that it is in the U.S. interest to maintain its commitments to the defense of South Korea.

The South Korean government has plausible reasons for believing that such a full-court press to counter U.S. retrenchment or withdrawal from the Korean Peninsula can be successful: South Korea has built a reservoir of good will in the U.S. Congress and may be able to mobilize constituent pressure by the Korean American community. American public-opinion polling by organizations such as the Chicago Council on Global Affairs have shown consistent and solid levels of support in the United States for the alliance with South Korea in recent years, given the nature of the threat both countries face from North Korea.

Second, in the event that redoubled South Korean efforts to shore up American commitments to the alliance were to fail, South Korea would have little choice but to strengthen its options for self-defense to compensate. These efforts would almost certainly include higher defense spending, possibly including the development of an indigenous nuclear weapons capability to counter that of North Korea. South Korea could also face a deteriorating economic environment due to its inability to secure wide access to global consumer markets on its own, necessitating outreach efforts to other countries such as Japan and China for help with economic stabilization measures.

Third, American retrenchment would have a direct impact on South Korean domestic politics given that South Korean conservatives have been consistently pro-American and have benefited the most from long-standing U.S.-ROK alliance ties. The impact on South Korean political leadership would be to strengthen Korean progressives, who would be more open to improving relations with a rising China and would work hard to promote multilateral security mechanisms in Northeast Asia to the extent possible. As was illustrated under the Roh Moo-hyun and George W. Bush administrations, the combination of a progressive Korean government and a conservative American administration has the potential to generate tensions that could facilitate the unraveling of the U.S.-ROK alliance, particularly if there are clashes in the two governments' priorities and threat perceptions or if U.S. commitment to the maintenance of the alliance with South Korea comes under pressure or is drastically curtailed.

DETERMINANTS OF SOUTH KOREAN STRATEGIC CHOICE

This book has identified the following determinants of South Korea's future strategic choices. First, South Korean foreign-policy opportunities expand when the international security environment is benign, enabling South Korea to pursue its foreign-policy goals through a wider variety of options and with greater flexibility and autonomy. For instance, Roh Tae-woo's pursuit of Nordpolitik at the end of the Cold War and Kim Dae-jung's pursuit of the Sunshine Policy in the late 1990s were aided by a more relaxed regional security environment and involved South Korea's active efforts to enlist its neighbors' cooperation in moving toward the goal of enhanced stability in inter-Korean relations.

Second, South Korea is able to act more autonomously when its policy preferences align with those of the United States and when Seoul has Washington's backing. South Korea's establishment of new diplomatic relationships with the Soviet Union and China, its alignment with the Clinton administration in the initial phase of Kim Dae-jung's pursuit of expanded engagement with North Korea, and Lee Myung-bak's Global Korea policies all benefited from a close relationship with and support from the United States. Roh Moo-hyun's pursuit of greater autonomy through the "balancer" policy, in contrast, did not enjoy similar success, in part because of domestic opposition but also because of policy differences between the Roh and Bush administrations.

Third, the degree of domestic political consensus between progressive and conservative factions within South Korea is an important factor that influences the success or failure of South Korean foreign policy. Roh

Tae-woo's Nordpolitik policy enjoyed relative cooperation and support from progressive and conservative factions, and the Korea National Community Unification Formula drew from the ideas on both sides of the political spectrum. In contrast, Kim Dae-jung's policy of engagement toward North Korea was arguably hampered by his failure to bring conservatives with him to the inter-Korea summit in June 2000 and subsequently was constrained by the emergence of the South-South divide over North Korea policy following the summit. As shown throughout the book, however, domestic politics becomes a lesser factor when South Korea faces a deteriorating regional environment.

The most important factor constraining South Korea's strategic choices, despite its desires to be an autonomous actor and despite its expanded capabilities globally, is that it remains relatively less powerful economically and militarily than all of its immediate neighbors, with the exception of North Korea. This ongoing reality has prevented South Korea from pursuing independence through neutralization or internationalization through autonomy, as shown in figure 1.2, which charts the strategic choices that each South Korean president has made since the beginning of the Republic of Korea. The fact that South Korea has thus far never been willing to abandon the alliance with the United States is an indication that South Korean leaders have never truly regarded the option of autonomy as viable. South Korea simply has had no other choice but to rely on a great-power patron to achieve its strategic goals of security and prosperity. The most logical choice of patron is the United States, which remains the most powerful country in the world, shares democratic values with South Korea, and is relatively distant geographically from Northeast Asia.

A factor that could challenge South Korea's preference for alliance with the United States is a potential shift in the relative power of China and the United States. As detailed in chapter 9, there are several conditions under which South Korea might consider China as an alternative to the United States as a viable security guarantor for South Korea. First, China would have to surpass the United States in relative power, at least in Northeast Asia, even as the United States becomes unable or unwilling to guarantee South Korea's security. Second, China would have to become the primary architect, rule maker, and guarantor of the regional, if not international, order. Third, South Korea would have to write off the sunk costs invested in decades of alliance relations with the United States, dismantle the institutional bonds that link South Korean and American decision making in the security sphere, and overcome the differences between a democratic South Korea and a Communist China.

The primary wild card that might disrupt South Korea's established thinking regarding its security needs is the prospect of national unification, a long-held and enduring yet thus far illusory strategic goal that has been an essential objective for South Korean strategic thinkers. Obstacles that must be overcome for unification to be achieved include the feasibility of either unification via negotiations or unification via North Korean instability and collapse, but both pathways depend on developments inside North Korea that remain outside the control of South Korea to decisively influence, even as its power relative to that of North Korea continues to grow. Moreover, the conflicting interests of neighboring major powers serve as a further obstacle at the regional level to the feasibility of national unification. Some South Korean strategists may be encouraged by the idea that the realization of national unification could be one means of cutting the gap in relative power between South Korea and its neighbors sufficiently to overcome its historically weak position in the region, but it is unlikely that a unified Korea would become as strong as its major-power neighbors.

With an understanding of these factors, the United States should be able to enhance its own assessment of the durability of the U.S.-ROK relationship and the resilience of the common interests that have sustained the alliance for the past six decades.

SOUTH KOREA'S MIDDLE-POWER ASPIRATIONS

South Korea's middle-power aspirations have thus far contributed to the strengthening and broadening of the U.S.-ROK security alliance into a global and comprehensive partnership. Moreover, South Korean and American national capabilities and interests in global financial stability, global health, international development, energy security (including nuclear cooperation), and other nontraditional security areas have provided new opportunities for the United States and South Korea to work together to address common global challenges. Although there are conditions under which South Korea's middle-power aspirations could become a source of discord in the U.S.-ROK alliance, such conditions are unlikely.

South Korea's interests may not always be in harmony with U.S. interests. To the extent that South Korea's middle-power aspirations are focused on preservation of regional stability through enhanced cooperation with other middle powers so as to buffer against the possibility of Sino-U.S. conflict, however, its middle-power diplomacy is unlikely to conflict with U.S. interests. Alliance-based sunk costs, institutionalized cooperation, and common values are likely to sustain South Korea's strategic choice to ally with the United States unless or until it becomes apparent that South Korea lives in a made-in-China world and that the global, regional, and peninsular benefits of China's protection clearly outweigh the benefits of the U.S.-ROK alliance. In the meantime, South Korea's strategic decisions will continue to be shaped by the desire for autonomy yet constrained by the need for an alliance with the United States as its best means by which to sustain its security and prosperity and by which to pursue the strategic objective of Korean unification.

CHINA'S RISE AND THE U.S.-ROK ALLIANCE

The U.S.-ROK alliance will remain the anchor and platform that enables South Korea's pursuit of its fundamental strategic objectives as long as U.S. defense commitments remain credible and if the United States remains the most powerful actor in global affairs. However, to the extent that South Korea imagines a future in which a China-centered world order eclipses the current U.S.-centered world order, South Koreans may begin to hedge against the possibility that the United States will no longer be able to meet existing security commitments. Such hedging behavior may introduce new tensions in the bilateral relationship and would constitute a new test for the durability of the U.S.-ROK alliance. Moreover, China's desires to constrain the purposes and scope of the alliance to deter North Korea will likely result in periodic Chinese probes for weaknesses in the U.S.-ROK alliance. These probes could generate friction between the United

States and South Korea during situations in which China attempts to induce South Korea to make a premature or false choice between the current alliance with the United States and an uncertain future. Although the United States remains in a strong position to fend off such challenges from China today, the intensity and severity of such challenges will grow as China continues to rise.

A secondary factor likely to lead to the perpetuation of the U.S.-ROK alliance is that efforts to assert Chinese hegemony may drive South Korea into the hands of the United States or at least increase South Korea's desire for demonstrations of assurance from the United States. In this respect, the best strategy for maintaining South Korea's allegiance is to reinforce the credibility of alliance commitments, but in an understated fashion that allows China's efforts to assert itself to generate South Korean support for maintenance of a strong U.S.-ROK alliance. Indeed, China's attempt to interfere with South Korea's sovereign decision-making process with regard to the THAAD System and the consequential increase in South Korea public support for the system provide a clear example of dynamics that work to strengthen the durability of the U.S.-ROK alliance.

PREPARING FOR KOREAN UNIFICATION

Since the end of the Cold War, South Korea's desire to achieve unification has been strengthened by a decisive shift in power on the Korean Peninsula in favor of Seoul. Yet it is also North Korea's vulnerability that stands in the way of unification. Given the North's current economic and social conditions, unification would be extraordinarily expensive and could have seriously destabilizing consequences for the Korean Peninsula and beyond. Therefore, South Korea must seek a method for achieving unification that minimizes the potential risk to the country's security and prosperity.

The United States and South Korea have formally agreed on the desirability of Korean unification on the condition that it is led by Seoul and that a unified Korea would be a democracy and a market economy. The risks associated with this process are related primarily to quality of coordination and management of expectations. In particular, the United States should effectively coordinate on the priorities of stability and unification to ensure that the United States and South Korea not come into conflict with each other on the relative priority of these two shared objectives.

In the event that Korean unification becomes feasible, the United States has an interest in promoting regional stability by coordinating regional support for a peninsular transition from division to reunification and by managing the process in a way that minimizes the risks of unnecessary regional conflict among major powers. This coordination will require careful consultations with China and others on a regional mechanism through which all parties can cooperatively channel political and material support for Korean unification and regional stability in the context of a unified Korean Peninsula. Furthermore, coming to a consensus on the geopolitical orientation of a unified Korea acceptable to its neighbors will be the most important goal. The biggest question in such a process will likely revolve around whether a unified Korean state will continue to be allied with the United States or whether neighboring parties are able to agree to other arrangements that preserve the security and stability of a unified Korea and East Asia.

Reconciling these objectives could be problematic as events on the ground are likely to outpace strategic planning in a scenario of North Korean instability. If an opportunity for unification were to arise, a sudden surge of nationalism could push the South Korean government to act hastily in response to strong public sentiment; external attempts to influence South Korea could potentially backfire under such circumstances and would be unlikely to succeed. After all, most South Koreans do not see North Korea as a separate nation, although a growing number of younger-generation South Koreans might contest that proposition, making this issue one that will be influenced by domestic divisions within South Korea. The United States could face the choice of either having to prioritize strong support for South Korean actions and risk greater chance of conflict with China or to prioritize dialogue with China in an attempt to generate strategic understandings so as to preserve regional stability. Any choice the United States makes would have repercussions for its relations with postunification Korea.

In the near term, however, a unified Korea is likely to be best served by continuing its alliance with the United States, even if U.S. troops are reduced or are removed from the Korean Peninsula. In the long term, a U.S. security alliance with a unified Korea will be desirable unless a unified Korea proves strong enough to fend for itself or until Korea's neighbors are able to work out satisfactory cooperative security arrangements that are sufficiently robust to replace the alliance with the United States as the primary security guarantor on a unified peninsula. Given the strategic importance of the Korean Peninsula, though, a cooperative security arrangement will be difficult to achieve as long as U.S.-China tensions persist.

SELECT SOURCE DOCUMENTS

MUTUAL DEFENSE TREATY BETWEEN THE UNITED STATES AND THE REPUBLIC OF KOREA

October 1, 1953

The Parties to this Treaty,

Reaffirming their desire to live in peace with all peoples and governments, and desiring to strengthen the fabric of peace in the Pacific area,

Desiring to declare publicly and formally their common determination to defend themselves against external armed attack so that no potential aggressor could be under the illusion that either of them stands alone in the Pacific area,

Desiring further to strengthen their efforts for collective defense for the preservation of peace and security pending the development of a more comprehensive and effective system of regional security in the Pacific area,

Have agreed as follows:

ARTICLE I. The Parties undertake to settle any international disputes in which they may be involved by peaceful means in such a manner that international peace and security and justice are not endangered and to refrain in their international relations from the threat or use of force in any manner inconsistent with the Purposes of the United Nations, or obligations assumed by any Party toward the United Nations.

ARTICLE II. The Parties will consult together whenever, in the opinion of either of them, the political independence or security of either of the Parties is threatened by external armed attack. Separately and jointly, by self-help and mutual aid, the Parties will maintain and develop appropriate means to deter armed attack and will take suitable measures in consultation and agreement to implement this Treaty and to further its purposes.

ARTICLE III. Each Party recognizes that an armed attack in the Pacific area on either of the Parties in territories now under their respective administrative control, or hereafter recognized by one of the Parties as lawfully brought under the administrative control of the other, would be dangerous to its own peace and safety and declares that it would act to meet the common danger in accordance with its constitutional processes.

ARTICLE IV. The Republic of Korea grants, and the United States of America accepts, the right to dispose United States land, air and sea forces in and about the territory of the Republic of Korea as determined by mutual agreement.

ARTICLE V. This Treaty shall be ratified by the United States of America and the Republic of Korea in accordance with their respective constitutional processes and will come into force when instruments of ratification thereof have been exchanged by them at Washington.

ARTICLE VI. This Treaty shall remain in force indefinitely. Either Party may terminate it one year after notice has been given to the other Party.

IN WITNESS WHEREOF the undersigned Plenipotentiaries have signed this Treaty.

DONE in duplicate at Washington, in the English and Korean languages, this first day of October 1953.

JOINT STATEMENT OF NORTH AND SOUTH

July 4, 1972

Recently talks were held in Pyongyang and Seoul to discuss the problems of improving the South-North relations and of unifying the divided country.

Lee Hu-Rak, director of the Central Intelligence Agency in Seoul, visited Pyongyang in the period from May 2 to 5, 1972, and had talks with Kim Yong-Ju, director of the Organization and Guidance Department of Pyongyang, and Vice-Premier Park Sung-Chul, acting on behalf of Director Kim Yong-Ju, visited Seoul in the period from May 29 to June 1, 1972, and held further talks with Director Lee Hu-Rak.

With the common desire of achieving the peaceful unification of the nation as early as possible, the two sides engaged in a frank and open-hearted exchange of views during these talks and made great progress towards promoting mutual understanding.

In an effort to remove the misunderstandings and mistrust, and mitigate the heightened tensions that have arisen between the South and the North as a consequence of their long period of division and moreover to expedite unification, the two sides reached full agreement in respect of the following issues.

1. The two sides agreed on the following principles as a basis of achieving unification : First, unification shall be achieved independently, without depending on foreign powers and without foreign interference.

Second, unification shall be achieved through peaceful means, without resorting to the use of force against each other;

Third, a great national unity shall be sought first, transcending differences in ideas, ideologies, and systems.

2. In order to ease tensions and foster an atmosphere of mutual trust between the South and the North, the two sides have agreed not to slander or defame each other, not to undertake military provocations, whether on a large or small scale, and to take positive measures to prevent inadvertent military incidents.

3. In order to restore severed national ties, promote mutual understanding and to expedite independent peaceful unification, the two sides have agreed to carry out numerous exchanges in various fields.

4. The two sides have agreed to actively cooperate in seeking the early success of the South-North Red Cross talks, which are currently in progress with the fervent support of the entire nation.

5. In order to prevent the outbreak of unexpected military incidents and to deal directly, promptly, and accurately with problems arising between

the South and the North, the two sides have agreed to install a direct telephone line between Seoul and Pyongyang.

6. In order to implement the above items, to solve various problems existing between the South and the North, and to settle the unification problem on the basis of the agreed principles for unification, the two sides have agreed to establish and operate a South-North Coordinating Committee co-chaired by Director Lee Hu Rak and director Kim Yong Ju.

7. Firmly convinced that the above items of agreement correspond with the common aspirations of the entire Korean people, all of whom who are anxious for an early unification, the two sides solemnly pledge before the entire Korean nation to faithfully carry out these agreed items.

Agreed upon July 4th 1972
By Lee Hu-Rak, South side delegate,
Kim Yong-Ju North side delegate

INTER-KOREAN AGREEMENT ON RECONCILIATION, NON-AGGRESSION, AND EXCHANGES AND COOPERATION BETWEEN SOUTH AND NORTH KOREA

To enter into force as of February 19, 1992

The South and the North,

In keeping with the yearning of the entire Korean people for the peaceful unification of the divided land;

Reaffirming the three principles of unification set forth in the July 4 {1972} South-North Joint Communiqué;

Determined to remove the state of political and military confrontation and achieve national reconciliation;

Also determined to avoid armed aggression and hostilities, reduce tension and ensure peace;

Expressing the desire to realize multi-faceted exchanges and cooperation to advance common national interests and prosperity;

Recognizing that their relations, not being a relationship between states, constitute a special interim relationship stemming from the process towards unification;

Pledging to exert joint efforts to achieve peaceful unification;

Hereby have agreed as follows:

CHAPTER I. SOUTH-NORTH RECONCILIATION

Article 1. The South and the North shall recognize and respect each other's system.

Article 2. The two sides shall not interfere in each other's internal affairs.

Article 3. The two sides shall not slander or vilify each other.

Article 4. The two sides shall not attempt any actions of sabotage or overthrow against each other.

Article 5. The two sides shall endeavor together to transform the present state of armistice into a solid state of peace between the South and the North and shall abide by the present Military Armistice Agreement {July 27, 1953} until such a state of peace has been realized.

Article 6. The two sides shall cease to compete or confront each other and shall cooperate and endeavor together to promote national prestige and interests in the international arena.

Article 7. To ensure close consultations and liaison between the two sides, South-North Liaison Officers shall be established at Panmunjom within three (3) months after the coming into force of this Agreement.

Article 8. A South-North Political Committee shall be established within the framework of the South-North High-Level Talks within one (1) month of the coming into force of this Agreement with a view to discussing concrete measures to ensure the implementation and observance of the accords on South-North reconciliation.

CHAPTER II. SOUTH-NORTH NONAGGRESSION

Article 9. The two sides shall not use force against each other and shall not undertake armed aggression against each other.

Article 10. Differences of views and disputes arising between the two sides shall be resolved peacefully through dialogue and negotiation.

Article 11. The South-North demarcation line and areas for nonaggression shall be identical with the Military Demarcation Line specified in the Military Armistice Agreement of July 27, 1953 and the areas that have been under the jurisdiction of each side until the present time.

Article 12. To implement and guarantee non-aggression, the two sides shall set up a South-North Joint Military Commission within three (3) months of the coming into force of this Agreement. In the said Commission, the two sides shall discuss and carry out steps to build military confidence and control of major movements of military units and major military exercises, the peaceful utilization of the Demilitarized Zone, exchanges of military personnel and information, phased reductions in armaments including the elimination of weapons of mass destruction and attack capabilities, and verifications thereof.

Article 13. A telephone hotline shall be installed between the military authorities of the two sides to prevent accidental armed clashes and their escalation.

Article 14. A South-North Military Committee shall be established within the framework of the South-North High-Level Talks within one (1) month of the coming into force of this agreement in order to discuss concrete measures to ensure the implementation and observance of the accords on non-aggression and to remove military confrontation.

CHAPTER III. SOUTH-NORTH EXCHANGES AND COOPERATION

Article 15. To promote an integrated and balanced development of the national economy and the welfare of the entire people, the two sides shall engage in economic exchanges and cooperation, including the joint development of resources, the trade of goods as domestic commerce and joint ventures.

Article 16. The two sides shall carry out exchanges and cooperation in various fields such as science and technology, education, literature and the arts, health, sports, environment, and publishing and journalism including newspapers, radio and television broadcasts and publications.

Article 17. The two sides shall promote free intra-Korea travel and contacts for the residents of their respective areas.

Article 18. The two sides shall permit free correspondence, meetings and visits between dispersed family members and other relatives and shall promote the voluntary reunion of divided families and shall take measures to resolve other humanitarian issues.

Article 19. The two sides shall reconnect railroads and roads that have been cut off and shall open South-North sea and air transport routes.

Article 20. The two sides shall establish and link facilities needed for South-North postal and telecommunications services and shall guarantee the confidentiality of intra-Korean mail and telecommunications.

Article 21. The two sides shall cooperate in the economic, cultural and various other fields in the international arena and carry out jointly undertakings abroad.

Article 22. To implement accords on exchanges and cooperation in the economic, cultural and various other fields, the two sides shall establish joint commissions for specific sectors, including a Joint South-North Economic Exchanges and Cooperation Commission, within three (3) months of the coming into force of this Agreement.

Article 23. A South-North Exchanges and Cooperation Committee shall be established within the framework of the South-North High-Level Talks within one (1) month of the coming into force of this Agreement with a view to discussing concrete measures to ensure the implementation and observance of the accords on South-North exchanges and cooperation.

CHAPTER IV. AMENDMENTS AND EFFECTUATION

Article 24. This Agreement may be amended or supplemented by concurrence between the two sides.

Article 25. This Agreement shall enter into force as of the day the two sides exchange appropriate instruments following the completion of their respective procedures for bringing it into effect.

Signed on December 13, 1991

Chung Won-shik, Prime Minister of the Republic of Korea, Chief delegate of the South delegation to the South-North High-Level Talks

Yon Hyong-muk, Premier of the Administration Council of the Democratic People's Republic of Korea, Head of the North delegation to the South-North High-Level Talks

4. SOUTH-NORTH JOINT DECLARATION

June 15, 2000

In accordance with the noble will of the entire people who yearn for the peaceful reunification of the nation, President Kim Dae-jung of the Republic of Korea and National Defense Commission Chairman Kim Jong-il of the Democratic People's Republic of Korea held a historic meeting and summit talks in Pyongyang from June 13 to June 15, 2000.

The leaders of the South and the North, recognizing that the meeting and the summit talks were of great significance in promoting mutual understanding, developing South-North relations and realizing peaceful reunification, declared as follows:

1. The South and the North have agreed to resolve the question of reunification independently and through the joint efforts of the Korean people, who are the masters of the country.

2. For the achievement of reunification, we have agreed that there is a common element in the South's concept of a confederation and the North's formula for a loose form of federation. The South and the North agreed to promote reunification in that direction.

3. The South and the North have agreed to promptly resolve humanitarian issues such as exchange visits by separated family members and relatives on the occasion of the August 15 National Liberation Day and the question of unswerving Communists serving prison sentences in the South.

4. The South and the North have agreed to consolidate mutual trust by promoting balanced development of the national economy through economic cooperation and by stimulating cooperation and exchanges in civic, cultural, sports, health, environmental and all other fields.

5. The South and the North have agreed to hold a dialogue between relevant authorities in the near future to implement the above agreements expeditiously.

President Kim Dae-jung cordially invited National Defense Commission Chairman Kim Jong-il to visit Seoul, and Chairman Kim Jong-il will visit Seoul at an appropriate time.

Kim Dae-jung, President, The Republic of Korea

Kim Jong-il, Chairman National Defense Commission, The Democratic People's Republic of Korea

June 15, 2000

DECLARATION ON THE ADVANCEMENT OF SOUTH-NORTH KOREAN RELATIONS, PEACE, AND PROSPERITY

October 4, 2007

In accordance with the agreement between President Roh Moo-hyun of the Republic of Korea and Chairman Kim Jong Il of the National Defense Commission of the Democratic People's Republic of Korea, President Roh visited Pyongyang from October 2–4, 2007.

During the visit, there were historic meetings and discussions.

At the meetings and talks, the two sides have reaffirmed the spirit of the June 15 Joint Declaration and had frank discussions on various issues related to realizing the advancement of South-North relations, peace on the Korean Peninsula, common prosperity of the Korean people and unification of Korea.

Expressing confidence that they can forge a new era of national prosperity and unification on their own initiative if they combine their will and capabilities, the two sides declare as follows, in order to expand and advance South-North relations based on the June 15 Joint Declaration:

1. The South and the North shall uphold and endeavor actively to realize the June 15 Declaration.

The South and the North have agreed to resolve the issue of unification on their own initiative and according to the spirit of "by-the-Korean-people-themselves."

The South and the North will work out ways to commemorate the June 15 anniversary of the announcement of the South-North Joint Declaration to reflect the common will to faithfully carry it out.

2. The South and the North have agreed to firmly transform inter-Korean relations into ties of mutual respect and trust, transcending the differences in ideology and systems.

The South and the North have agreed not to interfere in the internal affairs of the other and agreed to resolve inter-Korean issues in the spirit of reconciliation, cooperation and reunification.

The South and the North have agreed to overhaul their respective legislative and institutional apparatuses in a bid to develop inter-Korean relations in a reunification-oriented direction.

The South and the North have agreed to proactively pursue dialogue and contacts in various areas, including the legislatures of the two Koreas, in order to resolve matters concerning the expansion and advancement of inter-Korean relations in a way that meets the aspirations of the entire Korean people.

3. The South and the North have agreed to closely work together to put an end to military hostilities, mitigate tensions and guarantee peace on the Korean Peninsula.

The South and the North have agreed not to antagonize each other, reduce military tension, and resolve issues in dispute through dialogue and negotiation.

The South and the North have agreed to oppose war on the Korean Peninsula and to adhere strictly to their obligation to nonaggression.

The South and the North have agreed to designate a joint fishing area in the West Sea to avoid accidental clashes. The South's Minister of Defense and the North's Minister of the People's Armed Forces have also agreed to hold talks in Pyongyang this November to discuss military confidence-building measures, including military guarantees covering the plans and various cooperative projects for making this joint fishing area into a peace area.

4. The South and the North both recognize the need to end the current armistice regime and build a permanent peace regime. The South and the North have also agreed to work together to advance the matter of having the leaders of the three or four parties directly concerned to convene on the Peninsula and declare an end to the war.

With regard to the nuclear issue on the Korean Peninsula, the South and the North have agreed to work together to implement smoothly the September 19, 2005 Joint Statement and the February 13, 2007 Agreement achieved at the Six-Party Talks.

5. The South and the North have agreed to facilitate, expand, and further develop inter-Korean economic cooperation projects on a continual basis for balanced economic development and co-prosperity on the Korean Peninsula in accordance with the principles of common interests, co-prosperity and mutual aid.

The South and the North reached an agreement on promoting economic cooperation, including investments, pushing forward with the building of infrastructure and the development of natural resources. Given the special nature of inter-Korean cooperative projects, the South and the North have agreed to grant preferential conditions and benefits to those projects.

The South and the North have agreed to create a "special peace and cooperation zone in the West Sea" encompassing Haeju and vicinity in a bid to proactively push ahead with the creation of a joint fishing zone and maritime peace zone, establishment of a special economic zone, utilization of Haeju harbor, passage of civilian vessels via direct routes in Haeju and the joint use of the Han River estuary.

The South and the North have agreed to complete the first-phase construction of the Gaeseong Industrial Complex at an early date and embark on the second-stage development project. The South and the North have agreed to open freight rail services between Munsan and Bongdong and promptly complete various institutional measures, including those related to passage, communication, and customs clearance procedures.

The South and the North have agreed to discuss repairs of the Gaeseong-Sinuiju railroad and the Gaeseong-Pyongyang expressway for their joint use.

The South and the North have agreed to establish cooperative complexes for shipbuilding in Anbyeon and Nampo, while continuing cooperative projects in various areas such as agriculture, health and medical services and environmental protection.

The South and the North have agreed to upgrade the status of the existing Inter-Korean Economic Cooperation Promotion Committee to a Joint Committee for Inter-Korean Economic Cooperation to be headed by deputy prime minister–level officials.

6. The South and the North have agreed to boost exchanges and cooperation in the social areas covering history, language, education, science

and technology, culture and arts, and sports to highlight the long history and excellent culture of the Korean people.

The South and the North have agreed to carry out tours to Mt. Baekdu and open nonstop flight services between Seoul and Mt. Baekdu for this purpose.

The South and the North have agreed to send a joint cheering squad from both sides to the 2008 Beijing Olympic Games. The squad will use the Gyeongui Railway Line for the first-ever joint Olympic cheering.

7. The South and the North have agreed to actively promote humanitarian cooperation projects.

The South and the North have agreed to expand reunion of separated family members and their relatives and promote exchanges of video messages.

To this end, the South and the North have agreed to station resident representatives from each side at the reunion center at Mt. Geumgang when it is completed and regularize reunions of separated family members and their relatives.

The South and the North have agreed to actively cooperate in case of emergencies, including natural disasters, according to the principles of fraternal love, humanitarianism and mutual assistance.

8. The South and the North have agreed to increase cooperation to promote the interests of the Korean people and the rights and interests of overseas Koreans on the international stage.

The South and the North have agreed to hold inter-Korean prime ministers' talks for the implementation of this Declaration and have agreed to hold the first round of meetings in November 2007 in Seoul.

The South and the North have agreed that their highest authorities will meet frequently for the advancement of relations between the two sides.

October 4, 2007

Pyongyang

Roh Moo-hyun, President, Republic of Korea

Kim Jong Il, Chairman, National Defense Commission, Democratic People's Republic of Korea

6. JOINT VISION FOR THE ALLIANCE OF THE UNITED STATES OF AMERICA AND THE REPUBLIC OF KOREA

June 16, 2009, Washington, D.C.

The United States of America and the Republic of Korea are building an Alliance to ensure a peaceful, secure and prosperous future for the Korean Peninsula, the Asia-Pacific region, and the world.

Our open societies, our commitment to free democracy and a market economy, and our sustained partnership provide a foundation for the enduring friendship, shared values, and mutual respect that tightly bind the American and Korean peoples.

The bonds that underpin our Alliance and our partnership are strengthened and enriched by the close relationships among our citizens. We pledge to continue programs and efforts to build even closer ties between our societies, including cooperation among business, civic, cultural, academic, and other institutions.

The United States–Republic of Korea Mutual Defense Treaty remains the cornerstone of the U.S.-ROK security relationship, which has guaranteed peace and stability on the Korean Peninsula and in Northeast Asia for over fifty years. Over that time, our security Alliance has strengthened and our partnership has widened to encompass political, economic, social and cultural cooperation. Together, on this solid foundation, we will build a comprehensive strategic alliance of bilateral, regional and global scope, based on common values and mutual trust. Together, we will work shoulder-to-shoulder to tackle challenges facing both our nations on behalf of the next generation.

The Alliance is adapting to changes in the 21st Century security environment. We will maintain a robust defense posture, backed by allied capabilities which support both nations' security interests. The continuing commitment of extended deterrence, including the U.S. nuclear umbrella, reinforces this assurance. In advancing the bilateral plan for restructuring the Alliance, the Republic of Korea will take the lead role in the combined defense of Korea, supported by an enduring and capable U.S. military force presence on the Korean Peninsula, in the region, and beyond.

We will continue to deepen our strong bilateral economic, trade and investment relations. We recognize that the Korea-U.S. (KORUS) Free Trade Agreement could further strengthen these ties and we are committed to working together to chart a way forward. We aim to make low-carbon green growth into a new engine for sustainable economic prosperity and will closely cooperate in this regard. We will strengthen civil space cooperation, and work closely together on clean energy research and the peaceful uses of nuclear energy.

Through our Alliance we aim to build a better future for all people on the Korean Peninsula, establishing a durable peace on the Peninsula and leading to peaceful reunification on the principles of free democracy and a market economy. We will work together to achieve the complete and verifiable elimination of North Korea's nuclear weapons and existing nuclear programs, as well as ballistic missile programs, and to promote respect for the fundamental human rights of the North Korean people.

In the Asia-Pacific region we will work jointly with regional institutions and partners to foster prosperity, keep the peace, and improve the daily lives of the people of the region. We believe that open societies and open economies create prosperity and support human dignity, and our nations and civic organizations will promote human rights, democracy, free markets, and trade and investment liberalization in the region. To enhance security in the Asia-Pacific, our governments will advocate for, and take part in, effective cooperative regional efforts to promote mutual understanding, confidence and transparency regarding security issues among the nations of the region.

Our governments and our citizens will work closely to address the global challenges of terrorism, proliferation of weapons of mass destruction, piracy, organized crime and narcotics, climate change, poverty, infringement on human rights, energy security, and epidemic disease. The Alliance will enhance coordination on peacekeeping, post-conflict stabilization and development assistance, as is being undertaken in Iraq and Afghanistan. We will also strengthen coordination in multilateral mechanisms aimed at global economic recovery such as the G20.

The United States of America and the Republic of Korea will work to achieve our common Alliance goals through strategic cooperation at every level. Proven bilateral mechanisms such as the Security Consultative Meeting and the Strategic Consultations for Allied Partnership will remain central to realizing this shared vision for the Alliance.

7. JOINT DECLARATION IN COMMEMORATION OF THE 60TH ANNIVERSARY OF THE ALLIANCE BETWEEN THE REPUBLIC OF KOREA AND THE UNITED STATES OF AMERICA

May 7, 2013

For six decades, the U.S.-ROK Alliance has served as an anchor for stability, security, and prosperity on the Korean Peninsula, in the Asia-Pacific region, and increasingly around the world. President Barack Obama of the United States of America and President Park Geun-hye of the Republic of Korea, meeting in Washington, D.C. on May 7, 2013, present this Joint Declaration in celebration of sixty years of bilateral partnership and shared prosperity. The two leaders affirm that the Alliance is well-placed to address the opportunities and challenges of the future.

The U.S.-ROK Alliance, forged in the Korean War and founded on the 1953 United States–Republic of Korea Mutual Defense Treaty, has evolved into a comprehensive strategic alliance with deep cooperation extending beyond security to also encompass the political, economic, cultural, and people-to-people realms. The freedom, friendship, and shared prosperity we enjoy today rest upon our shared values of liberty, democracy, and a market economy.

Building on the past sixty years of stability on the Korean Peninsula, we continue to strengthen and adapt our Alliance to serve as a linchpin of peace and stability in the Asia-Pacific and to meet the security challenges of the 21st century. The United States remains firmly committed to the defense of the Republic of Korea, including through extended deterrence and the full range of U.S. military capabilities, both conventional and nuclear.

This year also marks another milestone for our two nations—the first anniversary of the entry into force of the U.S.-Korea Free Trade

Agreement (KORUS FTA). This agreement embodies the positive evolution of our partnership and demonstrates how deeply the United States and the Republic of Korea are committed to a shared future of growth and prosperity. We are pleased to note the positive results of the KORUS FTA, including increased trade and investment between our two countries, and recognize its potential for expanding bilateral cooperation and business opportunities, including in the energy sector. Our two countries will fully implement the KORUS FTA to ensure that the agreement serves as an economic growth engine in both our countries.

We are pleased with the significant progress made in realizing the 2009 Joint Vision for the Alliance of the United States of America and the Republic of Korea, which lays out a blueprint for the future development of our strategic Alliance. We pledge to continue to build a better and more secure future for all Korean people, working on the basis of the Joint Vision to foster enduring peace and stability on the Korean Peninsula and its peaceful reunification based on the principles of denuclearization, democracy and a free market economy. In this context, the United States and the Republic of Korea will continue to work through the Alliance to bring North Korea in to compliance with its international obligations and promote peace and prosperity on the Korean Peninsula, including through the trust-building process initiated by President Park.

We share the deep concern that North Korea's nuclear and ballistic missiles programs and its repeated provocations pose grave threats to the peace and stability of the Korean Peninsula and Northeast Asia. Both the United States and the Republic of Korea are determined to achieve the peaceful denuclearization of North Korea and are working with other Six-Party Talks partners and the international community to insist that North Korea adheres to its international obligations and commitments. While we invite North Korea to take the path that leads out of isolation and to join the community of nations as a responsible member, we are resolved to continue to defend our citizens against North Korea's provocations by strengthening our comprehensive, interoperable, and combined defense capabilities, to include shared efforts to counter the missile threat posed by North Korea and integrated intelligence, surveillance, and reconnaissance systems. Because both the United States and the Republic of Korea share a deep concern for the well-being of the North Korean people, we encourage North Korea to invest in, and improve, the conditions for its citizens and to respect their basic human rights.

The peace and prosperity of both our nations are inextricably linked to regional and global security and economic growth. Based on the solid U.S.-ROK Alliance, we are prepared to address our common challenges and seek ways to build an era of peace and cooperation in Northeast Asia. The U.S.-ROK Alliance is an increasingly global partnership, and the United States welcomes the Republic of Korea's leadership and active engagement on the world stage, including in international fora. We will strengthen our efforts to address global challenges such as climate change and to promote clean energy, energy security, human rights, humanitarian assistance, development assistance cooperation, counter-terrorism, peaceful uses of nuclear energy, nuclear safety, non-proliferation, cybersecurity, and counter-piracy.

Our sixty years of partnership and shared prosperity have demonstrated that the strength of our Alliance stems from the close relationships between our peoples. The large Korean-American community in the United States not only serves as a significant link between our two countries, but also makes countless contributions to the strength and vitality of American society. We pledge to continue programs and efforts to build even closer ties between our societies, including cooperation among business, civic, academic, and other institutions.

As allies and Asia-Pacific nations, we look forward to shaping together the future of Asia for generations to come.

CHRONOLOGY OF IMPORTANT EVENTS IN SOUTH KOREAN STRATEGIC HISTORY

July 20, 1948	Syngman Rhee is elected president of South Korea.
August 15, 1948	The Republic of Korea (South Korea) declares its independence, with Syngman Rhee serving as its first president.
December 1, 1948	South Korea adopts the National Security Act.
December 8, 1948	The United Nations (UN) approves the recognition of the Republic of Korea with General Assembly Resolution 195.
June 28, 1949	The last U.S. combat troops are called home from Korea, leaving only five hundred advisers.
October 6, 1949	China and South Korea establish diplomatic relations.
January 12, 1950	In a speech, U.S. secretary of state Dean Acheson places South Korea outside the U.S. defense perimeter in Asia but Japan, Okinawa, the Philippines, and the Aleutians inside the perimeter to be defended.
June 25, 1950	The Korean War starts.
July 27, 1953	An armistice that ends the fighting in the three-year Korean War is signed by representatives of the UN, Korea, and China in Panmunjom. Lieutenant General

William K. Harrison represents the UN, and General Nam Il represents the Democratic People's Republic of Korea (North Korea). General Mark Clark, commander of the UN forces, adds his signature to the armistice agreement.

August 8, 1953   The United States and South Korea initial a mutual security pact.

April 28, 1960   Syngman Rhee flees South Korea with the help of the U.S. Central Intelligence Agency after being overthrown by a student-led revolution.

May 16, 1961   Park Chung-hee leads a military coup to become South Korea's leader.

June 22, 1965   Treaty on Basic Relations Between Japan and the Republic of Korea.

1965–1973   Some three hundred thousand South Korean troops fight alongside U.S. forces in Vietnam. In 1998, South Korea expresses regret to Hanoi for participation in the war.

January 19, 1967   North Korean artillery batteries fire on and sink Republic of Korea Navy ship PCE-56 off North Korea's east coast, killing thirty-nine South Korean sailors.

January 21, 1968   A group of thirty-one North Korean commandos invades the South undetected and makes its way to the Blue House of South Korean president Park Chung-hee in downtown Seoul but is stopped by the South Korean police and troops before the operation is able to succeed. Twenty-eight North Koreans and thirty-four South Koreans are killed in the resulting clash.

1970   Park Chung-hee launches efforts to acquire nuclear weapons.

April 1970   North Korea intercepts a South Korean fishing trawler and seizes its crew. Most of the crew are later repatriated, but Lee Jae-geun, owner of the trawler, is held for three decades before he escapes home.

April 27, 1971   In South Korea, Kim Dae-jung nearly defeats Park Chung-hee in the presidential election.

July 4, 1972   The Joint Communiqué of July 4 is the first major accord between the Koreas on unification since the Korean War ended with a fragile truce in 1953.

November 21, 1972   Park Chung-hee's Yushin Constitution is confirmed in a referendum, making him a dictator all but in name.

December 28, 1972   A North Korean navy ship seizes twenty-five South Korean fishermen aboard two boats. In 2013, Jeon Wook-Pyo, one of the twenty-five, escapes and makes it back to South Korea.

June 23, 1973   Park Chung-hee gives a special foreign-policy address aimed at China and the Soviet Union, stating that South Korea "will open its door to all the nations of the world on the basis of the principles of reciprocity and equality" and to "countries whose ideologies and social institutions are different" from those of South Korea.

August 15, 1974   Park Chung-hee escapes a North Korean assassination attempt in which his wife is killed.

April 23, 1975   South Korea ratifies the Treaty on the Non-Proliferation of Nuclear Weapons.

August 1975   North Korea seizes thirty-three South Korean fishermen near their maritime border. In 2006, Choi Uk-il, one of the thirty-three, escapes to China and returns home to South Korea.

Late January 1976   South Korea shuts down its nuclear weapons program in response to U.S. pressure.

August 18, 1976   Two U.S. Army officers are killed in Korea's Demilitarized Zone by a group of North Korean soldiers wielding axes and metal pikes.

October 26, 1979   Park Chung-hee is shot to death by the head of the Korean Central Intelligence Agency, Kim Jae-kyu.

December 12, 1979   Chun Doo-hwan leads a military coup and becomes South Korea's leader.

May 18–27, 1980   The people of Gwangju rise to protest for democracy and are violently put down by the South Korean military.

September 17, 1980   South Korea opposition leader Kim Dae-jung is sentenced to death. In 1981, the sentence is commuted to life imprisonment in Seoul.

May 1983   First high-level, official, face-to-face exchanges take place between South Korean and Chinese officials as they work to resolve a crisis involving a hijacked plane full of Chinese passengers that lands in South Korea.

September 1, 1983   Korean Airlines Flight 007 is downed by a Soviet jet fighter after the airliner enters Soviet airspace. Of the people aboard the Boeing 747, 269 are killed, including 61 Americans, among them Georgia representative Larry McDonald. On September 6, The Soviet Union admits to shooting down the plane.

October 9, 1983   North Korea attempts to bomb President Chun Doo-hwan and his cabinet and other top officials at a monument in Rangoon, Burma. Chun survives the attempt, but seventeen South Koreans, including the deputy prime minister, two other cabinet members, and two Burmese are killed.

1985   The volume of indirect trade between China and South Korea surpasses the volume of indirect trade between China and North Korea.

June 10–29, 1987   A nationwide democracy movement forces the Chun government to make a transition to democracy. Roh Tae-woo is elected the next president.

November 29, 1987	A Korean Air jetliner, Flight 858, is blown up by North Korean bombs planted on the plane, with the loss of all 115 people aboard.
July 7, 1988	Roh Tae-woo announces Nordpolitk.
September 17–October 2, 1988	Summer Olympics are held in South Korea.
September 11, 1990	South Korea and the Soviet Union establish diplomatic relations.
April 19, 1991	Soviet president Mikhail Gorbachev arrives in South Korea for talks with Roh Tae-woo.
September 17, 1991	The UN General Assembly welcomes new members Estonia, Latvia, Lithuania, North Korea, South Korea, the Marshall Islands, and Micronesia at the opening of its forty-sixth session.
December 6, 1991	Kim Hak Soon becomes the first Korean to publicly acknowledge her World War II past as a sex slave, or "comfort woman."
January 20, 1992	North Korea and South Korea sign the Joint Declaration of the Denuclearization of the Korean Peninsula, stating that neither will "test, manufacture, produce, receive, possess, store, deploy or use nuclear weapons."
February 12, 1992	South and North Korea sign a basic agreement designating the Northern Limit Line, promoting nonaggression in eventual reconciliation, and encouraging exchange and cooperation.
August 24, 1992	South Korea and China normalize relations.
February 25, 1993	In South Korea, Kim Young-sam wins the presidency to become the first democratically elected civilian in thirty-two years.
June 18, 1994	The leaders of North Korea and South Korea agree to hold a historic summit. The plans are disrupted by the death of North Korean leader Kim Il-sung on July 8.

December 3, 1997   South Korea strikes a deal with the International Monetary Fund for a record $55 billion bailout of its foundering economy.

December 18, 1997   Kim Dae-jung wins the presidential election and is the first opposition leader to be inaugurated in a peaceful, democratic transfer of power.

June 17, 1998   Hyundai's founder, Chung Ju-yung, goes on a trip to aid North Korea, taking 501 cows with him as a symbolic gesture.

June 22, 1998   In an event known as the Sokcho Submarine Incident of 1998, South Korea sinks a half-submarine belonging to North Korea and recovers the body of a crewmember wearing a wetsuit and carrying a grenade.

October 8, 1998   In Japan, Kim Dae-jung and Japanese prime minister Obuchi Keizo sign a landmark partnership agreement, the New Partnership for the Twenty-First Century, which includes Obuchi's expression of "remorseful and heartfelt apology" and Kim's acceptance of the apology and commitment on both sides to pursue a "future-oriented relationship."

1997–1998   The Asian financial crisis hits.

June 9–15, 1999   A naval clash between the North and the South occurs near Yeonpyeong Island, an incident known as "the first battle of Yeonpyeong."

June 13–15, 2000   The first inter-Korean summit is held.

September 1, 2000   South Korea repatriates sixty-three North Korean spies as a gesture of reconciliation.

September 25, 2000   In Jeju, defense ministers from the two Koreas, Cho Sung-tae and Kim Il-chul, meet and pledge to work for reconciliation.

October 24, 2000   U.S. secretary of state Madeleine Albright visits North Korea and meets Kim Jong-il.

March 7, 2001   Kim Dae-jung meets with President George W. Bush in Washington, D.C. Bush says he does not plan to resume talks with North Korea.

October 15, 2001   Japan's prime minister Koizumi Junichiro visits South Korea and expresses his remorse at Sodaemun Independence Park for the suffering inflicted by Japan's colonial rule.

May 31, 2002   The World Cup soccer tournament begins in Japan and South Korea.

June 13, 2002   A U.S. military vehicle in South Korea runs over two middle school girls, sparking mass protests.

June 29, 2002   Second inter-Korean naval clash near Yeonpyeong Island.

February 25, 2003   Roh Moo-hyun becomes South Korea's president.

April 9, 2003   The United States says it will move its main military base out of the capital of South Korea as soon as possible.

May 12, 2003   North Korea declares that the agreement with South Korea to keep the Korean Peninsula free of nuclear weapons, signed in 1992, is nullified, citing a "sinister" U.S. agenda.

May 16, 2003   President Roh Moo-hyun visits the United States.

June 5, 2003   The United States decides to pull its ground troops away from the Demilitarized Zone separating North and South Korea.

December 22, 2003   South Korea and Japan begin negotiations on establishing a free-trade agreement.

June 7, 2004   U.S. and South Korean officials announce plans to withdraw one-third of thirty-seven thousand U.S. troops from South Korea by the end of 2005.

December 2004   The Kaesong Industrial Complex opens as a potent symbol of reconciliation between North Korea and South Korea.

June 20, 2005   Japan–South Korea summit between Roh Moo Hyun and Junichiro Koizumi fails to reap progress on the Dokdo/Takeshima territorial dispute.

October 12, 2005   South Korean defense minister Yoon Kwang-ung says South Korea has proposed talks to take back wartime control of its military from the United States.

January 8, 2006   The United States and South Korea withdraw their last remaining staff from the site of two North Korean nuclear reactors, ending a decade-old construction project amid rekindled tension over the North's nuclear ambitions.

April 19, 2006   Japan defies South Korean protests and dispatches two ships to begin a maritime survey near the disputed Dokdo/Takeshima islets between the two nations, raising the stakes in the territorial standoff.

April 22, 2006   Japan and South Korea defuse a tense standoff over disputed waters, with Japan withdrawing a plan to survey the area and South Korea delaying plans to submit name proposals for underwater features.

September 28, 2006   South Korea and the United States agree on a program to reshape their military alliance and give Seoul a bigger role in countering North Korean attacks. The two sides sign new terms for the decades-old alliance after talks in Washington, D.C.

October 9, 2006   The UN Security Council officially nominates South Korean foreign minister Ban Ki-moon to be the next UN secretary-general.

October 20, 2006   South Korea defense minister Yoon Kwang-ung meets with U.S. defense secretary Donald H. Rumsfeld and agrees that Seoul will retake full wartime operational control of Korean forces from the United States sometime between 2009 and 2012.

November 16, 2006	South Korea says it will reverse its long-standing refusal to join international efforts criticizing North Korea's human rights record and vote in favor of a UN resolution against the Communist regime's alleged abuses.
December 14, 2006	South Korean diplomat Ban Ki-moon formally takes the reins of the UN.
January 1, 2007	Ban Ki-moon becomes the UN's eighth secretary-general.
April 2, 2007	South Korea and the United States agree to a free-trade pact with only minutes to go before a deadline.
October 2, 2007	The second inter-Korean summit begins. North Korean leader Kim Jong-il shows scant enthusiasm for the visiting South Korean president, while orchestrated crowds of thousands of North Koreans cheer the start of the second summit between the divided Koreas since World War II.
February 25, 2008	Lee Myung-bak takes office as president, promising greater prosperity both for his own nation and for impoverished North Korea if it will scrap its nuclear drive.
March 27, 2008	North Korea expels all eleven South Korean officials from a joint industrial estate just north of the border in retaliation for Seoul's new tougher line toward the Communist state.
April 21, 2008	Japanese prime minister Yasuo Fukuda meets with Lee Myung-bak, and both declare a new era of closer cooperation.
May 29, 2008	South Korea takes the final step to resume full imports of beef from the United States, which it banned in 2003 over fears of mad cow disease.
May 31, 2008	In the largest demonstration in a month of almost daily protests, tens of thousands of South Koreans

	rally against a government decision to import U.S. beef.
June 2, 2008	The South Korean government decides to delay the planned resumption of U.S. beef imports after a request from the ruling party and large weekend street protests.
June 21, 2008	South Korea decides to resume imports of U.S. beef after American and South Korean suppliers agree to block meat from older cattle, aiming to soothe health concerns that sparked weeks of demonstrations against new president Lee Myung-bak. More than ten thousand people rally in central Seoul to protest the U.S. beef imports.
December 13, 2008	Japan, China, and South Korea move to ward off the effects of the global financial crunch at a trilateral summit in Japan, while Tokyo and Seoul criticize North Korea for stalling denuclearization talks.
January 30, 2009	North Korea announces that it is scrapping agreements with South Korea on easing military tensions, accusing Seoul of pushing relations to the brink of war.
May 27, 2009	North Korea renounces its truce with the Allied forces signed in 1953 and threatens to strike any ships that try to intercept its vessels.
July 4, 2009	Attacks begin on more than two dozen Internet sites in the United States and South Korea, and some are disabled by hackers. South Korea's intelligence agency later says the attacks were possibly linked to North Korea. Some of the affected U.S. government websites, such as those of the Treasury Department, the Federal Trade Commission, and the Secret Service, are still reporting problems days after the attack started during the Fourth of July holiday.

July 9, 2009	South Korean websites are attacked again after a wave of website outages in the United States and South Korea that several officials suspect North Korea is behind.
September 26, 2009	In North Korea, 97 South Koreans reunite with 228 North Korean relatives at the Diamond Mountain resort. This is the first reunion in nearly two years.
October 10, 2009	China, Japan, and South Korea hold a trilateral summit in Beijing.
November 10, 2009	A badly damaged North Korean patrol ship retreats in flames after a skirmish with a South Korean naval vessel along their disputed western coast.
January 27, 2010	North Korea fires more than eighty shells into the sea near its disputed maritime border with South Korea, sparking an artillery exchange.
March 26, 2010	A South Korean naval ship sinks after an explosion, leaving 46 marines missing near Baengnyeong Island. Of the 104-member crew, 58 are rescued. A North Korean torpedo is later found to be the cause of the explosion.
May 20, 2010	A multinational team blames North Korea for sinking the South Korean corvette.
May 24, 2010	Lee Myung-bak cuts South Korea's trade with North Korea, vowing the latter will "pay a price" for the torpedo attack.
May 25, 2010	North Korea declares that it will sever all communication and relations with Seoul as punishment for blaming it for the sinking of a South Korean warship.
May 27, 2010	South Korean warships fire guns and drop antisubmarine bombs in a large-scale military exercise a week after Seoul accused North Korea of shooting a torpedo that sank a navy frigate in March. North Korea declares it will scrap an accord with the South

designed to prevent armed clashes at their maritime border and warns of "immediate physical strikes" if any South Korean ships enter its waters.

October 29, 2010 — North and South Korea exchange gunfire across their heavily armed land border.

October 30, 2010 — Hundreds of North and South Korean family members embrace each other in another round of reunions.

November 10, 2010 — U.S. president Barack Obama arrives in South Korea for the G20 summit. He says a strong, job-creating economy in the United States would be its most important contribution to a global recovery as he pleads with world leaders to work together despite sharp differences.

November 11, 2010 — The G20 summit opens in Seoul.

November 23, 2010 — North and South Korea exchange artillery fire after the North shells Yeonpyeong Island near their disputed sea border.

August 30, 2011 — South Korea's top court rules that it is unconstitutional for the South Korean government not to make efforts to resolve the "comfort women" issue with Japan.

October 12, 2011 — U.S. Congress approves free-trade agreements with South Korea, Colombia, and Panama.

October 18, 2011 — Japanese prime minister Yoshihiko Noda visits South Korea to improve bilateral relations.

March 26, 2012 — Leaders and top officials from fifty-three nations gather in Seoul for the Nuclear Security Summit.

May 13, 2012 — Leaders of China, Japan, and South Korea hold their fifth trilateral summit.

June 29, 2012 — Seoul backs off signing the South Korea–Japan General Security of Military Information Agreement.

August 10, 2012   South Korea's president Lee Myung-bak visits the
                   Dokdo/Takeshima islets.

October 7, 2012   South Korea announces that a U.S. accord has been
                   altered to allow the South to have ballistic missiles
                   with a range of up to eight hundred kilometers (five
                   hundred miles) to better cope with North Korea's
                   nuclear and missile threats.

January 30, 2013   South Korea launches a satellite into space from its
                   own soil for the first time. The satellite is designed to
                   analyze weather data, measure radiation in space,
                   gauge distances on Earth, and test how effectively
                   South Korean–made devices installed on the satellite
                   operate in space.

February 25, 2013 Park Geun-hye begins her term as South Korea's
                   president.

March 27, 2013   North Korea cuts its last military hotline with
                   Seoul.

April 8, 2013   North Korea says it will suspend operations at the
                   Kaesong Industrial Complex, which it has jointly
                   run with South Korea, and pull out more than
                   fifty-three thousand North Korean workers.

May 7–8, 2013   Obama meets with Park Geun-hye. She also ad-
                   dresses the two houses of the U.S. Congress.

August 14, 2013   After a series of talks, North and South Korea agree
                   to restart the joint Kaesong Industrial Complex.

September 5, 2013 North Korea agrees to restore the cross-border
                   military hotline with South Korea.

February 5, 2014   North Korea and South Korea agree to hold their first
                   divided-family reunions in more than three years.

March 25, 2014   In the Netherlands, U.S. president Barack Obama,
                   Japanese prime minister Abe Shinzo, and South
                   Korean president Park Geun-hye meet to discuss
                   the security threat from North Korea.

April 16, 2014	In South Korea, some 274 people are missing after the sinking of the Sewol passenger ferry in the Yellow Sea. It carried 475 passengers and crew, mostly high school students from Danwon High School in Ansan, on a school trip to Jeju Island. Only 174 are rescued. On July 18, the confirmed death toll is 294, with 10 still missing. A body recovered on October 28 raises the death toll to 295.
May 22, 2014	North and South Korean warships exchange artillery fire in disputed waters off the western coast.
July 3, 2014	Chinese president Xi Jinping begins a two-day visit to Seoul, marking the first time a Chinese leader has visited the South before visiting the North.
September 4, 2014	South Korea says it will create a joint military unit with the United States.
October 15, 2014	The first military talks between North and South Korea in more than three years end with no agreement.
November 10, 2014	South Korea says it has agreed to sign a free-trade deal with China that will remove tariffs on more than 90 percent of goods over two decades but will not include rice or autos.
March 26, 2015	South Korea joins the China-led Asian Infrastructure and Investment Bank.
August 2015	A minicrisis erupts along the Demilitarized Zone when South Korean soldiers are injured by mines planted by the North. The crisis is resolved through a direct talk between the two sides.
September 3, 2015	Park Geun-hye attends China's military parade in Beijing, standing alongside Xi Jinping and Vladimir Putin.
October 20–22, 2015	Another inter-Korean family reunion is held.
December 28, 2015	South Korea and Japan reach an agreement to resolve the "comfort women" issue.

July 7, 2016   In response to North Korea's fourth nuclear test and another intercontinental ballistic missile test, South Korean and the United States jointly agree to deploy the Terminal High-Altitude Area Defense System.

NOTES

1. SOUTH KOREA'S STRATEGIC CHOICES

1. For example, see In Kwan Hwang, "Neutralization: An All-Weather Paradigm for Korean Reunification," *Asian Affairs* 25 (Winter 1999): 195–207, http://www.jstor.org/stable /30172449, and Tae-ryong Yoon, "Neutralize or Die: Reshuffling South Korea's Grand Strategy Cards and the Neutralization of South Korea Alone," *Pacific Focus* 30, no. 2 (2015): 270–295.

2. STRATEGIC CHOICES UNDER AUTHORITARIAN RULE

1. For more on Rhee and military conflict with the North, see Victor D. Cha, *Powerplay: The Origins of the American Alliance System in Asia* (Princeton: Princeton University Press, 2016).
2. Min Yong Lee, "Vietnam War: South Korea's Search for National Security," in *The Park Chung Hee Era: The Transformation of South Korea*, ed. Byung-kook Kim and Ezra F. Vogel (Cambridge, Mass.: Harvard University Press, 2011), 426.
3. Young-ick Lew, *The Making of South Korea's First President: Syngman Rhee's Quest for Independence, 1875–1948* (Honolulu: University of Hawai'i Press, 2014).
4. See Cha, *Powerplay*.
5. "The Syngman Rhee Era, 1946–1960," Country Studies, Library of Congress, http:// countrystudies.us/south-korea/11.htm.
6. See Yong-pyo Hong, *State Security and Regime Security: President Syngman Rhee and the Insecurity Dilemma in South Korea, 1953–60* (New York: St. Martin's Press, 1999).
7. Chung Hee Park, *Our Nation's Path: Ideology of Social Reconstruction* (Seoul: Hollym, 1970), 34–107; Chung-in Moon and Byung-joon Jun, "Modernization Strategy: Ideas and Influences," in *The Park Chung Hee Era*, ed. Kim and Vogel, 125.

8. Chung Hee Park, *Korea Reborn: A Model for Development* (Englewood Cliffs, N.J.: Prentice-Hall, 1979), 129, 132, emphasis in original.

9. Ibid., 21.

10. Ibid., 22.

11. Chung Hee Park, *The Country, the Revolution, and I* (Seoul: Hollym, 1970), 166.

12. Moon and Jun, "Modernization Strategy," 120.

13. Quoted in Donald Kirk, *Korean Dynasty: Hyundai and Chung Ju Yung* (Hong Kong: Asia 2000, and Armonk, NY: M. E. Sharpe, 1994), 75.

14. Quoted in Nicholas Eberstadt, *Policy and Economic Performance in Divided Korea During the Cold War Era: 1945–91* (Washington, D.C.: AEI Press, 2010), 228.

15. Richard M. Steers, *Made in Korea: Chung Ju Yung and the Rise of Hyundai* (New York: Routledge, 1999), 52.

16. Kwang-il Baek, "The U.S.-ROK Security Relationship Within the Conceptual Framework of a Great and Small Power Alliance," *Journal of East and West Studies* 6 (1982): 118.

17. Taehyun Kim and Chang Jae Baik, "Taming and Tamed by the United States," in *The Park Chung Hee Era*, ed. Kim and Vogel, 58.

18. Ibid., 59.

19. Min Yong Lee, "Vietnam War: South Korea's Search for National Security," in *The Park Chung Hee Era*, ed. Kim and Vogel, 405.

20. Ibid., 407.

21. "Record of National Security Council Action No. 2430," in *Foreign Relations of the United States, 1961–1963*, vol. 22: *Northeast Asia*, ed. Glenn W. LaFantasie, Edward C. Keefer, David W. Mabon, and Harriet Dashiell Schwar (Washington, D.C.: U.S. Government Printing Office, 1996), document 230, https://history.state.gov/historical documents/frus1961-63v22/d230.

22. Kim and Baik, "Taming and Tamed by the United States," 65–67.

23. Ibid.

24. Ibid., 68–69.

25. Quoted in Lee, "Vietnam War," 409.

26. On the domestic response to Park's deployment of troops to Vietnam, see Edward Reynolds Wright and Suk-choon Cho, eds., *Korean Politics in Transition* (Seattle: University of Washington for the Royal Asiatic Society, Korea Branch, 1975).

27. Quoted in Hong-koo Han, "South Korea and the Vietnam War," in *Developmental Dictatorship and the Park Chung Hee Era: The Shaping of Modernity in the Republic of Korea*, ed. Byeong-cheon Lee (Paramus, N.J.: Homa & Sekey, 2006), 261.

28. Lee, "Vietnam War," 415.

29. Ibid., 416.

30. Ibid., 412–413.

31. Ibid., 419.

32. Jong-pil Kim, "How Korea Got Free Phantoms," *JoongAng Ilbo*, August 11, 2015, http://koreajoongangdaily.joins.com/news/article/article.aspx?aid=3007795.

33. Quoted in Jung-hoon Lee, "Normalization of Relations with Japan: Toward a New Partnership," in *The Park Chung Hee Era*, ed. Kim and Vogel, 438.

34. "Visit of Prime Minister Sato, January 11–14, 1965," background paper, January 4, 1965, Japan and the United States, 1960–1976, JU00414, Digital National Security Archive, 2, http://search.proquest.com/dnsa/docview/1679105117/23430DAAD5CF46E6PQ/2 ?accountid=37722.

35. Donald Stone Macdonald, *U.S.-Korea Relations from Liberation to Self-Reliance: The Twenty Year Record* (Boulder, Colo.: Westview Press, 1992), 129–130.

36. Lee, "Normalization of Relations with Japan," 450–451.

37. Lee, "Vietnam War," 407.

38. Victor D. Cha, *Alignment Despite Antagonism: The U.S.-Korea-Japan Security Triangle* (Stanford, Calif.: Stanford University Press, 1999), 28–35.

39. Lee, "Vietnam War".

40. Quoted in Don Oberdorfer and Robert Carlin, *The Two Koreas: A Contemporary History* (New York: Basic Books, 2013), 11.

41. Quoted in ibid.

42. Governments of the Republic of Korea and the Democratic People's Republic of Korea, "The July 4 South-North Joint Communiqué," July 4, 1972, http://peacemaker.un.org/sites /peacemaker.un.org/files/KR%20KP_720704_The%20July%204%20South-North %20Joint%20Communiqu%C3%A9.pdf.

43. Ibid.

44. Oberdorfer and Carlin, *The Two Koreas*, 25.

45. Ibid.; Jong-dae Shin, "DPRK Perspectives on Korean Reunification After the July 4th Joint Communiqué," North Korea International Documentation Project, Woodrow Wilson International Center for Scholars, July 2012, document 1, https://www .wilsoncenter.org/publication/dprk-perspectives-korean-reunification-after-the-july -4th-joint-communique.

46. "Memorandum of Conversation," July 1971, in *Foreign Relations of the United States, 1969–1976*, vol. 17: *China 1969–1972*, ed. Stephen E. Philips and Edward C. Keefer, (Washington, D.C.: U.S. Government Printing Office, 2006), document 139, https:// history.state.gov/historicaldocuments/frus1969-76v17/d139.

47. "Memorandum of Conversation, Beijing, October 22, 1971, 4:15–8:28 p.m.," in *Foreign Relations of the United States, 1969–1976*, vol. E-13: *Documents on China 1969–1972*, ed. Steven E. Phillips and Edward C. Keefer (Washington, D.C.: U.S. Government Print-ing Office, 2006), document 44, https://history.state.gov/historicaldocuments/frus1969 -76ve13/d44.

48. Shin, "DPRK Perspectives on Korean Reunification After the July 4th Joint Communi-qué," document 2, http://digitalarchive.wilsoncenter.org/document/114018.

49. Im Hyug Baeg, "The Origins of the Yushin Regime: Machiavelli Unveiled," in *The Park Chung Hee Era*, ed. Kim and Vogel, 233–235.

50. Quoted in Jong-pil Kim, "The Start of the Yushin Era Brings Pushback with It," comp. Young gi Chun and Bong moon Kim, *JoongAng Ilbo*, July 30, 2015, http://koreajoon-gangdaily.joins.com/news/article/article.aspx?aid=3007225.

51. For example, see Kim Sung-hwan 김성환, "Park Chung-hee Was Going to Resign After Publicly Revealing Nuclear Weapons in '81" "박정희, 81년 핵무기 공개 후 전격 하야할 생각

이었다," *Seoul Economy* 서울경제, November 8, 2010, http://economy.hankooki.com/lpage /politics/201011/e20101108113554931120.htm.

52. Myung-lim Park, "The Chaeya," in *The Park Chung Hee Era*, ed. Kim and Vogel, 372–400.

53. "Memorandum of Conversation, Washington, March 27, 1975, 5 p.m.," in *Foreign Relations of the United States, 1969–1976*, vol. E-12: *Documents on East and Southeast Asia, 1973–1976*, ed. Bradley Lynn Coleman, David Goldman, David Nickles, and Edward C. Keefer (Washington, D.C.: U.S. Department of State, 2011), document 265, https://history .state.gov/historicaldocuments/frus1969-76ve12/d265.

54. Kang Choi and Joon-Sung Park, "South Korea: Fears of Abandonment and Entrapment," in *The Long Shadow: Nuclear Weapons and Security in 21st Century Asia*, ed. Muthiah Alagappa (Stanford, Calif.: Stanford University Press, 2008), 377–378; Michael J. Siler, "U.S. Nuclear Nonproliferation Policy in the Northeast Asian Region During the Cold War: The South Korean Case," *East Asian Studies* 16, nos. 3–4 (1998): 71–74.

55. Sheila Miyoshi Jager, *Brothers at War: The Unending Conflict in Korea* (New York: Norton, 2013), 413.

56. Pyong-choon Hahm, "Korea and the Emerging Asian Power Balance," *Foreign Affairs* 50, no. 2 (1972): 339, https://www.foreignaffairs.com/articles/asia/1972-01-01/korea-and -emerging-asian-power-balance.

57. For details, see Kee Kwang-seo 기광서, "Park Chung-hee Government's Foreign Policy Toward the Soviet Union and China—an Analysis of Presidential Records" "박정희 정부 의 대중, 소 외교정책—대통령 기록을 분석을 중심으로," *Journal of Asiatic Studies* 아세아연구 58, no. 2 (2015): 78–105.

58. Ibid.; Jae Ho Chung, "South Korean Strategic Thought Toward China," in *South Korean Strategic Thought Toward Asia*, ed. Gilbert Rozman, In-Taek Hyun, and Shin-wha Lee (New York: Palgrave Macmillan, 2008), 156.

59. Quoted in Chae-jin Lee, *China and Korea: Dynamic Relations* (Stanford, Calif.: Hoover Press, 1996), 105. By 1972, approximately 38 percent of Korean National Assembly members favored normalizing relations with China, as noted in Chung, "South Korean Strategic Thought Toward China," 155.

60. Chung-hee Park, "President Park's Special Foreign Policy Statement Regarding Peace and Unification," June 23, 1973, http://eng.unikorea.go.kr/content.do?cmsid=1889&mode =view&page=10&cid=32077.

61. Byung-Joon Ahn, "South Korea and the Communist Countries," *Asian Survey* 20, no. 11 (1980): 1102, http://www.jstor.org/stable/2643912.

62. Jae Ho Chung, *Between Ally and Partner: Korea-China Relations and the United States* (New York: Columbia University Press, 2007), 31.

63. Ibid., 32; Ahn, "South Korea and the Communist Countries," 1102–1103.

64. Siler, "U.S. Nuclear Nonproliferation Policy."

65. Quoted in Jong-pil Kim, "Korea Plays Cat-and-Mouse with Nukes," *JoongAng Ilbo*, August 10, 2015, http://koreajoongangdaily.joins.com/news/article/Article.aspx?aid=3007693.

66. "South Korea: Nuclear Developments and Strategic Decisionmaking," U.S. National Security Archive, intelligence report, excised copy, June 1978, 13, http://nautilus.org/wp -content/uploads/2011/09/CIA_ROK_Nuclear_DecisionMaking.pdf.

67. Shim Yung-taek 심용택, *Baekgom Rising Toward the Sky* 백곰 하늘로 솟아오르다 (Seoul 서울: Giparang 기파랑, 2013), 29.

68. Choi and Park, "South Korea," 275.

69. See Scott Snyder and Joyce Lee, "Infusing Commitment with Credibility: The Role of Security Assurances in Cementing the U.S.-ROK Alliance," in *Security Assurances and Nuclear Nonproliferation*, ed. Jeffrey W. Knopf (Stanford, Calif.: Stanford University Press, 2012); Sangsun Shim, "The Causes of South Korea's Nuclear Choices: A Case Study in Nonproliferation," Ph.D. diss., University of Maryland, 2003, 44–48.

70. Siler, "U.S. Nuclear Nonproliferation Policy," 62; Hyung-a Kim, *Korea's Development Under Park Chung Hee: Rapid Industrialization, 1961–79* (London: Routledge Curzon, 2004), 166.

71. Shim 심, *Baekgom Rising Toward the Sky* 백곰 하늘로 솟아오르다, 29.

72. "U.S. National Security Council Memorandum, ROK Weapons Plans," National Security Adviser Presidential Country Files for East Asia and the Pacific, Box 9, Korea (4), March 3, 1975, History and Public Policy Program Digital Archive, Gerald R. Ford Presidential Library, Ann Arbor, Mich., http://digitalarchive.wilsoncenter.org/docu ment/114628.pdf?v=7b0fb5ebe54ofe21b3072690ad1e5161.

73. Kim, "Korea Plays Cat-and-Mouse with Nukes."

74. Quoted in Alexandre Debs and Nuno Monteiro, *Nuclear Politics: The Strategic Causes of Proliferation* (New York: Cambridge University Press, 2017), 383.

75. "U.S. Department of State Memorandum, Approach to South Korea on Reprocessing," National Security Adviser Presidential Country Files for East Asia and the Pacific, Box 9, Korea (9), July 2, 1975, History and Public Policy Program Digital Archive, Gerald R. Ford Presidential Library, http://digitalarchive.wilsoncenter.org/document/114620; "US National Security Council Memorandum, Approach to South Korea on Reprocessing," National Security Adviser Presidential Country Files for East Asia and the Pacific, Box 9, Korea (9), July 8, 1975, History and Public Policy Program Digital Archive, Gerald R. Ford Presidential Library, http://digitalarchive.wilsoncenter.org/doc ument/114621.

76. "Memorandum of Conversation, Seoul, August 27, 1975," in *Foreign Relations of the United States, 1969–1976*, vol. E-12: *Documents on East Asia and Southeast Asia, 1973–1976*, ed. Coleman et al., document 272, https://history.state.gov/historicaldocuments/frus 1969-76ve12/d272.

77. "U.S. Department of State Cable, ROK Nuclear Reprocessing," National Security Adviser Presidential Country Files for East Asia and the Pacific, Box 11, Korea–State Department Telegrams, to SecState—NODIS (8), December 10, 1975, History and Public Policy Program Digital Archive, Gerald R. Ford Presidential Library, http://digitalar chive.wilsoncenter.org/document/114611.

78. Kim, "Korea Plays Cat-and-Mouse with Nukes."

79. Sung Gul Hong, "Search for Deterrence: Nuclear Option," in *The Park Chung Hee Era*, ed. Kim and Vogel, 488. South Korea under Park began to produce some of its own military hardware by 1973, as noted in Yong Sup Han, "South Korea's Military Capabilities and Strategy," in *Korea: The East Asian Pivot*, ed. Jonathan D. Pollack (Newport, R.I.: Naval War College Press, 2006), 222. Backed by a U.S. military assistance

program worth $1.5 billion, the Ministry of National Defense implemented an aggressive military modernization project from 1971 to 1975.

80. Ibid.

81. Etel Solingen, *Nuclear Logics: Contrasting Paths in East Asia and the Middle East* (Princeton: Princeton University Press, 2007), 84.

82. Shim, "The Causes of South Korea's Nuclear Choices," 111–116.

83. Siler, "U.S. Nuclear Nonproliferation Policy," 75–78.

84. Han, "South Korea's Military Capabilities and Strategy," 222–223.

85. Ronald Reagan, "Joint Communiqué Following Discussions with President Chun Doo Hwan of the Republic of Korea," February 2, 1981, American Presidency Project, http://www.presidency.ucsb.edu/ws/?pid=44223.

86. Brian Bridges, *Korea and the West* (New York: Routledge and Kegan Paul, 1986), 6.

87. Michael Getler, "Viewing Maneuvers from the 'Royal Box'; President of South Korea, Weinberger Observe Exercises Under Very Tight Security," *Washington Post*, April 1, 1982.

88. Quoted in Bridges, *Korea and the West*, 60.

89. Quoted in Im Chun-gun 임춘건, *Nordpolitik and Korean Politics' Policy Choice* 북방정책과 한국정치의 정책결정 (Paju 파주: Korean Studies Information 한국학술정보, 2008), 90, translated by Sung-tae (Jacky) Park.

90. Quoted in ibid., translated by Sung-tae (Jacky) Park.

91. Henry C. K. Liu, "Part 10: The Changing South Korean Position," *Asia Times*, February 7, 2007, http://www.atimes.com/atimes/Korea/IB07Dg01.html.

92. Yasuhiro Izumikawa, "South Korea's Nordpolitik and the Efficacy of Asymmetric Positive Sanctions," *Korea Observer* 37, no. 4 (2006): 616.

93. Ibid.

94. United Press International, "China to Let Seoul Try Hijackers in Return for Jet and Passengers," *New York Times*, May 9, 1983, http://www.nytimes.com/1983/05/09/world/china-to-let-seoul-try-hijackers-in-return-for-jet-and-passengers.html.

95. Chung, *Between Ally and Partner*, 34.

96. Christopher Wren, "China's Quiet Courtship of South Korea," *New York Times*, March 11, 1984, http://www.nytimes.com/1984/03/11/weekinreview/china-s-quiet-courtship-of-south-korea.html.

97. Izumikawa, "South Korea's Nordpolitik," 618.

98. Ibid., 616–617.

99. Ibid., 616.

100. Richard Halloran, "Seoul Proposing an Exchange of Envoys with North Korea," *New York Times*, January 22, 1982, http://www.nytimes.com/1982/01/22/world/seoul-proposing-an-exchange-of-envoys-with-north-korea.html.

101. Hyung Gu Lynn, *Bipolar Orders: The Two Koreas Since 1989* (London: Fernwood, Zed Books, 2007), 159.

102. Oberdorfer and Carlin, *The Two Koreas*, 117.

103. Kyudok Hong, "South Korean Strategic Thought Toward Asia in the 1980s," in *South Korean Strategic Thought Toward Asia*, ed. Rozman, Hyun, and Lee, 36.

3. ROH TAE-WOO AND KIM YOUNG-SAM: NORDPOLITIK AND DEMOCRATIZATION

1. International Monetary Fund, World Economic Outlook Database, n.d., https://www
.imf.org/external/pubs/ft/weo/2016/01/weodata/index.aspx; World Bank, World Data
Bank, World Development Indicators, n.d., http://databank.worldbank.org/data/re
ports.aspx?code=NY.GDP.MKTP.CD&id=af3ce82b&report_name=Popular_indicat
ors&populartype=series&ispopular=y.

2. Kyudok Hong, "South Korean Strategic Thought Toward Asia in the 1980s," in *South
Korean Strategic Thought Toward Asia*, ed. Gilbert Rozman, In-Taek Hyun, and Shin-
wha Lee (New York: Palgrave Macmillan, 2008), 233–235.

3. Samuel Huntington, "Democracy's Third Wave," *Journal of Democracy* 2, no. 2 (1991),
http://www.ned.org/docs/Samuel-P-Huntington-Democracy-Third-Wave.pdf.

4. Jae-sung Chun, "Evaluation of the Nordpolitik: The Inception of a Korean Diplomatic
'Grand Strategy,'" in *Reconsidering the Roh Tae-woo Era*, ed. Won-taek Kang (Paju,
South Korea: Nanam, 2012), 215–216.

5. The sources of these tensions might have been ameliorated or even removed if a summit
meeting between Kim Il-sung and Kim Young-sam brokered by Jimmy Carter during his
effort to mediate escalating U.S.-DPRK nuclear tensions in June 1994 had been realized.
The United States instead remained committed to negotiations with North Korea during
Pyongyang's succession process, but Kim Young-sam, cognizant of South Korean domestic political pressures, refused to express condolences to North Korea on Kim Il-sung's
death and compared North Korea under Kim Jong-il to a broken airplane.

6. See Jae-jung Suh, *Power, Interest, and Identity in Military Alliances* (New York: Palgrave
MacMillan, 2007).

7. See Gab-je Cho, *Oral Memoir of Roh Tae-woo* (Seoul: Chogabjedotcom, 2007).

8. Geun Lee, "Roh Administration's Nordpolitik," in *Reconsidering the Roh Tae-woo Era*,
ed. Kang, 181–189.

9. Lee Hongkoo, interview by the author, July 2015, Seoul.

10. As listed in Ji-hyung Kim, "The Development of the Discussions on Unification During
the Early Post–Cold War Era: Competition and Coexistence Between the Government
and Nongovernment Sector," *International Journal of Korean History* 17, no. 1 (2012):
171–203.

11. Ham Taek-young 함택영 and Nam Goong-gon 남궁곤, *Korean Foreign Policy: History
and Issues* 한국 외교 정책: 역사 와 쟁점 (Seoul 서울: Social Criticism 사회평론, 2010),
378–379.

12. Kim Chong-hwi, interview, quoted in Lee, "Roh Administration's Nordpolitik," 179.

13. Hong-choo Hyun, "Hyun Hong-choo, ROK Ambassador to USA, 1990–1993," in *Am-
bassador's Memoir: U.S.-Korea Relations Through the Eyes of the Ambassadors*, comp. Korea
Economic Institute of America (Washington, D.C.: Korea Economic Institute of
America, 2009), 60–61.

14. Tae-woo Roh, *Roh Tae-woo's Memoir: The Grand Strategy in Transition* (Seoul: Chosun
News Press, 2011), 144.

15. Ham 함 and Nam 남, *Korean Foreign Policy* 한국 외교 정책, 396–398.

16. Kim Hang Hun 김항훈, *The Yesterday and Today of South Korean Foreign Policy* 한국 외교 의 어제와 오늘 (Paju 파주: Korea Studies Information 한국학술정보, 2013), 172–173.

17. Cho, *Oral Memoir of Roh Tae-woo*, 55, 60.

18. Don Oberdorfer and Robert Carlin, *The Two Koreas: A Contemporary History* (New York: Basic Books, 2013), 158.

19. Quoted in ibid., 157.

20. Roh, *Roh Tae-woo's Memoir*, 193.

21. Ibid., 210.

22. Quoted in Oberdorfer and Carlin, *The Two Koreas*, 160.

23. Roh, *Roh Tae-woo's Memoir*, 215–217.

24. Quoted in Oberdorfer and Carlin, *The Two Koreas*, 154–165.

25. Ibid., 166–169.

26. Roh, *Roh Tae-woo's Memoir*, 222–224.

27. Scott Snyder, *China's Rise and the Two Koreas: Politics, Economics, Security* (Boulder, Colo.: Lynne Rienner, 2009), 28–29.

28. Ham 함 and Nam 남, *Korean Foreign Policy* 한국 외교 정책, 398–399.

29. Jae Ho Chung, "South Korean Strategic Thought Toward China," in *South Korean Strategic Thought Toward Asia*, ed. Rozman, Hyun, and Lee, 160.

30. Uk Heo and Terence Roehrig, *South Korea Since 1980* (Cambridge: Cambridge University Press, 2010), 185.

31. Ham 함 and Nam 남, *Korean Foreign Policy* 한국 외교 정책, 400.

32. Quoted in Oberdorfer and Carlin, *The Two Koreas*, 190.

33. Chung, "South Korean Strategic Thought Toward China," 44. See also Ham 함 and Nam 남, *Korean Foreign Policy* 한국 외교 정책, 398–399.

34. Samuel S. Kim, *The Two Koreas and the Great Powers* (Cambridge: Cambridge University Press, 2006), 75.

35. Jae Ho Chung, *Between Ally and Partner: Korea-China Relations and the United States* (New York: Columbia University Press, 2007), 69–74.

36. Ibid., 73.

37. Roh, *Roh Tae-woo's Memoir*, 255.

38. Cho, *Oral Memoir of Roh Tae-woo*, 63–66, 104.

39. Chung, *Between Ally and Partner*, 90 (quote from Hwang), 91.

40. Quoted in Young-june Park, "South Korea's Diplomacy and the Evolution of Korea-Japan Security Relations, 1965–2015," *Seoul Journal of Japanese Studies* 2, no. 1 (2016): 117, http://s-space.snu.ac.kr/bitstream/10371/97040/1/06_PARK%20Young-June.pdf.

41. Tae-woo Roh, *The Collection of President Roh Tae-woo's Speeches*, vol. 2: *1989. 2. 25–1990. 1. 31* (Seoul: Presidential Secretariat, 1990), 341–343.

42. World Economic Outlook Database, International Monetary Fund, "Report for Selected Countries," October 2016, http://www.imf.org/external/pubs/ft/weo/2016/02 /weodata/weorept.aspx?pr.x=25&pr.y=13&sy=1980&ey=2021&scsm=1&ssd=1&sort=c ountry&ds=.&br=1&c=512%2C672%2C914%2C946%2C612%2C137%2C614%2C546 %2C311%2C962%2C213%2C674%2C911%2C676%2C193%2C548%2C122%2C556%2C912

%2C678%2C313%2C181%2C419%2C867%2C513%2C682%2C316%2C684%2C913%2C273
%2C124%2C868%2C339%2C921%2C638%2C948%2C514%2C943%2C218%2C686%2C963
%2C688%2C616%2C518%2C223%2C728%2C516%2C558%2C918%2C138%2C748%2C196
%2C618%2C278%2C624%2C692%2C522%2C694%2C622%2C142%2C156%2C449%2C626
%2C564%2C628%2C565%2C228%2C283%2C924%2C853%2C233%2C288%2C632%2C293
%2C636%2C566%2C634%2C964%2C238%2C182%2C662%2C359%2C960%2C453%2C423
%2C968%2C935%2C922%2C128%2C714%2C611%2C862%2C321%2C135%2C243%2C716
%2C248%2C456%2C469%2C722%2C253%2C942%2C642%2C718%2C643%2C724%2C939
%2C576%2C644%2C936%2C819%2C961%2C172%2C813%2C132%2C199%2C646%2C733
%2C648%2C184%2C915%2C524%2C134%2C361%2C652%2C362%2C174%2C364%2C328
%2C732%2C258%2C366%2C656%2C734%2C654%2C144%2C336%2C146%2C263%2C463
%2C268%2C528%2C532%2C923%2C944%2C738%2C176%2C578%2C534%2C537%2C536
%2C742%2C429%2C866%2C433%2C369%2C178%2C744%2C436%2C186%2C136%2C925
%2C343%2C869%2C158%2C746%2C439%2C926%2C916%2C466%2C664%2C112%2C826
%2C111%2C542%2C298%2C967%2C927%2C443%2C846%2C917%2C299%2C544%2C582
%2C941%2C474%2C446%2C754%2C666%2C698%2C668&s=NGDPD&grp=o&a=.

43. Stockholm International Peace Research Institute, Military Expenditure Database,
https://www.sipri.org/databases/milex.

44. Brian Bridges, *Japan and Korea in the 1990s: From Antagonism to Adjustment* (Aldershot,
U.K.: Edward Elgar, 1993), 57.

45. Quoted in ibid.

46. C. S. Eliot Kang and Yoshinori Kaseda, "South Korea's Security Relations with Japan:
A View on Current Trend," in *Korea in the 21st Century*, ed. Seung-ho Joo and Tae-hwan
Kwak (Hauppauge, N.Y.: Nova Science, 2001), 235.

47. Cho, *Oral Memoir of Roh Tae-woo*, 52.

48. Roh, *Roh Tae-woo's Memoir*, 324–325.

49. Ahn Jung-shik 안정식, *Is an Autonomous North Korea Policy Possible for South Korea? Post–
Cold War Conflicts and Cooperation Between ROK and U.S. Policies Toward North Korea*
한국의 자주적 대북정책은 가능한가 탈냉전기 한미 대북정책의 갈등과 협력 (Seoul 서울:
Hanwool 한울, 2007), 72–73, translation by Sung-tae (Jacky) Park.

50. Hyun, "Hyun Hong-choo,," 52–55.

51. David Straub, *Anti-Americanism in Democratizing South Korea* (Stanford, Calif.:
Shorenstein Asia-Pacific Research Center, Stanford University, 2015), 39.

52. Ibid.

53. "Seoul Had Own Designs on N-Bomb," *Fay Observer*, March 31, 1994, http://www
.fayobserver.com/military/seoul-had-own-designs-on-n-bomb/article_cabc4cd5-8797
-57dc-9b8b-cb9dd97d6219.html.

54. "S. Korea Says U.S. Blocked Its Plan for N-Arms," *Deseret News*, March 28, 1994, http://
www.deseretnews.com/article/344169/S-KOREA-SAYS-US-BLOCKED-ITS
-PLAN-FOR-N-ARMS.html?pg=all.

55. Ham 함 and Nam 남, *Korean Foreign Policy* 한국 외교 정책, 390–392.

56. Clyde Haberman, "Korean Opposition, Declaring Extensive Fraud, Pledges to Keep
Fighting," *New York Times*, December 18, 1987, http://www.nytimes.com/1987/12/18/world

/korean-opposition-declaring-extensive-fraud-pledges-to-keep-fighting.html
?pagewanted=all.

57. "Rest in Peace, Former President Kim Young-sam," *Dong-A Ilbo*, November 23, 2015, http://english.donga.com/List/3/all/26/411805/1.

58. Ahn 안, *Is An Autonomous North Korea Policy Possible for South Korea?* 한국의 자주적 대북 정책은 가능한가, 84–85.

59. Thomas L. Wilborn, *Strategic Implications of the U.S.-DPRK Framework Agreement* (Carlisle, Pa.: Strategic Studies Institute, U.S. Army War College, 1995), 23, http://fas .org/nuke/guide/dprk/nuke/us_dprk.pdf.

60. Gi-Wook Shin, *One Alliance, Two Lenses: U.S.-Korea Relations in a New Era* (Stanford, Calif.: Stanford University Press, 2010), 168.

61. Quoted in Chae-Jin Lee, *A Troubled Peace: U.S. Policy and the Two Koreas* (Baltimore: Johns Hopkins University Press, 2006), 168.

62. Quoted in Ahn 안, *Is an Autonomous North Korea Policy Possible for South Korea?* 한국의 자주적 대북정책은 가능한가, 85, translated by Sung-tae (Jacky) Park.

63. Ibid., 94–97.

64. Ibid., 94, translated by Sung-tae (Jacky) Park.

65. U.S. Department of Defense, "U.S. Security Strategy for the East Asia–Pacific Region," February 27, 1995, http://nautilus.org/global-problem-solving/us-security-strategy-for -the-east-asia-pacific-region/.

66. Gilbert Rozman, *Strategic Thinking About the Korean Nuclear Crisis: Four Parties Caught Between North Korea and the United States* (New York: Palgrave Macmillan, 2007), 54.

67. Oknim Chung, "The Role of South Korea's NGOs: The Political Context," in *Paved with Good Intentions: The NGO Experience in North Korea*, ed. L. Gordon Flake and Scott Snyder (Westport, Conn.: Greenwood, 2003).

68. Philip Bowring and *International Herald Tribune*, "In South Korea, Mixed Feelings About Joining the Rich Club," *New York Times*, September 10, 1996, http://www.nytimes.com /1996/09/10/opinion/in-south-korea-mixed-feelings-about-joining-the-rich-club.html.

69. Quoted in Samuel S. Kim, "Korea's Segyehwa Drive: Promise Versus Performance," in *Korea's Globalization*, ed. Samuel S. Kim (Cambridge: Cambridge University Press, 2000), 244.

70. Lee, "Roh Administration's Nordpolitik," 178.

71. Paul Lewis, "South Korean Chief, at U.N., Calls for World Talks and Unification," *New York Times*, October 19, 1988, http://www.nytimes.com/1988/10/19/world/south -korean-chief-at-un-calls-for-world-talks-and-unification.html.

4. KIM DAE-JUNG AND THE SUNSHINE POLICY

1. Dae-jung Kim, *Kim Dae-jung's Three Stage Approach to Korean Reunification* (Los Angeles: Center for Multiethnic and Transnational Studies, University of Southern California, 1997), 9–13.

2. Ibid., 11–13.

3. Lee Hongkoo, interviewed by the author, July 2015, Seoul.

4. Dae-jung Kim, *Kim Dae-jung's Memoir*, vol. 2 (Seoul: Samin Press, 2011), 304.

5. Dong-won Lim, *Peacemaker: Twenty Years of Inter-Korean Relations and the North Korean Nuclear Issue: A Memoir* (Stanford, Calif.: Shorenstein Asia-Pacific Research Center, 2012), 165–166, 258.

6. Quoted in Kihl Young Hwan, *Transforming Korean Politics: Democracy, Reform, and Culture* (New York: M. E. Sharpe, 2005), 249.

7. Korea Institute of Public Administration, *Republic of Korea's Major Policies and Government Operation of Former Administrations*, vol. 6: *Kim Dae-jung Administration* (Seoul: Daeyoung Press, 2014), 66.

8. Ibid., 128–129.

9. Ibid., 66.

10. "Address by His Excellency Kim Dae-jung, President of the Republic of Korea," speech to a joint session of the U.S. Congress, 105th Cong., 2nd sess., June 10, 1998, https://www.gpo.gov/fdsys/granule/CREC-1998-06-10/CREC-1998-06-10-pt1-PgH4334.

11. Korea Institute of Public Administration, *Republic of Korea's Major Policies and Government Operation of Former Administrations*, 6:130.

12. Insung Kim and Karin Lee, "Mt. Kumgang and Inter-Korean Relations," National Committee on North Korea, November 10, 2009, http://www.ncnk.org/resources/briefing-papers/all-briefing-papers/mt.-kumgang-and-inter-korean-relations.

13. Moon, "Understanding the DJ Doctrine," 42.

14. Donald Kirk and the *International Herald Tribune*, "North Korea Sub Is Snagged Off South," *New York Times*, June 23, 1998, http://www.nytimes.com/1998/06/23/news/north-korea-sub-is-snagged-off-south.html.

15. Donald Kirk, "Four Killed as North and South Korean Navy Vessels Trade Fire," *New York Times*, June 29, 2002, http://www.nytimes.com/2002/06/29/world/four-killed-as-north-and-south-korean-navy-vessels-trade-fire.html.

16. Donald Kirk, "Slaughter on the 'Northern Limit Line,'" *Korea Times*, July 2, 2015, http://www.koreatimes.co.kr/www/news/opinon/2015/07/162_182065.html.

17. "Inter-Korean Vice-Ministerial Meeting to Be Held in July," *Korea Times*, March 10, 2000.

18. Governments of the Republic of Korea and the Democratic People's Republic of Korea, "South-North Joint Declaration," June 15, 2000, http://www.usip.org/sites/default/files/file/resources/collections/peace_agreements/n_skorea06152000.pdf.

19. Quoted in Young-jin Oh, "Kim Apologizes for Summit Scandal," *Korea Times*, February 14, 2003.

20. Moon, "Understanding the DJ Doctrine," 36.

21. Quoted in Calvin Sims, "Summit Glow Fades as Koreans Face Obstacles to Unity," *New York Times*, June 22, 2000, http://partners.nytimes.com/library/world/asia/062200korea-summit.html.

22. Quoted in Howard W. French, "Two Koreas Agree to First Meeting of Their Leaders," *New York Times*, April 10, 2000, http://www.nytimes.com/2000/04/10/world/two-koreas-agree-to-first-meeting-of-their-leaders.html.

23. Quoted in Steven Mufson, "Korean Summit Seen as Election Ploy," *Washington Post*, April 11, 2000, https://www.washingtonpost.com/archive/politics/2000/04/11/korean -summit-seen-as-election-ploy/98ed8575-0d47-4f7a-9450-f1a94d209263/.

24. Katharine H. S. Moon, *Protesting America: Democracy and the U.S.-Korea Alliance* (Berkeley: University of California Press, 2012), 40.

25. Quoted in "President Gives Details Behind Summit Declaration," Yonhap News Agency, June 15, 2000.

26. Korea Institute of Public Administration, *Republic of Korea's Major Policies and Government Operation of Former Administrations*, 6:124–125.

27. Richard V. Allen, "On the Korea Tightrope, 1980," *New York Times*, January 21, 1998, http://www.nytimes.com/1998/01/21/opinion/on-the-korea-tightrope-1980.html.

28. "KEDO Marks 'First Concrete' Pouring Milestone," *KEDO News*, August 7, 2002, https://kedo.org/news_detail.asp?NewsID=22.

29. Glenn Kessler, "South Korea Offers to Supply Energy If North Gives Up Arms," *Washington Post*, July 13, 2005, http://www.washingtonpost.com/wp-dyn/content/article/2005 /07/12/AR2005071200220.html.

30. Peter Maass, "The Last Emperor," *New York Times*, October 19, 2003, http://www .nytimes.com/2003/10/19/magazine/the-last-emperor.html; Jay Kim, "Repercussions of N. Korea's Long-Range Missile Launch," *Korea Times*, September 9, 2011, http://www .koreatimes.co.kr/www/news/opinon/2016/08/306_94569.html.

31. Federation of American Scientists, "Kumgchangni," January 16, 2000, https://fas.org /nuke/guide/dprk/facility/kumchangni.htm.

32. Yoichi Funabashi, *The Peninsula Question: A Chronicle of the Second North Korean Nuclear Crisis* (Washington, D.C.: Brookings Institution Press, 2007), 118–119.

33. David E. Sanger, "Korean Clash May Ruin U.S. Reconciliation Bid," *New York Times*, June 17, 1999, http://partners.nytimes.com/library/world/asia/061799korea-us.html.

34. Chung-in Moon, *The Sunshine Policy: In Defense of Engagement as a Path to Peace in Korea* (Seoul: Yonsei University Press, 2012), 24.

35. Quoted in Lim, *Peacemaker*, 188.

36. Stephen Bosworth, "USA Ambassador to ROK, 1997–2000," in *Ambassador's Memoir: U.S.-Korea Relations Through the Eyes of the Ambassadors*, comp. Korea Economic Institute of America (Washington, D.C.: Korea Economic Institute of America, 2009), 124.

37. Dae-jung Kim, "Address by President Kim Dae-jung of the Republic of Korea, Lessons of German Reunification and the Korean Peninsula," March 9, 2000, http://www .monde-diplomatique.fr/dossiers/coree/A/1904.

38. Quoted in Don Kirk, "U.S. Suffers a Setback in Its North Korea Policy," *New York Times*, February 24, 2003, http://www.nytimes.com/2003/02/24/international/asia/us -suffers-a-setback-in-its-north-korea-policy.html.

39. Moon, *Sunshine Policy*, 46; Don Kirk, "South Koreans Challenge Northerner on U.S. Troops," *New York Times*, August 7, 2001, http://www.nytimes.com/2001/08/07/world /south-koreans-challenge-northerner-on-us-troops.html.

40. Hee-young Song, "Skepticism," *Chosun Ilbo*, March 15, 2001.

41. Quoted in Mike Chinoy, *Meltdown: The Inside Story of the North Korean Nuclear Crisis* (New York: St. Martin's Press, 2008), 73–74.

42. Quoted in John Swenson-Wright, "Springtime in North Korea," *Guardian*, May 19, 2006, https://www.theguardian.com/commentisfree/2006/may/19/springtimeinnorth korea2?index=0.

43. Quoted in Chinoy, *Meltdown*, 132.

44. Quoted in James Brooke, "South Korea Criticizes U.S. Plan for Exerting Pressure on North," *New York Times*, December 30, 2002, http://www.nytimes.com/2002/12/31 /world/threats-responses-nuclear-politics-south-korea-criticizes-us-plan-for-exerting .html.

45. Bruce Cumings, "Unilateralism and Its Discontents: The Passing of the Cold War Alliance and Changing Public Opinion in the Republic of Korea," in *Korean Attitudes Toward the United States: Changing Dynamics*, ed. David I. Steinberg (Armonk, N.Y.: M. E. Sharpe, 2005), 97–98.

46. "Possibility of Unification Within 10 Years" "10년내 통일 가능성," public-opinion poll, Gallup Korea 한국갤럽조사연구소, November 11, 2002, http://www.gallup.co.kr/gallupdb /newsContent.asp?seqNo=398&pagepos=79&search=&searchKeyword=&selectYear=; Gi-Wook Shin, *One Alliance, Two Lenses: U.S.-Korea Relations in a New Era* (Stanford, Calif.: Stanford University Press, 2010).

47. Shin, *One Alliance, Two Lenses*.

48. David Straub, *Anti-Americanism in Democratizing South Korea* (Stanford, Calif.: Shorenstein Asia-Pacific Research Center, 2015), 2.

49. Don Kirk, "U.S. Dumping of Chemical Riles Koreans," *New York Times*, July 15, 2000, http://www.nytimes.com/2000/07/15/news/us-dumping-of-chemical-riles-koreans .html; Straub, *Anti-Americanism in Democratizing South Korea*, 69–88.

50. Kirk, "U.S. Dumping of Chemical Riles Koreans"; Ho-jeong Lee, "Calls to Boycott U.S. Goods Spread on Web," *JoongAng Ilbo*, March 4, 2002, http://koreajoongangdaily .joins.com/news/article/article.aspx?aid=1901090; Straub, *Anti-Americanism in Democratizing South Korea*, 133–156.

51. Straub, *Anti-Americanism in Democratizing South Korea*, 3–6; Shin, *One Alliance, Two Lenses*.

52. Doug Struck, "Resentment Toward U.S. Troops Is Boiling Over in South Korea," *Washington Post*, December 9, 2002, https://www.washingtonpost.com/archive/politics /2002/12/09/resentment-toward-us-troops-is-boiling-over-in-south-korea/142fa387 -a604-41a9-bcad-9bf3abd39515/; Straub, *Anti-Americanism in Democratizing South Korea*, 157–178.

53. Meredith Woo-Cumings, "Unilateralism and Its Discontents: The Passing of the Cold War Alliance and Changing Public Opinion in the Republic of Korea," in *Korean Attitudes Toward the United States*, ed. Steinberg, 56.

54. Victor D. Cha, "Anti-Americanism and the U.S. Role in Inter-Korean Relations," in *Korean Attitudes Toward the United States*, ed. Steinberg, 128.

55. Ibid., 130.

56. Moon, *Protesting America*, 46.

57. Ibid., 141–142.

58. Korea Institute of Public Administration, *Republic of Korea's Major Policies and Government Operation of Former Administrations*, 6:124.

59. "Kim Dae-jung's Live Interview with CNN," *Korea Times*, May 5, 1999.

60. Kim, *Kim Dae-jung's Memoir*, 2:342–351.

61. Lim, *Peacemaker*, 166.

62. Kang Won-taek, Kim Geun-taek, Kim Gi-sik, Kim Doo-kwan, Kim Min-woong, Kim Sung-jae, Kim Sung-hoon, et al., 강원택, 김근택, 김기식, 김두관, 김민웅, 김성재, 김성훈 외, *Thinking About Dae-jung Kim* 김대중을 생각한다 (Seoul 서울: Samin 삼인, 2011), 91–92.

63. Dae-jung Kim, "Speech of H.E. President Kim Dae-jung of the Republic of Korea ASEAN+3 Summit," Association of Southeast Asian Nations, 1998, http://asean.org /?static_post=speech-of-he-president-kim-dae-jung-of-the-republic-of-korea-asean3 -summit.

64. Termsak Chalermpalanupap, "Towards an East Asia Community: The Journey Has Begun," Association of Southeast Asian Nations, October 19, 2002, http://asean.org/towards -an-east-asia-community-the-journey-has-begun-by-termsak-chalermpalanupap/.

65. "Trilateral Meeting of Leaders of China, Japan, S Korea," *China Daily*, May 27, 2010, http://www.chinadaily.com.cn/china/2010-05/27/content_9899091.htm.

66. "Korea, China, Japan to Establish Trilateral Cooperation Secretariat in Korea," *Korea .net*, May 29, 2010, http://www.korea.net/NewsFocus/Policies/view?articleId=81417.

67. Dae-jung Kim, "Regionalism in the Age of Asia," *Global Asia* 1, no. 1 (2006), https:// www.globalasia.org/wp-content/uploads/2006/09/76.pdf.

68. Quoted in "Japan–Republic of Korea Joint Declaration: A New Japan–Republic of Korea Partnership Towards the Twenty-First Century," October 8, 1998, http://www.mofa.go.jp /region/asia-paci/korea/joint9810.html; "Japan's Rising Nationalism Enrages Asia," *Guardian*, July 15, 2001, https://www.theguardian.com/world/2001/jul/15/theobserver.

69. "Japan, South Korea Conduct Joint Military Exercise," Associated Press, August 4, 1999; Mark E. Manyin, *Japan–South Korea Relations: Converging Interests and Implications for the United States* (Washington, D.C.: Congressional Research Service, 1999), http://congressionalresearch.com/RL30382/document.php?study=JAPAN-SOUTH +KOREA+RELATIONS+CONVERGING+INTERESTS+AND+IMPLICA TIONS+FOR+THE+UNITED+STATES.

70. "Japan's Rising Nationalism Enrages Asia."

71. "S. Korea, Japan Resume Naval Drill," United Press International, September 12, 2002, http://www.upi.com/Business_News/Security-Industry/2002/09/11/SKorea-Japan -resume-naval-drill/UPI-20291031746470/?st_rec=80981111136441.

72. Norman D. Levin and Yong-Sup Han, *Sunshine in Korea: The South Korean Debate Over Policies Toward North Korea* (Washington, D.C.: RAND Center for Asia Policy, 2002), 127, http://www.rand.org/content/dam/rand/pubs/monograph_reports/2005/RAND _MR1555.pdf.

73. Ibid., 128.

74. Eric Johnston, "The North Korean Abduction Issue and Its Effect on Japanese Domestic Politics," Japan Policy Research Institute, June 2004, http://www.jpri.org/publica tions/workingpapers/wp101.html.

75. "President Kim Dae-jung Returns Home from Asian Trip," *Korea Herald*, November 20, 1998.

76. Jae Ho Chung, *Between Ally and Partner: Korea-China Relations and the United States* (New York: Columbia University Press, 2007), 115.

77. Kwan-woo Jun, "Seoul Reaffirms No Plan to Join U.S.-Led Theater Missile Defense Plan," *Korea Herald*, May 4, 1999.

78. "China Supports Korean Peace Regime Through Four-Party Talks; Zhu Says Korean Firms Welcome in Chinese Mobile Phone Market," *Korea Herald*, October 19, 2000.

79. Bonnie Glaser, Scott Snyder, and John S. Park, *Keeping an Eye on an Unruly Neighbor: Chinese Views of Economic Reform and Stability in North Korea*, working paper (Washington, D.C.: U.S. Institute of Peace, 2008), 11, https://www.usip.org/sites/default/files/Jan2008.pdf.

80. C. S. Eliot Kang, "The Four-Party Peace Talks: Lost Without a Map," *Comparative Strategy* 17, no. 4 (1998): 330, http://www.tandfonline.com/doi/pdf/10.1080/01495939808403151.

81. Scott Snyder, *China's Rise and the Two Koreas* (Boulder, Colo.: Lynne Rienner, 2009).

82. Peter Graff, "Putin Goes to Seoul as Korean Families Meet," *Moscow Times*, February 26, 2001.

83. Martin Fackler, "South Koreans Express Fatigue with a Recalcitrant North," *New York Times*, May 27, 2009, http://www.nytimes.com/2009/05/28/world/asia/28seoul.html.

84. Chan Yul Yoo, "South Korea's Sunshine Policy Revisited," *Korea Social Science Journal* 31, no. 2 (2004): 3, http://www.kossrec.org/wp-content/uploads/2015/04/유찬열최종본.doc.

85. Ministry of National Defense, Republic of Korea, *2010 White Paper* (Seoul: Republic of Korea, 2010), 18, https://www.nti.org/media/pdfs/2010WhitePaperAll_eng.pdf?_=1340662780.

86. Min Bok Lee, "Human Rights in North Korea," *Korea Focus* 9, no. 3 (2001), http://www.koreafocus.or.kr/design1/layout/content_print.asp?group_id=637.

87. Ibid., 73–75.

5. ROH MOO-HYUN'S BALANCER POLICY

1. Moo-hyun Roh, *National Security Strategy* (Seoul: Republic of Korea, 2005).

2. Jongryn Mo, "Grassroots Influences on the U.S.-ROK Alliance: The Role of Civil Society," paper presented at the workshop "Influence of Stakeholders on the U.S.-ROK Alliance," Center for U.S.-Korea Policy and the East Asia Institute, Seoul, February 22, 2010, 7, http://www.asiafoundation.org/resources/pdfs/JongrynMoROKCivilSociety.pdf.

3. Quoted in Chung-Bae Kim, "Visions and Tasks of a Cooperative Self-Reliant Defense," in *Security and Foreign Policy of the ROK Government*, ed. Su-hoon Lee (Seoul: Happyreading, 2007), 105.

4. Chung Kyung-hwan 정경환, "Problems of and Directions for Improvement in Roh Moohyun Administration's North Korea Policy" 노무현 정권 대북정책의 문제점과 개선방향, in *Evaluation of the Roh Mu Hyun Administration's North Korea Policy* 노무현 정권 대북정책의 평가 (Seoul 서울: Lee Kyung 이경, 2008), 20–21.

5. Blue House, Republic of Korea, *Peace and Prosperity National Security Policy* (Seoul: Blue House, Republic of Korea, 2004).

6. Ju-heum Lee, "Balanced and Pragmatic Diplomacy: Conceptual Background and Accomplishments," in *Security and Foreign Policy of the ROK Government*, ed. Lee, 73.

7. Shin-hong Park, "Before Roh–Bush Talks, Seoul Airs Balancing Role," *JoongAng Ilbo*, June 1, 2005, http://koreajoongangdaily.joins.com/news/article/article.aspx?aid=2576004.

8. Hoon Choi and Ji-soo Kim, "President Says Forces Are Being Strengthened," *JoongAng Ilbo*, May 20, 2004, http://koreajoongangdaily.joins.com/news/article/article.aspx?aid=2417226.

9. Chung-bae Kim, "Visions and Tasks of a Cooperative Self-Reliant Defense," in *Security and Foreign Policy of the ROK Government*, ed. Lee, 146.

10. Ibid., 104–147.

11. James Brooke, "A Quiet Foreign Invasion of Korea's Giants," *New York Times*, May 20, 2004, http://www.nytimes.com/2004/05/20/business/a-quiet-foreign-invasion-of-korea-s-giants.html.

12. Presidential Commission on Policy Planning, *Korea's Future: Vision & Strategy; Korea's Ambition to Become an Advanced Power by 2030* (Seoul: Seoul Selection, 2008), 323.

13. Quoted in David C. Kang, "South Korea's Embrace of Interdependence in Pursuit of Security," in *Strategic Asia 2006–07: Trade, Interdependence, and Security*, ed. Ashley J. Tellis and Michael Wills (Seattle: National Bureau of Economic Research, 2006), 162.

14. Quoted in Chung정경환, "Problems of and Directions for Improvement in Roh Moo-hyun Administration's Nordpolitik" 노무현 정권 대북정책의 문제점과 개선방향, 31, translated by Sungtae (Jacky) Park.

15. Su-hoon Lee, "Northeast Asian Cooperation Initiative of the Roh Moo-hyun Government," in *Security and Foreign Policy of the ROK Government*, ed. Lee, 22–36.

16. "Two Koreas Issue 'Peace Declaration,'" *Chosun Ilbo*, October 4, 2007, http://english.chosun.com/site/data/html_dir/2007/10/04/2007100461031.html.

17. Quoted in Man-bok Kim, Jong-chun Baek, and Jae-jung Lee, *Roh Mu-hyun's Conception for Peace on the Korean Peninsula: 10.4 South-North Summit Declaration* (Seoul: Tongil, 2015), 200.

18. Ham Taek-young 함택영 and Nam Goong-gon, 남궁곤, *Korean Foreign Policy: History and Issues* 한국 외교 정책: 역사 와 쟁점 (Seoul 서울: Social Criticism 사회평론 , 2010), 624–626.

19. Quoted in "Again Roh Fails to Consult the People," *Chosun Ilbo*, March 22, 2005, http://english.chosun.com/site/data/html_dir/2005/03/22/2005032261037.html.

20. Su-Hoon Lee, "South Korea's Middle Power Diplomacy," in *Asia's Middle Powers? The Identity and Regional Policy of South Korea and Vietnam*, ed. Joon-Woo Park, Gi-Wook Shin, and Donald W. Keyser (Stanford, Calif.: Walter H. Shorenstein Asia-Pacific Research Center, 2013), 104.

21. Tae-hyo Kim, "[Outlook] Creating 'Korea Style' Strategic Flexibility," *JoongAng Ilbo*, March 14, 2005, http://koreajoongangdaily.joins.com/news/article/article.aspx?aid=2541429.

22. Yong-sup Han, "Analysing South Korea's 'Defence Reform 2020,'" *Military Technology* 31, no. 10 (2007): 71–75.

23. Scott Snyder, *China's Rise and the Two Koreas: Politics, Economics, Security* (Boulder, Colo.: Lynne Rienner, 2009), 186.

24. Kim, Baek, and Lee, *Roh Mu-hyun's Conception for Peace on the Korean Peninsula*, 64–65.

25. Quoted in Cho Kyung-guen 조경근, "The Roh Moo-hyun Administration's Northeast Asia Balancer Diplomacy" "노무현 정부의 '동북아 균형외교 정책'," in *Evaluation of the Roh Moo-hyun Administration's Nordpolitik* 노무현 정권 대북정책의 평가, 74.

26. Lee, "Balanced and Pragmatic Diplomacy," 74.

27. "Roh's Aide Calls FTA with U.S. the Last Word on Seoul's Pro-American Policy," Yonhap News Agency, August 1, 2006.

28. Woosang Kim, "Breakup of Triangular Alliance Will Only Lead to Isolation," *Korea Focus* 13, no. 3 (2005), http://www.koreafocus.or.kr/design1/layout/content_print.asp?group_id=153.

29. Cho, "Roh Moo-hyun Administration's Balanced Diplomacy in East Asia," 98–99.

30. "Korea Wants to Have Its Cake and Eat It, Too," *Chosun Ilbo*, March 31, 2005, http://english.chosun.com/site/data/html_dir/2005/03/31/2005033161035.html.

31. Cho, "Roh Moo-hyun Administration's Balanced Diplomacy in East Asia," 32, 81–82.

32. Quoted in "Kim Dae-jung Tells New Uri Leaders to Accept Alliance," *Chosun Ilbo*, April 8, 2005, http://english.chosun.com/site/data/html_dir/2005/04/08/2005040861032.html.

33. Presidential Commission on Policy Planning, *Korea's Future*, 330–331.

34. As quoted in Lee, "Northeast Asian Cooperation Initiative of the Roh Moo-hyun Government," 16.

35. Ibid., 34–38.

36. Scott Snyder, "Middle Kingdom Diplomacy and the North Korean Nuclear Crisis," *Comparative Connections* 5, no. 3 (2003), https://csis-prod.s3.amazonaws.com/s3fs-public/legacy_files/files/media/csis/pubs/0303qchina_korea.pdf; Sung-han Kim, "Northeast Asian Regionalism in Korea," Council on Foreign Relations, December 2009, http://www.cfr.org/content/publications/attachments/NEAsiaSecurityKim.pdf.

37. Hosup Kim, "Evaluation of President Roh Moo-hyun's Policy Toward Japan," *Korean Journal of International Relations* 45, no. 2 (2005), http://koreafocus.or.kr/design1/layout/content_print.asp?group_id=256.

38. "Japan–Republic of Korea Summit Meeting," June 7, 2003, http://japan.kantei.go.jp/koizumiphoto/2003/06/07korea_e.html.

39. Ibid.

40. Quoted in Yong-kyun Ahn, "Controversy Surrounds Roh's 'Takeshima' Slip," *Chosun Ilbo*, July 22, 2004, http://english.chosun.com/site/data/html_dir/2004/07/22/2004072261039.html.

41. "'Takeshima Day' Bill Passes," *Chosun Ilbo*, March 16, 2005, http://english.chosun.com/site/data/html_dir/2005/03/16/2005031661023.html.

42. "Roh Warns of Diplomatic War with Japan," *Chosun Ilbo*, March 23, 2005, http://english.chosun.com/site/data/html_dir/2005/03/23/2005032361023.html.

43. "Leading the News: Seoul, Tokyo End a Face-off at Sea Over Remote Islets," *Wall Street Journal Asia*, April 24, 2006.

44. Nat Kretchun, "South Korea–Japan Political Relations in 2007: Roh and Abe's Path to Estrangement," in *SAIS U.S.-Korea Yearbook* (Baltimore: School of Advanced

International Studies, Johns Hopkins University, 2007), 100, http://uskoreainstitute.org
/wp-content/uploads/2010/05/YB07-Chapt8.pdf.

45. Scott Snyder to former Bush administration official, and official to Snyder, email, December 9, 2016.

46. Kim Hang Hun 김창훈, *The Yesterday and Today of South Korean Foreign Policy* 한국 외교 의 어제와 오늘 (Paju 파주: Korea Studies Information 한국학술정보, 2013), 465.

47. Yong-won Yoo and Jeong-rok Shin, "Roh Speech Stresses Self-Reliance," *Chosun Ilbo*, August 14, 2003, http://english.chosun.com/site/data/html_dir/2003/08/15/2003081561002 .html.

48. Seong-ho Sheen, "Strategic Thought Toward Asia in the Roh Moo-hyun Era," in *South Korean Strategic Thought Toward Asia*, ed. Gilbert Rozman, In-Taek Hyun, and Shin-wha Lee (New York: Palgrave Macmillan, 2008), 112.

49. Jae Ho Chung, "South Korean Strategic Thought Toward China," in *South Korean Strategic Thought Toward Asia*, ed. Rozman, Hyun, and Lee, 166.

50. Peter Hays Gries, "The Koguryo Controversy, National Identity, and Sino-Korean Relations Today," *East Asia* 22, no. 4 (2005): 3, http://www.ou.edu/uschina/gries/articles /texts/Gries2005KoguryoEAIQ.pdf.

51. Quoted in "What China's Northeast Project Is All About," *Chosun Ilbo*, September 30, 2009, http://english.chosun.com/site/data/html_dir/2008/05/30/2008053061001.html.

52. Gries, "The Koguryo Controversy," 3.

53. Jae Ho Chung, "China's 'Soft' Clash with South Korea: The History War and Beyond," *Asian Survey* 49, no. 3 (2009): 473, http://www.jstor.org/stable/10.1525/as.2009.49.3.468.

54. "What China's Northeast Project Is All About."

55. Hyun-jin Seo, "China-Korea Truce in Ancient Kingdom Feud," *Asia Times*, August 25, 2004, http://www.atimes.com/atimes/Korea/FH25Dg01.html.

56. Hyun-jin Seo, "Skepticism Lingers Over History Issue; Beijing Pledges Not to Stake Claim to Goguryeo in History Textbooks," *Korea Herald*, August 25, 2004, http://yale global.yale.edu/content/skepticism-lingers-over-history-issue.

57. Chung-in Moon and Chun-fu Li, "Reactive Nationalism and South Korea's Foreign Policy on China and Japan: A Comparative Analysis," *Pacific Focus* 25, no. 3 (2010): 349.

58. "Forced Repatriation for 70 Refugees," *AsiaNews*, November 11, 2004, http://www .asianews.it/news-en/Forced-repatriation-for-70-refugees-1881.html.

59. Duyeon Kim, "Korea-Russia Bilateral Trade Hits Record in 2006," *Arirang News*, February 26, 2007, http://www.arirang.co.kr/News/News_View.asp?nseq=69029.

60. Jung-rok Shin, "Korea, Russia to Form 'Comprehensive Partnership,'" *Chosun Ilbo*, September 21, 2004, http://english.chosun.com/site/data/html_dir/2004/09/21/2004092161028 .html.

61. Sheen, "Strategic Thought Toward Asia in the Roh Moo-hyun Era," 115.

62. Bong-jo Rhee, "The Implementation and Challenges of the Engagement Policy," in *Security and Foreign Policy of the ROK Government*, ed. Lee, 155.

63. Quoted in James Brooke, "North Threatens End of Armistice," *New York Times*, February 19, 2003.

64. Quoted in Chung-in Moon, "Diplomacy of Defiance and Facilitation: Six Party Talks and the Roh Moo Hyun Government," *Asian Perspective* 32, no. 4 (2008): 75.

65. Rhee, "The Implementation and Challenges of the Engagement Policy," 174, with figures provided by the Ministry of Unification.

66. Glenn Kessler, "South Korea Offers to Supply Energy If North Gives Up Arms," *Washington Post*, July 13, 2005, http://www.washingtonpost.com/wp-dyn/content/article/2005/07/12/AR2005071200220.html.

67. Sheen, "Strategic Thought Toward Asia in the Roh Moo-hyun Era," 104–105.

68. Noted in Hyo-jun Lee, "U.S. Bid for a Pullout Seen Unlikely to Pass," *JoongAng Ilbo*, February 27, 2003, http://koreajoongangdaily.joins.com/news/article/Article.aspx?aid=1940755.

69. Victor D. Cha, "Korea: A Peninsula in Crisis and Flux," in *Strategic Asia 2004–05: Confronting Terrorism in the Pursuit of Power*, ed. Ashley J. Tellis and Michael Wills (Seattle: National Bureau of Asian Research, 2004), 148–149.

70. Quoted in James Brooke, "Seoul Again Delays Vote on Military Backing for U.S. in Iraq," *New York Times*, March 28, 2003, http://www.nytimes.com/2003/03/28/international/worldspecial/seoul-again-delays-vote-on-military-backing-for.html.

71. Kim 김, *The Yesterday and Today of South Korean Foreign Policy* 한국 외교의 어제와 오늘, 420–421.

72. Ibid., 420–423.

73. Il-hyeon Jang, "SPI Talks Postponed to After U.S. Cabinet Reshuffle," *Chosun Ilbo*, November 21, 2004, http://english.chosun.com/site/data/html_dir/2004/11/22/2004112261028.html.

74. Quoted in Tong Kim, "Timing of OPCON Transfer," *Korea Times*, March 21, 2010, http://www.koreatimes.co.kr/www/news/opinon/2010/03/167_62736.html.

75. Kim 김, *The Yesterday and Today of South Korean Foreign Policy* 한국 외교의 어제와 오늘, 461–463.

76. Samuel S. Kim, *The Two Koreas and the Great Powers* (Cambridge: Cambridge University Press, 2006), 593.

77. Governments of the United States and the Republic of Korea, "Statement on the Launch of the Strategic Consultation for Allied Partnership," U.S. Department of State, January 19, 2006, https://2001-2009.state.gov/r/pa/prs/ps/2006/59447.htm.

78. Larry A. Niksch, *Korea: U.S.-Korean Relations, Issues for Congress* (Washington, D.C.: Congressional Research Service, July 21, 2006), 15, http://digital.library.unt.edu/ark:/67531/metacrs9488/m1/1/high_res_d/RL33567_2006Jul21.pdf.

79. "NK Human Rights," *Korea Times*, November 21, 2017, http://www.koreatimes.co.kr/www/opinion/2017/02/202_14138.html.

6. LEE MYUNG-BAK'S GLOBAL KOREA POLICY

1. Young-jin Oh, "Subdued Ode to Old Freedom Fighter," *Korea Times*, August 19, 2008, http://www.koreatimes.co.kr/www/news/opinon/2015/10/164_29618.html.

2. Park Byung-chul 박병철, "Lee Myung-bak Administration and Diplomatic Strategy Towards the U.S." "이명박 정부와 대미외교전략," in *Establishment of the Lee Myung-bak Administration and the Direction for Reunification Policies* 이명박 정부 출범과 통일정책의 방향 (Seoul 서울: Lee Kyung 이경, 2008), 80–81.

3. Blue House, Republic of Korea, *White Paper*, vol. 4: *Global Leadership and Improvement of National Status* (Seoul: Government of the Republic of Korea, 2013), 68–85.

4. Myung-bak Lee, "President of the Republic of Korea at the Sixty-Fourth Session of the General Assembly of the United Nations," September 23, 2009, http://www.un.org/ga /64/generaldebate/pdf/KR_en.pdf.

5. Myung-bak Lee, "Full Text of Lee's Address to U.S. Congress," Yonhap News Agency, October 14, 2011, http://english.yonhapnews.co.kr/national/2011/10/14/30/0301000000 AEN20111014001000315F.HTML.

6. Park 박, "Lee Myung-bak Administration and Diplomatic Strategy Towards the U.S." "이명박 정부와 대미외교전략," 53.

7. Blue House, Republic of Korea, *Global Korea: The National Security Strategy of the Republic of Korea* (Seoul: Blue House, Republic of Korea, 2009), 8.

8. Blue House, *White Paper*, 4:56–57.

9. Blue House, *Global Korea*, 12.

10. Ibid., 11.

11. James Ro, "President Lee Emphasizes Reciprocity in N. Korea Policy," Korea.net, September 22, 2009, http://www.korea.net/NewsFocus/policies/view?articleId=75167.

12. Ibid.

13. Jo-hee Lee, "Foreign, Unification Ministries at Odds," *Korea Herald*, January 4, 2008.

14. Blue House, *White Paper*, 4:70.

15. Ibid., 4:73–74.

16. Governments of the Republic of Korea and the United States, "Joint Vision for the Alliance of the United States of America and the Republic of Korea," June 16, 2009, https:// www.whitehouse.gov/the-press-office/joint-vision-alliance-united-states-america-and -republic-korea.

17. Quoted in Jongryn Mo and John G. Ikenberry, *The Rise of Korean Leadership* (New York: Palgrave Macmillan, 2013), 9.

18. Blue House, *White Paper*, 4:367.

19. Jill Kosch O'Donnell, "The Global Green Growth Institute: On a Mission to Prove Green Growth," Green Growth Quarterly Update II-2012, Council of Foreign Relations, November 2012, http://www.cfr.org/south-korea/global-green-growth-institute -mission-prove-green-growth/p29398.

20. Blue House, *White Paper*, 4:423–426.

21. Ibid., 417.

22. Myung-bak Lee, "How Korea Solved Its Banking Crisis," *Wall Street Journal*, March 27, 2009, http://www.wsj.com/articles/SB123811059672252885.

23. Myung-bak Lee and Kevin Rudd, "The G20 Can Lead the Way to Balanced Growth," *Financial Times*, September 2, 2009, http://www.ft.com/cms/s/0/55fd681a-97f3-11de -8d3d-00144feabdco.html#axzz3tQcrG4Og.

24. Mo and Ikenberry, *Rise of Korean Leadership*, 18–30; Colin Bradford, "South Korea as a Middle Power in Global Governance: 'Punching Above Its Weight' Based on National Assets and Dynamic Trajectory," in Colin I. Bradford, Toby Dalton, Brendan M. Howe, Jill Kosch O'Donnell, Andrew O'Neil, and Scott A. Snyder, *Middle-Power*

Korea: Contributions to the Global Agenda (New York: Council on Foreign Relations Press, 2015).

25. Blue House, *White Paper*, 4:59.

26. O'Donnell, "Global Green Growth Institute."

27. Blue House, *White Paper*, 4:423–426.

28. "South Korea 'Hints' at Delaying Command Transition Amid Security Concerns," Yonhap News Agency, January 20, 2010.

29. *North Korea Chronology 2010* (Brooklyn, N.Y.: Social Science Research Council, 2010), 50–51.

30. Ibid.

31. Anthony H. Cordesman and Aaron Lin, *The Changing Military Balance in the Koreas and Northeast Asia* (Washington, D.C.: Center for Strategic and International Studies, 2015).

32. Andrew Yeo, "China, Japan, South Korea Trilateral Cooperation: Implications for Northeast Asian Politics and Order," *East Asia Institute Briefing*, November 2012, 2, https://www.files.ethz.ch/isn/154972/2012110618151837.pdf.

33. Ibid., 3–5.

34. Min Gyo Koo, "Embracing Asia, South Korean Style: Preferential Trading Arrangements as Instruments of Foreign Policy," *East Asia Institute Issue Briefing*, November 2009, http://www.eai.or.kr/data/bbs/eng_report/2009111215515244.pdf.

35. Duk-kun Byun, "Seoul Declares Ambitious Diplomatic Initiative for Asia," Yonhap News Agency, March 8, 2008, http://english.yonhapnews.co.kr/national/2009/03/07/16 /0301000000AEN20090307003200315F.HTML.

36. Quoted in Mo and Ikenberry, *Rise of Korean Leadership*, 22.

37. Quoted in Associated Press, "Lee Pushes Better Ties with Japan," *Japan Times*, March 2, 2008.

38. Kenji E. Kushida and Phillip Y. Libscy, "The Rise and Fall of the Democratic Party of Japan," in *Japan Under the DPJ: The Politics of Transition and Governance*, ed. Kenji E. Kushida and Phillip Y. Lipsky (Stanford, Calif.: Shorenstein Asia-Pacific Research Center, 2013).

39. Ibid., 34.

40. Martin Fackler, "Japan Apologizes to South Korea on Colonization," *New York Times*, August 10, 2010, http://www.nytimes.com/2010/08/11/world/asia/11japan.html?_r=0.

41. Quoted in Ito Masami, "'Comfort Women' Issue Resolved: Noda," *Japan Times*, October 18, 2011.

42. Sun-ah Shim, "Court Says Seoul's Inaction Over Former Comfort Women Unconstitutional," Yonhap News Agency, August 30, 2011, http://english.yonhapnews.co.kr/na tional/2011/08/30/27/0302000000AEN20110830007951315F.HTML.

43. Seongho Sheen and Jina Kim, "What Went Wrong with the ROK-Japan Military Pact?" *East-West Center: Asia Pacific Bulletin* 176 (July 2012), http://www.eastwestcenter .org/sites/default/files/private/apb176.pdf.

44. Jae-soon Chang, "Lee Strongly Urges Japan to Resolve 'Comfort Women' Issue," Yonhap News Agency, December 18, 2011, http://english.yonhapnews.co.kr/national/2011 /12/18/43/0301000000AEN20111218001100315F.HTML.

45. Ralph A. Cossa, "Japan–South Korea Relations: Time to Open Both Eyes," Council on Foreign Relations, July 2012, http://www.cfr.org/south-korea/japan-south-korea -relations-time-open-both-eyes/p28736.

46. Sheen and Kim, "What Went Wrong with the ROK-Japan Military Pact?"

47. "S. Korea Postpones Signing Controversial Military Pact with Japan," Yonhap News Agency, June 29, 2012, http://english.yonhapnews.co.kr/national/2012/06/29/57/030100 0000AEN20120629008900315F.HTML.

48. Ibid.

49. Sang-Hun Choe, "South Korean's Visit to Disputed Islets Angers Japan," *New York Times*, August 10, 2012, http://www.nytimes.com/2012/08/11/world/asia/south-koreans -visit-to-disputed-islets-angers-japan.html.

50. Quoted in Evan Ramstad, "Tensions Rise Between Tokyo, Seoul Over Islets," *Wall Street Journal*, August 10, 2012, http://www.wsj.com/articles/SB10000872396390443991 70457758038136354502 6.

51. Masami Ito, "Tokyo Seeks ICJ Ruling on Takeshima," *Japan Times*, August 18, 2012, http://www.japantimes.co.jp/news/2012/08/18/national/tokyo-seeks-icj-ruling-on -takeshima/.

52. Blue House, *White Paper*, 4:125–126.

53. Ibid., 102.

54. Quoted in Michael Ha, "Chinese Official Calls Korea-US Alliance Historical Relic," *Korea Times*, May 28, 2008, http://www.koreatimes.co.kr/www/news/nation /2011/04/116_24932.html.

55. Suk-hee Han, "South Korea Seeks to Balance Relations with China and the United States," Council on Foreign Relations report, November 2012, http://www.cfr.org/south -korea/south-korea-seeks-balance-relations-china-united-states/p29447.

56. Jeremy Chan, "The Incredible Shrinking Crisis: The Sinking of the *Cheonan* and Sino-Korean Relations," in *U.S.-Korea Institute at SAIS: 2010 Yearbook* (Baltimore: School of Advanced International Studies, Johns Hopkins University, 2010), 24.

57. Jeremy Page, Jay Solomon, and Julian E. Barnes, "China Warns U.S. as Korea Tensions Rise," *Wall Street Journal*, November 26, 2010, http://www.wsj.com/articles/SB1000142 4052748704008704575638420698918004.

58. Scott Snyder and See-Won Byun, "Cheonan and Yeonpyeong: The Northeast Asian Response to North Korea's Provocations," *RUSI Journal* 156, no. 2 (2011): 76.

59. Jiyoon Kim, Karl Friedhoff, Chungku Kang, and Euicheol Lee, *Asan Report: South Korean Attitudes on China* (Seoul: Asan Institute for Policy Studies, July 2014), 18–19, http:// en.asaninst.org/contents/south-korean-attitudes-on-china/.

60. "China Fisherman Dies in Clash with South Korea Coast Guard," BBC, December 18, 2010, http://www.bbc.com/news/world-asia-pacific-12026765.

61. "China Blames S. Korea for Clash with Chinese Trawler," *Chosun Ilbo*, December 22, 2010, http://english.chosun.com/site/data/html_dir/2010/12/22/2010122200755 .html.

62. "South Korean Coastguard 'Killed by Chinese Fisherman,'" Reuters, December 12, 2011, http://www.reuters.com/article/us-korea-china-idUSTRE7BB03Z20111212.

63. "Four Fishing Inspectors Wounded," *Korea Times*, April 30, 2012, http://www .koreatimes.co.kr/www/news/nation/2012/05/117_110010.html.

64. Scott Snyder, "China-Korea Relations: Under New Leadership," *Comparative Connections*, 2013, 3, https://csis-prod.s3.amazonaws.com/s3fs-public/legacy_files/files/publi cation/1203qchina_korea.pdf.

65. Mansoo Lee, "Korea's Dynamic Economic Partnership with a Rising China: Time for Change," *Journal of International and Area Studies* 19, no. 2 (2012): 68, http://www.jstor .org/stable/43107240.

66. Quoted in "Lee Suggests 'Shuttle Diplomacy' with N. Korea," *Chosun Ilbo*, March 12, 2008, http://english.chosun.com/site/data/html_dir/2008/03/12/2008031261012.html.

67. Jae-nam Ko, "Preparations for Korea-Russia Dialogue and Future Tasks," *Analysis of Current International Issues*, May 2010, http://www.koreafocus.or.kr/design2/layout/con tent_print.asp?group_id=103069.

68. Cheong-mo Yoo, "S. Korea, Russia Agree on Gas Pipeline Project Involving N. Korea," Yonhap News Agency, September 29, 2008.

69. G. A. Ivanshetsov, "Comprehensive Review of Russia–Republic of Korea Relations," in *Russia–Republic of Korea Relations: Revising the Bilateral Agenda* (Moscow: Russian International Affairs Council, 2013), 10, http://www.slideshare.net/RussianCouncil/wp -russia-koreaen.

70. Ibid., 9–11.

71. Yoo, "S. Korea, Russia Agree on Gas Pipeline Project Involving N. Korea."

72. Ibid.

73. Kwang-Yeon Lee, "Pipeline Diplomacy: The Russia-DPRK-ROK Gas Pipeline Project," in *U.S. Korea Institute at SAIS: 2011 Yearbook* (Baltimore: School of Advanced International Studies, Johns Hopkins University, 2011), 105.

74. Hyun-kyung Han, "Lee, Medvedev to Discuss Pipelines," *Korea Times*, November 1, 2011, http://www.koreatimes.co.kr/www/news/nation/2011/11/116_97813.html.

75. Ministry of Unification, Republic of Korea, *White Paper* (Seoul: Republic of Korea, 2010), 18, http://eng.unikorea.go.kr/content.do?cmsid=1819.

76. Mo and Ikenberry, *Rise of Korean Leadership*, 15.

77. Blue House, *White Paper*, 4:60–61.

78. Quoted in Sung-ki Jung, "Big Ticket Inter-Korean Projects Put on Backburner," *Korea Times*, January 7, 2008, http://www.koreatimes.co.kr/www/news/nation/2009/09/120_16859 .html.

79. Young-hie Kim, "Lee and the North," *Korea JoongAng Daily*, December 28, 2007, http:// koreajoongangdaily.joins.com/news/article/Article.aspx?aid=2884398.

80. Blue House, Republic of Korea, *White Paper*, vol. 5: *Nordpolitik and Security Policies with Principle* (Seoul: Blue House, 2013), 101–102.

81. Ministry of Unification, Republic of Korea, "The Republic of Korea's Policy Toward North Korea," 2012, http://eng.unikorea.go.kr/cwsboard/board.do?mode=download&bid =1112&cid=32794&filename=32794_201408221407435220.PDF.

82. Jae-soon Chang, "S. Korea: N. Korea Not Cooperating in Shooting Probe," Associated Press, July 12, 2008.

83. Ji-hyun Kim, "Lee Gets Tough on Tourist Killing," *Korea Herald*, July 17, 2008.

84. U.S. Department of State, "Press Availability with Secretary Gates, Korean Foreign Minister Yu, and Korean Defense Minister Kim," July 21, 2010, http://www.state.gov /secretary/20092013clinton/rm/2010/07/145014.htm.

85. Ji-hyun Kim, "Seoul Holds Back Full PSI Support," *Korea Herald*, January 18, 2010, http://www.koreaherald.com/view.php?ud=20100118010.

86. "Grand Bargain," *Korea Times*, September 22, 2009, http://www.koreatimes.co.kr/www /news/opinon/2009/09/137_52267.html.

87. Blue House, *White Paper*, 4:61.

88. Sang-ho Son, "N. Korean Submarine Torpedoed Cheonan," *Korea Times*, May 20, 2010.

89. Blue House, *White Paper*, 4:197.

90. Quoted in "Govt. Sends Mixed Messages About N. Korea Policy," *Chosun Ilbo*, December 30, 2010, http://english.chosun.com/site/data/html_dir/2010/12/30/2010123001108.html.

91. "Obama Has Misgivings About Korea-U.S. FTA," *Chosun Ilbo*, February 15, 2008, http://english.chosun.com/site/data/html_dir/2008/02/15/2008021561013.html.

92. Blaine Harden, "In S. Korea, a Reversal on U.S. Beef Imports," *Washington Post*, June 4, 2008, A-12, http://www.washingtonpost.com/wp-dyn/content/article/2008/06/03/AR200 8060301714.html; Hyung-jim Kim, "South Koreans Rally Against U.S. Beef; Government Rejects Calls to Renegotiate Deal," Associated Press, May 6, 2008.

93. Jung-a Song, "S. Korea President Apologizes for US Beef Deal," *Financial Times*, May 23, 2008, 3.

94. Ibid.; Vershbow quoted in Jung-a Song, "Seoul Seeks New Talks on U.S. Beef," *Financial Times*, June 3, 2008, https://www.ft.com/content/f92de8dc-3185-11dd-b77c-0000779fd2ac.

95. Sang-hun Choe, "South Korea Ends Legal Hurdle for Importing American Beef," *New York Times*, June 26, 2008.

96. Blue House, *White Paper*, 4:90–92.

97. Hyuk-chul Kwon, "S. Korea's Ballistic Missile Firing Range May Increase," *Hankyoreh*, January 20, 2011, http://english.hani.co.kr/arti/english_edition/e_northkorea/459702 .html.

98. "Seoul Wants Missile Range to Cover Whole Peninsula," *Chosun Ilbo*, September 19, 2011, http://english.chosun.com/site/data/html_dir/2011/09/20/2011092000599.html.

99. Chen Kane, Stephanie Lieggi, and Miles Pomper, "Time for Leadership: South Korea and Nuclear Proliferation," *Arms Control Today*, March 2011, 22–28, https://www .armscontrol.org/act/2011_03/SouthKorea.

100. Sang-hun Choe, "South Korea and U.S. Differ on Nuclear Enrichment," *New York Times*, December 5, 2011, http://www.nytimes.com/2011/12/06/world/asia/south-korea -and-us-differ-on-nuclear-enrichment.html.

101. Gwang-lip Moon, "Another Nuclear Issue to Keep Seoul, D.C. Busy," *JoongAng Ilbo*, December 9, 2010.

102. Ibid.

103. Toby Dalton, "Will South Korean Nuclear Leadership Make a Difference in 2016?" *Asia Unbound*, September 16, 2015, http://blogs.cfr.org/asia/2015/09/16/will-south-korean -nuclear-leadership-make-a-difference-in-2016/.

7. PARK GEUN-HYE'S ASIAN PARADOX

1. Geun-hye Park, "A Plan for Peace in North Asia," *Wall Street Journal*, November 12, 2012, http://www.wsj.com/articles/SB10001424127887323894704578114310294100492.

2. Ibid.

3. Tae-hwan Kim, "Beyond Geopolitics: South Korea's Eurasia Initiative as a New Nordpolitik," *Asan Forum*, February 16, 2015, http://www.theasanforum.org/beyond-geopolitics -south-koreas-eurasia-initiative-as-a-new-nordpolitik/.

4. Trustpolitik was outlined most fully in an article Park published in *Foreign Affairs* during her campaign: Geun-hye Park, "A New Kind of Korea," *Foreign Affairs*, September–October 2011, https://www.foreignaffairs.com/articles/northeast-asia/2011 -09-01/new-kind-korea. See also Ministry of Foreign Affairs, Republic of Korea, *Eurasia Initiative*, 2013, http://www.mofa.go.kr/ENG/image/common/title/res/0707 _eurasia_bro.pdf.

5. "Full Text of Park's Inauguration Speech," Yonhap News Agency, February 25, 2013, http://english.yonhapnews.co.kr/national/2013/02/25/95/0301000000AEN20130225 001500315F.HTML.

6. Park, "A New Kind of Korea."

7. "Full Text of Park's Speech on N. Korea," Yonhap News Agency, March 28, 2014, http:// english.yonhapnews.co.kr/full/2014/03/28/40/1200000000AEN20140328008000315F .html.

8. Sarah Kim and Won-yeob Jeong, "Unification Committee Launched," *JoongAng Ilbo*, July 16, 2014, http://koreajoongangdaily.joins.com/news/article/article.aspx?aid=29 92086.

9. "Park's Office Chooses 'Bonanza' for Korean Word 'Daebak,'" Yonhap News Agency, February 20, 2014, http://english.yonhapnews.co.kr/news/2014/02/20/79/0200000000 AEN20140220008300315F.html.

10. Dae-jin Hwang, "Eleventh-Hour Agreement Saves Kaesong Industrial Complex," *Chosun Ilbo*, August 16, 2013, http://english.chosun.com/site/data/html_dir/2013/08/16 /2013081600868.html.

11. Chico Harlan, "For Some North and South Koreans, a Long-Awaited Family Reunion," *Washington Post*, February 20, 2014, https://www.washingtonpost.com/world/for-some -koreans-a-long-awaited-reunion/2014/02/20/2e6d916c-9a19-11e3-b1de-e666d78c3937 _story.html.

12. Sang-hun Choe, "In Unusual Trip, North Korean Aides Attend Games in South," *New York Times*, October 3, 2014, http://www.nytimes.com/2014/10/04/world/asia/north -korean-aides-south-games-kim-jong-un.html.

13. James Pearson and Ju-Min Park, "North, South Korea Reach Agreement to Ease Tensions," Reuters, August 24, 2015, http://www.reuters.com/article/us-northkorea-south korea-idUSKCN0QR02D20150824.

14. Quoted in "S. Korean FM Warns N. Korea Against Nuclear Test," Yonhap News Agency, April 22, 2014, http://english.yonhapnews.co.kr/northkorea/2014/04/22/50/0401 000000AEN20140422005000315F.html.

15. Elizabeth Shim, "U.N. Security Council Passes Sanctions on North Korea," United Press International, March 2, 2016, http://www.upi.com/Top_News/World-News/2016/03/02/UN-Security-Council-passes-sanctions-on-North-Korea/4621456934780/.

16. "Workers' Party in N. Korea Holds Seventh Congress," Korea Broadcasting Service, May 12, 2016, http://world.kbs.co.kr/english/event/nkorea_nuclear/now_02_detail.htm?No=2504.

17. See Ministry of Foreign Affairs, *Eurasia Initiative.*

18. Jeremy Page and Alastair Gale, "China President's Visit to South Korea Before North Seen as Telling," *Wall Street Journal*, June 27, 2014, http://www.wsj.com/articles/chinas-president-xi-to-visit-seoul-1403858327.

19. Jonathan Kaiman, "Who's Who (and Who Isn't) at China's Big Parade," *Los Angeles Times*, September 2, 2015, http://www.latimes.com/world/asia/la-fg-whos-who-china-parade-20150902-story.html.

20. Michael J. Green, "Korea in the Middle," *JoongAng Ilbo*, June 11, 2014, http://koreajoongangdaily.joins.com/news/article/article.aspx?aid=2990401.

21. Sungtae "Jacky" Park, "How China Sees THAAD," Center for Strategic and International Studies, March 30, 2016, https://www.csis.org/analysis/pacnet-32-how-china-sees-thaad.

22. White House, "Press Conference with President Obama and President Park of the Republic of Korea," April 25, 2014, https://www.whitehouse.gov/the-press-office/2014/04/25/press-conference-president-obama-and-president-park-republic-korea.

23. Sang-hun Choe, "Japan and South Korea Settle Dispute Over Wartime 'Comfort Women,'" *New York Times*, December 28, 2015, http://www.nytimes.com/2015/12/29/world/asia/comfort-women-south-korea-japan.html?_r=0.

24. Geun-hye Park, "Address to the Nation on the Agreement on the 'Comfort Women' Issue," *Korea.Net*, December 31, 2015, http://www.korea.net/Government/Briefing-Room/Presidential-Speeches/view?articleId=136045.

25. White House, "Remarks by President Obama and President Park of South Korea in a Joint Press Conference," May 7, 2013, https://www.whitehouse.gov/photos-and-video/video/2013/05/07/president-obama-holds-press-conference-president-park-south-korea#transcript.

26. White House, "Remarks by President Obama and President Park of the Republic of Korea in Joint Press Conference," October 16, 2015, https://www.whitehouse.gov/the-press-office/2015/10/16/remarks-president-obama-and-president-park-republic-korea-joint-press.

27. Mark E. Manyin, Emma Chanlett-Avery, and Mary Beth-Nikitin, *U.S.–South Korea Relations* (Washington, D.C.: Congressional Research Service, October 4, 2011), 8, http://fpc.state.gov/documents/organization/175896.pdf.

28. Jeyup S. Kwaak, "President Park Apologizes for Ferry Response," *Wall Street Journal*, April 29, 2014, http://www.wsj.com/articles/SB10001424052702304163604579530750831476112.

29. "Coping with Outbreaks of MERS," *New York Times*, June 20, 2015, http://www.nytimes.com/2015/06/21/opinion/sunday/coping-with-outbreaks-of-mers.html.

8. THE PARADOX OF SOUTH KOREA'S MIDDLE-POWER STATUS

1. See, for example, John J. Mearsheimer, *The Tragedy of Great Power Politics* (New York: Norton, 2014).

2. Quoted in Sunghan Kim, "Global Governance and Middle Powers: South Korea's Role in the G20," February 2013, http://www.cfr.org/south-korea/global-governance-middle -powers-south-koreas-role-g20/p30062.

3. Jongryn Mo and John G. Ikenberry, *The Rise of Korean Leadership* (New York: Palgrave Macmillan, 2013), 5.

4. See Colin I. Bradford, Toby Dalton, Brendan M. Howe, Jill Kosch O'Donnell, Andrew O'Neil, and Scott A. Snyder, *Middle-Power Korea: Contributions to the Global Agenda* (Washington, D.C.: Council on Foreign Relations Press, 2015).

5. Andrew O'Neil, "South Korea as a Middle Power: Global Ambitions and Looming Challenges," in Bradford et al., *Middle-Power Korea*, 76–77.

6. See Andrew F. Cooper, Richard A. Higgott, and Kim R. Nossal, *Relocating Middle Powers: Australia and Canada in a Changing World Order* (Vancouver: University of British Columbia Press, 1993); Bruce Gilley and Andrew O'Neil, "China's Rise Through the Prism of Middle Powers," in *Middle Powers and the Rise of China*, ed. Andrew O'Neil and Bruce Gilley (Washington, D.C.: Georgetown University Press, 2014), 8–13.

7. For instance, see Yul Sohn, "Searching for a New Identity: South Korea's Middle Power Diplomacy," *FRIDE Policy Brief*, no. 212 (December 2015), http://fride.org/des carga/PB212_South_Korea_middle_power_diplomacy.pdf.

8. Sook-Jong Lee, Chaesung Chun, Hyeejung Suh, and Patrick Thompson, *Middle Power in Action: The Evolving Nature of Diplomacy in the Age of Multilateralism* (Seoul: East Asia Institute, April 2015), 5–6, http://www.eai.or.kr/data/bbs/eng_report/201505011632276 .pdf.

9. Sohn, "Searching for a New Identity."

10. Andrew Carr, "Is Australia a Middle Power? A Systemic Impact Approach," *Australian Journal of International Affairs* 68, no. 1 (2013): 79–80.

11. Mo and Ikenberry, *Rise of Korean Leadership*, 1–16.

12. Myung-bak Lee and Kevin Rudd, "The G20 Can Lead the Way to Balanced Growth," *Financial Times*, September 2, 2009, http://www.ft.com/cms/s/0/55fd681a-97f3-11de -8d3d-00144feabdc0.html#axzz3tQc1G4Og.

13. Mo and Ikenberry, *Rise of Korean Leadership*, 17–30.

14. Colin I. Bradford, "South Korea as a Middle Power in Global Governance: Punching Above Its Weight Based on National Assets and Dynamic Trajectory," in Bradford et al., *Middle-Power Korea*, 8–20.

15. Mo and Ikenberry, *Rise of Korean Leadership*, 31–49.

9. KOREA BETWEEN THE UNITED STATES AND CHINA

1. Chung-in Moon, "China's Rise and Security Dynamics on the Korean Peninsula," paper presented at the conference "China, the United States, and the East Asian Order: Managing Instability," November 22–23, 2013, Beijing.

2. See Jae Ho Chung, *Between Ally and Partner: Korea-China Relations and the United States* (New York: Columbia University Press, 2007).

3. Miki Tanikawa and Don Kirk, "Mushrooms with Garlics and Tariffs," *New York Times*, April 17, 2001, http://www.nytimes.com/2001/04/17/business/mushrooms-with-garlic -and-tariffs.html.

4. Scott Snyder, *China's Rise and the Two Koreas: Politics, Economics, Security* (Boulder, Colo.: Lynne Rienner, 2009), 49, 63.

5. See Jae-ho Chung, "Dragon in the Eyes of South Korea," in *Korea: The East Asian Pivot*, ed. Jonathan D. Pollack (Newport, R.I.: Naval War College Press, 2004), 253–266.

6. Hyeong Jung Park, *Looking Back and Looking Forward: North Korea, Northeast Asia, and the ROK-U.S. Alliance*, working paper (Washington, D.C.: Center for Northeast Asian Policy Studies, Brookings Institution, December 17, 2007), https://www.brookings.edu /research/looking-back-and-looking-forward-north-korea-northeast-asia-and-the-rok -u-s-alliance/.

7. Jong-cheol Choi, "Strategic Flexibility of USFK and South Korea's Strategic Responses," *Korea Focus*, June 2006, http://www.koreafocus.or.kr/design1/layout/content _print.asp?group_id=101200.

8. Bae Geung Chan, "Moving Forward with Korea's 'Northeast Asian Cooperation Initiative,'" *Korea Focus*, November 2004, http://www.koreafocus.or.kr/design1/layout/con tent_print.asp?group_id=174.

9. Quoted in Michael Ha, "Chinese Official Calls Korea-US Alliance Historical Relic," *Korea Times*, May 28, 2008, http://www.koreatimes.co.kr/www/news/nation/2011/04 /116_24932.html.

10. "S. Korea Not in Dilemma Over Rivalry Between U.S., China: FM," Yonhap News Agency, March 30, 2015, http://english.yonhapnews.co.kr/national/2015/03/30/29 /0301000000AEN20150330003351315F.html.

11. Robert S. Ross, "Balance of Power Politics and the Rise of China: Accommodation and Balancing in East Asia," *Security Studies* 15, no. 3 (2006): 381.

12. David C. Kang, "Between Balancing and Bandwagoning: South Korea's Response to China," *Journal of East Asian Studies* 9, no. 1 (2009): 1–29.

13. "Editorial: Park Must Balance Diplomacy Between China and Japan-U.S. Alliance," *Mainichi*, September 5, 2015, http://mainichi.jp/graph/2015/09/05/20150905p2a00m 0na008000c/001.html.

14. Dingding Chen, "Is a China–South Korea Alliance Possible?" *The Diplomat*, July 9, 2014, http://thediplomat.com/2014/07/is-a-china-south-korea-alliance-possible/.

15. Ibid.

16. For examples, see Kang Choi and Ki-bum Kim, "Breaking the Myth of Missile Defense," *Seoul Times*, August 6, 2014, http://theseoultimes.com/ST/?url=/ST/db/read

.php?idx=12466; "Bad Neighbor," *Korea Herald*, August 7, 2016, http://www.koreaherald
.com/view.php?ud=2016080700276; "Reining in China's Illegal Fishing," *Korea JoongAng Daily*, June 8, 2016, http://koreajoongangdaily.joins.com/news/article/article.aspx
?aid=3019685; and "Pirates in the West Sea," *Korea Herald*, October 11, 2016, http://www
.koreaherald.com/view.php?ud=20161011000701.

17. Chung, *Between Ally and Partner*, 119–121.

18. Ellen Kim and Victor Cha, "Between a Rock and a Hard Place: South Korea's Strategic
Dilemmas with China and the United States," *Asia Policy* 21, no. 1 (2016): 112–113, https://
muse.jhu.edu/article/609180/pdf.

19. Sukhee Han, "The Rise of China, Power Transition, and Korea's Strategic Hedging,"
Institute of China Studies, University of Malaya, May 5–6, 2009, http://ics.um.edu.my
/images/ics/may2009/hansh.pdf.

20. U.S.-China Economic and Security Review Commission, *2014 Annual Report to
Congress* (Washington, D.C.: U.S.-China Economic and Security Review Commission,
2014), 435, http://origin.www.uscc.gov/sites/default/files/annual_reports/Complete%20
Report.PDF.

21. Gilbert Rozman, "Option 5: Rethinking Middle Power Diplomacy," *Asan Forum*, June
11, 2015, http://www.theasanforum.org/option-5-rethinking-middle-power-diplomacy/.

22. Jin Park, "Korea Between the United States and China: How Does Hedging Work?"
Joint U.S.-Korea Academic Studies 26 (2015), http://www.keia.org/sites/default/files/pub
lications/korea_between_the_united_states_and_china.pdf.

23. Chung-in Moon, "Theory of Balancing Role in Northeast Asia," *Chosun Ilbo*, April 12,
2005.

24. Quoted in "S. Korea Not in Dilemma Over Rivalry Between U.S., China."

25. Jin-kyu Kang and Yong-ho Shin, "Foreign Minister Under Fire for 'Blessing' Remark,"
JoongAng Ilbo, April 1, 2015, http://koreajoongangdaily.joins.com/news/article/Article
.aspx?aid=3002571.

26. Sukjoon Yoon, "Strategic Dilemma or Great Blessing?" Center for Strategic and
International Studies, April 13, 2015, https://www.csis.org/analysis/pacnet-23-strategic
-dilemma-or-great-blessing.

27. Byung Moo Hwang, "Maneuvering in the Geopolitical Middle: South Korea's Strategic Posture," *Global Asia* 9, no. 3 (2014): 43, https://www.globalasia.org/wp-content
/uploads/2014/09/583.pdf.

28. Seong-kon Kim, "Is Korea a Pawn on the International Chessboard?" *Korea Herald*,
March 1, 2016, http://www.koreaherald.com/view.php?ud=20160301000326.

29. Pyong-choon Hahm, "Korea and the Emerging Asian Power Balance," *Foreign
Affairs*, January 1972, https://www.foreignaffairs.com/articles/asia/1972-01-01/korea
-and-emerging-asian-power-balance.

30. David C. Kang, *East Asia Before the West: Five Centuries of Trade and Tribute* (New York:
Columbia University Press, 2012).

31. Jae-jung Suh, *Power, Interest, and Identity in Military Alliances* (New York: Palgrave
MacMillan, 2007).

10. UNIFICATION AND KOREAN STRATEGIC CHOICES

1. Ji-eun Seo, "Unification May Be Jackpot: Park," *JoongAng Ilbo*, January 7, 2014, http://koreajoongangdaily.joins.com/news/article/article.aspx?aid=2983129.

2. Quoted in Norman D. Levin and Yong-Sup Han, *Sunshine in Korea: The South Korean Debate Over Policies Toward North Korea* (Santa Monica, Calif.: RAND, 2002), 52.

3. Don Oberdorfer, "S. Korean Leader Makes New Overture to North," *Washington Post*, October 19, 1988.

4. Peter James Spielmann, "North Korea Proposes Northern-Southern Confederation," Associated Press, October 19, 1988.

5. Seong-ho Jhe, "Comparison of the South's Confederation Proposal with the North's 'Low Stage Federation' Proposal—from the Perspective of International Law," *International Journal of Korean Unification Studies* 12, no. 1 (2002): 165–197.

6. Hong-koo Lee, "Keep the Continuity Flowing," *JoongAng Ilbo*, February 19, 2013, http://koreajoongangdaily.joins.com/news/article/article.aspx?aid=2967302.

7. David E. Sanger, "In Nuclear Deal, Seoul Halts War Game with U.S.," *New York Times*, January 7, 1992, http://www.nytimes.com/1992/01/07/world/in-nuclear-deal-seoul-halts-war-game-with-us.html.

8. David E. Sanger, "Koreas Sign Pact Renouncing Force in a Step to Unity," *New York Times*, December 13, 1991, http://www.nytimes.com/1991/12/13/world/koreas-sign-pact-renouncing-force-in-a-step-to-unity.html?pagewanted=all.

9. Quoted in Hakjoon Kim, *The Domestic Politics of Korean Unification: Debates on the North in the South, 1948–2008* (Seoul: Jimoondang, 2010), 358.

10. Lorien Holland, "Forty-Five Years After North Korea Invaded South Korea, Young," United Press International, December 18, 1995, http://www.upi.com/Archives/1995/12/18/Forty-five-years-after-North-Korea-invaded-South-Korea-young/3077819262800/.

11. Don Kirk, "The Warnings from Korean History," *Time Asia*, July 3, 2000, http://www.cnn.com/ASIANOW/time/magazine/2000/0703/korea.viewpoint.html.

12. Kim, *Domestic Politics of Korean Unification*, 548–551.

13. Scott Snyder, "The End of History, the Rise of Ideology, and the Future of Democracy on the Korean Peninsula," *Journal of East Asian Studies* 3, no. 2 (2003): 199–224.

14. Anthony Faiola, "A Crack in the Door in N. Korea," *Washington Post*, November 24, 2003.

15. Seo, "Unification May Be Jackpot."

16. Sang-ho Song, "Candidates Struggle to Find Unique North Korea Policies," *Korea Herald*, October 24, 2012, http://www.koreaherald.com/view.php?ud=20121024001082.

17. Ji-eun Seo, "President Makes History in Dresden," *JoongAng Ilbo*, March 29, 2014, http://koreajoongangdaily.joins.com/news/article/Article.aspx?aid=2987120.

18. Jin-kyu Kang, "Two Koreas Reach Deal to Avoid Military Confrontation," *JoongAng Ilbo*, August 25, 2015, http://koreajoongangdaily.joins.com/news/article/article.aspx?aid=3008350.

19. Simon Tisdall, "WikiLeaks Row: China Wants Korean Reunification, Officials Confirm," *Guardian*, November 10, 2010, https://www.theguardian.com/world/2010/nov/30/china-wants-korean-reunification.

20. Sheila A. Smith, "North Korea in Japan's Strategic Thinking," *Asan Forum*, October 7, 2013, http://www.theasanforum.org/north-korea-in-japans-strategic-thinking/.

21. Georgy Toloraya, "A Neighborly Concern: Russia's Evolving Approach to Korean Problems," *38 North*, February 18, 2016, http://38north.org/2016/02/gtoloraya021816/.

SELECT BIBLIOGRAPHY

Ahn, Jung-shik. *Will Korea's Autonomous North Korean Policy Materialize? Post–Cold War Conflicts and Cooperation Between South Korea and U.S. Policies Toward North Korea.* Seoul: Hanwool, 2007.

Blue House, Republic of Korea. *White Paper.* Vol. 4: *Global Leadership and Improvement of National Status.* Seoul: Government of the Republic of Korea, 2013.

Bridges, Brian. *Japan and Korea in the 1990s: From Antagonism to Adjustment.* Aldershot, UK: Edward Elgar, 1993.

Cha, Victor D. *Alignment Despite Antagonism: The United States–Korea–Japan Security Triangle.* Stanford, Calif.: Stanford University Press, 1999.

Chinoy, Mike. *Meltdown: The Inside Story of the North Korean Nuclear Crisis.* New York: St. Martin's Press, 2008.

Cho, Gab-je. *Oral Memoir of Roh Tae-woo.* Seoul: Chogabjedotcom, 2007.

Chung, Jae Ho. *Between Ally and Partner: Korea-China Relations and the United States.* New York: Columbia University Press, 2007.

Cumings, Bruce. *Korea's Place in the Sun: A Modern History.* New York: Norton, 1997.

Hong, Yong-pyo. *State Security and Regime Security: President Syngman Rhee and the Insecurity Dilemma in South Korea, 1953–60.* New York: St. Martin's Press, 1999.

Izumikawa, Yasuhiro. "South Korea's Nordpolitik and the Efficacy of Asymmetric Positive Sanctions." *Korea Observer* 37, no. 4 (2006): 605–642.

Jager, Sheila Miyoshi. *Brothers at War: The Unending Conflict in Korea.* New York: Norton, 2013.

Kim, Byung-kook, and Ezra F. Vogel, eds. *The Park Chung Hee Era: The Transformation of South Korea.* Cambridge, Mass.: Harvard University Press, 2011.

Kim, Changhoon. *Korean Diplomacy: Yesterday and Today.* Paju City: Korean Studies Information Service, 2013.

Kim, Samuel S. *The Two Koreas and the Great Powers.* Cambridge: Cambridge University Press, 2006.

Korea Institute of Public Administration. *Republic of Korea's Major Policies and Government Operation of Former Administrations.* Vol. 6: *Kim Dae-jung Administration.* Seoul: Daeyoung Press, 2014.

Lee, Chae-Jin. *A Troubled Peace: U.S. Policy and the Two Koreas.* Baltimore: Johns Hopkins University Press, 2006.

Lim, Dong-won. *Peacemaker: Twenty Years of Inter-Korean Relations and the North Korean Nuclear Issue: A Memoir.* Stanford, Calif.: Walter H. Shorenstein Asia-Pacific Research Center, 2012.

Moon, Chung-in, and Chun-Fu Li. "Reactive Nationalism and South Korea's Foreign Policy on China and Japan: A Comparative Analysis." *Pacific Focus* 25, no. 3 (2010): 331–55.

Oberdorfer, Don, and Robert Carlin. *The Two Koreas: A Contemporary History.* New York: Basic Books, 2013.

Park, Chung Hee. *The Country, the Revolution, and I.* Seoul: Hollym, 1970.

——. *Korea Reborn: A Model for Development.* Englewood Cliffs, N.J.: Prentice-Hall, 1979.

——. "President Park's Special Foreign Policy Statement Regarding Peace and Unification." Ministry of Unification of the Republic of Korea, Seoul, June 23, 1973.

Presidential Commission on Policy Planning. *Korea's Future: Vision & Strategy; Korea's Ambition to Become an Advanced Power by 2030.* Seoul: Seoul Selection, 2008.

Roh, Tae-woo. *Roh Tae Woo, a Memoir: Grand Strategy in Transition.* Seoul: Chosun News, 2011.

Shin, Gi-Wook. *One Alliance, Two Lenses: U.S.-Korea Relations in a New Era.* Stanford, Calif.: Stanford University Press, 2010.

Snyder, Scott. *China's Rise and the Two Koreas: Politics, Economics, Security.* Boulder, Colo.: Lynne Rienner, 2009.

Straub, David. *Anti-Americanism in Democratizing South Korea.* Stanford, Calif.: Shorenstein Asia-Pacific Research Center, 2015.

INDEX